FROM THE PURITANS
TO THE PROJECTS

FROM THE PURITANS
PUBLIC HOUSING AND PUBLIC NEIGHBORS
TO THE PROJECTS

LAWRENCE J. VALE

HARVARD UNIVERSITY PRESS
Cambridge, Massachusetts, and London, England

Printed in the United States of America

First Harvard University Press paperback edition, 2007

Library of Congress Cataloging-in-Publication Data

Vale, Lawrence J., 1959–
From the Puritans to the projects : public housing and public neighbors /
Lawrence J. Vale.
p.   cm.
Includes bibliographical references and index.
ISBN-13 978-0-674-00286-9 (cloth: alk. paper)
ISBN-10 0-674-00286-5 (cloth: alk. paper)
ISBN-13 978-0-674-02575-2 (pbk.)
ISBN-10 0-674-02575-x (pbk.)
1. Public housing—Massachusetts—Boston—History.
2. Housing policy—Massachusetts—Boston—History.
3. Poor—Massachusetts—Boston—History.
I. Title.

HD7288.78.U52 M48 2000
363.5'85'0974461—dc21   00-035084

IN 1962, as a three-year-old enrolled at Chicago's Town and Garden nursery school, I watched the highrise towers of the Cabrini-Green public housing project take shape just down the block, making Sedgwick Street irretrievably more town than garden. Throughout the remainder of my childhood, my family took detours to avoid driving past this increasingly notorious neighborhood. When I moved to Boston as an adult, I noticed that aversion to public housing had been architecturally encoded into the city: the expansive windows of the Kennedy Library's public rooms faced every direction except that of the neighboring Columbia Point project; the observation deck of the John Hancock tower allowed views of the city's affluent neighborhoods and waterfront areas, but placed its service areas so as to block sight of neighborhoods that tended to be poor and black. These decisions were neither coincidental nor atypical.

After decades of bypasses and interrupted views, I have attempted in this book to investigate public housing more directly, to try to understand how "the projects" became the most vilified domestic environment in the United States and why their residents came to carry such a broadly shared stigma.

This book is concerned primarily with the shared struggles and larger cultural implications of American public housing. I am writing a second volume that attempts to do justice to the neighborhood specificity of particular public housing project sagas.

In the course of a project that has been an active if intermittent part of my endeavors for twenty years, I have accumulated many debts. In 1980–1981, when I first explored the intellectual history and prehistory of American public housing in an honors thesis at Amherst College, I gained immeasurably from the wise counsel of Barry O'Connell, Helen Searing, and Hugh Hawkins. Two decades later, I have many academic colleagues of my own to thank. At MIT these include Langley Keyes, Bernie Frieden, Gary Hack, Lois Craig, Dennis Frenchman, Bob Fogelson, Lloyd Rodwin, Phil Clay, Marty Rein, and, above all, Sam Bass Warner, Jr., who has served as my sounding board for five years and has generously helped me conceive and revise my manuscript.

Steady streams of students have assisted me with all phases of the research, including Anne Beamish, David Fernandes, Sharon Greenberger, Kristen Harol, Carla Morelli, Tony Petropulos, Lisa Rosan, Judy Su, Geneviève Vachon, and, especially, Dan Serda, whose knowledge of the vast library system at Harvard proved consistently invaluable. The assistance of librarians at both MIT and Harvard has been essential and ample, and I gratefully acknowledge the full cooperation of the helpful staff at the Massachusetts State Archives, the Boston Public Library, and the Boston Housing Authority. At Harvard University Press, I am thankful for the stewardship of Jeff Kehoe and the editing skills of Ann Hawthorne and Kate Brick.

My work has also benefited greatly from conversations and correspondence with many others, including Jack Bauman, Sidney Brower, Gordon Cavanaugh, John Davis, Susan Drucker, Gayle Epp, Roberta Feldman, Karen Franck, Rick Gentry, Gary Gumpert, Steve Hornburg, Michael Katz, Jeff Lines, Peter Marcuse, Oscar Newman, Ellen Pader, Wolfgang Preiser, Ruth Rae, Bill Rohe, Amy Schectman, Michael Schill, Wayne Sherwood, David Varady, and Dan Wuenschel. I am grateful, as well, for my mother's regular supply of clippings about Chicago public housing and for her newfound willingness to shop at the supermarket recently built at Cabrini-Green to replace some of the notorious highrises we once avoided.

Financially, this book has been supported by a Fellowship and publication subvention from the John Simon Guggenheim Memorial Foundation, as well as by funding from the Graham Foundation, the Edward H. and Joyce Linde Career Development Fund, the Mitsui Career Development Fund, and the MIT Provost's Fund for the Humanities, Arts, and Social Sciences. Taken together, these diverse sources have granted me time and assistance, while leaving me thankfully free of the intellectual burden of vested-interest sponsorship.

Ultimately, my greatest debt is to the ongoing support and partnership of Julie Dobrow, and to Mira, Aaron, Jeremy, and Jonathan, my private neighbors who were unwillingly born into the midst of this project but allowed me the space to think about "other people's houses."

CONTENTS

CONTENTS

ILLUSTRATIONS

TABLES

FROM THE PURITANS
TO THE PROJECTS

The "Public" in Public Housing

PUBLIC HOUSING has become a deeply embedded artifact of American culture, but it has entered the body politic more in the manner of a splinter—unintended, painful, and difficult to dislodge. This book seeks not to remove public housing, but rather to explain our collective discomfort with it. To do so entails exploring the nature and extent of public obligation to socially and economically marginal people in America, as expressed through more than 350 years of culturally produced decisions about how and where such people should live. In this historical context, the large, publicly owned housing projects built in every large American city during the mid-twentieth century may be seen not as a unique and isolated phenomenon, but as one manifestation of a continuing struggle. It is a struggle marked by a wide variety of partial and unsatisfactory resolutions dating back, at least in New England, to the time of the Puritans. Before there were public housing projects, there were model tenements, zoning laws, and philanthropic developers; there were settlement houses, working-class suburbs, and private charities; there were tax advantages for homeowners, land bounties for worthy veterans, and Homestead Act opportunities for thrifty pioneers; there were "Overseers of the Poor," pauper auctions, and laws of settlement; and there were almshouses, "bridewells," and "houses of industry." All of these helped to codify the relationships among land tenure, house form, and labor, and all were attempts at "improving poor people."[1] At least until the mid-1950s, sponsors of public housing projects shared this underlying aim, though in recent years most discussion about "improving poor people" in public housing has centered on strategies to enable them to leave it.

Nearly all of those who have written about public housing and identified its internal programmatic faults have viewed public housing as a subset of *housing;* my approach here reverses the direction of the lens, examining public housing as a subset of what it means to be *public.* The former concept is chiefly spatial, the latter chiefly economic. But the terms, though first formally joined during the New Deal, have never existed altogether separately in this country. Before one can interpret the saga of twentieth-century efforts to provide (or reform) public housing, it is crucial to understand what was meant by efforts aimed at housing the public in the three hundred years before programs existed that formally bore the "public housing" name.

The two terms appear together first in Britain. Under English common law, *public houses,* or publicly licensed inns, were charged with receiving all travelers able to pay for food, drink, and lodging. Thus the publicness of these houses was both mandatory in terms of social action and restrictive in terms of socioeconomic sorting. Eventually, by the nineteenth century, the English public house, then generally called a pub, came to be seen as a socially superior establishment, in contrast to alehouses, beerhouses, and ginshops, intended for a lower-class clientele.

The transmutation of public house into pub also serves as a reminder that meanings attached to words like *public* are far from static. In America as in England, both the institutions that act as public providers and the population targeted to benefit from them have undergone constant evolution. At the extremes, the theology-driven Puritan polity of early seventeenth-century Massachusetts Bay and the late twentieth-century federal welfare state have exercised public duties but conceptualized them in vastly different ways. The Puritans, whose state combined civil and ecclesiastical elements to maintain order, emphasized the potential spiritual possibilities of public assistance, in pursuit of what John Winthrop famously called "A Model of Christian Charity." The public, in this society, was neither a distant state bureaucracy nor an undifferentiated mass but a carefully bounded community of believers, elected by God to stand in harsh judgment of all miscreants. In the centuries since, the domains of law and religion have lost much of their initial overlap; instead of a Puritan elect, there is now an electorate.

Gradually and inevitably, the term *public* acquired many new meanings and manifestations. By the middle of the nineteenth century, unprecedented numbers of uneasily juxtaposed people—many of them afflicted by disease and impoverishment—crowded into industrializing cities, requiring government not just to license, but directly to sponsor new civil institutions to sustain order. In this continuum, the twentieth-century phenomenon of public housing should be seen as one public institution among the many that grew in tandem with the modern nation-state.

Publicly sponsored institutions distribute both rewards and sanctions, and public housing has inherited from both sides of the coin. On the reward side, the public housing project occupies a place among the interventions that include public schools, parks, libraries, baths, and hospitals. More painfully, it is descended from publicly sponsored "houses of correction" for those found to have engaged in deviant or dangerous behaviors, including prisons, mental asylums, and poorhouses. These various services and institutions—each located in carefully chosen environs—form a collective representation of the public charge, and function as extended arms of the government, sometimes reaching out with warm embrace, at others threatening with clenched fists.

Over the centuries, the term *public* has retained a central ambiguity, referring at once to the sponsor of an act or place (a public authority) and to the intended beneficiaries (the public). In a democracy, this ambiguity is resolved by a presumed common interest between sponsor and beneficiary in promoting the "public good." Yet such resolution is neither firm nor sustained. The notion of public-as-sponsor has changed immensely since the colonial era, as public authorities have multiplied, specialized, and diversified their functions. Likewise, the notion of public-as-beneficiary has also gained plural meanings, not only because jurisdictional responsibility has overlapped and shifted, but also because the various public authorities have been asked to respond to the claims of ever-widening and diversifying constituencies. Slowly but surely, the end of slavery, the rise of immigration, and the expansion of suffrage forced a diffusion of political power and privilege, a trend extended again by the civil rights movement and other efforts on behalf of gays, lesbians, and people with disabilities. Group by group, subgroup by subgroup, Americans have put themselves forward as deserving special consideration or even recompense for past inequity. In today's world of niche marketing and identity politics, it has become commonplace to speak of multiple publics—a notion inconceivable to the carefully bounded community of the old New England village. In our pluralist society, the notion of some single all-encompassing public has become highly contestable; it is easy to view public sponsorship as targeting some of the public much more than others.

Given these fundamental changes in the structure of government and in the demands of the governed, the concept of *public* must be situationally defined at every stage. Doing so reveals a perennial tension in the cultural roots of public housing. At the heart of the matter is a basic unresolved ambiguity in the American treatment of the public. In their mission to serve and protect all the people (the public good), public authorities must single out for special treatment some people whose condition or behavior threatens civil order; not merely those accused of crimes, but those afflicted with poverty or illness. Such people are told that publicly sponsored intervention, which might take the form of slum clearance of their substandard homes or entail their confinement to institutions, is for their own good, but it is also—simultaneously and fundamentally—expected to guard the public good. This ambiguity, which underlay nineteenth-century attitudes toward public health, continues to be relevant to twentieth-century public housing. The central question of this book is: How—and where—have the sponsors of government institutions reconciled their concern for social stability and their promotion of liberal values with their obligation to house the least advantaged? The answer involves probing the socioeconomic agenda of publicly sponsored places and institutions and examining how their placement affects the space of poverty in the American city. To do so is to reveal shifting relationships among the state, the market, and civil society, and to observe the spatial displacement of difference.

At all times, the assumption of public obligation is expressed through behavioral expectations, socioeconomic hierarchies, and spatial distribution. Whether public authorities build facilities to reward or to punish, each new institution is an attempt to articulate a broad set of rights and responsibilities. This codification of prescribed and proscribed behaviors is sometimes tacit, sometimes posted for all to see. Even those publicly provided amenities that appear most generous, such as Olmsted's parks, are no mere pleasure grounds; they too were built to provide the locus and the structure for inculcating behaviors felt to be conducive to the health, prosperity, and stability of the polity. The security and privacy of the broader community are guaranteed not simply by the granting of broad police powers, but also by the transformation and arrangement of the built environment. Power, in urban design as in physics, is the rate with which force is exercised through space.

When this force is publicly applied through the powers of eminent domain for public works such as bridges, tunnels, and public housing, it has had to be justified as serving a broad public purpose. The various ways in which housing and redevelopment authorities interpreted this public purpose seldom directly served those actually living in the area targeted for public action. When improved transportation was involved, for example, the officially promulgated tradeoffs were relatively straightforward: the private homes and businesses of the unfortunate few must be sacrificed for the good of safe mobility, daily efficiency, and enhanced prosperity of the many. In the case of public housing, which housing authorities often touted as direct replacement accommodation for those displaced from substandard dwellings, the presumed direct benefit for low-income residents also remained subservient to a diverse and shifting public agenda.

The publicness of public housing inheres in a broader set of presumed benefits and opportunities that stem only indirectly from public ownership or public management. With federal funds committed, public housing became subject to all federal laws, and thus a convenient conduit for multiple goals that had little more than a tangential relationship to housing. At various times, the tangled public agenda for public housing could promote not just housing, but also publicly funded employment, public open space, public health, and public action on civil rights. Especially when implemented in combination with slum clearance and urban renewal efforts, public housing projects became the most direct government mechanism for altering (or sustaining) the spatial distribution of the poor and their proximity to the nonpoor. Housing authorities have used the resulting project landscapes as laboratories for a half-century of federal, state, and local attempts to cope with, challenge, or perpetuate the combined effects of poverty, gender bias, and racism.[2] In addition to serving as an arena for playing out a wide variety of socioeconomic biases, public housing has also been a testing ground for theories of architecture, urban form, and neighborhood structure, reflecting and promoting much discussion about the capacity of the architectural environment to affect social behavior and moral development. As urban design, as social policy, and as economics, public housing injected public authority into domestic realms still regarded as resolutely private territory.

PUBLIC HOUSING AS AN AMERICAN PROBLEM

By comparison with other Western countries, support in the United States for subsidized low-income housing began belatedly and reluctantly, and has remained extremely limited. Today, less than 2 percent of the U.S. population resides in public housing, in contrast to at least 20 percent in other industrialized countries. In the United States, where the prevailing American individualist ethos is epitomized in ownership of a single-family home, public housing exposes a central tension in American culture. It raises uncomfortable questions about how Americans should live, where they should live, and with whom they should live, and forces government leaders to decide how to answer. Whether seen as a collection of physical artifacts or as an evolving set of policy ideas, public housing has been both a product and an instigator of bitter local, state, and national debates.

At the core, the controversy over public housing is a debate about the form and purpose of state-subsidized neighborhoods in a society that places ideological value on individual homeownership and the unfettered operation of private markets. In the United States, where individual liberties have long been given broad guarantees, government action in the field of housing has almost always worked to enhance these freedoms. In this context, the very concept of public housing introduces a special strain. As Clare Cooper Marcus commented more than twenty years ago, in a society in which personal identity and domestic place are thoroughly intertwined, public housing makes for a poor ideological fit:

> America is the home of the self-made man, and if the house is seen (even unconsciously) as the symbol of self, then it is small wonder that there is a resistance to the State's providing houses *for* people. The frontier image of the man clearing the land and building a cabin for himself is not far behind us. To a culture inbred with this image, the house–self identity is particularly strong. In some barely conscious way, society has decided to penalize those who, through no fault of their own cannot build, buy, or rent their own housing.[3]

While no opprobrium attaches to the majority of American families who annually receive tens of billions of dollars in federal housing assistance in the form of tax deductions tied to homeownership, for the small minority who live in public housing projects, the stigma of federal aid remains acute. It is a cruel but telling irony that what is called "subsidized housing" actually receives the *least* amount of government subsidy. Given the persistent cultural need to see questions of housing provision, like housing acquisition, as a private responsibility, a mortgage-subsidizing government must be the silent partner in individual initiative rather than a visible substitute for it. The public housing project contradicts this still-ascendant American tradition at every turn. Only by looking closely at the older ideological currents that flow through our national life can we begin to interpret the meanings loaded onto public housing even before the first projects were built.

Many historians and social scientists have sought to explain the slow emergence or limited efficacy of government-sponsored social institutions in the United States by referring to the tradition of national liberal values—the emphasis on individual freedom, private ownership, and voluntary organizations. Some, most notably Louis Hartz, have traced the ideological roots of this "American exceptionalism" to the development of a "new society" detached from the class conflicts embedded in the feudal structures of Europe.[4] The power and persistence of preindustrial national values, in this view, conditioned some of the cultural and social responses to industrialism. These general explanations, however, fail to explain the dynamic by which such national values enter into political debate and influence the fate of particular legislation and policies. As a half-century of challenges to the Hartzian conception of America have made clear, understanding the political complexity of decisionmaking in any era requires a more composite reading of American liberal ideology. That said, much of the history of subsidized housing policy in the United States does seem closely tied to national ideals about proper domestic behavior; efforts at housing reform have always been aimed at protecting chiefly those whose past actions or present circumstances could be judged worthy of aid. These judgments about worthiness—embedded in the language of legislation and in the words and actions of countless reformers—remain ideologically linked to a hierarchy of domestic settings, in which the single-family home on its own plot of land remains preeminent.

The persistent unwillingness of the American public (acting through its elected representatives) to commit to a large-scale program to house the country's low-income residents is both a product of ambivalence and a source of further contestation over which of the poor should be housed in the limited supply, what form this housing should take, and where it should be located.

HOUSING THE PUBLIC NEIGHBOR: OBLIGATION, PROXIMITY, AND FORM

The stigma attached to residence in late twentieth-century public housing projects is heir to a long American tradition of sociospatial disdain. Much of the recent writing about the systematic stigmatization of the American poor has focused on the social-control functions of public welfare benefits or on the ways in which antipoverty policy has worked against those it was meant to assist. These discussions, though central to an account of how stigma is produced, fail to explain the power of its place-based specificity when applied to a public benefit such as public housing. The functions and limits of American social provision must be seen not only in terms of the dynamics of obligation but also in terms of proximity and form.

Long before there were public housing projects, there were *public neighbors*, needy people unable or unwilling to meet the standards of industry or behavior in the community they had entered but whom community leaders nonetheless felt an obligation to assist or, since the early nineteenth century, to reform.[5] As the obligation to the public neighbor moved from a community responsibility motivated by Christian duty to a government responsibility grounded in a civic-minded search for public order, public neighbors were shunted increasingly farther away from the domains of the privileged.

By the second quarter of the nineteenth century, when deciding where to place these public charges, city officials could rely on a variety of new institutions to act as sorting mechanisms. Almshouses and reformatories provided the architectural and symbolic framework for attempts to classify the socioeconomically dependent according to the presumed cause of their dependency. Rather than attributing their condition to a providentially imposed fate that warranted a uniformly compassionate response, these new institutions and policies redefined much socioeconomic dependency as a moral condition, as the result of personal failings sometimes amenable to reform by forced labor or by transfer to more salutary environments.

Public housing projects are twofold heirs to such moral classification schemes. From the late 1930s through at least the mid-1950s, city leaders consistently used the projects to reward the most meritorious of the working poor. Instead of using public housing to assist the unemployed, housing authorities followed congressional intent and filled the first projects with stable two-parent families whose limited rent-paying ability was presumed to result from a temporary delay in upward economic mobility caused by the Great Depression, World War II, or the postwar housing shortage rather than from any inherent personal failing. Deliberately and repeatedly, housing authorities turned away a broad array of would-be public neighbors who were seen as presenting an unwelcome moral or financial risk. Since they were unable to afford decent private housing, the local authorities judged them too poor for public housing as well. Public housing was not intended to be a place for public neighbors. Those who really were unemployed or unemployable could, if eligible, seek solace from other New Deal programs, such as work relief or social security. As expected, the original cohort of carefully selected public housing tenants did not need this subsidy for long. Once they departed, however, housing officials could no longer evade their obligation to the neediest. Prodded by civil rights groups, by the mid-1960s most housing authorities dropped blanket restrictions against accepting unwed mothers and instead attempted to steer applicants into a new moral classification scheme. They informally divided the public housing supply into good projects and bad projects, depending on whether they served as domiciles for the "worthy" poor or as warehouses for those whose misfortunes (expressed through such things as welfare dependency, "broken" families, and delinquency) could be regarded as self-inflicted. As the reputations of individual projects became consolidated for good or ill, housing officials exercised great control over who could go where.

In short, public housing projects became another arena in which American society assessed, and then reassessed, the nature and extent of its obligation to assist public neighbors. Like the nineteenth-century public agencies, public housing authorities built their projects in ways that increasingly maximized their architectural distance from the dominant cultural ideal of the single-family home.

PUBLIC HOUSING IN BOSTON

While it is certainly an aim to speak more generally about the cultural origins and practice of public housing, this book draws its evidence chiefly from the city of Boston. Boston's long history affords a rare opportunity to explore the complete development of public housing in one place, to trace systematically the ideological currents flowing from the town's seventeenth-century poorhouse to the city's late twentieth-century public housing projects. Although other studies have documented the history of public housing in Chicago, Philadelphia, St. Louis, New York, and elsewhere, Boston's public housing experience has its own rich and peculiar personality.[6]

Part I of this book presents the three-hundred-year prehistory of American public housing, with particular reference to Boston. It is a kind of conceptual genealogy, examining attitudes toward housing public neighbors in the centuries before the government struggled over who among these people its publicly sponsored project neighborhoods should attempt to serve. This prehistory is structured to tell two parallel stories. Each is intended to lead to and converge upon the phenomenon of public housing as created in the 1930s. Chapter 1 follows one of these stories (a tale of institutions and techniques for coping with the poor) from the seventeenth century to the 1920s, whereas Chapter 2 traces a second trajectory (a tale of land policy and community design for rewarding and facilitating upward mobility) that begins in the late eighteenth century and is again carried forward to the New Deal era.

In every community, from the small towns of colonial New England to the large metropolises of the present, community leaders have attempted to codify the obligation of the broader polity to its dependent members, enacting laws and systems of social provision that both classify and locate the poor and unwanted. Chapter 1 examines social and spatial classification processes in seventeenth- and eighteenth-century Puritan New England, as well as the efforts of nineteenth-century Bostonians to classify and reform the impoverished and wayward through construction of public institutions located farther and farther from wealthier households. I continue this story through the nineteenth century and into the twentieth, examining efforts to improve tenement and neighborhood conditions. Here, instead of removing the poor from their communities and putting them in institutions, reformers left the poor where they found them, but tried to ameliorate the standards of their homes and their behaviors. In the effort to regulate tenements, reformers again struggled to define the proper scope of societal obligation to public neighbors, revealing an underlying ambivalence about whether these people were potentially good citizens who had been brought down by the evil circumstances of their environments, or irredeemable outcasts who deserved no proximate place to good citizens. Every act of reform, from building regulations to model tenements built by limited-dividend corporations, involved reforming not only tenements but their tenants. With the advent of the settlement house movement in Boston, from the 1890s through the 1920s, Robert Woods and his colleagues at South End House sought to reform not only individual buildings but entire neighborhoods, and to address not only physical surroundings but also social and educational needs. Settlement workers sought to Americanize immigrants both by the force of their own good example and by nurturing links to neighborhood-based institutions. The settlement view of neighborhoods anticipated the "projects" in its scale of intervention, and the settlement preference for working with the most upwardly mobile of the immigrant poor anticipated the aim of early public housing to reward only the most worthy among the needy.

Chapter 2 outlines a second important trajectory in the prehistory of public housing, one that focuses not on institutions that sought to punish and reform the poor, but on their converse—the ideologically grounded efforts to reward upwardly mobile workers with culturally preferred types of houses and neighborhoods. This reward system was premised on the belief that good citizens require good homes, and that the good home is one that is owned, not rented; an abode earned through hard work. From the Land Ordinance of 1785, inspired by Jefferson, through the various nineteenth-century initiatives to provide bounty lands to worthy veterans, to the Homestead Act of 1862, federal public lands policy sought ways to advance the ideological preference for single-family homes. From the mid-nineteenth-century onward, the ideological emphasis on the individualism and yeoman industriousness that the single-family home exemplified could be promoted as the morally pure alternative to the urban tenement. In Boston, late nineteenth-century and early twentieth-century reform efforts sought to redeem the poor by suburbanizing the most "worthy" of them into miniature versions of the homeownership dream. It was a marginally successful attempt to assimilate some slum-dwellers into the dominant system of housing rewards and values. Through the twentieth century, politicians promulgated the Christian virtue and patriotism inherent in single-family homeownership, while tax codes, zoning ordinances, realtors, and popular writers promoted the moral superiority attached to single-family homeownership. Despite the ideological push toward homeownership and the support for suburbanization, however, many reformers recognized the limitations of slum reform pursued through social action and middle-class example, and advocated wholesale replacement of such "blighted" areas with newly designed communities. I conclude Chapter 2 by examining the Anglo-American tradition of village-inspired community design that emerged during

Table 1 The Prehistory of Public Housing in Boston

YEAR	HOUSING REWARDS	HOUSING COPING MECHANISMS
1600		1601 Elizabethan poor laws
	1630 Winthrop's Puritans find "vacuum domicilium"	1630s ff. Settlement laws and "warning out"
		1637 First Alien and Sedition Act
1650		1657 Scot's Charitable Society founded
		1662 Almshouse on Boston Common
		1685 New almshouse/workhouse
	1692 Nuisance Ordinance to Protect Homes	1691 Bostonians elect overseers of the poor
1700		1721 Bridewell on Boston Common
		1724 Irish Charitable Society founded
		1739 Workhouse on Boston Common
1750	1785 Land Ordinance Act	
1800		1800 Leverett Street almshouse
		1818 McLean Asylum for the Insane
		1821 Quincy reports on poor relief
		1823 House of Industry and House of Correction, South Boston
		1834 Massachusetts counties require House of Correction
	1841 "Log Cabin Bill" (Preemption Act)	1840s Boston Lunatic Asylum
		1846 *Report of the Committee on the Expediency of Providing Better Tenements for the Poor*
1850		1852 House of Industry, Deer Island
		1854 Model Lodging House Association
	1855 Old Soldier's Act (public lands for veterans)	1857 Boston Board of Directors of Public Institutions formed
	1862 Homestead Act	1867 First tenement law passed, New York
	1870–1900 Streetcar suburb opportunities	1868 First tenement law passed, Massachusetts

YEAR	HOUSING REWARDS	HOUSING COPING MECHANISMS
		1875 *The Sanitary Condition of Boston*
	1880 ff. Federal pensions for veterans and widowed mothers	1870s ff. Model tenements
	1880 ff. Cooperative savings associations	1887 Massachusetts Bureau of Labor invents the term "unemployment"
	1880s ff. Building associations for working class	
	1890s Homestead clubs	1890 *How the Other Half Lives* (Riis)
		1891 Boston "Tenement Census"
		1893 *Civilization's Inferno* (Flower)
1900		1901 New York Tenement House Law
	1907ff. Tax laws reward homeownership	
	1910ff. Model working-class suburbs	
	1910ff. Small house movement	1910 *A Model Tenement House Law* (Veiller)
	1911 Massachusetts Homestead Commission (state-sponsored small houses)	
	1916ff. Zoning laws to protect single-family residences	1914ff. *A Model Housing Law* (Veiller)
	1918ff. World War I defense housing	
	1920 "Own Your Own Home" campaign	
	1922ff. "Better Homes Movement"	
	1931 President's Conference on Housing and Home Ownership	

the first decades of the twentieth century. These ideas, which coalesced most durably in Clarence Perry's "neighborhood unit" concept, combined the institutional focus of the settlement movement with an emphasis on residential superblocks. In form and scale, these new communities anticipated the urban public housing project and, also like the early projects, they often excluded the least advantaged. At every turn, tenement reformers, settlement workers, and community designers struggled to reconcile apartment living for the impoverished with the nation's dominant values favoring single-family homes and wide-open spaces.

Public housing, as locally implemented in Boston following the creation of the Boston Housing Authority (BHA) in 1935, represents a continuation of this ideological conflict by other means. Part II traces the controversial origins, racial tensions, disastrous decline, and ambitious partial revival of the BHA, examining institutional actions in relation to evolving national ideas about why public housing should exist, whom it should serve, and how it should look. Since the New Deal, the contested terrain of public housing has been buffeted by three contending rationales, which view public housing variously as primarily an exercise in humanitarian assistance, a venture in neighborhood design, or a tool for economic development. Conflicting motives and shifting agendas prevented consensus about who the intended beneficiaries of public housing should be, where it should be located, and what form it should take. Under these conditions, there could be little sustained progress in meeting any of the diverse objectives.

Chapter 3 examines the two major waves of public housing construction in Boston, which occurred just before World War II and in the early 1950s. In Boston, as in other cities where public housing construction got an early start, city leaders envisioned the projects as a new form of reward for good citizenship. They used the projects as a spatial and formal means to distinguish these "deserving poor" from the less worthy denizens of the surrounding slums. Public housing was intended to be a precursor to homeownership, a subsidized waystation to enable the industrious to save enough money to move upward on the scale of preferred domestic environments. The BHA justified the slum clearance that usually preceded the prewar construction as a service to slumdwellers that freed them from dangerous and indecent living conditions. Yet few of the evicted slumdwellers had the financial resources, the proper family structure, and the right citizenship to gain a place in the new public housing that the BHA constructed in place of their old neighborhoods, so the result, in effect, was a policy that promoted public neighborhoods without public neighbors. The selected groups who displaced them came with a publicly granted seal of approval from the Authority or firm political connections.

The second major burst of BHA project construction in Boston occurred between 1949 and 1954. Influenced by wartime defense housing efforts, public housing reemerged as a reward system for veterans and their families. Admissions standards included not only objective measures of need but also moralistic judgments about merit, measured by such criteria as a stable track record of earned wages, children born only after wedlock, service to the country in wartime, or service to the city during peacetime. As with the prewar projects, admission to public housing was a privilege, never a right.

Chapter 4 traces the BHA's struggle to manage its public housing once tenant preferences and civil rights pressures forced the Authority to accept a far more impoverished and decidedly more racially diverse cohort of public neighbors than had ever been envisioned. With twenty-five large family public housing projects already in place, located primarily in white neighborhoods and intended primarily for white occupancy, city officials turned instead to another priority: renewing the downtown to promote municipal fiscal stability and curb decentralization. During the early years of urban renewal, the projects held an ambiguous status; still regarded as a reward, they gradually also came to serve as a repository for public neighbors displaced by other forms of public action. As the preferred sorts of tenants gained the economic mobility to move out of the projects, and as segregation in them came under attack during the 1960s, the BHA faced mounting pressures to house single-parent and nonwhite families fairly and equally.

As the economic and racial composition of public housing changed during the 1960s and 1970s, neighborhood sentiment turned against it, and local support declined. With rent receipts tied to stagnating tenant incomes, and with inadequate state and federal subsidies, the poorly managed housing authority faced a fiscal crisis. The BHA deferred necessary maintenance, allowing many aging building systems to fail, and a frustrated polity often blamed the tenants themselves for the disorder of their projects. Now those inside rather than outside the projects were perceived as the socially disorganized slumdwellers. Instead of a system designed to keep public neighbors out, public housing increasingly became the place to consolidate them. Beginning in the 1960s, the BHA tried to deal with the growing stigma of its large family public housing projects by leasing private housing and entered into a variety of partnerships with private-sector development and management firms. None of these ventures, however, could divert attention away from the BHA's ever-pressing need to manage the twenty-five large family housing projects it had built between 1938 and 1954, and to cope with the massive needs of the public neighbors who continued to live in them. By the end of the 1970s, the whole system of Boston projects faced total institutional collapse, and the BHA was ordered into receivership.

Chapter 5, by way of conclusion, examines the partial success of efforts to re-suscitate the BHA and its projects during the period of the receivership, and briefly traces public housing reform efforts in the 1990s. In Boston, as in other American cities, the century closed with a trend to demolish large projects and to return more public housing to the working-class poor who first inhabited it. At the beginning of the twenty-first century, as at the beginning of the seventeenth, Boston officials still treat public neighbors with a well-worn ambivalence. In the public neighborhoods of the projects, social obligation and spatial stigma remain uneasily conjoined.

THE PREHISTORY OF
PUBLIC HOUSING

ONE

Coping with the Poor: Techniques and Institutions

SINCE THE TIME of the seventeenth-century Puritan villages, American communities have struggled to define the nature and extent of their ethical and jurisdictional responsibilities to public neighbors—those judged socioeconomically unable or unwilling to meet their community's standards of industry or behavior. The term *public neighbor* simultaneously encodes both social obligation and spatial proximity. Over the centuries, these matters of obligation and proximity have found expression in many different institutional and architectural forms—from almshouses to model tenements to settlement houses to public housing projects—and the jurisdictional and ethical issues have inevitably become more complex and more contested.

The jurisdictional struggle has centered on distinctions between stranger and neighbor, initially expressed through a variety of settlement laws that tried to limit public obligation to those individuals legally considered to be part of the community. Closely paralleling the jurisdictional struggle has been the ethical one, expressed through a variety of attempts to distinguish the public obligation to the "deserving" poor from the need to cope with those seen as undeserving. Local authorities have wished to assist those who worked but earned too little to support themselves, as well as those who were disabled, orphaned, elderly, and diseased. They have also, more reluctantly, expended public funds on those whose poverty apparently stemmed from their unwillingness to work (often characterized, until the mid-twentieth century, as able-bodied paupers, rogues, vagabonds, or "sturdy beggars"). As communities have grown in size and diversity, both the deserving/undeserving and the stranger/neighbor distinctions have proved more difficult to make, but this fact has never prevented communities from continuing to try.

In an increasingly pluralist America, decisions about the obligation, location, and form of assistance to the poor have reflected profound ambivalence toward those whose behaviors and group norms differed from once-prevailing white Anglo-Saxon Protestant practice (or ideals). Once such people had been allowed to enter a particular jurisdiction, that community was obliged to respond to their needs. But the ambivalence underlying that obligation revealed itself in the ways it was administered spatially.

Many historians of American poverty policy have treated the eighteenth- and nineteenth-century efforts to assist economically dependent people as background for discussion of twentieth-century relief and welfare programs. Yet it is also possible to see these earliest created conceptual frameworks as essential to understanding the history, politics, and form of low-income housing. Every decision about *how* to assist a public neighbor is a decision about *where* to do so. Whether intended to reinforce a decentralized house-based system of "outdoor relief" or to displace and consolidate the impoverished into peripherally located poorhouses and other residential institutions ("indoor relief"), decisions about public neighbors have always entailed decisions about housing.

Housing issues may also be seen as a fundamental aspect of public intervention. Poor housing conditions do more than contribute to the plight of the public neighbor; they also symbolize it, and draw societal attention to the existence of a problem. Poverty expresses itself not only through signs of ill-nourishment and ragged attire; it is also signaled by inadequacies of shelter. Poor housing gives poverty not just a personal but a spatial dimension. In America's urban areas, public neighbors have always been defined geographically, by reference to almshouse, ghetto, tenement, slum, and, eventually, housing project.

Actual distance from the more prosperous citizenry is reinforced by ideological distance from the owned single-family home on private land. As Herbert Gans has observed, "Everyday life is, among other things, a never-ending flow of moral surveillance."[1] Such surveillance is often trained on dwellings—judgments of self and others are closely bound up with how we assess houses and neighborhoods. Would-be housing reformers have almost always stressed not just matters of safety and sanitation but also questions of "decency." In a society whose laws and literature invest the single-family house with a kind of moral superiority, those without the means to obtain one have frequently been treated as morally inferior. We have linked substandard housing with anti-social behavior, and regarded better housing as socially transformative. Moral habits and spatial habitats became conjoined in a cycle of environmental determinism.

The public neighbor occupies the ambivalent middle ground of collective social engagement, considered neither a good citizen nor an irredeemable pariah. Though not wholly criminalized through banishment, imprisonment, or punishment, public neighbors are more likely to be tolerated as merely denizens than accorded respect as full citizens. Having emerged from both Christian duty and a concern for public order, the obligation to aid public neighbors remains a wellspring of mixed motives.

THE MORAL GEOGRAPHY OF PURITAN SPACE

The English Puritans who settled New England brought with them most aspects of the Elizabethan poor laws.[2] These laws helped to clarify the relationship between the individual and the state, declaring that those who could not support themselves must be supported by their communities through a combination of local taxation and parish-channeled charity. In contrast to continental traditions that emphasized confinement to institutions (such as workhouses, almshouses, and hospitals), the English approach to social welfare placed the burden of implementation on churchwardens and "overseers of the poor" in every parish, charging them with collecting taxes, relieving the "impotent," setting the able-bodied to work, and placing poor children in apprenticeship. Puritan leaders, who in England had championed many of the most comprehensive efforts at poverty relief, carried this predilection across the Atlantic.[3]

Even before landing in Boston in 1630, John Winthrop reminded his fellow passengers on the *Arbella* that God had arranged the condition of mankind such that "at all times some must be rich, some poor, some high and eminent in power and dignity, others mean and in subjection." Those accompanying Winthrop, though vocationally diverse and including both ordinary and indentured servants, were hardly impoverished. The Puritans had left behind the beggars, scavengers, and vagabonds that made up "England's visible poor."[4] Nevertheless, Winthrop, who himself came from the landed gentry, knew that the success of his idealized Christian community depended upon concern for the general welfare, the ability to "make others' conditions our own." In the most famous passage of his lay sermon, "A Model of Christian Charity," he aligned Puritan destiny with Matthew's evocation of "a city upon a hill." Often misinterpreted as a mark of haughty confidence, Winthrop used this urban geographical metaphor not to boast but to warn about the danger of overexposure to public criticism. The new settlement could become "a story and a by-word through the world," he worried, if it *failed* to create and sustain a community grounded in "Christian charity."⁵

Led by clergy who viewed the poor as perennially available for divinely demanded and divinely rewarded benevolence and charity, the early Massachusetts Puritans preferred to treat poverty relief as a face-to-face encounter among neighbors. Though the Puritans fully supported this community obligation as a centerpiece of Christian virtue, it eventually entailed considerable expense. The central question was not whether to accept the obligation, but how to decide who should receive aid. This, in turn, involved two related considerations: the townspeople who were eligible to vote had to decide both who was a member of the town and who, among these, was needy enough to incur the liability of town support.⁶ In New England, as in the England the Puritans had left behind, the poor laws attempted to limit or equalize the distribution of community financial responsibility by restricting the ability of indigent strangers to enter any town freely and remain there to dwell. Few strangers seemed likely to yield a commercial benefit to the community. Fearing to take in vagrants who would become an unwelcome public charge, Puritans accepted as public neighbors only those who were locally grown.

Unquestionably considered strangers, not neighbors, were the Native Americans. "God hath consumed the natives with a miraculous plague whereby the greater part of the country is left voide of inhabitants," John Winthrop matter-of-factly observed in 1629 while justifying his impending voyage.⁷ The Puritans' claim to this providentially cleared land was further justified by their having taken possession of the *vacuum domicilium* "by building an house there." By contrast, the "savage people ruleth over many lands without title or property; for they inclose no ground, neither have they cattell to maintayne it."⁸ The biblically grounded claim that the land belonged to those who dwelled and labored upon it transformed the humble home of the colonial pioneer into a sanctified gesture (Fig. 1.1). In the 1630s, settlers in Boston built and distributed themselves into 700 single-family homes, each with its own garden.⁹ John Foster's map of New England (1677) underscored the contrast by indicating English towns with miniature houses and church steeples, but marking Indian settlements only with trees. Though Boston's Puritans obtained a deed for their land from the Indians in 1684, this was an expedient formality, never intended to acknowledge that the natives had previously held a proper title under English law.

Excluded from vast areas of settlement by colonists who could not understand their "unsettled" ways and indifference to homeownership, the Indians were treated as strangers rather than neighbors, even before war with the Pequots broke out in 1637. When the Indians burned thousands of houses and destroyed

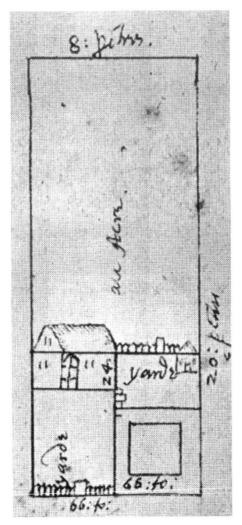

FIGURE 1.1 John Winthrop's house and garden, 1630. Winthrop's journal contains a page of sketches, including a plan of a house with front yard and one-acre rear garden.

dozens of whole towns during King Philip's War four decades later, the Puritan colonists lost not only hundreds of lives, but also the key symbols of their Englishness. As Jill Lepore puts it, "English possessions were, in a sense, what was at stake in the war, for these—the clothes they wore, the houses they lived in, and the things they owned—were a good part of what distinguished the English from the Indians." Even in more peaceful times, a society intent on finding ways to limit who should be counted as a public charge saw little reason to treat the Indians as potential public neighbors.[10] Instead, membership in a mutually supportive community was limited, and encoded in the very fabric of the town.

Puritan sociospatial practice gave New England towns their characteristic moral geography. At the moral, political, and spatial center was the meetinghouse, with the marketplace usually adjacent. Boston's first meetinghouse was constructed just up the street from John Winthrop's house, and in 1635 the Massachusetts General Court passed a law forbidding construction of any residence more than half a mile from a meetinghouse in any new settlement. Although the law proved impossible to enforce, the ideological intent remained clear: communities based on shared faith and cooperation needed to remain small and centered.[11]

WARNING OUT STRANGERS

During the seventeenth and eighteenth centuries the colonists adopted strict laws of settlement, intended to give each town the leeway to choose its inhabitants, and crafted to clarify the terms of obligation to them. In short, they attempted to enforce a residency requirement for public assistance, one that was designed to enable careful distinction between "inhabitants" and "unsettled" strangers.

Massachusetts town records from the mid-seventeenth century identify two major reasons for the rejection of newcomers: religion, and the perceived likelihood of early public dependency. Both forms of newcomer carried unacceptable costs for the community and were "warned out" of the town.[12] Thus the early settlements clearly signaled their jurisdictional unwillingness to accept public neighbors. These people arrived seeking to be neighbors, but were firmly rebuffed because their unacceptable beliefs or their unpredictable intents portended unwelcome private relations or public obligations.

In 1636, Boston town selectmen were granted the formal right to decide who would be admitted, and in 1637, they gained the power to screen all would-be sojourners "to keepe out such whose Lives were publickely prophane and scandalous [as well] as those whose judgements were Corrupt."[13] Governor Winthrop publicly defended this first American alien and sedition act by explaining that Massachusetts Bay was a "commonwealth . . . established by free consent," and that "the nature of such an incorporation ties every member thereof to seek out and entertain all means that may conduce to the welfare of the body, and to keep off . . . whatsoever appears to tend to our ruin or damage." Winthrop argued that it was therefore "lawful to take knowledge of all men before we receive them." The virtue of hospitality, he observed, "doth not bind further than for some present occasion, not for continual residence." As the governor would have it, "it is worse to receive a man whom we must cast out again, than to deny him admittance." Winthrop wished to guard the towns of Massachusetts against an influx of Antinomian heretics and non-Christians. Solomon Franco—Boston's first Jew—was warned out in 1649.[14]

Boston leaders feared not only doctrinal impurity but also financial liability. In 1647, the selectmen ordered—under threat of stiff fine—that any town inhabitant who "shall entertaine man or woman from any other towne or country as a sojourner . . . with an intent to reside here" must notify "the selectmen of the towne for their approbation within 8 dayes after their cominge to the towne." The sale of property to a stranger could be voided if transferred without prior town approval. Even newcomers judged acceptable underwent close financial scrutiny, and their admission sometimes required permanent sponsorship by a townsperson in the form of a bond holding the town free from the obligation to support the new neighbor, should he or she ever become dependent.[15]

With suspicion especially high regarding potential paupers arriving from overseas, Boston port officials denied some immigrants permission to disembark from their vessels and required that the vessel operators post bond for all others. In 1650, the Massachusetts General Court passed a law further restricting the entry of strangers by sea, stating that such people had been responsible for "great mischeifes and outrages" elsewhere. In 1655, following further complaints that strangers were continuing to enter Boston without the consent of the inhabitants and causing the town to be charged for their subsequent support, the General Court declared that the towns were under no obligation to provide aid. Responsibility for the relief and maintenance of those who entered "without the consent and allowance of the prudentiall men" (that is, the selectmen) rested with "those that were the cause of their coming in."[16]

Despite the various laws enacted to define the exact meaning of legal settlement in a town, and the wide powers available to warn out the undesirable, Boston's rapid growth brought an increase in the number of dependent poor. By the mid-1670s, according to historian Josiah Henry Benton, it had become "practically impossible" to enforce the exclusion of newcomers by physically preventing them from coming in or by warning them out. In practice, then, "warning out" did not always entail actual removal. During most of the eighteenth century, it consisted of a legal warning stipulating that, should they remain, the town would not support them in case of subsequent poverty. The stigma of having "been warned" persisted well after actual deportations ceased to be enforced. Even with such warnings in place, however, the need for public support of the poor continued to grow; the town's first private charitable society was already in place by 1657.[17]

Whenever private charity and kinship networks fell short in seventeenth-century Boston, aid to poor inhabitants became the responsibility of the selectmen. Until 1691, local officials dealt with their poor on a case-by-case basis, with each person's fate discussed at the town meeting, even though Boston was then the largest town in North America. Once the burden of this task threatened to derail the machinery of town government, however, Bostonians followed British practice and appointed separately elected "overseers of the poor." To minimize the burden of public relief, the justices, selectmen, and overseers of the poor undertook regular "walks" through the streets "for the purpose of discovering disorders and condition of living that might, if not changed, bring the inhabitants to dependency." According to a 1715 entry in the *Boston Selectmen's Records,* the object of such visits was to "inspect disorderly persons, new-comers, and the circumstances of the Poor and Education of their Children." By the middle of the eighteenth century, this task—following London precedent—was professionalized, with agents specially hired to seek out undesirable strangers, warn them out, and expedite their departure. These municipal bouncers were paid a set commission for each potential public neighbor thereby evicted. From 1721 to 1742, more than 500 strangers were warned out of Boston.[18]

POVERTY AMONG NEIGHBORS

For legally resident townspeople, the public response to poverty remained quite different. In seventeenth-century Boston, the home-grown dependent poor judged especially worthy were boarded in private houses, or, in rare cases, were allowed to live on their own at public expense. Some deserving poor received temporary assistance in cash or other forms.[19] At the same time, other sorts of impoverished people received harsher treatment. Robert W. Kelso's analysis of three hundred years of selectmen's and overseers' records describing poor relief in Massachusetts sets forth a litany of "ordinances and warnings and votes embodying shrewd Yankee bargains" aimed at "ridding the town" of the unwanted expenses associated with dependent families. This pattern of public assistance reveals an ever-hardening attempt to distinguish between deserving and undeserving public neighbors. In certain cases, town leaders counseled no public response at all; as Cotton Mather put it in the early eighteenth century: "For those who indulge themselves in idleness, the express command of God unto us is, that we shall let them starve."[20] Puritan leaders assumed that wayward conduct in defiance of family and church teachings was the cause of poverty and dependency, and the Massachusetts courts promulgated and upheld the harshest of admonitions and punishments. Willfully unemployed adults were "put out to service," with their children "disposed abroad for servants"—rented out "to the lowest bidder," all in the name of sparing further public expense. The universal custom in Massachusetts towns of the late eighteenth and early nineteenth centuries was to stage an auction, usually at a local tavern on the Saturday night following the annual town meeting. Kelso, having reviewed the records of many Massachusetts towns, presents a composite scene:

> Here, ranged about the table, sat the fathers of the town and such of those as by hard living and coarse thinking had arrived a place in life where they could speculate upon the bodily vigor and the probable capacity for hard labor of a half-witted boy, a forlorn-looking widow, or a halt and tottering old man. As they drained their liquor, the talk was not upon the sorrows of the poor or the hope that life, even the most humble, must hold for all men: it turned, rather, upon the odd shilling, the halfpence, the danger of the pauper dying whereby the bidder might lose a part of his equity.[21]

Among those allowed to remain as neighbors, idleness continued to be monitored and was subject to prosecution. Conviction, as stipulated in the Acts of 1692, entailed whippings and hard labor for adults, while their children were bound over to the town for use as apprentices. Actual public relief to those considered to be legitimate town inhabitants was parsed out in amounts just necessary to sustain life. With one's name and financial circumstances discussed at the town meeting and one's poverty forever inscribed in the town records, the stigma of "going on the town" was no doubt almost as demoralizing as the poverty itself. In the smaller towns in the eighteenth century, public relief often proceeded on the belief that short-term noncash assistance (such as the loan of a "town cow" or aid with house construction) would be sufficient to set an impoverished family on a more independent financial course. As Kelso observes, there was little attempt to distinguish among the causes of impoverishment: "Poverty was not differentiated from chronic pauperism and pauperism was akin to crime. The sturdy beggar, the idiot, the drunkard, and the widow who was only poor, were herded together under the same roof, the chief source of anxiety being the net cost of the establishment." In small towns this roof might be owned by a single individual, one who had successfully bid for the right to employ many of the town's paupers; in larger cities, where the poor were too numerous to be easily auctioned off, it was both necessary and more economical to rely on almshouses.[22]

ALMSHOUSES

Boston's first almshouse, which was probably the first in the American colonies, was constructed as a small woodframe structure on the eastern edge of Boston Common in 1662.[23] Some wanted it to serve as a house of correction for those who were "debauched and live idly"; while others thought it designed for "Honest Poor Peoples."[24] Both constituencies would be served. Its first occupant, "Mrs. Jane Woodcock, widow," took up residence in 1665, and soon had diverse company. When this structure burned down in 1682, the town meeting voted to build a larger and more durable facility. Speakers to the question decried the costs of poor relief, arising from the need to minister not only to the elderly and disabled and to those unable to find steady work but also to "persons & Families [that] misspend their time, in idlenesse & tipllinge with great neglect of their callings and suffer ye Children shamefully to spend their time in ye Streetes." To cope with this less worthy form of public neighbor, the new brick almshouse, completed in 1685, included a small workhouse intended to force public employment on the able-bodied poor.[25]

For the next several decades the almshouse/workhouse became the single repository for all who were unable to sustain themselves economically in the town. In 1694, the colony's "Act for the Relief of Ideots and Distracted Persons" laid more responsibility on town officials to provide for such people, and another law soon authorized the towns to institutionalize the most "furiously mad."[26] Heavy losses among Boston men in the Anglo-French wars of 1690 and 1711 led to an unusually high level of widowhood, and poverty was compounded by major fires in 1702 and 1711 coupled with a downturn in trade. In addition, as the region's political and economic capital and chief port, Boston received an increasingly unmanageable influx of destitute immigrants, free blacks, and refugees fleeing the conflicts with Indians on the New England frontier.[27]

Faced with diverse types of impoverished people, Boston's townspeople tried to address the problem on multiple fronts. In 1698 the town meeting appropriated £400 for materials and tools "To Sett and keep the poor people and Ill persons at work." Beginning in 1702, the town placed spinning wheels in the almshouse and periodically provided wool to keep them turning. Beyond the almshouse walls, the churches, together with charitable individuals and organizations, provided sources of private relief. In 1706 the town meeting doubled the number of overseers of the poor from four to eight; in 1715, it divided the city into eight wards to facilitate a division of responsibilities and quarterly visits by standing committees comprised of selectmen, justices, overseers, and constables. As dispensers of public relief, these committees committed funds to board some of the indigent with relatives; those without appropriate family were sent to the almshouse. Always, the "indoor relief" provided by Boston's almshouse remained clearly subordinate to public and private efforts to center responsibility for the poor on family and community. Taking in approximately 250 people annually, the almshouse was a domicile of last resort for chronically poor townspeople lacking "household support" and, on a temporary basis, "strangers in need— to prevent them from perishing."[28]

For more than half a century, the Boston almshouse—as the only remaining alternative to the jail—served two broad constituencies: the residue of widows, orphans, and the physically and mentally infirm not reached by private charity, and "the vagabond, the prostitute, the drunkard, and the loathsome syphilitic," for Suffolk County officials also used it as a bridewell. Only the "furiously mad" had separate sleeping quarters. Eventually, in 1713, the Boston town meeting directed the overseers of the poor to accept into the almshouse only "such are as proper objects of the charity of this town"; a year later as an interim measure the town meeting proposed erecting an actual partition through the building to separate the "sober and aged" worthy poor from "those put in for vice and disorder." Not until 1721 did Suffolk County purchase a piece of Boston Common next to the almshouse to build a separate bridewell for housing unruly servants and minor offenders, with part of the house also devoted to housing the insane. Plans to construct a separate "mad house" for the care of "distracted persons" did not materialize (Fig. 1.2).[29]

In 1739, using funds raised from public subscription, Bostonians constructed a 120-foot-long two-story brick workhouse next to the bridewell. Its promoters intended the workhouse to reinforce the settlement laws by serving as a deterrent to the migration of needy strangers and as a form of punishment for those accused of indolence. Its very existence bespoke the firm belief that some forms of destitution were self-imposed, and that failure to embrace the Yankee work ethic was grounds for community censure. The new strategy was to penalize the able-bod-

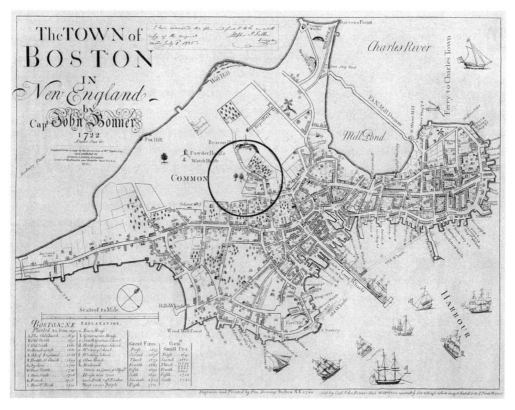

FIGURE 1.2 Bonner map of 1722. This map shows the location of Boston's almshouse and bridewell. Both are located on the northeastern edge of the Common, adjacent to the "Burying Place," now referred to as the Granary Burial Ground (see circle). This location, though only a short walk from major civic and commercial facilities, was on the periphery of developed lands.

ied poor by placement in this institution—where their labor could support the maintenance of the house—while retaining the almshouse for those who had a physical excuse to be without work, and relying on the jails and other houses of correction to incarcerate more serious criminal offenders.

It was soon apparent, however, that such firm distinctions were not easily applied. Despite the lingering expectation that townspeople could care for their own wayward members, the new workhouse did little to redress the broader problem of wandering "Rogues, Vagabonds [and] Common Beggars," and the almshouse continued to house a broad cross-section of the needy. Nor did the various facilities deter the arrival of impoverished strangers. A report in 1736 revealed that, of the eighty-eight persons residing in the poorhouse, only one-third were Boston-born, yielding much outrage that nearly £1,400 had been spent that year to support those "who are crept in among us." Another report by the overseers of the poor explained the financial problems of the workhouse by observing that it contained many "distracted, helpless & infirm people" who could not engage in productive labor. Despite persistent criticism about excessive expense, jurisdictional responsibility, and rising taxes, however, Boston could boast what was arguably eighteenth-century America's most complete system of poor relief.[30]

THE EXPANSION OF PUBLIC RESPONSIBILITY

During the course of Boston's first century, its leaders regarded public aid as a local responsibility, but struggled to define who should be considered "local." Unwanted strangers always constituted a problem, and when the first waves of homeless refugees from King Philip's War straggled into town in 1675, Bostonians sought outside assistance. Acknowledging the emergency, the Massachusetts General Court passed a special act providing funds for temporary relief from the provincial treasury to meet the expenses of Boston and other desperate towns unable to cope with so many "unsettled" new residents. This first act of relief sponsored extralocally was intended to meet a short-lived predicament, but was never repealed. Over time, town officials ignored the restricted nature of the original intent, and Massachusetts gradually augmented the terms under which the towns could expect reimbursement for support of the "Province-poor." By the mid-eighteenth century, Kelso contends, the expectation of outside aid led towns to relax their previously tight scrutiny and inspection of their more questionable new neighbors, who were often the former denizens of English prisons and poorhouses or wanderers from other colonies. Although towns continued to warn out their undesirable strangers so as to remain in legal compliance, they had far less incentive to take the additional expensive steps to ensure actual departure. Of equal import, the regional system carried no statutory requirement that the able-bodied work in exchange for their aid; with one system for treating the "Province-poor," it became increasingly difficult for town leaders to enforce work requirements on the locally reared ("settled") poor, especially since the two groups were often housed together.[31]

The ambivalence of early New Englanders toward housing their poor is reflected in two major surveys of poor relief in seventeenth- and early eighteenth-century Puritan Massachusetts. Historian David Rothman, focusing on the ministers' sermons, describes a society driven by Christian benevolence; while attorney Robert Kelso, immersing himself in the "chill and unsympathetic annals" of town boards and overseers, chronicles a society in which tolerance and community responsibility were coupled with ruthless stigmatization and resentful concern over expenses.[32] Both versions appear valid: in the Puritan conscience, paternalistic concern for the well-being of worthy dependent residents coexisted with contempt for the healthy unemployed and suspect stranger.

By the early eighteenth century, rapid population growth and mobility placed unprecedented strain on traditional systems of family and home care of the poor and disabled. Although neighborhood charity remained the rule rather than the exception, public neighbors, when jurisdictionally accepted at all, were housed in a trio of buildings on the townward edge of Boston Common. The Common itself was not central to the town, but the short, pedestrian-scaled distances of a tightly settled peninsula meant that even this somewhat eccentric location was only a five- or ten-minute walk from the town's civic and commercial core. In other words, during Boston's first century, obligation to the poor remained locally vested, and the town's public charges—even when institutionalized—were still allowed to be neighbors.

NEW INSTITUTIONS FOR INDOOR RELIEF:
WALLING IN PUBLIC NEIGHBORS

For most of the eighteenth century, arrangements for relief of Boston's poor continued to follow earlier practices: whenever practical, assistance was centered in neighborhoods, and the almshouse and workhouse remained small facilities for exceptional situations. In the early decades of the republic, however, Americans created a wholly new institutional system, one that partially shifted the jurisdictional obligation for housing undesirables away from the towns toward more centralized forms of government and, simultaneously, shifted the location of the institutionalized away from the homes of the more prosperous citizenry. Although the new institutions never even came close to becoming the numerically dominant form of poor relief, their ideological and symbolic presence became very powerful.

In the decades after 1820, Bostonians, New Yorkers, and Philadelphians led what became a nationwide "revolution in social practice," characterized by the simultaneous construction of penitentiaries for the criminal, asylums for the insane, almshouses for the poor, orphan asylums for homeless children, and reformatories for delinquents.[33] In all of these cases, the object of public action stood transformed. What had once been justified in terms of Christian obligation to respond to individual needs for shelter and sustenance now moved according to different principles. In contrast to prevailing seventeenth- and eighteenth-century American practice, public neighbors became objects of reform. Instead of maintenance, reformers now spoke of the possibility of cure.

In each newly constructed setting, promoters predicated this new institutionalization of care on a widely shared environmental determinism; architecture and organizational structure were deemed central to rehabilitation. Insanity, for example, was considered curable, if the insane could be housed in "a different kind of environment, which methodically corrected the deficiencies of the community." The asylum, in its architecture and in its routine, "would re-create fixity and stability to compensate for the irregularities of the society." Similar hopes spurred mass construction of penitentiaries, "free of corruptions and dedicated to the proper training of the inmate," where it would be possible to "inculcate the discipline that negligent parents, evil companions, taverns, houses of prostitution, theaters, and gambling halls had destroyed."[34] According to the Boston Prison Discipline Society, "There are principles in architecture, by the observance of which great moral changes can be more easily produced among the most abandoned of our race," and "the prospect of improvement, in morals, depends, in some degree, upon the construction of buildings." In a like manner, orphan asylums, reformatories, and almshouses were expected to redeem those they housed.[35]

Taken together, these institutions removed many categories of public neighbors from local responsibility in the hope of guaranteeing greater social tranquillity for the towns, and promoting, when possible, the rehabilitation of these public charges. In so doing, they created a new spatial base for public neighbors, one that in many cases turned locally known dependent people into displaced strangers. Because these reform impulses were often linked to the desirability of forced agricultural labor and to the benefits of outdoor activity, the new institutions required large plots of land, usually neither affordable nor available near the heart of a large settlement. Only by institutionalizing the problem people, paradoxically, could the overall anti-institutionalism that characterized the populist individualism of the Jacksonian age be permitted to flourish.

Although these institutions served only a minority of the Boston poor, and home relief remained numerically dominant, the new institutional layer had profound implications. To the extent that relief provision went both indoors and out of town, the dependent poor, who had long been considered a visible and inevitable part of the town community, were rendered invisible. In the colonial era even the almshouses architecturally resembled the regular houses of the town, and internal practices tried to mimic family routines. Now reformers delivered their indigents and miscreants to vast institutions, usually well isolated from dense concentrations of townspeople, and often consisting of imposing structures set out in ample grounds. Built and maintained at public expense, such institutions combined concern for the welfare of public neighbors with fearful insistence on their spatial isolation. Warning out had become walling in, a far more enforceable form of quarantine.

The long-standing view that a great deal of poverty was caused by willful indolence slowly gave way to the realization that dependency had many different sources. As the causes of poverty were brought into question, so, too, the prevailing practices of relief came under attack. In the secularizing and fluid society of the early American republic, more citizens challenged the belief that poverty was providentially imposed, and the old parochial insularity of the Puritans seemed increasingly incapable of providing for secure civic organization. With greater mobility of goods and labor, and increasing industrialization, the early New England assumption that responsibility extended only to the locally settled poor became an anachronism increasingly difficult to sustain.

In 1821 Massachusetts became the first of many states to establish a committee to investigate the conditions and relief of the Commonwealth's poor. Led by

Josiah Quincy, soon to be elected Boston's mayor, the committee produced a landmark report whose conclusions would help redirect relief policy in Massachusetts and elsewhere. Besides noting that the taxpayers of Boston were asked to relieve as many as 600 dependent people annually, the Quincy report sought to detail causes of dependency and how to cure them. Not surprisingly, the document revealed great ambivalence. On the one hand, it laid blame on the poor themselves, concluding that "of all causes of pauperism, intemperance, in the use of spiritous liquors, is the most powerful and universal." In this respect, the report confirmed the popular view stressing a distinction between the deserving poor (who were physically incapable of work) and the undeserving able-bodied, whose pauperism stemmed from their own indolence. Elsewhere, however, the report blamed the problem of dependency on the still-dominant practice of "outdoor relief"; supporting the poor at home discouraged initiative and gave them too much free time, encouraging them to partake in the vices present in the community. The Quincy report called this relief method "the most wasteful, the most expensive, and most injurious to their morals, and destructive of their industrious habits."[36] Although the report stopped short of urging the abandonment of all state-based relief in favor of reliance on private charities and did not advocate substituting institutional care for all forms of home relief, it opened the way for broader discussions of the subject.

Activist Bostonians, notably Joseph Tuckerman (Boston's first "minister to the poor") and Dr. Walter Channing (an obstetrician who delivered the babies of the poor at Massachusetts General Hospital), spoke out about the economic causes of poverty, pointing out that many of the poor were the hapless victims of unexpected fluctuations in job availability, low wages, or employment-related illness or injury. Moreover, they argued that the society bore responsibility for the environmental conditions under which the poor were forced to live, and that the availability of nearby vice was too great a temptation to the least provident among them. As Rothman puts it, "the charity sermon" that had characterized the Puritan response to poverty had shifted to a Yankee "analysis of the structure of the community."[37] Here, as with the concurrent movements toward asylums and penitentiaries, elimination of dependency was seen to require prior isolation from the environmental and social conditions in which pauperism could flourish. This impulse, which combined unease about the instability of the cities with growing distrust about the behavior of the poor, led to the unprecedented burgeoning of new institutions for "indoor relief."

In 1834 the Massachusetts General Court required each county to construct and maintain a house of correction. In so doing, the legislature shifted town responsibilities to a broader regional scale, helping to insure that the poor would be strangers to each other and to their keepers. At the same time, the new spatial scale of institutional reform targeted not poverty per se, but the broader list of undesirable behaviors that contributed to its most vicious manifestations. Under the new law local police, justices of the peace, and courts were empowered to commit "all rogues, vagabonds, and all idle persons going about in any town or place in the country begging, or persons using any subtle craft, juggling, or unlawful games or plays, common pipers, fiddlers, runaways, stubborn children, common drunkards, common night walkers, pilferers, wanton and lascivious persons, in speech, conduct or behavior, common railers and brawlers, such as neglect their callings or employment, misspend what they earn, and do not provide for themselves or for the support of their families."[38] This sweeping overview of undesirables suggests that misbehavior could come in many guises, but that public interest in the matter occurred only when misconduct caused such people to fail in their obligation to support themselves and their immediate families.

Although the various counties were slow to construct the new facilities, and the state continued to reimburse the towns directly, by 1865 fully 80 percent of those in Massachusetts who received extended relief "remained within an institution."[39] That said, the overall distribution of poor relief (including short-term assistance) stayed heavily skewed toward noninstitutional forms; in Massachusetts in 1870, approximately three persons per thousand received indoor relief whereas sixteen per thousand received aid outside an institution.[40] Still, with thousands of people institutionalized statewide in architecturally prominent facilities, the "revolution in social practice" remained highly visible.

ISOLATING THE ALMSHOUSE

What began in Boston in 1662 with the construction of a single almshouse as an undifferentiated repository for the indigent became transmuted, by the middle third of the nineteenth century, into a broad-based attempt to classify the various types of dependents, to reform them, and to remove them to those parts of town where their presence least threatened public and private development interests. The almshouse was shunted farther and farther from the town center. In 1790 a town committee complained that the structure on Boston Common was both too

small and no longer sufficiently peripheral. In 1798, with the completion of
Charles Bulfinch's State House nearly across the street, the almshouse found itself on the edge of a rapidly developing neighborhood that is today known as
Beacon Hill. The poorhouse immediately fell to gentrification pressures (Fig.
1.3). The town land on which the almshouse had stood was sold off to private individuals, who completed "the first of the improvements" in the area.[41] This development deal, in turn, helped finance a new Bulfinch-designed almshouse on
Leverett Street, in Boston's then-remote Barton's Point region (later known as the
West End), completed in late 1800 (Figs. 1.4–1.5).[42] That location marked just
about the last remaining out-of-the-way place on Boston's original Shawmut peninsula to put Boston's public neighbors. The new three-story facility, described
by contemporaries as a "large and expensive pile of buildings, which is so honorable to the liberality and beneficence of the town," was initially built entirely for
reception of "the infirm, diseased, aged, and children of both sexes." Soon, however, Boston's overseers of the poor sent in others considered by critics as less
worthy of "the comforts of such an institution."[43] Once again, concerns about
classification came to the fore. As ideas about institution-based reform evolved in

FIGURE 1.3 The New State House. In this view from the 1820s, the new nation's most lavish state
capitol occupies a site just opposite the northeast corner of the Common. The location of the former almshouse, bridewell, and workhouse—all torn down in the wake of gentrification—is ob-
scured by the large tree at the right of the image.

the early decades of the nineteenth century, the Leverett Street facility and its location quickly proved insufficient and inappropriate.

After more than a decade of debate over the indiscriminate mixing of paupers, pregnant women, and "lunatics" in the Leverett Street institution, the chaplain of the almshouse convinced two influential Boston physicians to lobby the legislature for construction of a general hospital that would accept all patients, regardless of their ability to pay. Eventually this resulted in the establishment of the Massachusetts General Hospital in 1818, but in keeping with the tenor of spatial resistance to public neighbors, Boston's leaders isolated the portion serving "lu-

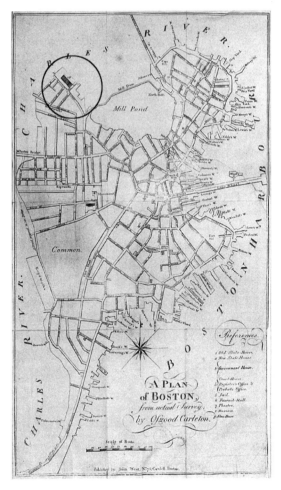

FIGURE 1.4 Location of Leverett Street almshouse. This detail from the Osgood Carleton map of 1800 shows the even more peripheral location of the new almshouse on Barton's Point.

natics." Substantially endowed by wealthy Bostonians and church-channeled bequests, the new McLean Asylum for the Insane opened not in Boston but across the water in Charlestown.[44]

THE HOUSE OF INDUSTRY

In 1821, the same year he chaired the committee that yielded the Quincy Report, Josiah Quincy also chaired a committee charged with making recommendations for the future of pauper relief in Boston itself. The general conclusions of this second report,[45] now rarely discussed, paralleled those of the Massachusetts-wide report, but stressed the need to establish a House of Industry in Boston, to supplement the Barton's Point almshouse. This more expansive alternative workhouse would be dedicated to providing for "the well directed labour of the poor." As increasing numbers of "vagrant and dissolute persons" took up residence at

FIGURE 1.5 Leverett Street almshouse, early nineteenth century. Completed in 1800 and demolished in 1825, this imposing 270-foot-wide structure was built of brick inset with marble and was considerably larger than the contemporaneous New State House. Each of its forty-eight rooms was designed for multiple occupancy. The center portion contained a 2,000-square-foot dining hall and, above this, at the focal point of the entire structure, a chapel. The basement was used for kitchens and workshops. The walled and gated complex had two yards, each approximately 80 by 280 feet.

the Leverett Street facility, the overseers had been forced to enlarge and convert its bath house building into a bridewell, "in which they have constructed small cells that are occupied by such disorderly persons as seem most to require to be punished by confinement." This practice had deprived the almshouse of "a part of its original accommodation indispensable to cleanliness and health" and substituted for it a place where confinement "must be temporary and occasional." Worst of all, hidden within a building complex originally intended to signal public benevolence toward virtuous unfortunates, the bridewell did nothing to convey an outward sense of discipline, since it relayed "no part of the terrors of such a place to persons abroad."

The "great defect" of the current almshouse, the committee concluded, was that it was "open to the indiscriminate influx of characters of all descriptions," and therefore did not easily permit the "different proportions of sympathy and solicitude" owed to the various "classes of poor [having] claims upon society." These classes consisted of "1st, the poor, by reason of age;—2nd, the poor, by reason of misfortune;—3rd, the poor, by reason of infancy;—4th, the poor, by reason of vice." With the single almshouse incapable of making the "great discrimination" in favor of the first three groups, two morally unacceptable alternatives were inevitable: either the "aged and virtuous poor" would be "reduced to the food, and made obnoxious to the severity, or the labour, to which the vicious are subjected," and thus suffer "degradation" and a "new and undeserved source of misery and misfortune," or, the "vicious" poor would be "permitted to enjoy the comforts, or partake of the indulgence, which is due to age and misfortune," and "public establishments [would] become thronged." Any perception that almshouse support could rival or surpass "the support to be obtained by labour" would lead to unacceptable consequences among the "vicious" poor. Once their "fear of poverty is diminished, and the shame of dependence obliterated," the almshouse would lose all power as a deterrent.

For Quincy's Boston committee, the only viable solution entailed construction of a separate facility, one located distantly enough to permit fifty acres of land conducive to forced agricultural labor, yet close enough to afford careful and frequent supervision by its trustees. In choosing a location for the proposed House of Industry, the committee at first favored a location on Deer Island, in Boston Harbor (Fig. 1.6). This particular island—where five hundred Christian Indians had been imprisoned "for their and our security" and put to work during King Philip's War in 1675–1676—certainly carried appropriate overtones of removal and control.[46] Upon actually visiting the site, however, the committee judged it "highly inexpedient" for a House of Industry, since the difficulty of reaching it during some seasons and weather conditions would make it awkward for the "constant supervision and inspection of a board of superintendents." This board was to be "composed of men, bred to business and accustomed to deal with men in the laborious walks of life" who "know what labour is" and "are capable of judging, by the eye, or by examination, whether neglect, or refusal to work, be through mere indolence, or real imbecility." Because such men were expected to incorporate their inspection duties into busy downtown schedules, they would require "easy and certain" access to the House of Industry, which a Deer Island location could never guarantee.

Moreover, the committee found the soil conditions on Deer Island "singularly

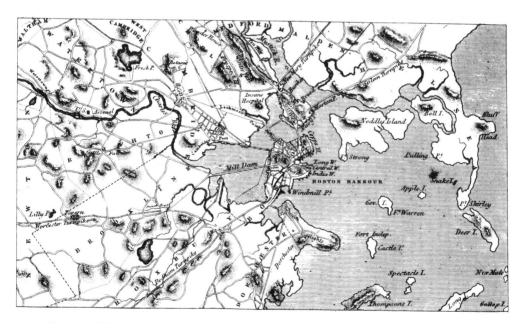

FIGURE 1.6 Boston and environs, 1820s. This map shows the dense development of Boston on its original peninsula. The Deer Island site proposed for new pauper institutions is at the far eastern edge. South Boston, where most of them ended up until the mid-nineteenth century, is the bridge-connected peninsula just south of Boston proper and is labeled "Dorchester Hights."

inauspicious" for agricultural productivity. In seeking the "economical employment of pauper industry," the committee wished to do everything possible to ensure success. With reform through hard work as its goal, promoters of the House of Industry sought to maximize the chances that "the paupers themselves may be made to take an interest, and even a pride, in the productive results of their garden, or cultivated field." Like their Puritan forebears, the Boston Protestants of the Quincy committee firmly believed that moral uplift came from working the land. At the same time, they shared the interest of both their ancestors and their contemporaries in reducing the taxes associated with municipal government administration.

Quincy's committee justified the new institution on both economic and moral grounds. Economically, they expected the House of Industry to generate "a great saving" over outdoor relief efforts while separating the "vicious poor" from "the aged and virtuous," and opening the opportunity for reform through hard work. For those public neighbors whose domestic failings were most egregious, the committee proposed what amounted to an alternative kind of "house," one premised on the restorative powers of country landscapes coupled with city-style inspection.[47] This deliberate combination of open space and strict surveillance would characterize many subsequent attempts at housing reform, including the design of public housing projects.

In 1821 the town of Boston authorized construction of both a House of Industry and a House of Correction, intended to serve complementary purposes.[48] The House of Correction was designed "for the restraint and employment of the idle and vicious poor, for habitual drunkards, beggars, and those condemned for petty offences, in the inferior courts of justice." By contrast, the House of Industry was "designed for the comfort, support, and relief, and as far as they are competent, for the employment of the virtuous poor, and of those alone who are reduced to seek this refuge, from misfortune or age or infancy."[49]

In 1823 the Boston House of Industry opened three miles from the city's commercial core in an underdeveloped section of South Boston, a newly annexed district located on a peninsula accessible by land in a roundabout way, but still isolated from it by water. Although the House of Correction and the House of Industry were to separate "idle and vicious" people from the "respectable and honest poor," the two institutions were built side by side and their architecture was nearly identical (Fig. 1.7).[50] Because city leaders expected denizens of both public houses to benefit from outdoor agricultural labor, each had access to more than fifty acres of yards and cultivated gardens, enclosed by a twelve-foot-high stockade. There were some differences, however: those in the House of Industry who had proved to be "of good behavior" were allowed out "occasionally to visit their friends, if they have any." And, on Thursdays they were allowed to receive visitors.[51]

Though less elaborately detailed than the Bulfinch-designed facility on Leverett Street (torn down in 1825), the new granite House of Industry shared most aspects of the earlier facility's spatial organization (Fig. 1.8). Like its predecessor, it was comprised of two large residential wings and a central protruding bay containing administrative and communal functions. At the top center of the structure was the chapel, breaking through the rest of the roof plane to signal its importance, with windows affording an unobstructed view of the distant church spires of Boston itself. Entrance to the building was gained on the second floor, reached by a rigidly symmetrical double exterior stair that enabled visitors to bypass the ground-floor kitchen. The middle two floors of the central bay housed

FIGURE 1.7 House of Industry and House of Correction, South Boston, ca. 1825. Unlike the single almshouse edifice at Leverett Street, the new facility was paired with a nearly identical structure intended as a city penitentiary. Together with other nearby institutions, this part of South Boston was turned into a reformer's colony, in which officials tried to classify various forms of dependency while also grouping all of these public neighbors together in an isolated area.

the superintendent's offices and living quarters, the apothecary's department, and other business facilities.

With the move out of Leverett Street, city officials had also embarked on a major administrative reorganization of Boston's poor relief system, creating a separate structure of authority for its "indoor relief" institutions. City officials vested oversight of the new facility in a board of directors; henceforth, the role of the overseers of the poor was confined to outdoor relief and the management of privately endowed charitable bequests. Architecturally, the elevated position of the administrative reception rooms seemed to mark this transition, signaling the institutional importance of the spatial juncture between resident superintendent and visiting inspectors.

This central administrative core also acted as an social barrier in the House of Industry between the women, who were confined to the facility's western wing, and the men, who were assigned to the eastern one. Necessary for internal supervision and for conveying the appearance of order to suspicious outsiders, this rigid symmetry belied the fact that male residents (both adults and chil-

FIGURE 1.8 House of Industry, South Boston, ca. 1834. The careful symmetry of building and landscape, as well as the artist's calculated inclusion of Boston's State House dome and major church spires flanking the house itself, gave an air of calm and respectability to the place, one that was wholly undermined by the despairing reports of its frustrated trustees.

dren) substantially outnumbered females. Within their respective sides of the institution, residents were assigned either to wards for the sick or to dormitory apartments containing from two to eight persons each. The two large attics, each lit only by five small dormers, contained lodgings for fifty to a hundred additional persons. On the ground-floor level—in addition to dining areas, storerooms, and the central kitchen—were the disciplinary areas: work rooms to enforce standards of industry, and a series of cells "for the punishment of refractory inmates."[52]

Despite such clear schemes of jurisdiction, classification, and discipline, the House of Industry, like its predecessor, quickly became an unclassified almshouse, where only a minority of denizens were able-bodied adult workers. In 1833 the House of Industry's trustees lamented that "Instead of a House of Industry, the place is a general infirmary, an asylum for the insane, a refuge for the deserted and most destitute children of the city." Writing in 1834, a correspondent for the *American Magazine of Useful and Entertaining Knowledge* described the House of Industry as "an asylum for the poor of all classes" and "a receptacle for men and women, whose imprudent and vicious course of life brings them into poverty and sickness."[53] As before, the public demand for places to ship the needy and undesirable had overwhelmed the capacity of the new specialized facilities to receive them.

Architecturally and socially, this overflow made a mockery of the well-controlled order conveyed by the published drawings. In addition to the main granite structure, by the early 1830s there was a variety of other structures intended to cope with the growing need to segregate and classify, and to keep up with the seasonal fluctuation in numbers—ranging from as few as 450 in the summer to as many as 660 in the winter. To keep children apart from contact with adults of "corrupt and vicious habits," the trustees authorized separate lodging and eating facilities. Reflecting the gender assumptions of the day, they built two schools— one for boys aged six to ten; the other for both boys and girls aged three to six, to which the older girls were also assigned. The schools did not need to continue much further, since children of "a suitable age" were soon "indented out to various occupations" where "a large majority of such prove faithful and respectable servants." Using thirty-five feet of space behind each wing of the main house, the city paid for construction of two new wooden houses two stories high, ninety feet long and twenty-five feet wide, the eastern one for men and the western one for women. Here, the board of directors placed all the public neighbors who could not be safely managed elsewhere: "colored persons, insane and idiots, syphilitic patients, and some others." In addition to these jumbled classifications of race and illness, the administrators of the House of Industry struggled with burgeoning numbers of foreign-born paupers. In 1833, even before the upsurge of Irish immigration, only about one-fourth of the house's adult residents were born in Boston, and three-quarters of the children had "non-American" parents.[54] Once again, the public neighbor was a dependent stranger, and the bonds of public obligation were strained.

In the simultaneous attempt to sort out the various types of dependency and to consolidate them in an out-of-the-way location, city authorities transformed parts of South Boston into a veritable village of reform, charitable, and penal institutions known at the time as the "City Lands" (Fig. 1.9). By the 1840s the House of Industry's neighbors included not only the House of Correction but also a House of Reformation (for juvenile offenders), the Boston Lunatic Hospital (intended to supplement the Charlestown facility), the School for the Feeble-Minded, a Small-pox Hospital and, nearby, the Perkins Institute for the Blind. In 1847 mounting local opposition to these institutions took the form of a harshly worded "Memorial" from a committee of Ward 12 inhabitants to Boston's mayor, aldermen, and common council.[55] In it, they complained that their district was exploited like a colony; South Boston had become "the Botany Bay of the city," a reference to the infamous British penal colony in Australia. "These institutions are among us but not of us. They give no business to South Boston. They employ none of our people. No one can enter the iron gate without a permit from the City Hall. Everything consumed in them comes from the City. They give us nothing but an undesirable name and an unpleasant association." Although they supported the value of these "blessed monuments of public charity," they resented their "great injury" to property values, and objected to "the *spirit* in which some of them have been thrust into our borders, as nuisances that would not be tolerated elsewhere." These nuisances were literally embodied in the "daily transit through our streets of the vehicle in which the unfortunate inmates of the House of Industry . . . are conveyed, pell mell, to and fro. In that cart are often seen, and seen too by the public eye, the wretched wrecks of humanity,—men and women, bloated, bruised and bloody,—bestowing upon each other obscene caresses, or blasphemy and blows, and exhibiting to our children a disgusting and demoralizing spectacle!" In this view, the stigma of the public neighbor threatened to stigmatize all who were caught in its path.

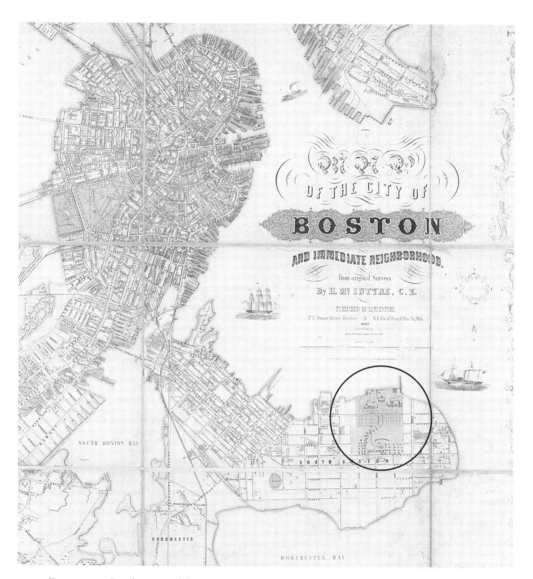

FIGURE 1.9 Development of the "City Lands," South Boston. The Henry McIntyre map of 1852 shows that the section of South Boston containing the House of Industry and the House of Correction also included a House of Reformation, a lunatic asylum, a hospital, and a nearby asylum for the blind.

In lamenting the "undesirable notoriety" that had accompanied the arrival of the new institutions, the citizens of Ward 12 stressed the contrast between themselves and the public neighbors sent to dwell with them. South Boston's own citizens were not people "who lived from hand to mouth, and wanted only a temporary lodging place," but "a class of intelligent and respectable persons of narrow means, but independent spirits, who wished to dwell in their own houses, and have elbow room about them, and pure air to breathe, and a wide prospect to enjoy." Thus, like their Puritan forebears, the South Bostonians defended their moral character by reference to the quality of their houses, "a very large proportion" of which were "owned by their occupants." In fact, they claimed, South Boston had higher rates of homeownership than any other ward. Moreover, "in the whole of the population there is not a single colored family, and not so many foreigners as in several other wards of the City." The foreigners who did live there were "for the most part, of that better class who will not live in cellars, or congregate together closely in order to keep each other warm." In sum, they declared, "South Boston has been sought as a residence by a very respectable class of persons, rather in spite of the policy which the City government has pursued with regard to the place, than in consequence of it."

In view of such demonstrable contrasts between themselves and their new public neighbors, the South Boston citizens' group called upon the City of Boston to remove the institutions, preferably to "one of the islands in the harbor." To argue the point, they noted "that the inmates would be as well accommodated in many respects; that the City land which they occupy would sell for about a half million dollars; that it would be covered in a few years with the habitations of substantial tax-payers; that the value of all the neighboring lands would be increased, and that one of the greatest obstacles to the development of the resources and capacities of this Peninsula would be removed." So too, they challenged past justifications for agricultural production in South Boston on economic grounds, claiming that "there is no reason for holding sixty acres of land as a garden for paupers, when one acre of it would sell for enough to buy a whole farm in one of the neighboring towns."

In urging the new island location, the South Bostonians nonetheless raised several concerns. First, such institutions should not be "thrust away out of sight"; there was great value in keeping them "where the public eye will require that both in architectural beauty, and in internal management, they shall meet the public approval." Second, it made no moral sense to relocate all the institutions in the same place: "many a widowed and broken down relic of an esteemed and useful citizen may be forced to seek an asylum in the Almshouse, and the bitterness of her lot should not be increased by having that asylum within the same enclosure as the House of Correction." Similarly, the "innocent children" of the orphan asylum should not have "constantly forced upon them disagreeable associations with convicts, with idiots, and with broken down paupers." Although these objections were phrased in terms of concern for the worthy poor, at base the South Bostonians distrusted an entire system that uprooted dependent people from their families and neighborhoods and turned them into a mass of strangers concentrated just beyond their own doorsteps. "Nature meant that men should live in families," they argued, "and it is unwise and injurious to herd hundreds and thousands of them together in vast buildings, especially if they are all (or a great majority) of a low grade of intellect, and are broken down and hopeless." In an argument that prefigured in sentiment, if not in phraseology, some of the concerns expressed about public housing projects 150 years later, the South Bostonians worried about the sheer concentration of poverty and misery: "Mixed up in the great mass of society, such persons may be of use; but selected out and congregated together, they act unfavorably upon each other; they create about them a moral atmosphere in which the spirit of true life is wanting, and which is injurious to all who breathe it." In such a system, all were bound to sink toward the least common denominator. Denying the possibility of protecting "the innocent" under such circumstances, the South Bostonians noted that the same people who insisted on the efficacy of classification "would shrink from building their own houses within such an enclosure, and from exposing their own families to such disagreeable and disadvantageous associations."[56] Whatever the future juxtaposition of the various institutions, these South Bostonians wanted the city's public neighbors out of South Boston.

Later in 1847 the Boston City Council's Committee on Public Buildings recommended the removal of the House of Industry and its sister institutions to Deer Island in Boston Harbor (Fig. 1.10).[57] The committee admitted that "neither the only, nor perhaps the principal, motive for erecting a new House of Industry, is to be found in the inadequacy of the old one." At base the move was undertaken to protect property values in South Boston by ridding it of its unwanted public neighbors. The city had an "interest . . . in the general increase of valuation" and was itself "a great co-proprietor with the citizens of South Boston," since the city, too, had "lands in the market."

In this way, a now familiar pattern repeated itself. City officials bowed before the economic arguments of South Bostonians just as they had twice previously for other citizens. With this justification, the Almshouse continued its centrifugal forced flight: from Boston Common to Barton's Point to South Boston to Deer Island.

The sum of these economically motivated moves showed just how far Boston's leaders had come from the seventeenth- and eighteenth-century communities of Christian congregations. By the mid-nineteenth century, the central operative body had become a civic community rooted in common fiscal interests of property taxes and land valuation. Rather than a community of artisans and merchants, this was a community of propertyholders who cheered publicly sponsored development whenever it could be privately steered. At the same time, the community still bore some resemblance to that of its Puritan antecedents, especially in its fearful distaste for certain kinds of strangers. In this context, development pressure from South Boston was not the only force acting on city leaders; the more sustained pressure came from immigration.

FIGURE 1.10 Deer Island House of Industry, ca. 1850. The grandeur and isolation of public houses for Boston's poor peaked in the construction of this massive turreted island fortress.

INSTITUTIONALIZING IMMIGRANTS

Between 1820 and the introduction of restrictive legislation in the early 1920s, more than 33 million immigrants arrived in the United States, and most headed toward the cities. During the last three-quarters of the nineteenth century, urbanizing immigrants transformed the industrializing cities of the Northeast and Middle West; by 1875, immigrants and their American-born children accounted for two-thirds or more of the population in such places. Until mid-century, immigration patterns depended a great deal on existing patterns of transatlantic commodity commerce, which helped account for a high influx of immigrants to New England from the British Isles and British America. Whereas German immigrants frequently came with greater resources, and moved disproportionately toward the Middle West, immigrants reaching Boston often could not afford to move more than walking distance beyond the port, and many did not even make it that far.[58]

Soaring Irish immigration in the late 1840s brought unprecedented numbers of immigrant paupers to Boston; by 1850 the vast majority of the inmates in the city's various institutions were first- or second-generation immigrants, overwhelmingly Roman Catholic and Irish. As a Committee on Public Buildings report noted, mass immigration "forced upon our charity a more destitute class of persons, and in a more sickly state, than we have ever received before." The influx not only overflowed the capacity of the House of Industry and associated temporary annexes, but also necessitated the establishment of a quarantine station on city-owned Deer Island in late 1847 for foreigners requiring city aid. As the Massachusetts legislature put it at the time, this was "a precautionary measure to ward off a pestilence that would have been ruinous to the public health and business of the city." From 1847 through 1849, city officials admitted 4,816 Irish immigrants to the island, 4,069 of them judged to be ill upon arrival. In 1849 the quarantine station was made permanent, and all vessels entering Boston Harbor with passengers or cargo considered to be "foul and infected with [a] malignant or contagious disease" were forced to make Deer Island their first stop. With the need for quarantine identified on both medical and economic grounds—needs that city officials believed would not diminish anytime soon—the committee proposed relocating the various other facilities to Deer Island as well. That decided, the committee reassured the rest of the City Council that this conglomeration would not eliminate the possibility of "classifying" the poor.[59]

Though affirming that the worthy poor could be separated from those of lesser character, the committee made clear that Deer Island was especially suitable for the latter sort. Not only was the island city-owned and amply endowed with buildable space; it already had a "fine quarantine ground, where alien paupers can be received with the greatest advantage to the City and least disadvantage to the navigation interest." Moreover, the site was sufficiently far from the shore that it required "no expenditure to render it secure," and security would be enhanced by allowing visitors only on the first Wednesday in January, April, July, and October. In contrast to the record of the South Boston House of Industry (from which 122 inmates "eloped" in 1849–50), swimming the strait from Deer Island would require "a remarkable combination of favorable circumstances" for even the most "daring and athletic" to manage an escape.[60] When the thousand-bed House of Industry opened on Deer Island in 1852, the old duty to "harbor the town's poor" carried a new double meaning.

At the same time, however, some old meanings lingered. The proponents of the new "House of Industry" on Deer Island used that term interchangeably with "Alms House." Although "House of Industry" connoted the requirement that the able-bodied poor be set to productive work, the directors began to acknowledge what their own records showed: most of Boston's incarcerated poor suffered not from laziness but from illness. During the fiscal year 1849–50, the lists of "Conditions and Employment" at the South Boston House of Industry were dominated by the "Sick and disabled" category and 327 inmates died; another 271 perished on Deer Island.[61] Clearly, the problem of poverty could not be very convincingly explained by lack of industry.

Attitudes toward immigrants in the city-owned institutions remained inseparable from more widespread beliefs about the threats such foreigners posed to the polity. For much of the nineteenth century in New England, city leaders could view immigration as an economically desirable and humanly benevolent aspect of industrialization, one that would strengthen American society. Even so, rampant anti-Irish sentiment had prevailed in Boston since its founding and, as in New York and Philadelphia, local nativist organizations had gained strength during the 1830s and 1840s. In 1852–53 groups with patriotic names such as "The Sons of '76" and "The Order of the Star Spangled Banner" joined together to form the "American Party," a national organization intended to protect Anglo-Saxon-Protestant hegemony. This group—commonly known as the "Know-Nothing Party" because of its members' declarations of secrecy about their activities—

swept to power in the Massachusetts legislature, pledging a program of "Temperance, Liberty, and Protestantism" to forestall what one house member called "Rome, Rum, and Robbery."

In Massachusetts as elsewhere the Know-Nothing movement collapsed after the elections of 1854, but anti-Catholic sentiment in Boston remained virulent. Thomas O'Connor comments, "Although religious and cultural clashes took place in other nineteenth-century American cities such as New York, Philadelphia, and Baltimore, the age and strong traditions of the Boston community, the homogeneous character of its Anglo-Saxon population, and the unmatched Puritan revulsion toward all things Roman Catholic raised the intensity of anti-Irish sentiment in Boston to incredible levels." Until well into the second half of the twentieth century, "Catholic children in Irish neighborhoods would be reared in the catechism of hate that instructed them never to forget the bigotry of Protestants, who had confined them to institutions and asylums, and the cruelty of Brahmins, who had posted on factory gates and workshop doors the signs that proclaimed for all to see: 'No Irish Need Apply.'"[62] With prejudice and poverty conjoined, the prospects were dim.

Even before the Civil War, city and state officials in the Northeast began to equate the terms *poor* and *immigrant*. In 1850 Boston city officials complained that port authorities in New York were actively exporting some of their own unwanted immigrants by supplying them "with the means of reaching Boston." In Massachusetts the foreign-born soon constituted five-sixths of those chargeable to the state, and an 1857 state report asking "Why has Massachusetts so many paupers?" answered its own question: "Because we have a larger proportion of foreigners from which they are made."[63] In 1859 a committee of the Boston Board of Aldermen charged with assessing the performance of the overseers of the poor reported that 8,000 people had been aided "outdoors" during the preceding year, at a time when the combined Deer Island institutions housed only 1,300 individuals, partly because the overseers of the poor had been unable to limit aid to "our own settlement poor." The committee recommended exporting more people to state almshouses outside the city. In addition to concern over municipal finances and jurisdictional responsibility, the committee found moral fault with the prevailing practice of outdoor relief. In addition to its undesirable role as a welfare magnet at a time of high immigration, they argued, outdoor relief "fosters among large classes a willingness to rest for support upon the industry of others, . . . deadens the natural sense of disgrace at dependence, and encourages habits of indolence, intemperance and mendacity."[64] In short, poorly regulated outdoor relief inevitably aided the wrong kind of public neighbors; institutionalization provided a far more reliable means of classification and reform, especially if this institutionalization could be shunted off to someone else's jurisdiction.

For the poor who remained publicly housed within Boston, the attitude of public authorities remained ambiguous at best. With construction of the Deer Island facilities, some portion of Boston's public neighbor problem could be neutralized through the act of maximum isolation coupled with architectural intimidation, but it was soon clear that the institutions fell far short of their intended reformatory functions. In 1857 Boston city officials established a municipal Board of Directors of Public Institutions as a first attempt to centralize and rationalize the administration of public welfare. Still, the managers of the various eleemosynary institutions continued to convey a message of ambivalence, as if powered by an alternating current of compassion and hostility for those they housed. Moreover, as is so often the case with architecturally imposing institutions, their construction coincided not with the height of their power but with the commencement of their eclipse. Although most of the institutions remained standing, the reform impulse dissipated after the Civil War. Increasingly, these places served chiefly custodial functions, intended to incarcerate the least well-off for whom there was little expectation of recovery. Especially as such institutions came to house predominantly immigrant populations, incarceration became a convenient means to control deviant and dependent people.

Even once various investigations documented the harsh conditions of the almshouses and other facilities during the last half of the nineteenth century, few challenged the underlying propriety of partial reliance on indoor relief. "The general public," observes Rothman, "seemed prepared to accept the various flaws that boards of charities uncovered, in part convinced that life in the almshouse was less corrupting than life in a slum, in part worried that unless the poorhouse was considerably less comfortable than the households of the lowest classes, it would reward and encourage idleness."[65] At a time when separate institutions were built for the criminal, the insane, the orphaned, and the delinquent, many among the dependent poor who overlapped with these various constituencies were subjected to parallel treatment. As more and more public neighbors arrived as immigrant strangers, the role and composition of poorhouses changed. In Boston, community officials accepted their obligation to assist such people, but tried to do so by distancing them from other Bostonians. Even though noninstitutional forms of poverty relief remained the ascendant mode, the whole notion of public assistance had become conflated with ideas about reform, restraint, and removal. The walls erected around the public neighbor became increasingly difficult to breach.

TENEMENT REFORM: REGULATING PUBLIC NEIGHBORS

Institution-based forms of "relief" for economically marginal people constituted only one part of the nineteenth-century efforts by Bostonians to reform the living conditions of the impoverished. For every wayward immigrant shipped off to Deer Island, scores of others remained on the Boston peninsula itself, largely confined to tenement house districts. There too, the impulse toward behavioral reform continued, initially through various efforts at tenement regulation and, by the turn of the century, by neighborhood-based settlement house efforts to inculcate "American standards" of conduct.

Gradually, driven by the great industrial capitalist transformation of America that occurred during the nineteenth century, the assumption of public responsibility toward dependent people devolved away from the local community of neighbors toward ever more centralized government aid. The term *public* increasingly connoted matters of expansive scale, whether expressed by the complex public bureaucracies created to manage burgeoning cities or by the range of distressed people seen to need public assistance. In this context, the movement to build privately sponsored neighborhood-focused settlement houses marked both an acknowledgment that urban neighbors could no longer be counted on to care for their own without outside assistance, and a sincere attempt to re-center and restore a dissipating gemeinschaft. At the same time, however, the settlements themselves added yet another new institutional layer to neighborhood social relations. Larger government, coupled with continued growth of citizens' groups claiming to act in the public interest, ensured that full consideration of "public health" would entail not simply the removal of those found offensive to publicly sponsored institutions but also systematic citywide and neighborhood-specific attempts to regulate and reform public neighbors in their own homes.

Tenement reform has long been discussed principally in terms of New York. In part, this is because New York suffered from America's largest tenement problem, making it an obvious subject for scholars, but mostly it is because New Yorkers themselves inaugurated many of the most visible and influential reform efforts, beginning with the first tenement law in 1867. It is impossible to raise the subject of tenement reform without mentioning the investigative photojournalism of Jacob Riis and the legislative triumphs of Lawrence Veiller. Riis's classic photojournal, *How the Other Half Lives* (1890), alerted a nation to the scourge of tenement life, while Veiller—the mastermind behind the 1901 New York Tenement House Law—helped spark nationwide efforts at housing reform through publication of *A Model Tenement House Law* (1910) and *A Model Housing Law* (1914, revised 1920). Veiller argued that the "health, safety and welfare of the people" depended on regulating the "light and ventilation, sanitation, fire protection, maintenance, alteration, improvement and use" of their dwellings.[66] The 1901 law and the two "model law" books became the source of nearly all American housing legislation in the first part of the twentieth century.

Despite the pre-eminence of New York leaders, however, it would be misleading to suggest that the efforts in New York were qualitatively different from those in Boston and other large American urban centers. In fact, writing in 1900, Veiller declared that "After New York, Boston has the worst tenement house conditions of any American city."[67] In Boston, as in New York, the decades of efforts to reform the tenements are inseparable from the efforts to reform their tenants. To many middle-class urban Americans of the mid-nineteenth century, the immigrant poor crammed in their tenement districts seemed an even greater threat than the indigents and deviants who populated the burgeoning array of new prisons, asylums, and almshouses. Theirs was an increasingly dominant and unsettling presence in the public realm, one that promised to alter the balance of local political power and posed a public health problem of unprecedented scale and severity.

As always in matters of public health, there is a fundamental ambiguity about whether the "public" object of concern is those who already suffer from the problem, or those who might be presumed to suffer in the future—either physically or economically—if that problem were to be allowed to persist and spread. In this sense, humanitarianism is inextricably linked to self-preservation, or at least self-interest. This ambiguity of motive, in turn, is the wellspring of ambivalent reform.

In the minds of most Bostonians, Sam Bass Warner, Jr. has argued, the city's inner area of low-income housing had become "an unknown and uncontrolled land," a faceless zone that was "out of reach of middle class supervision." Most important, "the concentration in a solid two-mile area of foreign languages, poverty, sweatshops, and slum housing gave the suburban middle class a sense of hopelessness and fear."[68] The fear that eventually sparked tenement reform would seem to be of three related kinds: first, that tenement conditions promoted the spread of epidemic disease that could engulf a non-tenement population; second, that tenement life nurtured the "microbe of criminality" that could escape and threaten the broader economic vitality of the city; and third, that tenement residence fostered immoral behaviors. These people posed a triple threat: a social problem with corporal, economic, and moral dimensions. On any or all of these three counts, they needed to be counted as public neighbors.

EXPOSING AND REGULATING BOSTON'S TENEMENTS

Wherever established populations grappled with massive foreign immigration, city officials and charitable organizations organized repeated investigations of slum conditions. Nationally, the campaigns for tenement reform in New York and Boston took the lead but, by the turn of the twentieth century, similar crusades had emerged in Chicago and elsewhere, even as the northeastern cities with a half-century headstart still struggled. As David Culver stated in his history of tenement reform in Boston, "evils exposed in the 1840s were still being exposed fifty years later."[69] In Boston, as in New York, the story of tenement reform is inseparable from the perception of an immigrant threat to the "American" way of life. The tenement, as the domestic base of this public threat, was seen simultaneously as cause, symptom, and symbol of such problems.

Faced with a settlement originally built on a 780-acre peninsula (approximately the size of New York's Central Park), nineteenth-century Bostonians leveled the city's hills to fill out its boundaries in a vain attempt to keep abreast of the demand for development. To serve the more prosperous and facilitate the movement of goods, they built bridges to neighboring communities, allowing for the possibility of suburban commutes as early as the 1830s.[70] With the sharply accelerating influx of very low-income Irish immigration after 1840, however, the central part of the city grew by unprecedented numbers.

Desperate to escape the famine of 1845–1849 that followed the potato blight, tens of thousands of Irish converged on Boston. The city housed fifty thousand Irish by 1855, a number twice the size of the *entire* town's population only fifty years before. The Irish-born quickly came to constitute nearly 40 percent of the city's residents. Many other large American cities—Brooklyn, Cincinnati, St.

Louis, Chicago, and New York—experienced similar percentages of foreign-born residents by 1870, but the Boston growth was unusually early, single-sourced, and concentrated.[71] This "great mass of Irish," historian Oscar Handlin found, were largely segregated "within the narrow limits" of Boston itself. Imprisoned by their poverty (which often had been exacerbated by the costs of obtaining trans-Atlantic passage), these mostly unskilled workers—like their counterparts in other cities—clustered near the most likely opportunities for unskilled day labor, the districts nearest to the markets, warehouses, and wharves (Fig. 1.11).[72]

In contrast to preindustrial cities where the poor were relegated to the periphery and the rich claimed the convenience and prestige of the center, the mid-century rise of American industrialization and the corresponding press of immigration drove many wealthier families outward. Advances in surface transportation—

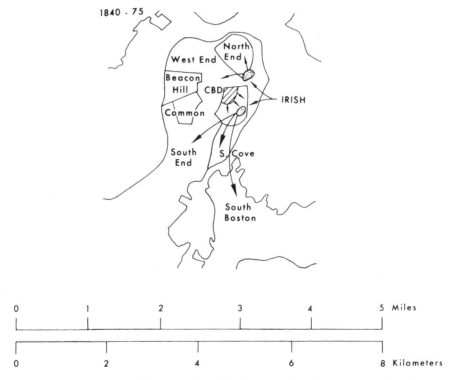

FIGURE 1.11 From 1840 to 1875 Boston's Irish immigrants only gradually spread inland from the districts closest to waterfront employment.

first rail then streetcars—accelerated the fringeward movement of families whose incomes and working hours permitted a longer journey to work, while enabling new immigrants to occupy the densified remains of older residential quarters at the edge of the commercial center. Often the wealthy abandoned central-city residential areas in the expectation that the expanding urban commercial centers would soon engulf them; in the interim, however, developers subdivided these houses and their lots for multifamily occupancy by immigrants.[73]

As an important industrial center, Boston typified such growth patterns, and its residential conditions worsened rapidly. In 1846 concerned citizens sounded the first alarm. The *Report of the Committee on the Expediency of Providing Better Tenements for the Poor* warned that Boston already faced conditions as bad as the slums of Europe, with some districts harboring a "density of population surpassed, probably, in few places in the civilized world." Since the immigrants could not afford the expense or inconvenience of relocation to the city's periphery, the *Report* concluded, the only solution was to build better tenements "near the present ground of their labor." At the same time, the committee struggled over which type of poor the new tenements should house, since the tenement population contained both "incipient paupers" ("those who are liable to become a charge on charity") as well as tenants who were "poor, but industrious, and independent." The committee resisted any commitment to "collateral arrangements" (such as lending out tools, "finding them employment during the dull season," or supplying these near-paupers with food and clothing "at a small advance on wholesale prices"). Instead, they wished any new city intervention to be in service of "justice" rather than charity, and wanted to do nothing "which might tend, in the slightest degree, to induce a spirit of dependence, or take away, however little, the feeling of self-respect, which is the chief support of the poor man." The *Report* closed with a plea to improve relations between "the landlord and the poorest class of tenants."[74]

This early call to build better tenements was little more than a request for better-behaved investors and better-behaved tenants. Nothing about it carried either the force of law or the promise of subsidy, and private enterprise continued to seek the most profitable and intensive use of the land. As Handlin shows, this meant converting decrepit former mansions and disused warehouses into tenements, often sublet in complex ways that benefited distant owners and negligent sub-landlords, while subjecting immigrant tenants to "merciless inflictions."[75] At the same time, construction of large new warehouses displaced low-rent dwellings and forced further overcrowding, yielding situations in which whole families—sometimes even two—packed themselves into a single room out of desperation.[76]

Such intense housing demand and lax regulation led to the gradual in-fill of any potentially habitable portion of the central city. Neighborhoods once laid out with detached houses gave way to slums, as "enterprising landowners utilized unremunerative yards, gardens, and courts to yield the maximum number of hovels that might pass as homes . . . Every vacant spot, behind, beside, or within an old structure, yielded room for still another." The compiler of the first *Boston Atlas* in 1861 found "so tangled a swarm" that he "gave up the attempt to map such areas, simply dismissing them as 'full of sheds and shanties.'" In mid-nineteenth century Boston, thousands of the poorest residents lived in cellars entirely below ground and subject to periodic flooding, while others lived stooped in tiny attics. As Handlin concludes, unlike New York, "The one evil of which Boston houses were free was excessive height, for most had only two or three stories—a blessing not to be underestimated."[77] By 1900, however, many narrow streets in Boston's densely populated North and West Ends were flanked by buildings of at least five floors.

In Boston, hardly a year passed during the second half of the nineteenth century without the release of a committee report documenting the conditions of tenement dwellings and their effects on public health. The various reports counted up the casualties and set out the justifications for further regulation, but often used language that treated the immigrant poor as a single collective public neighbor. The *Report of the Committee of Internal Health on the Asiatic Cholera* (1849), for instance, characterized the worst parts of the slum as "a perfect hive of human beings . . . in many cases, huddled together like brutes, without regard to sex, or age, or sense of decency" (Fig. 1.12).[78] Similarly, the Massachusetts Bureau of Statistics of Labor voiced despair about people "packed like figs in a drum."[79] For some Bostonians, such reports yielded a mass portrait of "the dangerous classes" and suggested no reason to scrutinize the economic sources of individual deprivation.

At all times, public health matters were closely allied to fear of civic unrest and economic instability. As the dispirited Brahmin nativist Charles Eliot Norton wrote in 1852, many Bostonians were afraid "lest the sea of ignorance which lies around us, swollen by the wave of misery and vice which is pouring from revolutionized Europe upon our shores, should overflow the dikes of liberty and justice, and sweep away the most precious of our institutions."[80] Norton viewed the density of the tenement district as a necessary part of the dike that protected the affluent from dangerous seepage, but such tenements needed emergency repairs.

In 1860 a group of Boston volunteers formed the Boston Sanitary Association and led the push for state-mandated public health regulation. They linked the

FIGURE 1.12 Burgess's Alley in the Fort Hill District, late 1840s. As sheds, outhouses, and other structures filled up the courts behind the original brick structures, such dense immigrant tenement districts became what one investigation termed "a perfect hive of human beings."

cause of statewide sanitation to a variety of economic and moral issues, and justified creation of a Board of Health as a financial necessity, not just a humanitarian gesture. Asking the General Court to regard each human being as "a matter of profit and value," they described each child born as "a machine begun," and argued that all deaths that occurred before the age of fifteen—the point at which that child was expected to engage in productive labor—represented potential lost income, a calculation that also applied to wages lost due to illness. Worst of all, they warned, there was a direct connection between short life expectancy and social unrest, since stability depended in large part on the watchful presence of "men who are over forty." Repeated attempts to establish a state Board of Health eventually gained legislative approval in 1869.[81]

The Massachusetts legislature passed its first Tenement House Law in 1868, almost identical to the more famous one passed the preceding year in New York. It established minimum standards for ventilation, cleanliness, and waste disposal, but provided little structure for enforcement, placed no restrictions on lot coverage, and continued to assume that private enterprise alone would insure an adequate low-rent housing supply. The 1868 law was amended by the Building Law of 1871, which initiated a requirement for building permits in advance of construction, and prohibited construction of buildings more than thirty feet high on narrow streets, both of which brought much-needed caution to the siting of new construction.[82] A year later, in the aftermath of Boston's devastating Great Fire, the city's first independent Board of Health began annual tenement house inspections, making frequent visits to those places and persons judged substandard: "The effect of frequent inspections," the Board reported in 1877, "is to improve the habits of many of the occupants, whose dislike at being annoyed by notices from City Hall is greater than that of keeping clean, and, choosing the lesser evil, they keep clean."[83]

In 1875, high death rates in tenement districts prompted Boston's health authorities to produce a report, *The Sanitary Condition of Boston*, which singled out Boston's Irish immigrants: "A considerable portion of our yearly mortality is the result of morbid tendencies inherent in our foreign population, and imported by them into our midst." Even when deaths occurred among the "so-called 'native' population" of Boston, the Board of Health judged these "more or less remotely attributable to a foreign, or more correctly, to a Celtic source."[84] In the health politics of 1870s Boston, even those whose residence was "remote" were not safe.

MODEL TENEMENTS FOR MODELING TENANTS

Between the 1850s and the 1920s, reformers in many American cities—initially drawing on English precedent—set out to improve tenants by constructing "model tenements." Alfred T. White was the "undisputed evangelist of the model-tenement gospel" after the Civil War, and his Improved Dwellings Company organized the construction of a promising series of limited-dividend structures in Brooklyn beginning in the late 1870s. In New York, other early ventures included the Improved Dwellings Association, the Tenement House Building Company, and the City and Suburban Homes Company, launched in 1896. Philadelphia boasted the Octavia Hill Association (founded to implement its namesake's principles of friendly rent collection and vigilant management), as well as its subsidiary, the Philadelphia Model Housing Company. Other notable organizations included Jacob Schmidlapp's Cincinnati Model Homes corporation and, in the nation's capital, the Washington Sanitary Improvement Company and the Washington Sanitary Housing Company. There were also significant early semi-philanthropic ventures ("limited-if-any-dividend corporations") bankrolled in Chicago by Julius Rosenwald and by the estate of Marshall Field. Taken together, however, the model tenement movement proved disappointing; its advocates failed to attract sufficient interest among the "large-hearted rich," and produced less than one percent of the country's new tenements.[85] Despite its shortcomings in practice, the model tenement movement revealed a great deal about the ideas and ideals of nineteenth-century housing reformers.

The most precocious of these ventures occurred in Boston. In 1854 a group of Boston Brahmins set up the Model Lodging House Association, erecting several five-story brick buildings featuring multiroom apartments with indoor plumbing. They charged rents comparable to those prevailing in less savory buildings, while still returning 6 percent annual interest to their investors.[86] This venture accommodated only forty families, however, and these families—with rare exception— were among the better-off of the American-born working class. Another parallel effort later in the decade, sponsored by the estate of wealthy merchant Abbott Lawrence, added only another twenty apartments, and again priced itself beyond the reach of the most needy.[87] In 1871, however, Dr. Henry Bowditch—who had campaigned for the creation of the Massachusetts Board of Health and would serve as its chairman for a decade—organized a group of wealthy Bostonians to found the Boston Co-operative Building Company, the first model housing organization of its kind in the United States.

Vowing not to perpetuate the practice of building tenements, the Company's directors sponsored construction of small single-family homes with large sets of rules. They agreed to admit "all applicants of good character, and of habits of neatness," and targeted homes to "American mechanics and those in sympathy with them," thereby evading both recent immigrants and those who lacked a substantial annual salary.[88] Ignoring the portion of the poor that constituted the greatest economic problem or civic threat, they extended their sense of obligation only to those thought worthy of the largesse.

Soon, however, Bowditch and his colleagues resolutely turned to a more pressing problem: the redevelopment—in both physical and moral terms—of a notorious tenement house. Bowditch chose the tenement mockingly referred to as the "Crystal Palace," a place the Massachusetts Bureau of Statistics of Labor described as an "abode of nastiness, robbery, drunkenness, prostitution, and every moral abomination, where riot, disorder, quarrels and police-jobs were the daily, nightly and hourly work." Bowditch called this home for three hundred persons "the kindergarten of future crime; a nuisance to the neighborhood and all living in it." The reformers commenced work on a variety of fronts: they patriotically rechristened the tenement house as "The Lincoln Building"; replaced the cellar grog-shop with the Anglicized "Holly-Tree Coffee Room" and banned the sale of liquor; introduced new ventilation shafts through the structure, closed the basement apartments, and cleaned the whole building; and reduced overall occupancy by one-third. Most important, in a building containing only about sixty apartments, they evicted fifty-three families during the first three years of operation. Even as the Boston Co-operative Building Company accepted the obligation to assist the most troublesome class of public neighbors, its management team sought to help only cooperative tenants.

Early on, the Company and its agents targeted the moral development of the building's youth. They gave each child a Christmas present of a bank book with the first ten-cent deposit already recorded, and met with them every two weeks to encourage further savings and "thrifty habits." They established sewing classes for girls and a small industrial school to occupy older tenement boys, who were otherwise "liable to become drinkers of beer, night prowlers, and the future burglars and desperadoes of the community." For the first three years, the directors believed that their "efforts at humanizing the tenants" were making headway, noting that tenant "needs" were beginning to "rise above those of animals." With equal ambivalence they observed that the building, yards, and corridors were kept "as clean as two hundred men, women, and children of the Celtic race will permit them to be kept."

Faced with an inability to sustain a profit and an incapacity to transform wholly the character of their tenants, the Company's directors chose not to exercise an option to renew their lease after the fifth year of operation, and the experiment ended. Ultimately, Bowditch concluded that the whole concept of the "large tenement house, occupied by the lowest classes who are accustomed to filth" was not worth perpetuating even in a redeveloped state because it was "in itself bad for the health and morality of the community." The directors placed some blame on the inadequacy of police protection and on the unchecked depredations of outsiders, but mostly they blamed the apartment house itself: "A building of so great a size and constructed as the Lincoln Building is, with passages, stairways, and water conveniences in common," they charged, "was totally unfit for the proper lodging of those human beings who need the oversight of others to keep them." Model tenement or not, "such a place must necessarily lead to filth, vice, and crime; and with filth, will come disease and death." The common corridors and shared facilities of the tenement house engendered contact that was both unwholesome and unsupervisable, the worst possible combination for public neighbors in need of "oversight."[89] Although Boston's model tenement movement gained some renewed impetus in the 1880s with the establishment of the Improved Dwellings Association, many housing reformers believed that the only real model for tenements was the single-family home; anything less would only unleash the worst aspects of the tenants.[90]

Still, sanitarians and housing reformers saw no easy exit from the tenement house problem itself, as documented by such reports as, "Sanitary Inspection of Certain Tenement-House Districts," 1887–88, and a more exhaustive "Tenement Census" conducted in 1891. The first investigation, led by Dwight Porter, an assistant professor of civil engineering from MIT, called for greater care in the enforcement of sanitary regulations, but stopped short of proposing mandatory destruction of those places found to be in worst violation. Porter favored further private-sector efforts to produce model tenements, stressing the need to improve not only the engineering systems of the buildings but the sanitary habits of the tenants, many of whom were "the very offscourings of the countries whence they came."[91] Porter's report preceded the publication of Jacob Riis's *How the Other*

Half Lives by only a few months; both contributed to a climate in which tenement house reform—in Boston, as in New York—was front-page news. In 1893 Benjamin O. Flower, Boston's closest equivalent to Riis, published *Civilization's Inferno; or Studies in the Social Cellar*, an indictment of tenement conditions in the North End: it sold 50,000 copies.[92]

CIVILIZATION'S INFERNO AND PROGRESSIVE AMBIVALENCE

In his book and in the pages of *Arena*, the seminal muckraking journal he edited, Flower gathered together the whole conflicted leading wedge of progressive reform, combining sympathy for the plight of the slum-dweller with calls for immigration restrictions. Like most reformers, he justified action using a variety of different rationales. Not only were the tenement districts "reservoirs of physical and moral death," he warned readers of *Civilization's Inferno*, they were also "an enormous expense to the State" and a "reality whose shadow is at once colossal and portentous." In "time of social upheavals," he concluded, "they will prove magazines of destruction" since hundreds of "slowly starving" families lived within "rifle-shot of the gilded dome of the State House and the palaces of Beacon Hill." For Flower, justice alone could prevent "a bloody cataclysm." As both penumbra and arsenal, the tenement district boded ill.

The frontispiece of Flower's book graphically presaged his argument (Fig 1.13). Rather than a single undifferentiated social mass, Flower described a "social cellar" containing three distinct levels. Interweaving the metaphor of the townhouse with the metaphor of heaven and hell, he dually infused the inferno of civilization with domestic and Christian symbolism. In the illustration, a theatrical curtain is pulled back to reveal the social whirl of ballroom dancing on the top level, separate and oblivious from the progressively darker strata that lay below. The first lower level shows a world of "patient toil" populated by sturdy workingmen faced with unprecedented competition for scarce jobs; beneath this is the economic purgatory and "uninvited poverty" of the worthy widow and other unfortunates; and, at the very bottom, the "darker zone" of the inferno itself: "a subterranean, rayless vault—the commonwealth of the double night." Flower's spatial metaphor translated the old distinction between the deserving and the undeserving into a hierarchy (or, perhaps, lowerarchy) of environmental zones: one where "virtue and integrity remain," the other where "under-world vice and crime mingle with poverty." In his opinion, the tenement house was both cause and symbol of a larger socioeconomic disorder.

Even as he emphasized the moral distinction between the vicious subterranean poor and the "illuminated inner temple" of the more virtuous, Flower faulted American property tax policy for permitting the schism: "so long as landlords have comparatively low taxes to pay for old, rickety, disease-laden, and vermin-infected rookeries, they will not replace them with clean, healthful, or more commodious buildings; and while vacant lots adjacent to a city are lightly taxed, land speculators will hold them out of the reach of the poor. Thus, our present system of taxation acts as a two-edged sword." Flower traced corruption to the "irresist-

FIGURE 1.13 *Civilization's Inferno,* a literary excursion into Boston's "Social Cellar," mixed Christian and domestic symbolism.

ible power of environment," but also identified economic causes for poverty, empathetically observing the insecurity of Boston's poorest citizens: "Over their heads perpetually rests the dread of eviction, of sickness and of failure to obtain employment, making existence a perpetual nightmare, from which death alone brings release." He even related drunkenness not only to character defects or slum conditions but to "the inability to find work."

At the same time, like most other slum reformers of the day, Flower blamed Boston's most recent immigrants for tenement conditions. In contrast to the "great moral worth and intellectual independence" of earlier settlers who represented "a distinct gain to the young republic," he now observed that "every ship laden with immigrants must necessarily feed the fire which threatens the destruction of free government." The threat was at once both social and economic. "Every incoming army from the slums of Europe," Flower wrote, "places the breadwinners of America in a more hopeless condition." With the arrival of "foreign cheap labor, the Americans must sink to the frightful social environment of this class or starve." Flower embraced the environmental determinism of his reform-minded peers, seeing the tenements as "morally infected" environments. His choice for the "most feasible immediate measure" was familiar: more model tenements. Unlike many of his contemporaries, however, he also warned that a permanent solution would eventually require "radical economic changes."[93]

Flower's dire assessment of the political economy of Boston's tenement districts reflected a growing engagement with the economic roots of poverty in Massachusetts by both public and private agencies. In 1869 Massachusetts was the first state to establish a Bureau of Statistics of Labor, and the very term *unemployment*—which referred both to the condition of being unemployed and to the social problem that existed when workers were unable to find jobs—made its first American appearance in print in the Bureau's 1887 *Annual Report*. As Alexander Keyssar argues, "for the first time in American history, the phenomenon of 'involuntary idleness' had become sufficiently widespread or important or visible to need its own name and to be measured." Although unemployment had long existed in Massachusetts before statistics were kept, until the 1820s the problem was masked by widespread agricultural and artisanal self-employment, the integration of agriculture and manufacturing, the availability of frontier land, and by what Keyssar terms the "social and communal relationships that enveloped economic activity."

With the rapid industrialization of the Massachusetts economy in the four decades preceding the Civil War and the mid-century arrival of "an Irish proletariat," the situation changed. By 1875, Keyssar points out, "more than 85 percent of the people who worked in 'manufactures and mechanical industries' were employees," their wages dependent on the decisions of others. Massachusetts developed a substantial and active labor reserve, "a collection of men, women, and children who rarely had as much work as they needed or wanted and who consequently were available when the employers of the Bay State had need of them." With the rise of industrial capitalism and its periodic market downturns, then, working Bostonians had come "to need continuous work while, at the same time, they had lost control over its continuity."

In Boston, the various private charitable organizations such as the Boston Provident Association and the Associated Charities, as well as church and ethnic groups and the publicly sponsored overseers of the poor, gave some assistance to the unemployed, but unemployment per se was not the principal motive for their aid. Instead, these organizations directed their obligations to those public neighbors judged demonstrably *unemployable,* due to age or disability. According to Keyssar, in late nineteenth-century and early twentieth-century Massachusetts, "most jobless workers had no contact whatsoever with charitable or relief agencies," and "coping with unemployment was essentially a private affair, a challenge confronted by families, a burden shared with kin, friends, and neighbors."[94] At the same time, growing city and state recognition of unemployment as a central component of poverty slowly began to infiltrate the highly moralized rhetoric of the tenement reform movement, and even affected the way that Boston's charities classified those they professed to assist.

The Associated Charities of Boston tabulated its own assessment of the causes of Poverty based on an analysis of 991 of its cases from the year 1890–91. By the standards of today's social science, this analysis (see Table 2) is a methodological nightmare. The researchers assumed that "trained investigators" acting in "a scientific way" could reliably categorize the causes of poverty into two broad categories of "Misfortune" and "Misconduct," and could further taxonomize these into various subcategories, each pointing to a mutually exclusive proximate cause.[95] As an index of perceptions, however, it suggested that fully two-thirds of the causes of poverty (at least among those Boston families the Associated Charities chose to assist) stemmed from matters judged to be largely beyond the control of the impoverished, and that poverty did indeed have some important economic roots. At the same time, the survey results could be used self-servingly by chari-

Table 2 Causes of Poverty in Boston, 1890–91

CAUSES INDICATING MISCONDUCT	PERCENT
1. Drink	19.2
2. Immorality	
3. Laziness	
4. Inefficiency/Shiftlessness	7.6
5. Crime/Dishonesty	1.5
6. Roving Disposition	.6
Subtotal	28.9

CAUSES INDICATING MISFORTUNE	PERCENT
1. Lack of Normal Support	
a. Imprisonment of Breadwinner	1.6
b. Orphans/Abandoned Relatives	1.1
c. No Male Support	7.2
2. Matters of Employment	
a. Lack of Employment	14.1
b. Insufficient Employment	6.0
c. Poorly Paid Employment	.5
d. Unhealthy/Dangerous Employment	.7
3. Matters of Personal Capacity	
a. Ignorance of English	.7
b. Accident	3.6
c. Sickness or Death in Family	23.2
d. Physical Defect	2.5
e. Insanity	.7
f. Old Age	3.8
Subtotal	65.7
Not Classified	5.4
Total	100.0

Source: The Church Social Union, "Poverty and Its Causes," pub. no. 25 (Boston: The Church Social Union, May 15, 1896), pp. 8–11.

ties to counter charges that they primarily and improvidently dispensed assistance to shiftless, roving, drunken criminals.[96] Even in this new willingness to include some forms of unemployment on the "worthy" side of the balance sheet of poverty, rather than to code it all as laziness, the fundamental ambivalence underlying the obligation to public neighbors remained unaltered.

In the early 1890s, armed with the vast documentation assembled by Boston's Tenement Census, leaders from groups such as the Better Dwellings Society, the Anti–Tenement House League, and even the Associated Charities echoed Benjamin Flower's cries for improved housing conditions. On the whole, however, the Tenement Census served to contain outrage, since it concluded that Boston's slums were never so widespread as to "absorb entire precincts," and that the worst slum conditions affected "comparatively few persons." If the average Bostonian learned anything from the venture, it was probably the widely quoted assertion that Boston's overall tenement problem was less severe than that prevailing in other large cities.[97] In such an atmosphere, state and municipal interest waned, and once again private volunteerism ventured into the breach.

Leading Brahmins founded the Twentieth Century Club, whose Municipal Reform Department appointed its own Tenement House Committee, chaired by Robert Treat Paine. In the winter of 1896–97, this Committee visited hundreds of tenements and, in 1898, published a pamphlet entitled, *Some Slums in Boston*, which generated much discussion. This time the outrage, generated not by a government report but by the actions of prominent citizens, gained the full attention of both Boston's mayor and its Board of Health. In 1897, following precedents in London and New York, this Board had been granted the power to condemn tenements, but had not yet chosen to do so. With new evidence of horrific conditions and the political support to address them, however, the Board embarked on a more activist course, ordering the abandonment and demolition of more than 150 dwellings during the next four years.[98] Property rights were no longer quite so inviolate, but neither was there yet much challenge to the practices of the private market. As the century closed, the composite message was clear: government had a role in housing reform, but it was one characterized by regulation and spot demolition, rather than by slum clearance and large-scale construction. Moreover, with Boston's housing problem still seen as a matter of public health rather than private wealth, regulation of tenements invariably translated as regulation of tenants.

SETTLEMENT HOUSES: DOMESTICATING PUBLIC NEIGHBORS

While tenement reformers in large American cities fought for legislation to prevent the repetition of poor construction in individual new buildings, a second and more multifaceted movement arose to study and take action on the broader questions of neighborhood environmental quality raised by slum conditions. In contrast to the charity workers of the time, who gave assistance to individual paupers, the workers in the various urban settlement houses addressed their assistance primarily to the working class, seen as suffering from a "poverty of opportunity." Whereas the charitable agencies acted out of philanthropy, the guiding impulse of settlement house leaders was environmental amelioration by means of supplemental social services.[99] Settlement workers grappled directly with the social problems of impoverished immigrant groups, and sought every possible way to exemplify and inculcate middle-class American standards of behavior without completely extinguishing those more admirable cultural contributions of each group that remained safely strange. In their role as interpreters, settlement workers tried to identify and nurture the sorts of public neighbors who were most deserving of outside private and governmental support. At the same time, however, they stopped short of becoming advocates for the immigrant, and instead acted out of the same profound ambivalence that motivated other reformers.

The work of Jane Addams and her colleagues at Hull House in Chicago has remained the most widely remembered legacy of the settlements. Her counterparts in other cities regarded Addams as both "chief interpreter" and "pre-eminent leader" of the movement; others referred to her as "Saint Jane" and "an American abbess," and she eventually won a Nobel Peace Prize.[100] By the turn of the century, led by Addams, Florence Kelley, and Julia Lathrop, Hull House stood ready to take on the full range of "enemies which the modern city must face and overcome would it survive," including "insanitary housing, poisonous sewage, contaminated water, infant mortality, the spread of contagion, adulterated food, impure milk, smoke-laden air, ill-ventilated factories, dangerous occupations, juvenile crime, unwholesome crowding, prostitution, and drunkenness."[101] In a movement dominated by women, other large cities also had charismatic settlement leaders, yet the central intellectual spokesperson was Robert A. Woods of Boston.

In seven books and innumerable articles and lectures, Woods set out the most cogent explanations of settlement philosophy.[102] The work of Woods and his settlement house associates remains crucial to the present discussion not simply because it centers on the social problems of low-income housing in Boston, but because these struggles reveal the same perennial ambivalence that would later color attitudes toward public housing in Boston and nationwide. The settlement movement played a seminal role in establishing the neighborhood—rather than the individual building—as the appropriate unit for housing reform, and it consolidated the belief that such reform must encompass social and moral intervention as well as architectural design. Through examining the writings and actions of those who were among the most sympathetic toward the plight of the American urban poor, it is possible to see how judgments about individual shortcomings became transmuted into the intractable racial and ethnic problems that continue to plague American cities.

In the second half of the nineteenth century whole sections of many large cities were viewed as dominated by non-American people. Woods, together with his frequent collaborator, Albert J. Kennedy, claimed that immigration was the chief "cause of disintegration in neighborly relations" in the American city.[103] They argued that high-density foreign habitation carried profound social and political dangers: "When, as in the case of certain parts of Boston and New York, 1,200 people are crowded on an acre, it is difficult to individualize one's immediate neighbors sufficiently to be on human terms with any considerable portion of them." These nonindividuated neighbors comprised a mass public of "nomadic factory hands who form no neighborhood ties, join no neighborhood associations, and involve themselves in no effort for community betterment." To bring such "kaleidoscopic shiftings of men and conditions"[104] into close domestic proximity served only to unleash "deep-seated antagonisms, bred through centuries of provincial as well as national experience in Europe."[105] To nervous reformers in the downtown tenement districts and to prosperous individuals on the suburban periphery, these immigrant districts with their seemingly reckless melange of otherness could be seen as a kind of collective public neighbor. In this view, the public obligation to intervene was a necessary societal response to the arrival of dangerous strangers. Woods, like Addams and other self-described settlement "pioneers," sought to interpret these neighbors by serving as resident anthropologists and civic activists. They looked outward to humanize them in the eyes of wealthier classes at the same time as they looked inward to reform their physical, moral, and educational environments.[106]

Born out of a collaboration among universities, churches, and philanthropists in England, the settlement idea spread to the United States in the late 1880s. Established first in New York, houses soon opened in Boston, Pittsburgh, Philadelphia, Chicago, and elsewhere. By 1911, when the movement seems to have peaked in influence if not in numbers, there were nearly four hundred settlements, distributed across cities in thirty-six states.[107] Professor William Jewett Tucker of the Andover Theological Seminary established Boston's first settlement, Andover House, in October 1891, and maintained that "The whole aim and motive is religious, but the method is educational rather than evangelistic."[108] For Tucker, the "united purpose" of the House was "to increase the moral valuation of the neighborhood" by developing it from within through long-term residence; by cooperating with existing neighborhood organizations, seeking "influence, not power"; by making use of "the true missionary disposition and temper" but without proselytizing; and by seeking "improvement through self-help, not patronage."[109] In keeping with such principles, Andover House was renamed South End House in 1895 to emphasize its location in a Boston neighborhood rather than the exurban headquarters of its initial ecclesiastical sponsor. Tucker later became president of Dartmouth College, and Robert Woods served as head resident of the House from 1891 until his death in 1925. Moreover, demonstrating that his leadership had become national as well as local, Woods served as co-secretary (with Albert Kennedy) of the National Federation of Settlements, created in 1911 and headquartered at South End House.

WRESTLING ANGELS

In *The City Wilderness*, published in 1898 as the first volume detailing the methods and achievements of South End House, the thirty-four-year-old Woods set out his vision of a cooperative kind of social work, through which "A neighborhood is first permeated with friendly influence."[110] In another early essay, however, Woods expressed the desired relationship slightly differently, asserting that "every visitor" should enter the neighborhood from the settlement as "a wrestling angel." This latter image of tough beneficence calls to mind the Christian charity obligations of the seventeenth and eighteenth centuries, and expressed Woods's own approach much more accurately than his many other more wholly ingenuous formulations, in which the visitor is "simply a neighborly caller."[111] Willing to wrestle with the immigrants as well as to befriend them, the residents and volunteers of South End House pinned their hopes on the power of their own good example.

Woods and South End House undertook an astonishingly wide variety of initiatives, and helped to bring about many significant reforms at all scales, from the neighborhood to the national. Not a public institution itself, its representatives nonetheless called for public action on a wide variety of housing matters, and successfully fought for other kinds of public neighborhood amenities for its surrounding district, including a bath, playground, gymnasium, and branch library.[112] With their bills paid by prominent Brahmins, South End House residents became actively involved with "investigation" and "objective study of neighborhood, district, and city conditions," and also undertook numerous kinds of interventions to ameliorate problems. Efforts at district improvement, undertaken during the first twenty years of the house, included surveys, public testimony before various civic commissions, campaigns for tenement law reform, assistance with code enforcement, and service in the directorate of a model buildings company. Residents of the house worked with other district improvement associations to upgrade the sanitary services of the South End by serving as a center for processing complaints; and they worked with city agencies to establish a new neighborhood playground and to maintain other play areas on vacant lots, while providing "direction" for their use. Going beyond the tenement reform impulse, the settlement workers regarded the space between tenement houses—like the space between tenants—as a potential source of positive social interaction and learning.

Similarly, they worked with the local public schools "through visitation, meetings with teachers, conferences, [and] work for backward children," and promoted industrial education. They worked with unions to arbitrate strikes, held conferences on labor matters, assisted in the formation of new unions representing various women's interests, and joined forces to bring about the local public bath house. They restructured political institutions and campaigned for bipartisan issues, cooperating with "the better grade of politicians in the neighborhood" while conducting studies into the corruption of political machinery. They engaged in relief work and worked on studies of unemployment during the depression of 1893, helped distribute coal during the strike of 1902, and initiated a few small business ventures. They worked on public health issues such as the anti-tuberculosis campaign, maintained a resident nursing service, founded a dispensary for the sale of milk to infants, and helped with a variety of local exhibits on proper medical and dental health. Led by Woods's own special concern over issues of temperance (he chaired the board of the State Hospital for Dipsomaniacs), the settlement played a leading role in legislative regulation of saloons in advance of prohibition, and kept a close watch over local drinking establishments. At the same time, Woods's colleagues worked to establish a variety of alternative neighborhood social and recreational activities, including sponsorship of picture exhibits, lecture courses, and concerts. And, as is obvious from the plethora of book-length publications that remain easily available, Woods and his South End House associates played a leading role in disseminating the ideas of the settlement movement across the country and abroad, through their studies, books, college lecturing, public meetings, and conferences.[113]

TREATING POVERTY AND OTHER THREATS

Although driven by a humanitarian imperative to improve the living conditions of the poor, settlement workers—like others who have aided public neighbors since the seventeenth century—frequently stressed the self-interest of the nonpoor. They challenged the consciences of the wealthy, but also warned them of dangers to their health, their political system, and their economic well-being. Their early study of the "city wilderness" provided "indisputable evidence that the health, comfort, and morals in the city's more comfortable sections are acutely threatened by evils bred under tenement conditions." It revealed tenement workshops full of men, women, and children "engaged in stitching garments or preparing edibles" while suffering from measles, diphtheria, and tuberculosis, demonstrating how the slum could become the breeding ground for broader metropolitan scourges: "Carlyle's dictum made early in the nineteenth century that the plague which begins in the lodge proceeds, as though directed by supreme intelligence itself, to the mansion, was confirmed in our own times."[114] Charles D. Underhill, a physician who worked with South End House, argued that "the evil effects of overcrowding reproduce themselves in geometrical ratio, and soon will, if they do not already, imperil the health and morals of the city's population." He appealed to the long-term financial self-interest of wealthier citizens, insisting that improvements to tenement neighborhoods, "although apparently very expensive, eventually increase the rent and therefore the tax valuation of the district improved."[115]

From the viewpoint of South End House, however, the more immediate threat to financial stability in turn-of-the-century Boston was political corruption fueled by ward-based machine politicians. Settlement staff noted that "'Land on Saturday, settle on Sunday, school on Monday, vote on Tuesday' is a proverb among the teachers," and Woods clearly distrusted the immigrants' choice of candidate.[116] Writing in 1903, he charged that a "demoralizing political régime bred in the midst of an alien, ill-favored way of life" was fast becoming a risk to "the prosperous classes . . . and even at times threatens important downtown business interests."[117] Woods, while certainly calling for greater compassion, also phrased his appeal in terms of a social and economic threat.

All this but further confirms the fundamental conservatism of the settlement venture. Woods and his colleagues saw a city where "employers and workmen, taxpayers and the mass of voters, Protestants and Catholics stand in an attitude of armed neutrality toward each other." They sought disarmament by bringing the "civilizing influence"[118] of the American middle class back into the city center, and pushed for informed consensus rather than class solidarity. By sending in settlement workers as middle-class emissaries, however, the bulk of Boston's "respectable suburban population" did not need to live there themselves. They could protect their "community of interest" by supporting surrogate neighbors.[119]

PROCESSING AMERICANS

To Robert Woods, the immigrants in Boston's slums were "Americans in Process." That process was assimilation, and its chief agents were to be the settlement residents and volunteers. Settlement leaders wrote in an era when the very term *American* held an especially restrictive meaning. To them, being an American was seen as the alternative to being Irish or Negro, and was even contrasted with those who were "third generation through foreign ancestry." Being an American was a concept that accepted no multicultural hyphens. Rather than encompassing all those who lived and worked in the United States or even all those who were born in it, full rights to the designation, if achieved at all, were reserved for those who could approximate the norms of third-generation white Anglo-Saxon Protestants, most of whom were middle-class suburbanites. The loaded term *American* combined in one standard ideas about race, ethnicity, religion, longevity of residence, class, tenure status, and spatial location.

Intervention on behalf of Americanizing immigrants formed the heart of the settlement agenda. Nationwide, a survey conducted in the early 1920s revealed that fully 92 percent of settlements were "placed among immigrants."[120] Having established proximity, the settlement residents sought to domesticate these neighbors in a dual sense. The goal was Americanization—the replacement of foreign customs by domestic standards—to be achieved by physical and moral reform of the home. The settlement house was more than an outpost on the urban frontier; it was a model for an alternative moral order.

In a book published to assess the national settlement movement as a whole, Woods and Kennedy set out "An Experimental Definition of the American Standard of Living," intended to communicate the attitudes and goals of many settlement leaders. Under the main headings of Language, Food, Room, Cleanliness, Clothing, Association, Child Nurture, and Moral Idioms, they grouped standards that covered a wide variety of physical, social, and moral comportments, both within the home and beyond its confines. To meet "the American Standard," a family must rely on the English language; secure sufficient domestic space to allow the family to meet together and dine in a single room at least once a day; participate in "group observance of holidays and festivals"; and adopt a "general attitude of hope and opportunity toward communal activities." Settlement workers combined this concern for communal space with a standard of no more than two persons per bedroom, "with additional space where necessary to insure decent privacy." They expected "standard" Americans to bathe and change underclothes at least weekly, and to wear "inconspicuous" clothing. Children were to be provided with "constant oversight" and the relations between men and women were to be conducted with a "certain consideration . . . which is difficult to describe but which everyone recognizes." In short, they set the "American Standard" in direct counterpoint to their understanding of the prevailing practices among immigrants, seen as illiterate, ill-fed, overcrowded, dirty, ragged or garish in appearance, civically isolated, inconsiderate, and lacking in ambition.

Above all, attainment of the "American Standard" involved commitment to the ideal that upward class mobility was possible, if parents would only be watchful for "the appearance of ability or talent" among their children, and ready to "sacrifice convenience or substance in order to provide education and opportunity for advancement." As Woods and Kennedy concluded, "America has always refused to contemplate continued existence of a lower class. It has preferred to regard anything below its standard as a temporary stage in an upward process which will be passed through within a relatively few years. This is a unique contribution made by our country to the world and must be actualized."[121] Such optimism about mobility—the willful fantasy that all Americans are (or soon will be) middle class—has certainly never been fully actualized, but surveys suggest it has remained a powerful part of American self-perception throughout the twentieth century.

Other contemporary observers, however, refused to accept the settlements' goals at face value. Thorstein Veblen went so far as to charge that while "the solicitude of 'settlements' . . . is in part directed to enhance the industrial efficiency of the poor . . ., it is also no less consistently directed to the incubation, by precept and example, of certain punctilios of upper-class propriety in manners and customs." Veblen saw the settlement "vogue" as largely self-serving, an attempt by the wealthy to "authenticate the pecuniary reputability of their members, as well as gratefully to keep them in the mind of their superior status by pointing to the contrast between themselves and the lower-lying humanity in whom the work of amelioration is to be wrought."[122] Though Veblen accurately detected the moralizing that infused the settlement agenda and acknowledged the extent to which the settlement workers were themselves among the chief beneficiaries of their own actions, this is far too narrow an encapsulation of the movement's significance. While there was certainly some over-reliance on the import of "punctilios," the settlement leaders' belief in self-actualization and economic progress through assisted education encompassed a broad and powerful assimilationist agenda.

Assimilating and Restricting Immigrants

Whatever the rhetoric about care for communities and insistence on working with the poor as individuals, the settlement's welcome was far from unambiguous. The first twenty years of publications to emerge from South End House residents are riddled with stereotypes, often of the most prejudicial variety. Especially in these early years, the discussion of immigrant groups tended to individualize them chiefly at the level of "race traits." As Barbara Miller Solomon comments, settlement workers assumed that humans were endowed with "fixed and rigid" hereditary characteristics, and that it was therefore possible to make "permanent judgments" about ability and character.[123] Even so, Woods's version of what Emerson once approvingly called the American "smelting-pot" was decidedly more accepting of diversity than were the superheated versions concocted by more aggressive Americanizers who feared the decline of Anglo-Saxon racial stock and the endangerment of the American way of life.

That way of life was also threatened at the ballot box. The Boston Irish had consolidated their footholds in city politics during the 1860s and 1870s and, in 1884, spearheaded the election of Hugh O'Brien as the city's first Irish Catholic mayor. Although O'Brien's fiscal conservatism and penchant for public works

made him in many respects almost indistinguishable from his Yankee predecessors, prosperous Yankees feared the growing influence of Irish politicians
in almost every ward. Displaced by an expanding central business district, the
Irish had begun to spread outward from central Boston, both northeast toward
Charlestown and East Boston, and south and southwest toward South Boston
and the recently annexed districts of Roxbury and Dorchester, thereby creating a
metropolitan city of ethnic neighborhoods that left the Yankees engulfed in their
midst. At the same time newer immigrants—who appeared to Yankees, O'Connor
writes, as "swarthy Italians, black-bearded Jews, inscrutable Orientals, and a mot-
ley collection of Poles, Lithuanians, Greeks, and Syrians [who] spoke a babel of
incomprehensible tongues, dressed in weird costumes, consumed strange foods,
and followed entirely different customs"—took the place of the Irish in the
center-city districts of the North and West Ends (Fig. 1.14). Taken together, the
increased political and spatial visibility of the Irish and the burgeoning presence of new kinds of foreigners seemed to threaten not only Anglo-Saxons, but
Protestant American culture as a whole. With the Irish insisting on independent
parochial schools and other immigrant groups arriving in unprecedented numbers, many Brahmins worried that Anglo-Saxons might no longer manage to assimilate and Americanize the increasingly unfamiliar groups landing on their
shores.[124]

Francis A. Walker, an Amherst College–educated economist, provided the statistical justification for such inchoate fears. From the 1870s through the 1890s,
Walker developed and promulgated arguments, based on census data, demonstrating how the various European immigrant groups with their prolific child-
bearing—far from being absorbed into Yankee society—were instead replacing
it.[125] Walker animated his prose with far more than cold statistics; he paired concern over rampant growth of immigrants with sweeping generalizations about the
inadequacies of their domestic habits and habitats. In contrast to the life of the
old Yankee world where "the house had been kept in order, at whatever cost, the
gate hung, the shutters in place, while the front yard had been made to bloom
with simple flowers," he saw a netherworld of foreigners with "houses that were
mere shells for human habitations, the gate unhung, the shutters flapping or fall-
ing, green pools in the yard, babes and young children rolling about half-naked
or worse, neglected, dirty, unkempt."[126] For Walker, the link between "immigration and degradation" was clear—the foreigners were unable to comprehend the
American standard, and were dragging the Americans down with them.

In 1894, a handful of young Brahmin Harvard graduates took such sentiments to their logical conclusion, and formed the Immigration Restriction League of Boston. Within a year, there were parallel branches set up across the country, from New York City to San Francisco, from Alabama to Montana. Surprisingly, perhaps, Robert Woods—the chief interpreter of Boston's immigrant poor—himself became an important member of the League's executive committee. Woods's deep-seated ambivalence about the waves of newcomers seems best explained as the frustration of a man whose life was spent helping immigrants, but who saw his work threatened by the pace and sheer diversity of the influx. Woods struggled not against immigrants but for ways to manage their "flood," to use the popular aquatic metaphor that frequently washes through his writings.[127] He wished the settlements, as the moral equivalent of municipal public works, to engineer ci-

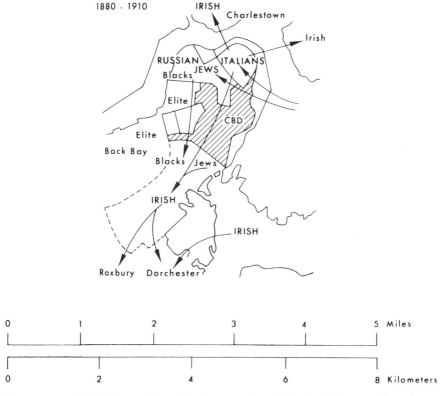

FIGURE 1.14 As the Irish moved out of the innermost city neighborhoods between 1880 and 1910, other immigrant groups replaced them.

vility by flood control of public neighbors. More callous restrictionists, however, turned such ambiguous xenophobia into overt racism, and the League's views increasingly interbred with those of eugenicist organizations such as the National Association of Mental Hygiene, The Commission on the Alien Insane, the American Genetic Association, and the American Breeders Association. Eventually, Congress passed the landmark National Origins Act of 1924, which established annual quotas for immigrant groups based on 2 percent of their American prevalence in 1890; after 1929, total immigration was fixed at 150,000 per year, again allocated according to earlier proportions of residency. As Solomon observes, by backdating the quotas to reflect a period before southern and eastern European immigration had reached full speed, "the intent was clear: to preserve the Teutonic composition of the American people in its present proportions so that the descendants of the foreign-born would never dominate the Yankees."[128] The long history of free immigration had been defeated by a revival of deeply rooted Puritan suspicions about strangers who threatened civic and economic order.

Black Neighbors: An Unassimilated Public

Although Robert Woods became entangled in national struggles over immigration, the most intractable problem for the residents of South End House was what they referred to as the "delayed assimilation" of Boston's low-income blacks.[129] The published assessments from the late 1890s were the most harsh, rooted in popular stereotypes about "animal propensities" and the like, rather than the product of careful and sustained empirical observation.[130] In 1910, with most Boston blacks headed toward the South End and already gone from the city center (where they had served Beacon Hill elites from the "back side" of the hill), a report sponsored by South End House concluded that Boston was not a "healthy or suitable home for the Negro race." Settlements, in this view, had a responsibility to aid those who had already come, but should do nothing to tempt more blacks to migrate from the southern farms where they naturally belonged.[131] In 1914, after nine years of research, former South End House resident John Daniels published a history of Boston's blacks, affirming the prevalent view that they were inferior but educable. At the end of more than four hundred pages of text, Daniels concluded: "The final diagnosis of the Negro's case must be, then, that when weighed in the scale he is found wanting, in the point of fundamental moral stamina." Still, Daniels optimistically opined, his "present incapacities . . .

appear to be not those of the lower orders of creation as compared with man, but rather those of the growing child compared with the mature adult."[132]

It has taken much of the twentieth century to begin to redress the damage done by such early racist analyses. Only in the 1970s did more careful studies of Boston's black population reveal that, far from the nefarious caricature of animalistic licentiousness and obliterated family lines, black household structure in late nineteenth-century Boston "was strikingly stable in comparison with other elements of the population."[133] In hindsight, it is clear, many of the judgments made about blacks and immigrants by the early settlement investigators made up in racism what they lacked in rigor. If Robert Woods's hope that "The isolated philanthropy of one generation becomes the organized social work of the next, and perhaps the public charge of the third" did in some measure come to pass, it is also the case, as Sam Bass Warner has commented about Woods's work, that "one generation's social science . . . is another's sermons."[134] In any case, the Boston settlement experience provides yet more evidence of the racial schism that would continue to penetrate housing and neighborhood policy throughout the twentieth century.[135]

The percentage of blacks in Boston's population had remained remarkably constant throughout the nineteenth century and beyond; in 1790, blacks had comprised approximately 4 percent of Boston's population, a proportion that would not again become as large until 1950.[136] Despite the small and relatively stable proportion, however, the actual numbers were growing steadily. As a result, there were attempts to force curtailment of black immigration to Boston during the early nineteenth century "on the ground that poverty, disease, and crime were rife among them." Although antebellum Boston became the moral center of the abolitionist movement and, after the war, a popular destination for freed slaves, some prominent Boston citizens complained about "the increase of a species of population which threatened to become both injurious and burdensome," and took note of the disproportionately high black occupancy of prisons, poorhouses, and "all public establishments" of Massachusetts. In reality, as subsequent studies found, there was little evidence to fuel such fears; black reliance on Boston's public institutions and private charity was disproportionately small, and was declining throughout the last third of the nineteenth century (though this ability to "provide for their own" could certainly be interpreted as a perceived necessity as well as a preference). On the other hand, by the turn of the twentieth century, Massachusetts blacks were incarcerated for crimes in numbers far greater than their share of the population.[137] In any case, no restrictions were imposed to keep black migrants and refugees out of the state since, as Daniels put it, "the troubling of the Puritan conscience" prevailed.[138]

By the time the settlements took an active interest in Boston's black population, its numbers had surpassed ten thousand, following forty years of decadal growth increases of between 38 and 68 percent. Though blacks still constituted only about 2 percent of the city's population at the turn of the century,[139] Woods and his colleagues perceived a neglected problem, one in which the settlements could help. He believed that the "Negro problem" was "manageable . . . if the Negroes can be considered as an unassimilated social factor analogous to the different immigrant nationalities." Recognizing that "the feeling of aversion on the part of the whites" was increasing, Woods sought ways to educate "the people of the city as a whole, including the colored population," to view "the color line . . . as simply a much more extreme form of the cleavage which separates the different types of immigrants from the natives and from one another." Assimilation, in other words, was the only answer: "the Negro must adopt the method," Woods ambiguously concluded, "or rule himself out of the game."[140]

Epitomizing the "separate but equal" doctrine of the day, South End House first formed a separately located "Center for Work among Negroes" in 1902. This Center moved twice again before being independently established as the Robert Gould Shaw House in 1908, named after the white transplanted-Brahmin leader of an all-black Civil War regiment.[141] "Established to give colored people the same privileges that other settlements are giving people of other races," the Shaw house did not formally "shut out other races," even though the intent to separate was wholly clear. The stated goals of the Shaw House, initially run by women and staffed primarily by female volunteers, were "to secure better opportunities for the Negro—industrially, educationally, and socially—by helping him to become better fitted for larger opportunities; to lessen prejudice by bringing about a better understanding between the white and colored races; and to achieve its purpose through the co-operation of both white and colored."[142] In 1914 Daniels reported that the Shaw House workers themselves were evenly divided between blacks and whites, and that there were even "several leading Negroes" on its managing board, but conceded that "the great majority of those who take advantage of the institution are Negroes."[143]

The Boston effort to establish a separate mechanism for settling with blacks seems to have been one of the most proactive efforts in the country at this time, yet its deliberate segregation provided an important foreshadowing of future struggles. Despite the Great Migration of southern blacks to northeastern and midwestern cities that gained strength during World War I and its aftermath, settlement leaders in all parts of the United States generally preferred to ignore their black neighbors. No more than a half-dozen settlements were designated for blacks before the Second World War; few others attempted more than token efforts at integration; and some even closed their doors rather than serve a local constituency that had become newly black.[144] In Boston, it was relatively easy for settlement leaders to remain focused on immigrant whites, since black population growth occasioned by the Great Migration was three times smaller than that experienced in Philadelphia, five times smaller than New York's, eight times smaller than Chicago's, sixteen times smaller than Cleveland's, and forty times smaller than Detroit's.[145] In Boston, from the standpoint of settlement leaders, the treatment of blacks remained unresolved—part of a much larger perennial problem: how to decide which public neighbors were worthy of aid.

ASSESSING THE NET WORTH OF THE POOR

Although Robert Woods seems to have been less prone to racial and ethnic labels and libels than some of his settlement house colleagues, he remained centrally interested in finding other ways to judge the comparative worth of the poor. Like other reformers, Woods sought ways to seek out, distinguish, and support the deserving poor, those whose poverty stemmed from "sickness or misfortune." Rather than engage in wholesale judgments about race traits, he sought more fine-grained moral and behavioral distinctions between "the honest unemployed" and the "loafer or the vagabond" with whom the worthy people were all too often confused. Reflecting back on the origins of the settlement movement, Woods recalled that the need to make moral judgments about the poor immediately asserted itself. The initial residents naively looked upon everyone "as belonging by choice to the ranks of honest labor," he recalled, but "almost before they knew it, residents found themselves besieged by various camp-followers of poverty. Tramps, chronic loafers, beggars, cheats, ne'er do wells, sought to make gain of the optimism of young reformers."[146] The settlement workers faced poverty in many guises, ranging from forms "which are an obvious expression of physical and moral degeneracy" to more ambiguous "cases of sporadic misery traceable directly to low-grade family life, incapacity to bear responsibility, and shiftlessness." Frequently, Woods and Kennedy commented, they were "impelled to assist far from worthy head of households in order to safeguard children with whom they had already become friends." Gradually, however, their prolonged presence in the neighborhood enabled them to form sounder judgments about the virtue of those they aided, assisted in part by learning from the way the neighbors themselves could "distinguish economic hardship clearly traceable, not to defects of character but to accident, sickness, death, unemployment, unforeseen responsibility, [or] fluctuation of industry."[147] Faced with such a range of need, settlement workers operated on the basis of triage, establishing a hierarchy of worthiness among the various types of poor, including an action plan for removing those least capable of being saved.

For Woods, the effective work of both charities and settlements could not take place unless "much of the social wreckage" was first "dredged out." He wrote in 1898 that "No civilized community undertakes to carry within its corporate life the criminal and the lunatic," but argued that Boston's South End "attempts to carry three equally dangerous types—the confirmed pauper, the confirmed prostitute, [and] the confirmed drunkard." "Persons of these types," he argued, "must be dealt with upon the principle of the habitual criminal act, the length of term rapidly increasing with each commitment, and reaching ere long a sentence that will last until the persons either are cured or die." In addition, reiterating a viewpoint with clear Puritan antecedents, Woods called for efforts to get Boston put on "every tramp's black list" by making it widely known that all who enter the city must gain meals and lodgings only by "hard work." This, he believed, could "relieve the South End of the cheap lodging house incubus," especially if accompanied by the destruction of other "dark, noisome, rear-tenement buildings," which served as "the most fertile breeding places of pauperism and its accompanying degradation."[148] His ultimate goal, in short, was to incarcerate or otherwise eliminate from Boston all of the undeserving poor. Though warning out was no longer possible, Woods still wished to identify those paupers to whom the community owed no obligation. In this way, Woods and the Brahmin urban reformers retained both the Puritan's troubled conscience and his willingness to seek the expulsion of the unproductive or undeserving poor.

In keeping with the aspect of the American standard that emphasized individual initiative, Woods looked forward to civilized urban neighborhoods where "only the industrious would remain to grow old." This elderly remainder, he continued, could if necessary be "pensioned under a veteran's discharge" with "little fear of demoralizing the younger generation." Best of all, he wrote,

> With the worst fathers and mothers removed, and those with like tendencies threatened by a similar fate, the work of child saving would be greatly simplified . . . By removing these specially difficult factors from the poverty equation . . ., it would be much easier to conduct forms of relief for those who have honorably fallen out of the struggle for subsistence, temporarily or permanently. There would be free scope for broadly devised private, cooperative and municipal measures of assistance to families overcome by some domestic catastrophe, to workmen forced into the ranks of the unemployed and to industrial veterans who have worthily ended their term of service. All such effort, since early Christian days, has had its dignity from the side of human compassion.[149]

In Woods's interpretation of Christian duty, all pretense of a nonjudgmental stance toward the causes of poverty was forsaken; compassion was due only to those who had honorably and worthily fallen. Even when assessing the personal responsibility of the worthy poor for their economic plight, Woods struggled with contradictory impulses.

Boston's first settlement had faced its "baptism of fire" during the depression that began in 1893, and Woods fully understood the human impact of protracted unemployment: "Any lurking element of sentimentality, of superficiality, of mere palliation, was burned away," he later recalled. "No person who has lived here through these years," he wrote in 1898, "could question its actuality and seriousness." Living among the depression's victims, he could empathize with "respectable families of working people" who had been brought into "severe straits," yet he could not fully blame the structure of the economy for their fate. Instead, while he allowed that "it is by no means merely the moral delinquent that suffers," he also saw industriousness as an adequate deterrent to the threat of unemployment: "It is not the most efficient workman, to be sure, who is thrown aside."[150] Ultimately, he believed that most problems of industry were rooted in personal, rather than corporate, misbehavior. In coming to terms with the proper level of public obligation to impoverished neighbors, Woods's ambivalence underscored the constant and unrelenting tension between the responsibility of individuals and the duty of communities.

THE SOCIAL LEGACY OF THE SETTLEMENTS

As a chapter in the unfolding odyssey of the American attempt to cope with the poor, the settlement movement remains unsettling. Sometimes its Progressive-era leaders succeeded in humanizing immigrants and blacks in the eyes of suspicious white nativists, but they also extended damaging stereotypes and established precedents for segregated housing and neighborhood assistance. In any case, their activities provided both direct and indirect prodding toward greater action by all levels of government on matters of housing and urban reform.

From the beginning, the settlement leaders made choices about where they wished to intervene, and with whom. They made disparaging comments about those deemed most unassimilated and unreachable, and chose to locate among the more upwardly mobile of the working poor rather than amidst the worst of the tenements and lodging houses. They willfully ignored portions of the public, or addressed them separately. Though many settlement workers through the 1920s liked to think of themselves as "neighbors," the class-based divisions and paternalist assumptions always worked against the formation of informal and reciprocal community relationships. Instead, the settlements introduced a new hybrid spatial arrangement for implementing didactic reforms: part outdoor relief, since it dealt with neighbors where they lived, but also part indoor relief, since it provided them with an institutional base. The new institution, however, requested only voluntary engagement rather than incarceration, and was deliberately located for the convenience of its neighbors, rather than premised on the obligation to isolate them from civil society.

The settlement house, as a nascent "neighborhood center,"[151] addressed public neighbors on their own turf (even if not always on their own terms), and this remains its most salient legacy. The early settlements not only catalyzed positive changes in individual neighborhoods, but introduced an alternative paradigm of urban intervention. Not content to devise new ways to destroy or regulate tenement districts, settlement leaders stressed the need to work with and educate their tenants. Anticipating the ecological principles of the Chicago School sociologists, they tried to re-establish the kinds of community support networks that had withered under urban densities and anonymities. Even at their most empathetic, however, the South End House studies revealed new and deeper individual and neighborhood pathologies, which served only to intensify the collective ambivalence.

As a stage in the evolution of approaches to public neighbors, the Boston settlement experience between the 1890s and 1920s bears considerable relevance for the subsequent development of public housing. With the neighborhood as the unit of investigation, settlement leaders considered not only the conditions of individual buildings but the broader socioeconomic environment in which good American citizenship could best be nurtured, thereby anticipating both the scale and the social purpose that would later animate construction of "the projects." Moreover, by choosing to work with the most upwardly mobile and socially redeemable among the working poor—while emphasizing the threat to public safety and finances wielded by less reputable types—settlement leaders perpetuated the idea of a clear division within the ranks of public neighbors. Their approach reconsidered the nature of the public obligation to the least advantaged: they saw public obligation as triggered not only by threats but also by opportunities. Given adequate social and moral education and neighborhood enrichment, it would be possible to assist and reform many of the poor without actually having to remove them from their tenements.

For other reformers, however, ideas of neighborhood enrichment suggested a fundamentally different course. Rather than upgrade the civic and educational infrastructure of the tenement district and leave old residential patterns substantially intact, they favored starting anew. Rather than accept the proposition that individuals could be upgraded by supportive middle-class contact, they reiterated two well-worn but under-exercised alternatives: either more tenements should be demolished or more tenement dwellers should be suburbanized. As Boston's nascent City Planning Board concluded in 1918, "the housing problem . . . is largely a question of improving tenement house conditions or encouraging the decentralization of population by proper suburban development."[152] In either view, the institutional reforms and social interventions of the settlements were but the starting point for a more fundamental realignment of urban slum environments and their populations.

IDEAL TENEMENT DISTRICTS

Gradually, during the first three decades of the twentieth century, urban reformers in Boston and elsewhere moved from a piecemeal tenement regulation mentality toward an ethic of planned slum clearance. Lawrence Veiller called this a "perfectly natural and logical step" but, despite increased legal powers and ample European precedent, large-scale use of slum clearance did not occur until the 1930s. The British had viewed slum clearance as a desirable social policy as early as the mid-nineteenth century, leading to a series of laws culminating in the Housing of the Working Classes Act of 1890, and other European countries had followed suit with modest efforts. However, in the United States even more than in Europe, slum clearance remained mostly a matter of rhetorical posturing rather than action. For districts closest to the commercial center, land-acquisition costs were exorbitant; courts upheld the rights of landlords to evade demolition unless their buildings were a demonstrable "nuisance"; and any attempt at mass evictions risked creating political havoc by shifting the poor from one tenement district to another, without producing any improved housing on the razed sites.[153]

While large-scale slum clearance efforts lagged, city leaders in Boston staked out a compromise: pursuit of the ideal tenement district. During the early years of the twentieth century this included some sporadic enforcement of condemnation powers, but a shortage of inspectors, a political unwillingness to prosecute some landlords, and a lack of affordable housing alternatives limited progress. Still, with stronger building codes in place, the city did succeed in removing many wooden tenements and in-fill houses by 1910, a success that also had the effect of raising rents and reducing the supply of housing at a time of peak immigration.[154] In 1915, Massachusetts legislators and voters passed and ratified an amendment to the Commonwealth's constitution empowering the state "to take land and to hold, improve, subdivide, build upon, and sell the same, for the purpose of relieving congestion of population and providing homes for citizens . . ." Further legislation, following English and New York precedent, permitted "excess takings"—allowing the government to use eminent domain powers to obtain adjacent parcels beyond what was absolutely required for a public project. In 1918 Boston Planning Board chairman Ralph Adams Cram spoke publicly about "scrapping the slum,"[155] and the Board proposed "a definite and complete general plan" to provide for "the improvement in living conditions."

Acknowledging the long-term persistence of tenements, the Board called for "public provision, at whatever expense, . . . to work toward the development of an ideal district." For the most part, this constituted little more than another plea for more stringent tenement regulation laws, but it also bespoke a new willingness to pursue the ideal through partial neighborhood clearance. Proposed improvements centered on city efforts to widen streets and introduce "public open spaces" into the "dead centers" of Boston's congested North End blocks. As the Planning Board put it, redemption of such areas would permit "a breath of fresh air for the overworked mothers and the somewhat numerous babies of the district," while the costs would be "in part offset by increase in values of adjacent properties." Justifying this approach, the Board pointed to precedents in New York, where slum blocks had been replaced by parks, but Boston's efforts continued to fall well short of the scale of clearance managed elsewhere.

As much as the Board wished to promote an ideal alternative to the prevailing pattern of tenement houses, it also looked forward to the day when "it will prove practicable to provide homes elsewhere with greater individual advantages." Cram argued that while a certain number of people would always want to live in the city, "great numbers . . . would be better off if they lived in the suburbs, or even in the surrounding towns where living conditions could be made more consonant with the principles of decency and righteousness."[156]

In linking slum reform to suburban ideals at a time when the city's population was already beginning to decentralize, Boston's City Planning Board articulated a long-standing cultural vacillation. One impulse led away from the city completely, toward suburban houses or even rural homesteads, which were seen as rewards for worthy workers. The other impulse led toward urban neighborhood design. Both directions entailed progressively greater public subsidy for housing and land development, and both enabled sponsoring institutions to choose which public neighbors they wanted to assist.

TWO

Rewarding Upward Mobility: Public Lands, Private Houses, and New Communities

THE LONG STRUGGLE to come to terms with public neighbors in early New England towns and the subsequent struggle to cope with the scourge of urban tenement districts are manifestations of a much broader ideology of American individualism and community development. In a society constructed from communities of individualists and imbued with a Puritan-inspired work ethic, public support for private land development has long remained central. In turn, communities have always distributed shared resources to meet public obligations. To accommodate such norms, a society's housing stock serves two central purposes: constraint and reward. As one form of constraint, Boston's leaders relegated many of the city's most marginal people to places outside the private housing market, rehousing troubled and troubling neighbors and immigrants in a variety of poorhouses and asylums. Alternatively, they permitted the poor to remain housed by private landlords but sought increased legal leverage to reform tenement conditions, or moral leverage to "Americanize" tenant behavior by sending middle-class emissaries to establish nearby settlements. These coping mechanisms were key aspects of an expanding effort to perpetuate the social stability of the polity, yet together they represent only one side of the housing issue.

The emerging American society also used housing as a way to symbolize and actualize a system of parallel rewards for good citizenship. From the semi-mythical draw of public land bounties and homesteads on the western frontier to pro-

motion of a more accessible suburban arcadia of small houses for worthy workers, public authorities and private groups promulgated the ideal of the single-
family home as a moral counterweight to the urban tenement. Such new opportunities further marginalized those who were forced into domestic dependency by
emphasizing alternative models of habitation that were theoretically available to
all, dependent only on open space, hard work, and individual self-reliance. Taken
together, these deeply felt attitudes toward private houses and public lands form
another essential intellectual strand of the prehistory of public housing. In the
century and a half before there was something formally called public housing,
American leaders—whether they were politicians, novelists, or taste-making architects—repeatedly extolled the ideals of the private house.

Walt Whitman, writing in 1868, captured perfectly the ideological expansive-
ness of the nineteenth-century American vision, while noting the paradoxical
place of the constricted and ill-housed poor within it. "The true gravitation-hold
of liberalism in the United States," he predicted in *Democratic Vistas*, "will be a
more universal ownership of property, general homesteads, general comfort—a
vast, intertwining reticulation of wealth." For Whitman, only the aggregate "safety
and endurance" of this network of "middling property owners" could knit and
hold together "a great and varied nationality, occupying millions of square miles."
For those left outside this American quilt, however, the prognosis was dire: "democracy looks with suspicious, ill-satisfied eye upon the very poor, the ignorant,
and on those out of business. She asks for men and women with occupations,
well-off, owners of houses and acres, and with cash in the bank—. . . and hastens
to make them."[1] In her haste, lady democracy left many public neighbors behind.

FRONTIER INDIVIDUALISM ON PUBLIC LANDS:
LEAVING BEHIND PUBLIC NEIGHBORS

The ambivalent treatment of public neighbors in America had its origins in colonial practices, but faced new challenges with the formation of the independent
American republic. Once the various original component states had agreed to
cede their western land claims to the federal government—and once the government expanded the American domain through further purchases and annexations—the question of public neighbors became fused with the question of public lands. As a place to dispatch urban public neighbors, the publicly owned

frontier appealed to those who characterized these misfits either glowingly or disparagingly. Those who distrusted their character believed that the daunting tasks and opportunities of frontier life would permanently insure against idleness; those who saw public neighbors as worthy unfortunates viewed public lands as a system of federal rewards for good behavior. In either case, from bounty lands to homesteads, the laws that expressed federal preferences for housing the public housed an ideology as well.

INDIVIDUALISM AND EARLY LAND-USE REGULATION

Well before the tenement laws that gained strength and momentum in the first two decades of the twentieth century, two major pieces of legislation—the Land Ordinance of 1785 (which set the tone for the disposition of public lands in the Western territory) and the Homestead Act of 1862 (which promoted the settlement of such lands by individual households)—established the fundamental basis for government regulation and organization of American domestic life at the national level. This social and physical order, established first in the vast countryside but later imported into the cities, both enshrined the myth of the yeoman farmer toiling to develop his own plot of land, and asserted his moral superiority.

The notion of a society of self-sufficient and economically independent farmers can be traced to Aristotle. More than two thousand years later, Thomas Jefferson believed that America had the abundant resources necessary to realize it. The yeomen farmers of Jefferson's era had emigrated from England, Scotland, and Ireland after having lost their ancestral lands to parliamentary enclosure acts, and could therefore equate the renewed ownership of land with liberty itself, as could many German immigrants. Jefferson thought the American independent yeoman farmer the very antithesis of the European peasant; not a servant but the foundation of the country. In 1785 he wrote, in a letter to James Madison, "The small landholders are the most precious part of a state."[2] For Jefferson, as for John Adams and Madison, the possession of private property signaled the supreme expression of individual freedom. One of the chief purposes of government, all three believed, was to protect such property. Madison, in particular, feared the power of factions and believed that a good way to insure a stable political order was to enable as many citizens as possible to own a stake in the land.

In his adulation of the yeoman landowner, Jefferson combined notions of patriotism, moral rectitude, and independent strength to describe a vision of the model American citizen. In *Notes on the State of Virginia,* he wrote that "Those who labor in the earth are the chosen people of God, if ever He had a chosen people . . . Corruption of morals in the mass of cultivators is a phenomenon of which no age nor nation has furnished an example." For Jefferson, those who could not rely on "their own soil and industry . . . for their subsistence" were rendered dependent, and "Dependence begets subservience and venality, suffocates the germ of virtue and prepares fit tools for the designs of ambition."[3] Jefferson here describes a new kind of environmentalism—even, perhaps, an environmental determinism. In contrast to the older emphasis on the sacred quality of the Puritan religious *community*, the Jeffersonian vision of sacred space and divinely rewarded behavior credits land, property ownership, and labor for making a "chosen people" virtuous.

Jefferson's ideal of a nation of yeoman farmers gained its first and most important physical representation with passage of the Land Ordinance of 1785.[4] The legislation emerged from a committee that Jefferson headed in 1784 and, though Jefferson himself did not play a formal role in Congress's subsequent adoption of the Ordinance, it certainly bore his intellectual stamp. Jefferson's committee included three Southerners and only two New Englanders, but their recommended system of land subdivision owed most of its characteristics to the prevailing practices of eighteenth-century New England. Under this more restrictive system of "township planting," careful surveys by local or colonial officials generally preceded private settlement, and titles were granted only for land within such townships.[5] The insistence on a variant of the New England method to serve the needs of the new nation bespoke a great interest in the perpetuation of order, yet did so while still stressing the centrality of individual initiative.

Although the Land Ordinance of 1785 explicitly aimed to raise funds for reducing the national debt incurred during the course of the Revolution, the strategy also established expectations about the way Americans should settle their expanding domain. The Ordinance was about settlement in at least two senses: pacification (by treaty or by musket) of unsettled Indians, viewed not as public neighbors but as enemies; and peopling of the land by those expected to take their place. By regularizing the rights to property, it reiterated long-standing legal concerns about the establishment of "settlement."

The Land Ordinance provided the authorization, the method, and the geometry for a survey of lands north and west of the Ohio River, a vision that would—during the course of the next century—eventually guide the pattern of land sales and settlement all the way to the Pacific Ocean, yielding a vast and nearly regular grid spanning three-quarters of a continent (Fig. 2.1). This megastructure was composed of six-mile-square townships, which were in turn subdivided into thirty-six sections of 640 acres each. Jefferson wished to divide America's land into as many equal farmable parcels as possible to reflect a democratic dispersal of political and economic power. As Daniel Webster made clear in 1820, the "political wisdom" of such land subdivision invested "the great majority of society in the protection of the government." Webster's contemporary Thomas Hart Benton told Congress that the alternative would be inimical to American values: "Tenantry is unfavorable to freedom. It lays the foundation for separate orders in society, annihilates the love of country, and weakens the spirit of independence."[6] Then as now, American leaders promoted widespread land ownership and homeownership as a bulwark against political extremism.

In cities, Jefferson also favored the use of a grid as a way to reduce development density and improve public health. In a letter of 1805, he wrote of the need to "[build] our cities on a more open plan," and envisioned a checkerboard arrangement. "Let the black squares only be building squares," Jefferson proposed, "and the white ones be left open, in turf and trees. Every square of houses will be

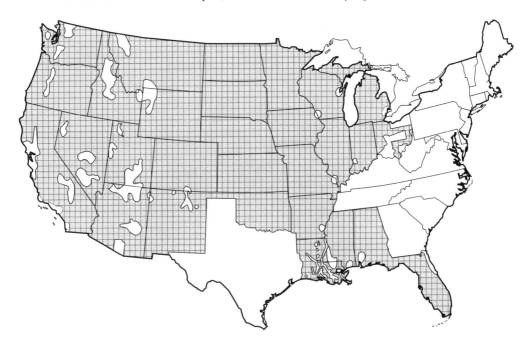

FIGURE 2.1 The Jeffersonian grid eventually influenced land development from the Ohio River to the Pacific Ocean.

surrounded by four open squares, and every house will front an open square. The atmosphere of such a town would be like that of the country, insusceptible of the miasmata which produces yellow fever."[7] Jefferson's vision, rooted in the interrupted grids found in the plans for New Haven (1638), Philadelphia (1682), and Savannah (1733), would reappear in various city design guises for many decades to come. Ultimately, even the form of the modern public housing project owes much to Jefferson's desire to regulate and inculcate the healthful effects of "open" space in dense cities. Though the connection to eighteenth-century land policy is certainly not direct, the impulses are far from wholly dissimilar.

The pattern of land sales and settlement that followed the Ordinance of 1785 and several decades worth of subsequent land acts compromised Jefferson's vision in many ways, yet a commitment remained to prevent the public domain from coming under the control of a few large landholders.[8] Federal policy retained a commitment to provide for sales of both large township-sized parcels and smaller quarter-section (160-acre) farms. Though many voiced concerns about unjust profiteering by absentee owners who gained from the improvements made to adjoining parcels, the overall system became a prodigious mechanism for passing public lands into private ownership, and even the presence of large ownership units often enabled speculators to "subdivide and sell at a long credit to poor men who could not afford to purchase directly from the government."[9] By the middle of the nineteenth century, it was possible to partake of a quarter-quarter section, and the farmers' dream of "forty acres and a mule" was born.

For all their apparent emphasis upon the individual, the framers of the early land acts also advocated independence and self-sufficiency at the communal level. Instead of a series of single-family islands on the prairie, they envisioned individual lots grouped into townships of thirty-six sections, with each of these subdivisions functioning as a kind of mini-republic with its own public school and other facilities. In this way, the township concept militated against the decentralizing force of a uniform grid, suggesting that even yeoman farmers must learn to live together. Significantly, though, the system also implied that such communities could arise only if each family was securely based on its own plot of land.

In fundamental ways, the framework set up for settling the "West" was a broad development scheme that sought to impose a geometric and a political order on chaotic parts. Like the urban slum-clearance efforts of the next century, nineteenth-century land policy tried to rationalize physical form, both to facilitate the sale and transfer of property, and to protect such property from attacks by the dispossessed. In the earliest years, little land was actually transferred, in large part because the native population had not relinquished its claims to lands the American government saw fit to "dispose." As a result, there was special incentive to use land as a reward for military service. The government could pay off indebtedness with its most plentiful currency and, at the same time, plant well-armed outposts who could be expected to secure the land in the process of settling it.

LAND BOUNTIES FOR WORTHY VETERANS

The practice of rewarding service in war with land grants is an ancient one, and was continued both in colonial America and in the aftermath of the Revolutionary War.[10] In a letter of June 1783, George Washington requested that Congress set aside public lands for veterans of the war "in certain proportions, agreeable to their respective grades." For Washington, the reward of public land conveyed the promise of future public benefits: "This plan of colonization . . . would connect our governments with the frontiers, extend our settlements progressively, and plant a brave, a hardy, and respectable race of people as our advanced post, who would be always ready and willing (in case of hostility) to combat the savages and check their incursions."[11] Acting in this spirit, the Ordinance of 1785 stipulated that the Secretary of War could provide such grants but, due to controversies over the location of the land reserves and nature of the intended beneficiaries, the plan did not pan out as expected: "The soldiers, in general, returned to their own homes and accustomed habits and few of them took any interest in lands in the wilderness except to assign their warrant, for a nominal consideration, to some restless settler or visionary speculator. The military reserve, therefore, instead of being peopled with hardy veterans contained large unoccupied tracts, while its cheap lands impaired the sales of the public domain."[12]

During the course of the first half of the nineteenth century, however, Congress extended and further democratized the notion of land grants for services. Eventually, the Old Soldiers Act of 1855 retroactively covered all phases of military service under the national government since the Revolution, and offered a quarter-section to anyone (including sailors, marines, flotillamen, chaplains, teamsters, and remarried widows) who could provide evidence of at least fourteen days' service. In all, Congress passed four acts between 1847 and 1855, granting over 60 million acres of public lands to more than a half-million veterans, widows, and heirs.[13] Rather than a source of revenue for the treasury, the distribution of public lands became a tool for socioeconomic development and a form of pension for exemplary citizens.[14] Even though most veterans preferred to convert their bounties into cash by selling their warrants rather than using them to move their families to the frontier, the mid-century bounty system is ideologically significant.[15]

There were limits to the willingness of the federal government to deploy its public lands for such public purposes, however. Beginning in 1848, Dorothea Dix, a mental health advocate, led a six-year fight to convince Congress to use proceeds from selected land sales to fund facilities for the care of the indigent insane, only to have the legislation vetoed by President Franklin Pierce in 1854. Pierce applauded the humanitarian aims of the plan but believed federal support for mental asylums would set a dangerous precedent: "If Congress has power to make provision for the indigent insane . . . it has the same power for the indigent who are not insane." Once the federal door was opened to the worthy poor, it would be impossible to keep out those of less deserving claim, and Pierce was unwilling to consider "making the Federal Government the great almoner of public charity throughout the United States." Thus, this most direct attempt to leverage the pattern of frontier settlement into a public subsidy to house the nation's least advantaged came to naught.[16] Pierce phrased his veto chiefly on constitutional grounds, but it marked a further reluctance of government to provide charity to those who had performed no previous public service.

The notion that direct federal housing support should be given as a reward for worthy behavior seems of seminal importance. Although it is surely a long way from the settlement of the nineteenth-century frontier to the redevelopment of America's twentieth-century inner cities, the spirit of mid-twentieth-century Congressional action to give preference in public housing to veterans (not to mention the long-standing informal local practice of reserving apartments for local police and firefighters) is much in the spirit of these earliest acts of federal land policy.

HOMESTEADS IN THE LAND OF THE FREE

The model of the rural yeoman received its greatest boost with passage of the Homestead Act of 1862, a law designed to encourage Americans to claim their own quarter-section of the western grid. Land which, under the various earlier land acts, had been sold by the United States government to its citizens or donated in grateful compensation for military service, was now available free of charge to nonveterans too, provided that it was inhabited and developed over a period of at least five years, at which time full title to the land could be obtained. Passage of the Homestead Act made it obvious that the ultimate objective of American land legislation had been irretrievably altered.[17] What once had been a system premised on revenue generation for the federal treasury now rested on the intrinsic value of settlement and ownership itself. In the eighteen years of debates that preceded passage of the Act, no one better expressed the political value of the homeownership ideology than Andrew Johnson, who saw the civicly engaged farm owner as a latter day Cincinnatus:

> The enactment of the Homestead Act would create the strongest tie between the citizen and the government. He [the homeowner] would with cheerfulness contribute his proportional part of the taxes to defray the expenses of the political system under which he lives. What a powerful league it would form between him and the government. What a great incentive it would be to obey every call . . . At the first summons of the clarion note of war, his plow in fact would be left standing in its half-finished furrow, the only plow horse would be converted into a war steed, his scythe and his sickle would be thrown aside, and his home armor buckled on, and with a heart full of valor and patriotism, he would with alacrity rush to his country's standards.[18]

Johnson, like Jefferson before him, assumed that once Americans owned a piece of land, they would want to farm and develop it; the Homestead Act made this progression a matter of law.

Such legal assurance was sorely needed. Between 1820 and 1860 the gap between ownership and occupancy steadily widened; most settlers claimed their land under the doctrine of "squatter's rights," but ignored the portion that required them to settle and improve the land.[19] Even so, during the first half of the nineteenth century, Congress gradually liberalized its perception of the squatter—most conclusively with passage of the Pre-emption Act of 1841 (known informally as the "log cabin bill"), which guaranteed the squatters' right to buy their claims from the government in advance of public auction. No longer seen as trespassers who violated the laws of the Union, the families who pre-empted the survey and land auction system through precocious settlement became regarded as public benefactors "whose bravery and whose sacrifices had opened great areas to peaceful settlement and who merited well of the nation."[20] In other words, as the myth of the yeoman pioneer grew, the nation's laws were changed to accommodate it.

Similarly, the moral value of the individual home became a popular theme in American literature, epitomized by *From Log Cabin to White House* (1881), which told the story of James Garfield's rise to the Presidency by reference to the progressively higher statuses of his homes. Indeed, the humble log cabin gained a mythical status during the course of the nineteenth century, transformed from mean outpost into cultural icon by successive waves of nostalgic novelists and commentators who had never lived in them. It constituted one strand of the literary attempt to symbolize the virtues of rural innocence and character-building hardship (a strand that conveniently ignored the fact that men such as John Wilkes Booth and Jesse James were also raised within log cabin walls).[21] In a country that largely abandoned the feudal practice of inherited homesteads even among the wealthy, each generation was more wholly left to reinvent itself. Rather than receiving an actual house, literary historian Jan Cohn has argued, most Americans gained a "symbolic inheritance" instead. Americans passed along not the house itself but "the house as a model, a lesson, an incentive." Moreover, Cohn concludes, "With each step in the symbolization of the American house, the tenement dweller, in fact the renter, was pushed further out of the mainstream of American life."[22]

As an enticement to individual homeownership, the Homestead Act was charity in the service of Jeffersonian liberty: freely given, yet paired with a carefully constructed sense of future responsibility for making land into a useful national resource. As Galusha Grow—often called "The Father of the Homestead Law"—put it: "I do not understand the principles of this bill to be based on almshouse bounty or that the Government is to be converted into a bounty-dispensing machine to relieve the wants and distresses of the country. I understand that it is a policy which will furnish the best facilities for cultivating the wilderness, to make it answer the happiness and the welfare of the race."[23]

RURAL HOMESTEADS FOR THE URBAN POOR

The Homestead Act was more than a strategy for rural settlement; it was also an indicator of preferred policies for dealing with ill-settled cities. Historian Eric

Foner notes that in the mid-nineteenth century, "The basic Republican answer to the problem of urban poverty was neither charity, public works, nor strikes, but westward migration of the poor, aided by a homestead act."[24] This implied that impoverishment and unemployment in the cities (such as that following the Panic of 1857) could best be prevented by providing the poor with an outlet that could give them economic independence, transform them from dependency into prosperous yeomen and, as Congressman Owen Lovejoy put it, "greatly increase the number of those who belong to what is called the middle class."[25] Lovejoy's colleague Grow viewed homesteads as assuring that "the national commonage would go to the toiling millions."[26]

That the "toiling millions" could ever have been transformed into millions of industrious yeomen, each on his own plot of land, simply by passage of such an act now seems naive, given that the Act provided no training in farming and that the gift of land was an incidental item on a lengthy list of expenses.[27] At the time, however, the westward exhortations of Horace Greeley and other journalists found congenial company with the free labor ideology of the Republican Party. For Greeley the public lands were "the great regulator of the relations between Labor and Capital, the safety valve of our industrial and social engine." In addition, Foner argues, this "safety-valve conception of the public lands, popularized a half-century later by Frederick Jackson Turner, was accepted as a reality by antebellum Republicans."[28]

In Boston, the directors of the Houses of Industry and Reformation shared the vague hope that some portion of the destitute would willingly forsake the city. Noting a temporary decline in the percentage of immigrant arrivals needing charitable assistance in Boston from 1849 to 1850, the Directors hoped that this meant more of these low-skilled workers had "pushed their fortunes westward" in response to "guidance of wiser counsels" and the "stern teachings of experience." Only a move to the inland countryside, the directors believed, would keep them from "congregating . . . around the seaboard towns and cities, increasing the public burdens . . . with no chance of relieving their own necessities."[29] Similarly, in 1859 a Boston City Council report complained that Boston and other Atlantic coast cities were saddled with the dregs of European immigration: Whereas "the intelligent, enterprising, and such that have the means, pass rapidly onward to the West," among those who remain "are large numbers of the aged, infirm and destitute." Part of the problem was that Boston's "countless" sources of charity, its "admirably managed public institutions," and its extensive system of "out-door relief to persons who have no legal claim to it" served as an unfortunate magnet, inviting "the wretched and helpless from all quarters of the globe to come and partake of her bounty." For Boston to continue to encourage "persons without self-respect or proper spirit of independence" to "take up their residence on our crowded seaboard" was entirely unnecessary, and grounded in "erroneous views of what is demanded by Christian benevolence." Instead, it was nothing less than "the part of humanity to speed them on their way" to the "new settlements of the West" where "the demand for every species of labor is far greater." Moreover, Boston's immigrant poor were "accustomed, in their own country, to a rural life," and getting them out of a city that had nearly two thousand drinking establishments and "social excitements" would greatly reduce their "great temptations to intemperance." Ultimately, the report recommended using almshouses as "distributive centres" to export Boston's least productive citizens: "young and old could be sent west, placed on farms or at mechanical employments, and would soon cease to be chargeable to the public."[30]

These proposals from Boston officials in the 1850s stopped short of endorsing a Homestead Act but clearly indicated the desirability of increased emigration from Eastern cities, and confirmed the moral uplift expected to accompany the rigors of rural employment.[31] Modest efforts to encourage the Boston Irish to emigrate to the western territories failed, however. As Thomas H. O'Connor has argued, the center of the city retained important appeal for a "gregarious people, devoted to clan, family, and religion, with little experience in large-scale farming and no inclination to see their sons and daughters scattered to the four winds. They preferred to remain in Boston, close to their friends, their relatives, their priests, their sacraments, and their pubs . . . The small piece of turf they had carved out along the shabby waterfront might be unsightly and unsanitary, but it was *theirs,* and they did not intend to give it up."[32]

Although the Homestead Act ultimately did little to alter the terms of urban poverty back East, the very discussion of homesteads for the "toiling millions" reaffirmed the distinction between the worthy working poor and those poor who failed to toil at all. The Act, at least in theory, expanded the range of individuals thought deserving of public aid, but did so with the usual expectation that such aid would reinforce the characteristics of good citizenship.

The influence of the Homestead Act—its capacity to perpetuate idealized yeoman citizenry—did not stem primarily from its success as a program for housing a great number of Americans. Although the Act contributed to hundreds of thousands of family-owned homesteads by 1900, it was dwarfed by other aspects of federal land policy; between 1860 and 1900, huge grants to railroads, wagon roads, states, and territories totaled nearly 500 million acres, while homesteads accounted for only 16 percent of western land acquisition. In all, less than half of the land claimed under the Act actually remained with the homesteader long enough to reach final patent; the rest succumbed to various forms of speculation, subject to the volatile boom and bust of nineteenth-century land markets. Most settlers bought new private residential land from larger interests, rather than gaining it directly through the Homestead Act.[33] Like the Land Ordinance of 1785, the Homestead Act carried symbolic meanings that transcended actual behavior. As Daniel Feller has observed, "The bucolic ideal had a stronger hold on men's imaginations than on their actions . . . The settler ideal portrayed the American not as he was but as he wished to think of himself."[34] The Act—as embodied in the lives of farmer, miner, and cowboy folk heroes, and as portrayed in Western novels and films—attained near mythical status by the twentieth century. In force until 1935, when President Roosevelt withdrew all public lands from private entry in order to promote conservation, it was not formally repealed until 1976.[35]

The power of the rugged individualist myth persisted even in the face of countervailing trends. As Theda Skocpol's study of early federal social protection efforts makes clear, the individualists of the late nineteenth century were not always left to their own devices. Between 1880 and 1920, federal veterans' pensions became "the keystone of an entire edifice of honorable income supplements and institutional provision for many northern Americans who were long-standing citizens."[36] In this, it is worth noting not only the comparative largesse of federal commitment toward veterans and widowed mothers with children but the way federal intervention remained premised on a confluence of economic need and moral worth.

Even though self-sufficiency remained incomplete, the homesteader personified frugality and independence in a land of widely separated houses, and held out the promise of an idealized spatial and economic order in which the need to support public neighbors would disappear. By requiring citizenship, expensive westward migration, and sustained hard work, the Homestead Act raised the expectation that public lands would house only those of highest private character.

HOMESTEADS IN THE BOSTON SUBURBS:
ESCAPING PUBLIC NEIGHBORS

In Boston, the lure of the Western homestead usually entailed a journey only as far as the Western suburbs. As industrialism released its pastoral counterweight during the second half of the nineteenth century, Boston's dense pedestrian-scaled merchant city became a sprawling industrial metropolis. In so doing, Sam Bass Warner has argued, it "split into two functional parts." One part became "an industrial, commercial, and communications center packed tight against the port," while the other, aided by the annexation of Roxbury, Dorchester, Charlestown, West Roxbury, and Brighton between 1867 and 1873, formed "an enormous ring of residences and industrial and commercial subcenters." As impoverished immigrants continued to stream into the city center, crowding into tenements that required disproportionate policing and public health expenditures, the city's political and commercial leaders sought to help upwardly mobile workingmen take advantage of a rise in real wages by leaving their tenements for more pastoral refuge in the burgeoning outer belt. New forms of transportation and new types of financing made it possible to separate the most thrifty workers from the mass of potential public neighbors, and to reward them with a home of their own.

For much of the nineteenth century, the preferred type of new residential construction in Boston had followed the precedent of Georgian London, with blocks formed by parallel rows of attached masonry structures. From Bulfinch's Tontine Crescent of 1793 to the rowhouses of the South End and the newly filled Back Bay at mid-century, the city grew with gridded streets divided into frontage lots. Prior to the mass annexations of 1867–1873, these districts represented the outer edge of Boston proper, and their development received substantial government support. From the city-developed South End to the state-developed Back Bay (where one section was sold at a time, and the proceeds used to fill in the next block), large-scale neighborhood development to serve the well-to-do was never fully private. In the Back Bay, where opulence and cultural amenities contributed to the early and rapid decline of the South End, the Commonwealth of Massachusetts set a minimum price for lots to guarantee both ample revenues and upper-class occupancy, and the state legislature reserved tracts for educational, scientific, and cultural institutions.[37] Driven by this broad public-private partnership, by the end of the nineteenth century Brahmin Boston had a new civic nucleus around Copley Square. Safely distant from the teeming immigrant tenements, even the street names—Marlborough, Newbury, Berkeley, Hereford and the like—all explicitly recalled places in England.

Gradually, other successful Bostonians sought refuge even farther afield. By 1870, Warner writes in *Streetcar Suburbs,* technological developments in surface transportation and balloon-frame wooden construction made it increasingly possible for many middle-class city dwellers to pursue "a mounting interest in the rural ideal." This movement toward a commuter culture, facilitated by thousands of family homes constructed by amateur builders between 1870 and 1900, yielded a new outer city comprised of neatly planted suburban streets. Wooden houses with open space on all four sides, frequently occupied by only a single family, became commonplace. Warner comments, "In an era so devoted to private money-making it seems hardly an accident that streets of row houses with more or less identical swell fronts were abandoned for a suburban style of individualized houses, arranged in such a way as to produce for the public the gratifying view of a prosperous street."[38]

The new suburban opportunities embraced by many middle-class Boston families depended not only on adequate income, but on the feasibility of separating home from workplace. For those in Boston's "central middle class," with stable employment in a fixed location in the city core, the streetcar lines provided appropriate commuting routes, enabling them to forsake the brick rowhouses of the West End or newly constructed South End and to venture as much as six miles farther out, where they could now afford to live in a single-family detached house. For many in Boston's lower middle class—including small shopkeepers, salesmen, skilled artisans, and construction workers—long and often irregular hours or mobile job locations discouraged such long-distance commuting. This combination of constraints and opportunities contributed to increased segregation by income.

For the lower middle class, new opportunities were concentrated in the inner suburbs, just beyond the perimeter of the old walking city. This most numerous segment of the middle class, estimated to comprise 20 to 30 percent of Boston's population, had less to spend on housing, and faced higher land costs. Builders met their demands either with very small single-family homes clustered together or, more often, barely detached two-family homes and three-deckers, which vainly attempted to mock the appearance of their more amply situated but unreachably priced model: the picturesque house on its garden lot.[39] Robert Woods called this ring of changing neighborhoods between the downtown tenement districts and the suburban fringe "The Zone of Emergence." In this zone, homeownership was possible for many, thereby marking "one of the surest indications that emergence is an emergence indeed." Homeownership stood as "a symbol that the newcomers [were] 'taking possession of the land'" and constituted "one of the great educational forces in American life."[40] "Emergence," then, was not simply a spatial movement away from the tenement district but a fuller socio-economic shift, symbolized by homeownership.

Long before Woods, other prominent Bostonians advocated relocation to single-family homes even for the lowest classes. As early as the 1820s, Joseph Tuckerman, a Unitarian clergyman who as "minister-at-large" visited the tenements of the city's impoverished, insisted that new suburban houses were the only means to reduce the congestion of the central city. Countering this view, the city committee established to evaluate housing options for the city's poor concluded in 1846 that mass suburbanization of the least advantaged was both unaffordable and impractical: even if suburban homes could be economically obtained, the laborer would be disinclined to live far from his work. Also, they saw little likelihood that railroad companies would be willing to provide trains for low-income commuters, since "it might prove annoying to the passengers . . . to have numbers of laborers assembled at the Depots." Moreover, the 1846 report warned, allowing such workers to settle in the suburbs could hurt land values and "discourage the settlement of a richer class." Despite such caveats, the committee favored limited "experiments," since "just so far as the laborers *can* be induced to remove from the city, it must benefit themselves and the public."[41]

SMALL HOUSES FOR WORTHY WORKERS

Despite their underlying ambivalence, Bostonians undertook a variety of small-scale attempts to promote low-cost suburbanization and homeownership. In 1854, Horace B. Sargent's pamphlet *Homesteads for City Poor* contended that philanthropic developers could attain a 12 percent annual return for participation in such ventures while, for the exurbanized poor, the results would be even more substantial: "Dignity, manhood, moral and political independence breathe in the very name of freehold . . . The title deed is both a reward and an omen of thrift." With an owned homestead, poverty would be "safely launched upon the limitless sea of prosperity."[42]

Sargent's dreams for the poor remained unfulfilled, but other organizations focused on housing progress for upwardly mobile "workingmen." During the 1850s and 1860s a variety of Boston-based cooperative savings and loan organizations, including the House and Land Association and the American Loan Fund Association, served approximately one thousand Boston families. Despite redoubled efforts, however, by 1890 savings and loan associations had fewer than two thousand borrowers, equal to about 2 percent of Boston's families. With pressures on railroads to introduce cheap "workingmen's trains" and new state-mandated financial mechanisms to permit easier credit, numerous Homestead Clubs also helped spread homeownership, at least for the middle class. Still, an increasingly large portion of the houses were priced outside the middle-income market. Even though the number of building and loan associations in Boston rose from three in 1880 to fifty-two in 1928, these continued to serve more upper-income homebuyers; it was not until the burgeoning of government-backed mortgage-credit systems during the 1930s and thereafter that homeownership became more widely affordable to middle-income Bostonians.[43] In the meantime, the savings and loan organizations offered no shortage of optimistic publicity.

In addition to the efforts of the loan associations themselves, prominent individuals such as the activist Reverend Edward Everett Hale championed single-family homes for worthy workingmen. In a variety of sermons, speeches, essays, stories, and books, Hale stressed the need for "the workingmen of our cities" to own "homesteads." He argued that "LAND is the great civilizer" and called for Bostonians (and other city dwellers) to "aim high" since civilization itself required "a separate house, owned by the tenant, with windows on each side, ready ventilation, and a patch of land large enough for the ornament at least of the home, [and] perhaps for the occupation of the children." Such homes were "at every man's command," Hale claimed, as long as "he does not drink or steal." Extolling "the magnificent system of the Land Laws of the United States," he championed their small-scale suburban equivalent, observing that those laws "give exactly the encouragement to the Western emigrant that I would secure for the emigrant whom I would lead from Lucas Street into Dorchester to-day." He recognized that this "ideal condition of home life for workingmen" was more easily attained in smaller towns and cities, but claimed that it also ought to be possible to "have this treasure within forty minutes of his workshop in the city of New York, Boston, Philadelphia, or Chicago."[44] All that was needed to serve such Hale fellows, was that they be well met by cheap trains and Homestead Clubs.

Private developers of a philanthropic bent, such as Robert Treat Paine, undertook a variety of projects to provide new housing for Boston's "substantial workingman," although his housing served rather insubstantial numbers. In addition to his abiding concern with tenement reform, Paine took special interest in promoting ways for "workingmen of sterling character and thrifty habits" to escape such tenements and attain ownership of a "small house." These houses, Paine believed, "promote the independence of character and life, which lies at the root of thrift." For Paine, the small house was not merely a better shelter; it was a perpetual inspiration to harder and more productive work. "A poor workman," he told the American Social Science Association in 1881, "seized with the desire to save and own a house, puts his soul into his work, and quickly learns how to do better work and faster work, and so rises to the top of his trade, and often finds chances opening out wider and higher—till he is surprised at his own success. The spirit of saving has developed the earning power." In this way, he contended, "the prosperity of the masses of the people is not only measured by their accumulation of property, but is in fact caused by it." At the same time, such worthy endeavors could also directly benefit their investors. He pointed to the positive results of Boston co-operative savings associations, inspired by Philadelphia practice and first authorized under Massachusetts law in 1877, which had yielded annual returns of between 7 and 11 percent. Most important, however, was the benefit to the borrower, who was taught "the art of getting ahead" and set on a "path [that] leads to independence." Given such possibilities, Paine insisted, "no American has any right to be poor."[45]

Acting on these ideas, between 1886 and 1890 Paine and his family financed and supervised the construction of a large Roxbury subdivision comprised of miniaturized single-family two-story rowhouses, each with approximately 600–800 square feet of living space, built on constricted alleys instead of forty-foot streets. This approach, in imitation of the widespread practice of cooperative building companies in Philadelphia and philanthropic builders in England, proved a distinct failure in Boston. "Built a full decade after the main body of the middle class had ceased building row houses for itself," Warner observes, their cramped quarters exuded "a strong philanthropic air." Paine was more successful in his next effort, undertaken by the Workingmen's Building Association, a division of his cooperative bank. This time, again in Roxbury, he doubled the house sizes (and the prices), and constructed a hundred detached wood-frame structures, on then-fashionable curvilinear streets that followed the contours of the land (Fig. 2.2).[46]

A variety of small efforts to promote low-cost housing for Boston's working-class families continued into the early decades of the twentieth century. Paine commented, "So far as an impulse is given to scatter the population out into the healthier suburbs and into the small, separate, detached suburban homes, each with its little plot of land, instead of the fearful overcrowding of families in the huge new tenement houses, students of the social welfare of the people must certainly rejoice."[47] One group of reformers founded the People's Building Association in 1893 to help poor workers buy homes in the suburbs with low weekly payments spread across fifteen to twenty-one years, but the venture foundered under pressure of the depression that immediately followed. A decade later, the Economic Club of Boston again called for cooperative building associations to provide accessible and affordable suburban residences for workers.[48]

FIGURE 2.2 Workingmen's Building Association model single-family house, 1891.

WOODBOURNE: COTTAGES FOR COMMUTERS

The Boston Dwelling House Company took up this challenge and, in 1912, broke ground on the "model suburb" of Woodbourne. Located in the city's Jamaica Plain section and built on thirty acres of the former Minot Estate, it was conveniently near a streetcar line and only a short walk from the Forest Hills terminus of the Boston Elevated Railway (which afforded a five-cent, fifteen-minute ride into the center of the city). Organized by banking executive Robert Winsor, Jr., its board of directors included many prominent Boston Brahmins as well as the city's cardinal. They sought "to point the way to home ownership for persons with limited incomes," and to do so "not in the spirit of charity, but in the spirit of good citizenship." Though the Company's investors certainly expected "a moderate financial recompense," they saw the venture as a great civic and moral experiment in "scientific housing." Claiming that "ninety-nine families out of a hundred long to own a home," they wished to provide the financial structure that would make this possible for those who had "heretofore considered the owning of a home an impossibility."[49] The Company offered a financing plan that made it possible to purchase a $5,000 house with 10 percent down and mortgage payments of only $50 per month. Woodbourne included a few apartments, but the bulk of the plan consisted of more than a hundred tiny two-story houses, most of which were detached single-family dwellings, some as small as 600 square feet (Figs. 2.3–2.4).

Woodbourne immediately garnered lots of good press. The *Boston Herald* lauded the fact that the site was far from the city's "congested districts" yet was "still within easy access of places of employment"; the *Boston Traveler* praised the plan as "a scientific demonstration" of "proper housing" for "the city's great army of workers"; and a magazine sponsored by the bricklayers industry emphasized the brick and stucco construction of the houses, seeing this as a way to check the advance of the wooden three-decker, whose "insidious march, like a fell disease, has ruined most of the real estate around the city." In contrast to these "slovenly developments" (each with three apartments but only one owner) that formed "vast areas of construction as combustible as a Philippine village," Woodbourne offered "individually owned cottages" for "a respectable class of citizens."[50] The three-decker "disease" was a double contagion, since it fostered both the spread of fire and the spread of tenancy. Woodbourne, by its form and its financing, promised to relieve both symptoms.

THE SPIRIT OF THE SMALL HOUSE

Woodbourne captured the spirit of many other efforts to extend the dominion of the "small house" during this period. As World War I was ending, *Architectural Record* devoted an entire issue to examples of such houses from around the nation, noting that "the laboring man is coming into his own." Commenting that "the position and conditions of manual labor workers, the toiling masses, are a National as well as a community concern," A. D. F. Hamlin concluded that "we are learning that a healthy, happy worker in a decent home is worth more, both to the State and to his employers, than one who is an unhealthy, unhappy wanderer from one factory and slum to another factory and slum."[51] For the worker truly to "come into his own," he needed to come into his own *house*.

From the point of view of *Architectural Record*'s correspondent, the small single-family house, unlike the flat, served as "a shrine, a temple, a castle, a bond," and was essential to the full realization of the "home-idea." For Hamlin, the term "flat" was an especially apt way to describe apartment life, since it suggested the

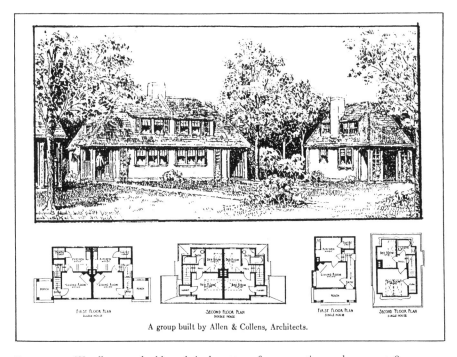

A group built by Allen & Collens, Architects.

FIGURE 2.3 Woodbourne; double and single cottages for commuting workers, ca. 1916.

mere two-dimensional existence that remained once "the variety and spice of life in one's own house" had been squeezed out.[52] In this view, housing the "workingman" in a single-family home promoted domestic tranquillity, and countered poverty in both aesthetic and economic dimensions. With house form so intertwined with cultural expectations, it is hardly surprising that the earliest example of direct government subsidy for low-income housing construction was also undertaken with a rich variety of motives.

STATE-SPONSORED SMALL HOUSES

Just as the high-profile Woodbourne venture began in Boston, the Massachusetts legislature got into the act as well. Not content to leave small house development entirely in the hands of private companies, the Commonwealth authorized direct state involvement in attempts to provide miniaturized lots and houses for worthy workingmen. Appropriately enough, however, the assistance was extremely small-scale. In 1911, the state legislature passed an act leading to the creation of the Massachusetts Homestead Commission (MHC). This resonantly named organization called for appropriations to support an "experiment . . . in providing wholesome, low-cost homesteads" (defined as "small houses and plots of

FIGURE 2.4 Woodbourne, 600-square-foot house.

ground") for "mechanics, factory employees, laborers, and others," and Massachusetts cities were authorized to obtain land for the purpose of teaching agriculture to former tenement dwellers.[53]

The MHC stressed that too few homesteading opportunities existed for Americans, that private methods would never suffice to build more in the absence of state encouragement, and that "therefore the State should experiment to learn whether it is possible to build wholesome dwellings within the means of low-paid workers." In its annual reports, the Commission detailed "the wretched and repulsive conditions in which thousands of families live," stressing their deleterious effects, including deteriorated health, "lessened efficiency," "moral and mental deficiency," and a "lowered standard of citizenship," while sounding further warnings about "their injurious effects on the general public health and well-being." Indeed, Commission members insisted, "it would be impossible to imagine a strong and energetic race coming from generations habituated only to contact with stone pavements, wooden floors and brick walls." The solution was to "take families from the congested districts, plant them in small houses, detached or otherwise, but with a garden plot, and give them a real chance in the fresh air and sunshine, with dirt to dig in and to grow things in, and with outdoors for the children to play in, and with a stake in the world." Nurturing this stake required rehousing the urban tenement population at a density of no more than eight houses per acre, on lots of 40 × 100 feet, in which the house itself occupied only 40 feet of the lot depth. The rest of the lot would be devoted to the character-building and income-boosting exercise of raising vegetables and chickens (Fig. 2.5).[54]

With only limited funds allocated to bankroll its aims, however, the MHC produced scant results: a dozen houses in Lowell. Still, historian Roy Lubove comments that these garden homes "might be described as America's first 'public housing' project." Although this assessment may be grandiose, or at least premature, the mini-experiment did mark an important milestone in the reluctant evolution of state aid, and did so in a way that affirmed the much-touted superiority of the detached single-family home. Moreover, the Homestead Commission made significant headway on other matters: it helped redirect the Commonwealth toward greater consideration of regional growth patterns and density controls, and it played a large part in launching Boston's City Planning Board, a precursor to the full-scale municipal zoning that was in force by the 1920s.[55]

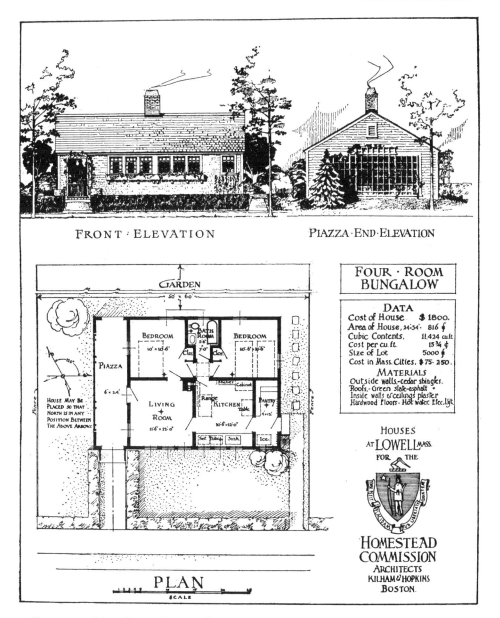

FRONT · ELEVATION PIAZZA·END·ELEVATION

GARDEN

BEDROOM BATH ROOM BEDROOM

PIAZZA

HOUSE MAY BE PLACED SO THAT NORTH IS IN ANY POSITION BETWEEN THE ABOVE ARROWS

LIVING ROOM

KITCHEN PANTRY

PLAN
SCALE

FOUR · ROOM
BUNGALOW

DATA
Cost of House $ 1800.
Area of House, 24·34'·   816 ⨍
Cubic Contents,   11,424 cu.ft.
Cost per cu. ft.   15¾ ¢
Size of Lot   5000 ⨍
Cost in Mass. Cities. $75· 250.

MATERIALS
Outside walls-cedar shingles.
Roofs,· Green slate-asphalt ·
Inside walls & ceilings plaster
Hardwood Floors· Hot water. Elec. lgt.

HOUSES
AT LOWELL MASS.
FOR THE

HOMESTEAD
COMMISSION
ARCHITECTS
KILHAM & HOPKINS
BOSTON.

FIGURE 2.5 Massachusetts Homestead Commission, housing for workers, Lowell, Massachusetts, 1918. The plan, very optimistically listed as 816 square feet, requires a solar orientation that promotes daylight in the kitchen and living room, as well as adequate sunshine for garden cultivation.

RESIDENTIAL DISTRICTS: ZONING OUT PUBLIC NEIGHBORS

In the twentieth century, many disparate groups and individuals acted to secure the elevated status of the single-family home. They did so not simply to affirm its positive values, but to exclude a variety of other people and practices judged less worthy. With house form and moral character so intertwined—and public dependency associated with rental tenements rather than with owned single-family homes—it became possible to zone out potential public neighbors by reference to the architectural character of their houses.

The nation's first large-scale zoning regulations, in California and New York, were phrased in terms of building types, but were rooted in racial and ethnic concerns. California's pioneering laws were enacted, in part, to keep Chinese out of "American" neighborhoods, while New York City's landmark ordinance of 1916 was implemented, in part, to check the advance of Jewish garment factories upon upscale Fifth Avenue shops. As Seymour Toll puts it in *Zoned American,* from the laundry-owners of California to the garment workers of New York, "the immigrant is in the fiber of zoning."[56] More surreptitiously, privately developed subdivisions for many decades relied on restrictive covenants to exclude "all non-Caucasians from occupancy, except as domestic servants."[57]

Zoning also served as a reward system, enshrining the position of the single-family house. Even before zoning, there were legal mechanisms in place to protect preferred house types from undesirable incursions. As early as 1692, the town of Boston passed nuisance ordinances, based on the common-law maxim that owners could do what they wished with their property as long as it caused no injury to neighbors. These early laws, though not yet coddling the single-family house since the town was at that time a jumble of mixed land-uses, were nonetheless intended to keep "any trade or employment which is a nuisance or hurtful to the public health, or is attended by some noisome odors" out of residential neighborhoods.[58] More than two centuries later, this early impulse reached full fruition in Boston and across the nation. The zoning codes of the twentieth-century American city placed individual houses at the apex of ranking—almost invariably labeled as "A-1" or some similar exalted designation—and frequently classified apartments in the same category as commercial businesses.

In 1926, the landmark Supreme Court decision in *Village of Euclid v. Ambler Realty Co.* overturned a lower court to affirm the constitutionality of such zoning regulations. In upholding this Cleveland suburb's right to place restrictions on the use of a developer's land, the Court also gave notice that similar ordinances across the country (including New York's, upon which Euclid's was closely based), could also be upheld as valid exercises of the government's "police power," intended to protect public health, safety, or welfare. Though the case turned on the constitutionality of a town's right to restrain a realty company from developing its land for more profitable industrial uses, it was argued not simply in terms of lost potential revenues but also in terms of the exclusive privileges accorded to those who dwell in single-family homes. Ambler's lawyers maintained that Euclid's zoning ordinance worked against public purposes because the zone of single-family homes blocked lower-status families from "the refreshing access" of Lake Erie and "the better air of the wooded upland." Instead, they contended, "All the people who live in the village and are not able to maintain single-family residences . . . are pressed down into the low-lying land adjacent to the industrial area, congested there in two-family residences and apartments, and denied the privilege of escaping for relief to the ridge or lake." The Ambler argument pointed directly to the underlying socioeconomic divisiveness of Euclid's ordinance, which excluded not only industrial and retail establishments but also apartment buildings from its prime residential districts.

In rendering its majority opinion, the Supreme Court completely rejected this line of argument. While repudiating the inviolability of Ambler's own private property claims, Justice Sutherland defended the property rights of homeowners, pointing out that "the development of detached house sections is greatly retarded by the coming of apartment houses," and noting that such inclusion "has sometimes resulted in destroying the entire section for private house purposes." Sutherland further described the apartment house as a "mere parasite, constructed in order to take advantage of the open spaces and attractive surroundings created by the residential character of the district." Such a view upheld the position that apartments ought properly to be regarded as a form of "business or trade," and thereby excluded from residential districts.[59] In other words, the very concept of "residential district" excluded multiple dwellings completely; in the eyes of the law, these places were the owner-landlord's place of business rather than the resident's home.

In practice, however, at least during the 1920s and 1930s, cities honored the sanctity of the "residential district" only for higher-income neighborhoods of owned homes. As Marc Weiss found, zoning regulations operated both to protect high-income areas from threats to property value and to promote greater diversification of economic development in those areas where the incomes of residents were lower:

> Where residential areas were planned for or built up with expensive single-family houses, *protection* to facilitate or to preserve this particular form of high property values was considered to be a worthwhile objective; in middle-income residential areas, *promotion* of higher-density, higher-value multifamily apartment buildings, hotels, stores, offices, and other residential and commercial uses was combined with the necessary *protection* of those uses from industrial "nuisance" encroachment; in low-income residential areas, *promotion* of industrial uses was the primary objective, with absolutely no *protection* of the local working-class population.[60]

Even as the codes were structured to promote whatever form of development sustained the highest land values, this principle was inflected to favor the culturally preferred and morally sanctioned house forms of the upwardly mobile. Built into the practice of municipal zoning, as well as written into deed restrictions, the value of the highest-priced single-family home achieved the highest possible protection.

The ideological preference for the single-family owned home thus encompassed not only a preference for single versus multiple dwellings but also a preference for ownership over tenancy. Allan Heskin comments in *Tenants and the American Dream*,

> Tenancy has never been a desirable position for residents of the United States. The drive to own has obsessed the people from the yeoman farmer to the modern suburbanite. Being a tenant had never been part of the "American Dream," and the status of tenants in this society has never been secure or comfortable. Tenants have been, in an essential way, the unpropertied in a society in which property is central. In that tenants' immediate interests seem to lie in opposition to those of property, their issues appear to present conflicts basic to the ideological fabric of the country.[61]

Although any detached home was judged superior, the owned home remained the ideal. Constance Perin, in *Everything In Its Place*, shows that the legal constraints placed upon those who rent persist to this day and represent an important incentive for single-family homeownership. "The secondary status of the tenant is perpetuated in the various anachronisms of real property law, especially in terms of landlords' minimal obligations and tenants' maximum liabilities. The basic value of owning is the freedom from the landlord's right of entry to inspect his premises, as well as in freedom from the customary restrictions in leases against personalizing rented quarters."[62] Even the term "landlord" carried the anachronistic ring of feudal privilege.

The frontier myths, nurtured by nineteenth-century novels and by more than a century of rural land development policies, gained new power in the urbanizing America of the twentieth century. In early rural America, the preference for ownership had been generated in part by the co-location of home and business; in an urban context without farmable lands, the ideology persisted but the house itself became its central distinguishing feature. As Manuel Castells puts it, the ideology of the individual urban house is based on the "compensatory myth of a rediscovery of a peaceful country life."[63] Throughout the twentieth century, some of that compensation has come in the form of multiple tax breaks for the homeowner. Since the first federal income tax legislation of 1907, property taxes and interest on a home mortgage have been tax deductible, incentives for ownership that have no parallel for renters. Fundamentally, though, the compensatory myth of homeownership is rooted in its cultural mystique, its ability to provide pastoral roots and moral superiority.

That the myth rushed ahead of the reality is well illustrated by the accelerating but still rather limited rise of homeownership rates in Boston. One study that traced the tenure and mobility patterns of a sample of Bostonians from 1880 onward found that only 7 percent were homeowners in 1880, rising to 25 percent by 1900 and 35 percent by 1910, as increasing numbers moved farther out from the city center.[64] This trend certainly testifies to the rapidly burgeoning opportunities for ownership made possible by suburbanization, but also suggests that for Bostonians (as for those in many other cities), only a minority of families achieved the dream of homeownership during the early part of the twentieth century. Until the full panoply of federal financial assistance packages was put into effect during the New Deal and postwar period—leading to the current situation in which approximately two-thirds of American families own their own homes—the rhetoric of homeownership well exceeded the reach.[65]

Disseminating the Homeownership Ideology

During the first decade of the twentieth century, the preference for owned homes appeared not only in the tax codes and political speeches; more pervasively, it entered the minds of the average citizen through the media and the self-interested promotion of the various builders' organizations. To read through these articles, reports, advertisements, and editorials is to see nineteenth-century ideals about the ties among home, hearth, morality, and country reiterated to middle-class America in the period immediately before the first large-scale efforts in government-subsidized low-income housing. From the realtor's pitch to the home magazine's essay, public opinion about homes was both shaped and measured.[66] Especially during periods of international strife, actual or imagined, the home could be lauded as proof of the superiority of individualism to anarchosyndicalism or other socialist or communist movements. Invariably, the home periodicals stressed the joys of self-sufficiency, and sought to emphasize the moral necessity of the family, neighborhood, and Christian community.

The fight for the owned home soon spread well beyond the pages of such journals. In 1919 and 1920, the National Association of Real Estate Boards (NAREB) and other industry groups joined forces with the U.S. Department of Labor to launch the "Own Your Own Home" campaign, part of a concerted effort to make increased rates of nonfarm homeownership the central and single-minded goal of American housing policy. A Boston newspaper demonstrated the spirit of this quest, by printing an "OWN YOUR OWN HOME RESOLUTION" in its "book of homes" supplement:

> I believe in the American home and its eternal power for good; I believe that it is my individual duty and privilege to own a home under the Stars and Stripes; I believe that Boston is one of the great home cities of the world; I solemnly resolve to make my best efforts during 1920 to become a homeowner in this great city, and thereby satisfy the cravings of my own heart and the desire of those dear to me in life; to make my own prosperity more secure, and also to stimulate through home ownership the industrial and commercial life of my own city.

Part credo, part sacred and patriotic proclamation, part civic and economic boosterism, the campaign was all hype, yet it pressed on in all seriousness. With homeownership having been achieved by only about 35 percent of nonfarm families in Massachusetts (ranking it forty-first among the various states and territories), Boston and the rest of the Commonwealth had a long way to go.[67]

Throughout the 1920s, the "community builders" themselves—with full federal approval—took the lead in promoting the ideological aims and political benefits of enhanced homeownership.[68] NAREB's chief propaganda effort in 1922, entitled *A Home of Your Own*, couched its strongest plea in the language of the independent yeoman. This twenty-page booklet impugned the moral and sexual inadequacy of renters by noting that homeownership "puts the MAN back in MANHOOD" and enabled one to be "completely self-reliant and dominant." Conversely, continued tenancy suggested an inability "to be your own man," since it entailed "[turning] over to others the control of the place that is the center of your whole personal and family life" (Fig. 2.6). The whole publication played upon the traditional American dislike of dependence, depicting home-

FIGURE 2.6 The National Association of Real Estate Boards (NAREB) promoted home-ownership in 1922 with the slogan, "You are either your own man or you are someone else's man."

ownership as a kind of rite of passage into a bold frontier manhood. NAREB treated the small semi-urban or suburban lot as if it were a nineteenth-century homestead tract, identified gardening with "miner's gold fever," and even implied that the self-reliance of ownership could be accompanied by economic self-sufficiency, entirely from backyard cultivation. The realtors invoked the Jeffersonian notion that value derived not only from ownership but from working the land, extolled the owned home as a bastion of morality in a world of dangerous and dissenting ideas, and praised the homeowner as an inward-driven pilgrim sanctified by daily trips to his "mecca." In a passage that explicitly distinguished privately owned homes from their morally deficient alternatives, NAREB promised protection from "the unwholesome and not infrequently contaminating ideas of the floating classes that predominate in the close-in rental districts."[69] In this way, NAREB defended homeownership not only as an index of self-esteem and control, but as a mechanism of class segregation (Figs. 2.7–2.8).

FIGURE 2.7 According to NAREB, homeownership was the key to workplace productivity and worthwhile domesticity.

In drawing such a sharp distinction between owners and renters, NAREB's booklet treated the single-family residential district as a sacred redoubt designed to keep the unworthy at bay. All renters could be found guilty by spatial association simply because they dwelled in "close-in rental districts" where "unwholesome" and "contaminating" transients "predominate." Because their "floating" housing tenure precluded them from establishing stable roots in the soil or in the community, NAREB stigmatized renters as unsettled dependent people, even if they had not yet obliged the state to assist them. If the custom of "warning out" had persisted into the twentieth century, this encroaching collectivity of unwanted and dangerous tenants would have been the first to be warned, at least to the extent that NAREB's neo-Puritan leadership had any say in the matter. NAREB's booklet, like its other homeownership publications, highlighted the psychological segregation of those who could not attain the exalted citizenship of

The Owned Home Makes Life More Worth While in Every Way

the homeowner, a status lauded as the twentieth-century version of the Puritan visible saint.

NAREB's wholesome homeowner, like the rugged frontier pioneer upon whom he was modeled, took full personal responsibility for the way he was housed, requiring little assistance from others. The role of government was simply to establish sufficient zoning and building regulation to assure the stability, safety, and sanitation of his neighborhood. Secure in his castle, the agencies of local government would intervene only to patrol, and periodically to clean, his moat.

The National Association of Real Estate Boards was but one constellation in a

**Have you a home for
your little fairy?**

FIGURE 2.8 NAREB advertised the benefits to every member of the family of homeownership over renting.

"Does Brown own his home?
No, he rents. Haven't you
seen him scratch matches on
the wall paper?"

No drudgery here.

What woman does not yearn
for her own garden and
flowers?
The outdoor work of caring
for them, and the sunshine,
help to keep her young.

firmament of movements intended to transmute the owned home into a heavenly presence. In 1922, the U.S. Department of Labor joined forces with the home-boosting organization known as Better Homes in America, Inc., to launch the Better Homes movement. With Herbert Hoover as its president until 1927 and Calvin Coolidge as the chair of its advisory council, this organization sought to encourage "better living conditions . . . by holding up high standards in home-building, home furnishing, and home life," while urging "old fashioned thrift" for homeownership, "the improvement of home lots, the promotions of home gardens, and the dissemination of information for home makers of moderate means."[70] By 1930, despite the disruption of the Great Depression, the Better Homes movement boasted local councils in more than 7,000 towns and cities across the country.

Even the Depression-induced threat to the privately owned home did not initially prompt federal support for public housing or even instigate a restructuring of government intervention in the mortgage industry. Instead, Hoover convened the "President's Conference on Home Building and Home Ownership" in December 1931, and the reports of its various committees, published the following year, all affirmed the vitality of the homeownership ideology. Above all, the conference represented a platform for Hoover's own views about the connection between the single-family home and good citizenship, ideas he had publicly expounded for many years. In his address, he affirmed the "wide distinction between homes and mere housing," and remarked that the country's "immortal ballads, *Home, Sweet Home, My Old Kentucky Home,* and *The Little Gray House in the West,* were not written about tenements and apartments." Secretary of Commerce Robert Lamont, as conference co-chairman, echoed the neo-Jeffersonian language of the President even more pointedly, asserting, "It is doubtful whether democracy is possible where tenants overwhelmingly outnumber home owners . . . The need to protect and guard the home is the whip that has proved, beyond all others, efficacious in driving men to discharge the duties of self-government."[71]

The Conference placed its emphasis squarely upon promoting ownership, completely disregarding the poor quality of housing available and affordable for purchase. As one journalist concluded, "Fundamentally Mr. Hoover is not interested in housing; he is interested in ownership . . . Mr. Hoover still thinks in terms of the old-fashioned individual and independent house, built more or less to order; and failing this, he is willing to let the individual purchaser take his chances with the botched and worthless stuff that is available on the market."[72] Significantly, the Committee on the Relationship of Income and the Home came up with no challenges to the President, despite Edith Elmer Wood's findings in *Recent Trends in American Housing* that two-thirds of the population of the country could not afford to rent or buy new houses of sound planning and good construction.[73] Only the Committee on Large-Scale Operations came up with anything newsworthy. Their report suggested, "By continuing to pay lip-service to the old-fashioned, individually built, free-standing one-family house, our pres-ent builders have not, as a rule, worked with efficient units." Far from a rejection of single-family houses, this was a recommendation that they be planned in larger tracts, an observation that prefigured the importance of merchant builders after World War II. Most important, the committee refused to concede that large-scale housing required government subsidy, though they realized that it might not be too far down the road: "This committee is firmly of the opinion that private ini-tiative backed by private capital is essential, at the present time, for the successful planning and operation of large-scale projects. Still, if we do not accept this chal-lenge, the alternative may have to be government-housing." For a committee that counted Executive Vice President Herbert U. Nelson of NAREB among its mem-bers, this admission was momentous indeed.[74] Equally portentous was the report of the Business and Housing Committee, which suggested keeping an "open mind" to the possibility that "the lowest wage earning group should be provided with homes at government expense."[75]

On the whole, however, the various reports gave little more than passing atten-tion to the problems of low-income areas or to the possibility of government as-sistance, except to the extent that such problem people might further undermine the social and financial stability of more prosperous areas. The report of the Committee on Blighted Areas and Slums offered further evidence that federal in-terest in America's urban poor centered more on the fiscal plight of America's cities than on the condition of the poor themselves. Phrased purely in economic terms, it began with the simple assertion, "Slums cost money." What followed was yet another articulation of the old cliché that the slum dweller creates the slums, a position that permitted no discussion of the larger questions of poverty, racism, and unemployment. Manuel Elmer, head of the Department of Sociology at the University of Pittsburgh and co-author of the report, dismissively listed types of slum dwellers in an appendix: "We find here the queer, the unadjusted, the radical, the 'Bohemian' and the criminal," and commented that "It has been accurately said that the slum is the 'neighborhood of lost souls.'" At another point in the report, paternalism and distrust combined even more graphically: "Like a migrating flock of black birds resting and feeding temporarily, so groups of immigrants as well as individual families and isolated individuals stop in this transitional area on their way up or down the social scale. Each of these waves of people leaves a residue of poverty-stricken, socially unadjusted, maladjusted defectives and delinquents which gradually accumulates into a slum population."[76] A committee that would equate the various types of America's poor with bird droppings certainly offered little hope for sensitive rehousing.

By 1932, the nineteenth-century language of institutional classification and reform could be wielded not as a means to sort and cure the poor, but as a way to consolidate and attack them. Taken as a whole, the committee reports clearly implied that slums should simply be torn down and replaced with private homes and correspondingly higher land values. Hoover's conferees wished to extend middle-class homeownership into city centers without any corresponding attempt to address the needs of the low-income population. In this context, slum-dwellers could be perceived as undesirable public neighbors even if they had not actually requested public assistance. Simply by virtue of where and how they lived, their presence was judged to be an economic drain on municipal budgets due to low tax receipts and high public expenditures (for such things as fire and police protection and medical care). Whether a stranger or a local, whether a "maladjusted defective" or a "delinquent" or simply a "poverty-stricken" family, the whole flock of bad black birds could be considered fiscally unwelcome.

COMMUNITIES BY DESIGN: DISPLACING PUBLIC NEIGHBORS

Just as the American ideology of the single-family home influenced efforts to reform tenement conditions, undergirded attempts to "process" Americans through the settlement movement, pervaded the formulation of public lands policy, supported suburbanization, and guided zoning ordinances, so too the ideals of the home permeated efforts to design new communities in ways that would clear slums and deconcentrate cities. The socio-environmental principles that ultimately inspired public housing in the United States are often traced to Europeans such as Walter Gropius and Le Corbusier, yet they have their own domestic ideological roots.

This is not to suggest that American thinking about housing and neighborhood design lacked outside influence. Although the vast subject of British and European contributions to the development of working-class housing proto-types during the first three decades of the twentieth century lies beyond the bounds of a book attempting to trace American themes, such efforts form an important backdrop. From the early twentieth-century designs for English garden cities to the Bauhaus-inspired housing schemes of the 1920s and the subsequent manifestos of CIAM (Congrès Internationaux d'Architecture Moderne), designers attempted to enhance and regulate the amount of open space between dwellings in new communities. Many concerned themselves with the challenges of *Existenzminimum,* and devised minimum housing standards for various *Siedlungen* and garden apartments while embracing "scientific" site-planning for proper solar orientation, ventilation, and optimum density.[77]

Many of these site-planning principles grew out of prior model tenement legislation, much of it American. As early as the 1890s, American architectural critic Montgomery Schuyler proposed designing apartment blocks with wide separation to permit greater light penetration and air movement.[78] Although European practice such as Ernst May's work in Frankfurt-am-Main, J. J. P. Oud's Kiefhoek housing estate in Rotterdam, and Karl Ehn's Karl Marx Hof in Vienna yielded seminal examples of housing form, Americans drew on a different cultural history to interpret the meaning of urban open space, and sought to house a different kind of worker.

In charting the genealogy of American public housing, one must look for ancestors whose practices linked neighborhood sociology and urban design. These come in many different guises: retrograde efforts to reintroduce elements of village society and form to American cities, a first abortive foray by the U.S. federal government into housing and community design during World War I, and several endeavors by private groups to design model communities using the "neighborhood unit" during the 1920s. All these efforts shared at least one key tenet: a belief that sound neighborhood design would yield environments conducive to productive labor and family success. In such places, there was no room for the dependent poor.

TENEMENT DISTRICT AS URBAN VILLAGE

As wholehearted adherents to the regulatory reform movements that sought to bring higher standards of light and ventilation to individual tenements, those who concerned themselves with broader questions of neighborhood improvement attempted to find common ground between the reality of the tenement district and the ideals of America's rural individualist heritage. As Allen Davis has noted, even city-focused settlement reformers, influenced by John Ruskin and William Morris, "talked at times as though they wanted to restore the rural village." In the early years, many settlement leaders actually left their city neighborhoods during the summer months: "Ellen Starr was constantly irritated by the dust and dirt at Hull House and loved to go to a clean New England village. Robert Woods maintained that the city was no place even for a settlement conference, and Lillian Wald said of New York, 'this is an awful city to live in.'"[79] These were reluctant urbanites, who revered—and idealized—both the physical form and the social structure of the village.

The village image they had in mind was highly specific and resolutely Yankee. By contrast, they viewed the village life of the immigrants' European past as an empty peasantry—part of the problem, not the solution—since old village ties worked against the adoption of American values. Worried that ethnically grounded loyalty "usually [found] a radius wider than that of a city district" and was "rather indifferent to strictly local interest,"[80] settlement workers tried to superimpose an Americanizing neighborhood social structure upon the ethnic enclave in an attempt to induce its fragmentation.

Robert Woods especially admired the order of the early New England village, which combined the privacy and rectitude of the home with the civic engagement implied by the town common and its flanking institutions. "The settlements," he averred, "are able to take neighborhoods in cities and by patience bring back to them much of the healthy village life, so that the people shall again know and care for each other."[81] In *The Settlement Horizon,* Woods sought to bring national unity to the settlement movement, but nonetheless stressed how its "American origins" were "everywhere" motivated by "the Puritan tradition of moralized community action, New England village life out of which the fabric of our civilization was built, [and] the town-meeting which contains the germ of American government."[82] In all this, Woods's palpable nostalgia for the New England villages of his college and seminary years was mixed, metaphorically and otherwise, with his romantic images of pioneers settling a "city wilderness." The oddity of the juxtaposition is, however, less interesting than the fact that so many other housing activists, at the time and in the decades that followed, seem to have shared his sentiments—a retrograde ruralism that would ultimately influence the design of public housing projects.

In the Boston area, this spirit motivated both the state-sponsored initiatives of the Massachusetts Homestead Commission in Lowell as well as the small houses for workers built in Woodbourne. Though the Lowell experiment entailed a more standard subdivision into private lots and gardens, Robert Anderson Pope intended his plan for Woodbourne to be a true "community design" (Figs. 2.9–2.10), and Robert Woods himself served as one of the Boston Dwelling Company's trustees for the venture. Not simply a way to make small houses affordable and accessible to Boston's workers, the designers also provided a network of shared open spaces linking playgrounds and parks to the rear of the houses. As one account described it in 1913, in contrast to the usual dense conglomeration of three-deckers, Woodbourne provided "uninterrupted sunlight and air." The cottages were laid out in groups, "each having its own garden plot of rather limited size but with rights in large open squares or playgrounds which assure not only plenty of air and sunlight but ample playing space for children." Pope's plan, in its emphasis on brick and stucco-faced cottages, irregular curving streets, and

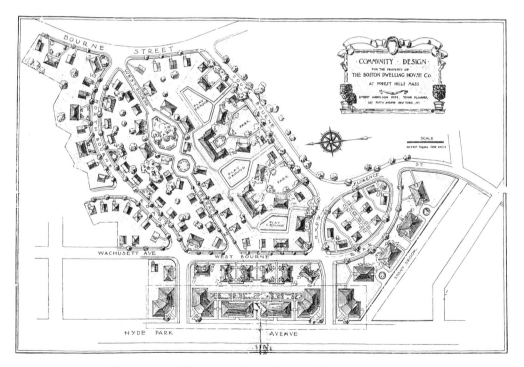

FIGURE 2.9 Woodbourne's "Community Design," 1912. Robert Anderson Pope's site design combined small houses with a large network of public open spaces.

connected open spaces, drew heavily on the English Garden City precedents derived from Ebenezer Howard's seminal tract, *Garden Cities of To-morrow* (1902), as interpreted by Barry Parker and Raymond Unwin in Letchworth (begun in 1903) and Hampstead Garden Suburb (begun in 1907) and, in America, by Grosvenor Atterbury's plan for Forest Hills Gardens in Queens (begun in 1910).[83] Woodbourne was much smaller than these other Anglo-American efforts, and entirely lacked a civic or retail component, with its thirty acres separated from major thoroughfares. Still, its promoters claimed it was "so large that it automatically guarantees itself against injury by the possible lowering of the character of the outside surroundings."[84] Two decades later, this idea that redevelopment must occur in large chunks in order to guard against future injury caused by downward market pressure from neighboring areas would become a guiding principle behind the promotion of large public housing projects in slum-clearance areas.

THE FIRST PUBLIC NEIGHBORHOODS:

COMPANY TOWNS FOR UNCLE SAM

With small-scale "village"-building efforts underway by private and philanthropic organizations during the late nineteenth century and first decades of the twenti-

FIGURE 2.10 The brick paths wind past houses and shared open areas off Southbourne Road in Woodbourne.

eth, and some progress being made on tenement regulation by cities and states, it took a national emergency to get the federal government involved. That first emergency was not the Great Depression, but World War I, which made it necessary to "intervene in the housing market in order to nurture the health, comfort, and productivity of the nation's workers."[85]

This first federal commitment to housing working-class Americans entailed the construction, sponsorship, or control of tens of thousands of dwelling units across the country. Like American intervention in the war itself, federal aid was reluctant, successful, and short-lived. As the nation geared up to enter the war in 1917, the various war production industries suffered from "crowded and insanitary housing" that caused "heavy labor turnover" as well as "inefficiency and discontent on the part of those operatives who . . . put up with unwholesome conditions and remained on the job." Despite the evident problem, private housing interests waged numerous battles on the home front to deny it. As Edith Elmer Wood observed, even after an August 1917 Council of National Defense conference decided that "the Government would have to intervene," many resisted the idea that such housing should be permanent. Faced with protests by tenement house owners who claimed they "would be ruined by the competition," federal officials made it "abundantly clear that this was a war policy only and did not commit the Government to anything in peace time." Unconvinced, private housing interests preferred to have the federal government "subsidize the transportation lines to bring workers from a distance," and charged that direct federal intervention in housing operations would be "highly dangerous and subversive."[86]

Given such controversies, it was not until the summer of 1918 that the federal government completed the last of the authorizing legislation and appropriations to fund its two industrial housing organizations, the United States Shipping Board's Emergency Fleet Corporation (EFC) and the Department of Labor's United States Housing Corporation (USHC). Roy Lubove called this "glacial slowness" in launching a housing program one of "the major administrative bungles" of the entire war, considering its importance to war production, but praised the quality of much of what did get built. In general, the USHC built and administered its projects directly, whereas the EFC—much less controversially—lent money to realty companies established by its ship-building companies, with the expectation that these companies would repay the loans and own the developments after the war. As it turned out, however, the time between the first availability of appropriations and the signing of the Armistice was all of 109 days.[87]

Despite such a narrow window of opportunity, advance planning enabled the

USHC to start 128 projects in 71 communities, and to begin construction on forty of these. Ultimately, the USHC's Town Planning Division, headed by Frederick Law Olmsted Jr., completed twenty-seven of these projects, housing 6,000 families and 7,000 single individuals in dormitories, hotels, and boarding houses. During the same brief period, the EFC authorized construction of twenty-eight projects including another 9,500 family dwellings and accommodations for 7,500 single persons. In total, the fifty-five projects supplied new housing for an estimated 95,000 war workers and their families.

With most private-sector building activity suspended, these government housing organizations could count on the availability of many of the country's most prominent architects and planners, such as Frederick Ackerman, Henry Wright, and Robert Kohn, all of whom would play leading roles in community planning efforts during the 1920s and again in the New Deal Public Works Administration, of which Kohn became director of housing. In 1920, a reviewer writing in *Architectural Record* went so far as to declare the 1919 Report of the USHC a signal "event in the literature of American architecture," praising not only the "extraordinary success" of the war housing but also the care with which the USHC set out its design principles in the report.[88] Christian Topolov has commented, "workers' housing, until then the province of small builders, small landlords and speculators, or employers hardly aspiring to be 'models,' was suddenly in the hands of the most eminent professionals and reformers of the architectural establishment. The stage was set for experimentation on a grand scale."[89]

The USHC and EFC built not only houses but entire "model villages," in many cases drawing explicitly on English garden city practice, and taking clear note of Raymond Unwin's seminal pamphlet *Nothing Gained By Overcrowding*, which argued in favor of lower building densities on both social and financial grounds.[90] EFC architect Electus Litchfield called his design for Yorkship Village in Camden, New Jersey "a romantic opportunity" to demonstrate that, "through providing proper homes for its employees, an industrial corporation could lay the foundation for a contented and efficient body of workers."[91] In a similar manner, *Architectural Record*'s correspondent pointed out that the model environment built for workers in Bridgeport, Connecticut would "exert a commensurate influence upon the people who live there—counteracting the slovenly and vicious tendencies of the usual tenement environment and leading them along the first steps of the way to the higher grades of American working-life."[92] Once again, supporters justified better housing for workers not just on aesthetic and sanitary grounds, but on the determinist capacity of good housing to promote economic gain and insure civil peace for the broader society.

Even as environmental determinism found new applications in realm of war housing, not all kinds of workers were assigned to equally auspicious sorts of environments. The USHC and EFC used criteria for working-class housing formulated by Lawrence Veiller, which specified light and sanitation requirements. These criteria stipulated that tenements and apartment houses were "generally considered undesirable," and would be accepted "only where the Housing Board is convinced that local conditions require or justify their use."[93] Tenements or no tenements, issues of class and income still determined which kinds of workers were provided with which kinds of housing.

Housing activist Edith Elmer Wood strongly objected to the USHC requirement stipulating that the number of bedrooms provided should be based on family income rather than on family size, but this was just one small way that the housing program attempted to distinguish, and then spatially segregate, different types of workers from one another. As one speaker put it to a congressional committee holding hearings on "Housing for Employees of Shipyards" in 1918: "The type of house, of course, we try to base on the wage of the man . . . [T]hat is the main consideration."[94]

The USHC staffed its Real Estate Division with representatives of NAREB—later to be one of the chief lobbying groups against public housing—and they resisted any explicit form of rental subsidy to tenants on the grounds that it would constitute unfair competition to private local landlords. The USHC resolved the issue of rent levels "'as best it could' by combining a number of contradictory criteria: the market value of the housing, the predominant rent levels of the locality, and the wages and living situation of the tenant."[95] Under pressure to set rent levels low enough so that the intended residents could afford to live in the new housing, the USHC stopped short of intermixing types of housing. This decision, correspondingly, also tended to keep apart the various types of workers. In addition to complete racial segregation, the wartime housing projects often featured separate housing types for unskilled workers, semi-skilled workers, and skilled workers, with each type located at increasing distance from the factory itself.

The U.S. Housing Corporation developments planned near the Fore River Shipbuilding Company in Quincy, Massachusetts perfectly illustrate the correspondence between job classification and spatial position (Fig. 2.11). As it geared up for the war effort, this company (a subsidiary of Bethlehem Steel) dramatically reoriented the residential and employment pattern of its immediate area. Its workers and their families added an estimated 40,000 to the population of greater Boston, and the company desperately needed both housing and transportation improvements to insure efficient operation.[96] The shipyards were located on the waterfront a few miles southeast of Boston, and the USHC stepped in to sponsor new housing construction to serve many hundreds of war workers, built on four unoccupied sites to the north and west of the plant.

Closest to the workplace (far bottom left of Fig. 2.11) the USHC built a "Dormitory Group" for unskilled workers. Agency standards specified that each dormitory room be 82.5 square feet, including a toilet. The dormitory buildings containing these rooms were constructed as a series of twenty-one identical rectangular structures—each about one hundred feet long—arranged on a rigid grid, and adjacent to a large common cafeteria ("mess hall") and a smaller recreation building. There were several related reasons for this particular juxtaposition of dwelling type, workplace, and community institutions. First of all, these were the sex-segregated domiciles of a cadre of nonunion workers who were either single or living far apart from their families, and who were held to this particular locality only by their jobs. To keep them, and to keep them productive, meant keeping them close by. As Topolov comments, for a labor force that worked long hours and in shifts, "dormitories eliminated travel time, reduced fatigue and the temptations associated with it, and lowered the costs of meals and laundry; it could thus be supposed that they promoted the rational use of wages and of nonworking time."[97]

By contrast, the USHC situated skilled workers in two clusters of single-family houses located more than a half-mile inland from the shipyard gates, on the far side of Pilgrim Parkway (Fig. 2.12). For these workers, assumed to have come with their families, the USHC's planners wished to provide not only for relative ease of pilgrimage to the workplace, but also for a peaceful family life for the worker's wife and children at home (an environment also intended to sustain the worker himself when off-duty). The larger of the two housing areas abutted the optimistically named Victory Park and a proposed school, and the smaller high-end housing area was but a short walk from the Fore River Club (a recreation center for higher-status workers).

At base, however, the principal reason for locating dwellings at some distance from the shipyards resulted from the need to insure the houses' future market-

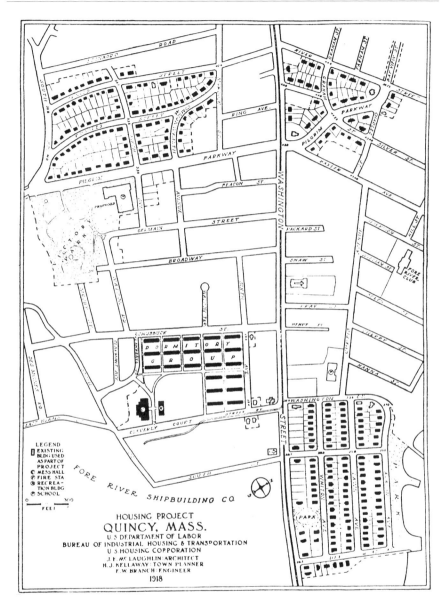

FIGURE 2.11 In the U.S. Housing Corporation's system for accommodating and classifying World War I workers in 1918 at the Fore River Shipbuilding Company, Quincy, Massachusetts, dormitories for unskilled workers are closest to the factory (bottom left); two-family houses (lower right) were for semi-skilled workers; and single-family detached homes predominated in the projects shown at the top of the map.

ability. With the relationship of the householders to the Fore River employer uncertain after the war, and immediate proximity to industry a distinct disadvantage to property values, Congress had insisted that the USHC build and site its houses to maximize their sales potential. It took little imagination to sense that single-family homes located on secondary roads in close proximity to parks and schools would carry the widest future appeal. Not wishing to tie war workers to the area on a long-term basis, the government agencies did not advocate sale of these houses to their occupants during wartime, but certainly wished to foster this option for the future. Inserted into the midst of a "prosperous middle-class population, pleasantly housed," the new USHC developments did their best to fit in with the prevailing norms of their Quincy neighbors.[98]

The fourth USHC housing development in Quincy was a grid of houses located just to the north of the shipyards, and intended for semi-skilled workers. Here, everything from houses to parks was scaled down from the more spa-

FIGURE 2.12 "Housing for War Needs," Quincy, Massachusetts, 1918. Architect James McLaughlin's single-family brick houses for Fifth Avenue each featured ample open space on all sides and a homey porch, just as specified in Lawrence Veiller's guidelines.

cious provisions of the upscale western neighborhoods. These were to be small houses—USHC guidelines allowed them to be as tiny as 616 square feet—reflecting both the ideological preference for the detached house and the economic reality of limited incomes. Across the country, construction of small single-family homes constituted fully 85 percent of the USHC's total housing program.[99]

The wartime housing ventures, in Quincy as elsewhere, were but one part of the ongoing adulation of small houses. Such houses made it possible to make life in a single-family home affordable to more workers, yet the moral dimension of the quest always remained firmly linked to every form of economic argument. With the ascent to a proper home came the expectation of both proper behavior and enhanced productivity. Concerned about housing "the right kind of worker," Veiller's wartime housing guidelines encoded a profound ambivalence. The guidelines stipulated "maximum sizes" for bedrooms, not simply to insure affordability, but also to prevent misuse by their residents. As Veiller put it, "the bedroom that is too large encourages the taking in of roomers and lodgers and is used practically as a dormitory."[100] As with the attempt by Woods and Kennedy to devise a set of "American standards" for judging the proper domestication of the immigrants, so too Veiller's standards sought to protect "the workingman" from his own worst tendencies.

In addition to their affirmation of the American ideological preference for single-family homes, the war housing experiments also embodied another Anglo-American tradition. Since these housing projects were organized on explicitly corporate lines, their philosophical roots remained embedded in the calculated paternalism of the company town, where the link between contented workers and efficient operations was no mere general principle but a place-focused necessity. These were neighborhoods closer in spirit and appearance to Pullman Village than to New Deal housing projects. This was housing for "the right kind of workers," Veiller said—for those who were productively engaged in matters affecting the national interest. This was not yet public housing in name, but it did share much of the underlying premise that would characterize the New Deal stage of the program. If the federal government was to ride to the rescue of working-class housing, it would do so saddled with a tacit stipulation: this housing was to be a temporary reward for good people engaged in worthy work. Moreover, it was to serve as a means to separate them from the negative influences of their neighbors and neighborhoods.

In administering these first publicly sponsored neighborhoods, the USHC's managers treated war workers with the same ambivalence that characterized past model housing efforts. At one extreme, Topolov found, tenants were met with "surveillance and hand-to-hand disciplinary combat," even if they were among the more skilled workers: "Tenants were selected on the basis of testimonials to their morality elicited from foremen; rent was collected weekly, by means of visits to the house where this was materially feasible, rather than by direct withholding from wages; and visits of inspection were the rule." At the same time, despite such high levels of suspicion, USHC managers also tried to foster a system of self-regulation, under which tenants were afforded representation on key management bodies,[101] a clear advance over the usual nineteenth-century practice. This tension between the inculcation of paternalist control and the encouragement of independent tenant responsibility would re-emerge when the government tried to administer public housing. That possibility, however, remained well in the future.

With the war's end, a substantial amount of the authorized industrial housing stood incomplete, while the rest was occupied by workers soon to be out of government service. Many housing proponents hoped that the unfinished "housing projects" would still be built, and that the completed houses would be sold off either for co-operative ownership, or managed by limited-dividend corporations introduced to facilitate the availability of government-backed credit. Instead, the government housing program faced an immediate Congressional backlash, a "vituperative campaign" not only to dissolve the initiatives but to discredit them. The House Committee on Public Buildings and Grounds excoriated the USHC for its laggard demobilization, while its Senate counterpart launched an effort to demonstrate that the organization had been wasteful and inefficient. The Senate committee lambasted the USHC for making a demonstration of "model housing," complaining that "Congress certainly did not intend . . . to enter into competition in architectural poetry with any other nation or private organization." Moreover, the senators charged, the quality provided was well in excess of what workers were accustomed to receiving and was not "necessary for the loyal mechanics to be housed." They even complained about the "'orientation' of the blocks," as if even consideration of daylight penetration was an idea deserving reproach.[102] The real orientation problem was, of course, a political one: in the "Red scare" climate of the day, Congress saw the USHC's construction, ownership, and management of housing as intolerably socialist. By the end of 1920 all federal housing efforts were entirely shut down, with little prospect for resumption.

As their various housing and community design projects were terminated or sold off, the USHC's leaders defended themselves by stressing the extent to which their products—far from dangerous anomalies—were conceived and constructed with a careful eye toward postwar marketability. The 1919 USHC Report so beloved by architects went into great detail about site planning techniques and attempts to achieve pleasing vistas and architectural variety, noting the need to avoid making "one set and formal design" that looked like "a penal or charitable institution." Equally important, the report explained, the USHC had successfully resisted efforts to make all the houses "so different, and each so unusual" that the result resembled "a village on the stage." Both approaches shared a common flaw: "neither kind of development would find a ready market," because "people in this country want to live in independent, self-sufficient homes of their own in a real, complete American town, which they understand and run in their own way, and they do not want their houses to be, or look like, parts of an artistic or sociologic experiment."[103] With federal ownership and management rescinded, the individualist ideology could rush in to fill the breach. Independence and self-sufficiency could still triumph over the appearance of charity or penology, and worthy Americans could still run a real town rather than watch a village simulacrum.[104]

As the House Committee on Buildings and Grounds put it in 1919, federal intervention in housing had been "purely and simply . . . an emergency measure demanded by the exigencies of war," and only this "could have justified Congress in entering upon such an undertaking."[105] Veiller, as a major champion of efforts to regulate the private housing market without government intervention into housing supply, expressed much the same view in the 1920 edition of *A Model Housing Law*: "It has seemed to many that the building of houses for workingmen by the Federal Government was an undue interference with the rights of the individual, and those of a conservative mind have feared greatly the inauguration of such a policy and what might come from it. But war changes everything." So, too, for Veiller, war's end changed things yet again. Although he praised efforts to design sound housing that would "attract and *hold* the right kind of workers," he affirmed his belief in the primacy of regulatory reforms: "We must make it impossible for builders to build dark rooms in new houses before we urge the government to subsidize building."[106]

Despite its abbreviated life, this first federal initiative in working-class housing served as a precedent for later public housing programs in at least four ways: it emphasized that housing should be seen as a subset of community design; it viewed this housing in the context of the broader ideology of the single-family home; it insisted that this kind of housing was for stable and "respectable" workers with families; and it sparked sustained discussion—outside of government circles, at least—of more active federal intervention on all fronts, from home mortgage subsidies to housing projects. Though it would be another fifteen years before all of these ideas could be realized in combination, the wartime efforts helped bring together many of the people who would take the lead.

THE NEIGHBORHOOD UNIT

In the years before the exigencies of the Great Depression once again forced the federal government to reconsider the nature of its involvement in housing, many private individuals and groups tried to build on ideas from the prewar garden suburb ventures and the wartime USHC and EFC communities.[107] Often embracing social ideals percolating out of the settlement movement, these housing activists—many with direct settlement connections—greatly helped to clarify the terms of neighborhood design by testing the emerging theory of the "neighborhood unit."

While no one expected any kind of literal importation of the New England village into the slums of Boston, settlement leaders understood that any approximation of this village-based social structure required a corresponding spatial reconceptualization of neighborhood form and amenities. To Robert Woods, the urban neighborhood was the appropriate scale for taking action: it "is large enough to include in essence all the problems of the city, the State, and the Nation" yet "small enough to be a comprehensive and manageable community unit." For him, the neighborhood was a "political and moral unit" for Americanization.[108] Woods devoted little intellectual energy himself to envisioning this unit in urban design terms, but architects and planners soon stepped forward with community designs that tried to connect neighborhood form and social programming.

In 1909 the Russell Sage Foundation hired Clarence Perry to study the community center and settlement movements, and his investigations led to widely influential proposals about the ideal form that neighborhoods should take. From his study of institutions, Perry gained respect for the importance of school, religious, and community facilities in residential areas; from the English garden city movement and its American interpreters, Perry appropriated ideas about distributed open space, mechanisms for coping with the presence of the automobile, and concepts for the distribution of land-uses. Perry developed his concept of the *neighborhood unit* over many years, but it gained prominence with the publication of the New York Regional Plan of 1929, in which a discussion of its principles appeared in monograph form. He subsequently extended the ideas in two books, *The Rebuilding of Blighted Areas* (1933) and *Housing for the Machine Age* (1939).[109] Even critics of the neighborhood unit concept acknowledge that it has for more than a half-century "been virtually the sole basis for formally organizing residential space."[110]

Perry began his discussion of the neighborhood unit by stressing the necessary connection between dwellings and community institutions: "Parents require much more than a house and lot. They need a school, a playground, groceries and drug stores, and perhaps a church. They want their children to associate with children from homes which hold similar standards to their own. They wish to live away from the noise of trains, and out of sight of the smoke and ugliness of industrial plants. They desire, if possible, to have their home in a district where each dwelling devotes a fairly equal amount of space to yard, shrubbery, and general outdoor amenity."[111] Perry's account of the ideal unit of neighborhood design is thus not just a diagram for a walking-distance community; it is an assertion of the virtues of class-based homogeneity, an affirmation that the good neighborhood is one where standards are shared, and houses and lot sizes are equal. As Shelby Harrison, Director of the Social Division of the New York Regional Plan wrote in the introduction to Perry's monograph, Perry sought to recapture the ideal of the village environment: "The purpose in undertaking this inquiry into neighborhood unity and life has been to discover the physical basis for that kind of face-to-face association which characterized the old village community and which the large city finds so difficult to re-create."[112]

Perry extolled the virtues of the neighborhood unit scaled to fit with the enrollment of a local primary school, but devised several types of such units, each seemingly intended to accommodate a narrow range of incomes. While it was clear that his preference was for units comprised of "modest homes in the suburbs," he also set out design guidelines for an "Industrial Section" unit, "An Apartment-House Unit" and a unit to be built following clearance of a "Slum District" (Figs. 2.13–2.15). The "Apartment-House" neighborhood unit bore partial resemblance to the one based on single-family homes, featuring a network of streets centered on a "community center" and school, and outfitted with playgrounds, parks, two churches, peripheral areas for both "local business" and

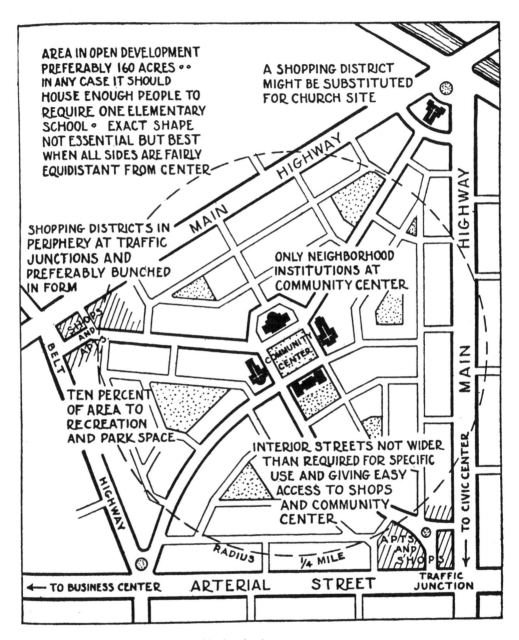

FIGURE 2.13 Clarence Perry's neighborhood unit, 1929.

"general business," as well as a theatre and arcade. For the slum-clearance unit—redeveloped into a "Five Block Apartment Development," however, all resemblance to the "single-family district" disappears. Here, the emphasis is on near-total suppression of interior streets to eliminate "exposure to traffic dangers." There is still provision for a school, auditorium, gymnasium, and arcade of shops—all facing the perimeter "boundary streets," but gone are the churches and conspicuous community center. Instead of a town common flanked by institutions, this neighborhood unit is centered on a "main central court" equal in size to "Gramercy Park, Manhattan, with its surrounding streets." The size comparison is a telling one since, of course, the proposed court would have no such "surrounding streets" with their attendant public use. This was to be an enclave

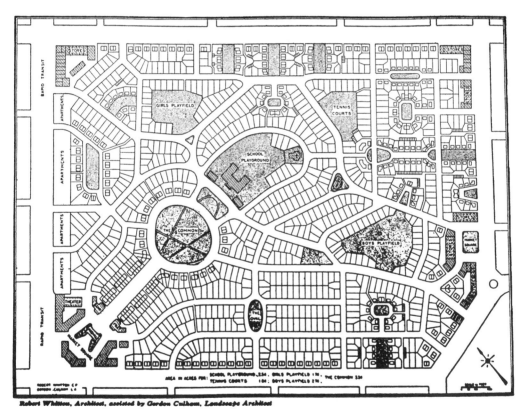

Robert Whitten, Architect, assisted by Gordon Culham, Landscape Architect

FIGURE 2.14 A neighborhood unit of single-family homes. Though inspired by the needs and circumstances of New York City, the 160-acre subdivision exactly corresponded to the "quarter section" of the western Jeffersonian grid.

even more private than its precedent, with exclusive use architecturally secured by the provision of sole access from the surrounding buildings themselves. As Perry put it, "The common space must . . . be practically surrounded by the buildings, or it will be difficult to preserve the enjoyment of it to the residents." These were not to be apartments for those displaced from the slums, but instead contained suites of up to fourteen rooms; suites clearly intended for higher-income families who wished protection from any slums and slum-dwellers that might remain on the other side of the boundary streets.[113]

Most of the site plans and photographs in Perry's 1929 monograph showed the work of other Americans. As Harrison put it, "There is nothing revolutionary about the neighborhood-unit scheme"; its purpose was "to direct attention to certain tendencies in city planning which are already evident in this country and abroad," and to bring them under "the correlating influence of a definite social objective."[114] Most directly, Perry's writings of the 1920s and 1930s reflected his own experiences as a resident of Forest Hills Gardens, the Queens development sponsored by his ongoing employer, the Russell Sage Foundation. His neighbor-

FIGURE 2.15 Perry called this neighborhood unit of apartment houses "dignified" and "blight resisting," adding that "if the area of rehabilitation is large enough, an internal charm can be created." As the desolate expanse of largely undifferentiated open space suggests, however, the pursuit of "dignity" and "charm" yielded the cultivated antithesis of the lively urban streetscape.

hood unit concept also incorporated concepts realized in many other contemporaneous Anglo-American community planning efforts, especially Clarence Stein and Henry Wright's designs for Sunnyside Gardens, Queens (1924–1928) and for Radburn, New Jersey (1928–1933), developed by the limited-dividend City Housing Corporation under the auspices of the Regional Planning Association of America (RPAA) (Figs. 2.16–2.17).[115] Embodying aspects of Perry's concept, these places—one located within a New York City grid and the other designed for unconstrained exurbia—marked a fundamental rethinking of the American residential neighborhood. For cities and for suburbs, communitarian designers converged on shared visions of car-free, pedestrian-oriented, civicly enriched, and economically homogeneous superblock precincts.

Drawing on settlement praxis, Perry grounded his vision of "community life" in civic institutions rather than retail opportunities. He explicitly expunged commercial activity from the core of neighborhood plans and neighborhood theory-building, relegating shopping to the status of a peripheral service. Nonetheless, Perry's generic neighborhood unit plan still included interior secondary streets and did not eliminate retail activity completely. Many of those who actually built such neighborhoods, however, corrupted and oversimplified the idea to the point of single-use superblocks. As applied to public housing projects during the next several decades, this kind of thinking often resulted in places that were not only auto-free but also community-free.

For Perry himself, the plan of Forest Hills Gardens, where he lived, "either compelled association or made it easy and enjoyable"; an attractive feature, since this brought together a "more or less homogeneous group of residents." That homogeneity was insured, at least initially, by careful selection: "prospective purchasers were required to give references," Perry observed, "and their former status was looked into with a view to discovering whether they would make congenial members of the colony." Much of this congeniality was channeled into the activities of the Gardens Corporation, a homeowners' organization that "mobilized public sentiment" to enforce a wide range of deed restrictions and community rules, and successfully fought off lawsuits to introduce new multifamily housing to their neighborhood.[116] As Lewis Mumford comments, Forest Hills Gardens was "meant to serve as a working-class community," but was "destined by the very generosity of its housing to become an entirely middle class, indeed upper middle class, community."[117]

Perry's message was about more than the codification of neighborhood units;

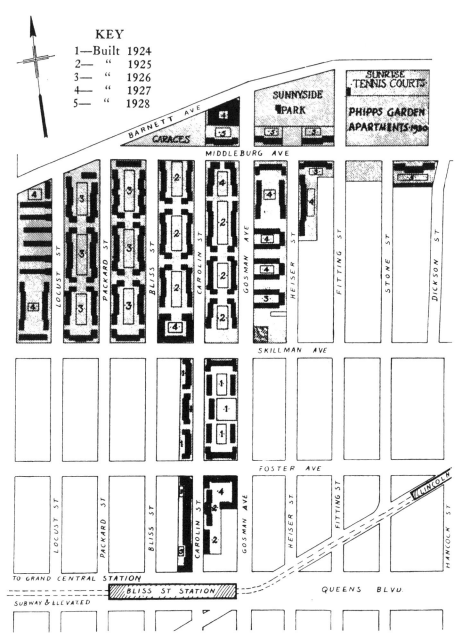

FIGURE 2.16 Clarence Stein and Henry Wright's Sunnyside Gardens in Queens worked within the New York City grid, but still assembled superblocks with housing on the perimeter and shared open space in the center.

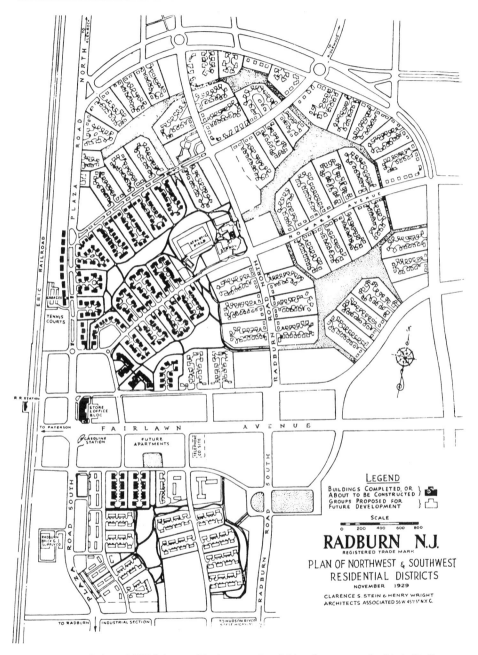

FIGURE 2.17 Stein and Wright's superblocks expand tenfold and move to suburbia in Radburn, New Jersey.

it was also about who should live in such units, and where they should be built. Perry thought the neighborhood units worked best if inhabited by a homogeneous population, and he contended that the "most efficient way of rehabilitating 'downtown' slum districts was to rebuild them with dwellings suitable for families whose heads were employed in nearby financial and business sections." Displacing the poor from the city centers would, in turn, "utilize the potentially high land values of central slums and enable a large number of workers to live near their offices."[118]

Despite decades spent promulgating drawings of apartment communities, Perry remained deeply suspicious of multifamily buildings. "Brought up in a single-family house, and still residing in one," he admitted that he was "naturally biased in favor of that form of living," adding that this preference was shared "by many people now tenants in apartments." In *Housing for the Machine Age*, he contrasted the close social relations possible in the village-like circumstances of a single-family home district with the distance that persists when people dwell in apartment buildings. Only in "village districts," he contended, can neighbors easily determine "what people are like." Here, they will know "the day and the hour when the new family puts out its wash, how often the postman calls, what time the husband goes to work, how often a fire is built in the front room, who the callers are, the children's actions while at play, the way they are dressed for school, the hour the family retires, the hour it gets up," and so on. In the "ordinary apartment house," by contrast, "residents come and go for months without ever seeing the people who live under the same roof. If the solitary dweller is held in bed by illness there is no signal—such as the absence of the smoke that usually issues from the chimney, to apprise neighbors and bring their willing aid. The very congestion of family compartments, their lack of a distinctive and personal atmosphere, their anonymity—all these conditions are hostile to the neighborly life."[119] Paradoxically, Perry observed, those who dwell in closest proximity are most mutually insulated from community scrutiny, yet also most vulnerable to neighborly disruption. Conscious of the potential for misbehavior as well as the danger of undetected distress, he emphasized the advantages of a benevolent watch, seen as the exclusive property of single-family districts.

THE POLITICAL ECONOMY OF THE URBAN SUPERBLOCK

Although the garden suburb efforts of Stein and Wright, with their emphasis on limited dividend corporations and their preference for peripheral locations, differed greatly from the slum-clearance center city focus of Perry and the other proponents of the New York Regional Plan, both groups shared a central belief in the importance of the superblock. Radburn and its successors carried the neighborhood unit and its superblocks into the design of suburban subdivisions and new towns,[120] whereas Perry's emphasis on slum-clearance schemes came to typify the approach taken in the center of cities. As a planning tool, the superblock could be defended on three major grounds simultaneously—its economy, its accommodation of amenities, and its articulation of boundaries. Taken together, it could be a tool for both inclusion and exclusion, though the emphasis was always on the latter.

As an economic tool, proponents pointed out that the superblock could yield substantial savings on the cost of streets and services, especially when coupled with the cost effectiveness of large-scale repetitive construction. Simultaneously, it maximized open space and daylight, providing for both recreation and better health. At Radburn, Stein claimed, "the savings in expenditure for roads and public utilities" realized through the development of 35- to 50-acre superblocks was what "paid for the parks."[121] Such presumed economy of infrastructure costs, harkening back to Unwin's insistence that "nothing [is] gained by overcrowding," would serve to justify superblocks for many decades, though usually without reinvestment of such "savings" into the creation of parks. As the future design of public housing projects would make clear, the goal of economy could easily outstrip the temptation for amenity.

The much-touted social benefit of arranging a neighborhood into a hierarchy of open communal spaces had its corollary in concern about public health. The same volume of the New York Regional Plan that featured Perry's neighborhood unit immediately followed this with a monograph proposing standards for "sunlight and daylight" in urban areas. Citing a variety of almost entirely American references, the report concluded that the "preponderance of evidence supplied by leading authorities pointed to . . . a definite relationship between sunlight and health," describing sunlight as a "beneficial agent" for the prevention and cure of rickets and tuberculosis, and for the prevention of other diseases "through the destruction of harmful disease germs and through the general strengthening of the powers of resistance." In consequence, the authors specified minimum standards for sunlight in every living and sleeping room, to be achieved through improved house orientation and street layout.[122] Four years later, Perry justified the size of his model slum-clearance proposal by observing that "It is large enough to permit the replanning of blocks so as to enable the maximum exposure of apartments to light and open spaces."[123] These stated goals of economy, amenity, and health were all in service of a deeper motive, however: the wish to set boundaries on territory that had been safely purged of the dependent poor.

Perry paid particular attention to the question of neighborhood unit boundaries, contending that "visible limits enable the public to see a local community as such and to recognize it as a distinct entity" worthy of a "special name." Gaining "identity" and "definiteness of character," he argued, depended on "the degree in which all factors of the development are brought under the control of a single management, guided by one co-ordinated, comprehensive plan." The neighborhood unit was "a village engulfed by an expanding city"; its superblocks not only promoted a healthful enclave, but ensured the security of this exemplary space from the people, cars, and slums that threatened it from all sides. The surrounding arterial streets were not mere edges or channels for through traffic, but "also the walls of the neighborhood cell." "Like fences around a house site, they show the precise domain for whose care and appearance responsibility is assumed by the occupant community." In turn, such walls "set it off from adjacent areas which may have different standards of residential upkeep" and "help to protect a neighborhood from any blight which may exist in the adjoining territory."[124] The neighborhood unit and its superblocks offered a way to segregate pedestrians from cars, "apartment-house units" from tenements and, ultimately, desirable neighbors from undesirable ones.

In 1933, with the Great Depression well underway, Perry focused in a more sustained way on the challenge of transforming slums into neighborhood units. In so doing, he sought to deliver as much as possible of the American individualist tradition to the design of multifamily housing, and aimed to make sure that the individuals so served were worthy of the effort. In the foreword to Perry's treatise, *The Rebuilding of Blighted Areas,* General Secretary Lawrence Orton of the Regional Plan Association stressed that this volume presented "not 'just another housing project,'" but a demonstration of "the attainability of a quality of apartment house life that is as yet unknown in American cities, large or small." The goal, he made clear, was to mimic the advantages of the detached single-family home while surpassing it in terms of proximate amenities: "As respects light and air, every suite is on a par with the average single-family dwelling and, as respects outlook, well above it. Children can reach playgrounds, and youths, athletic fields with no danger from traffic. Housewives have markets close at hand but there is no blight from the proximity of business buildings. Movies, lectures, dances, theatricals, bowling, swimming and billiards—for these and many other recreations and diversions adequate provision is made right in the housing scheme." This alternative to the slum, in short, combined "comfortable shelter and the services required for efficient homemaking" with "the facilities required for the cultural and social life of the family."[125] Perry, however, clearly believed that improved family life was inseparable from improved families. In the slum-clearance mindset, it was not enough to assume—as tenement reformers often did—that the newly designed environment would improve the behavior of tenants; it was often also necessary to replace the original tenants with others thought more worthy of the improved surroundings.

Perry's etiology of "blight" reveals much about the prevailing conception of social and physical change in urban areas. He saw blight as beginning with a "residential blemish" caused by changes from residential to nonresidential uses, and by shifts from single-family to multifamily occupancy, all involving greater lot coverage and height. Over time, as such changes multiplied, the original owners no longer wished to accept "the annoyances coming from the grocery traffic or swarms of children" and the "lowering of social status from the changed circumstances." Overwhelmed by this "infection," most owners would move away and "lease their properties to families of less exacting standards or lower incomes" who would "frequently . . . be of a different race." "In any case," he continued, "the chances are that they would differ in character, habits or status from the rest of the neighborhood, would irritate the families next door and eventually cause them to move. The new tenants would probably, in turn, cause a similar dislocation, and thus the blight would spread." Ultimately, "less and less exacting families are willing to occupy the houses until the lowest social levels are reached. When the district finally becomes filled with the city's jetsam . . . the name 'slum' is applied to it and agitation for its clearance begins."[126] For Perry, as for many others, a slum was defined by its presumed social character, not just its observable physical attributes: the slum was that portion of the city occupied by public neighbors, those ill-understood people whom an ambivalent society resisted yet felt obligated to aid.

As a result, when it came to slum clearance and replacement housing, the goal was not only to replace the housing but to replace the neighbors, and to do so on a very large scale. Aiding the slum dwellers meant getting them out of the slums, but that action also came with a more self-serving advantage: it opened up the redeveloped slums for more upscale occupancy. For Perry, codifying the prevailing view of the time, this process of neighborhood transformation had to occur in the largest possible units. Because the decline of a neighborhood was a slow process, a long and continuing series of individual acts, piecemeal rehabilitation would be insufficient; instead, Perry wrote, "radical treatment [is] required." Municipal zoning, though "of fundamental social importance," was an inadequate remedy since in built-up areas "it has the effect of freezing into permanence any defects which existed in the original layout or composition of the neighborhood." Moreover, zoning did nothing to prevent neglect and deterioration on the part of individual owners.[127] Ultimately, the twin concerns of greater economy and still greater distrust combined to insure that districts were transformed socially as well as physically. "Re-creation of a blighted district cannot generally be accomplished by merely replacing the old dwellings with new structures," Perry concluded. "To meet the heavy costs of demolition and new construction, another class of tenants with somewhat higher incomes must usually be brought into the district."[128] For Perry, slum clearance made everyone a winner: new residents benefited from the superior living environment; developers and their investors benefited from the superior incomes of the new residents and their corresponding effect on local businesses and property values; and former slum-dwellers benefited from the chance to escape unhealthful living conditions.

Uncertain about where such slum-dwellers would be rehoused, Perry nonetheless remained convinced that any move was in their best interest. He recognized that the American individualist ethos as expressed through the home "stands upon a peculiarly high eminence in public sentiment," and he acknowledged that "any proposal to put a man out of his house causes instant vibration of a fundamental chord in the national character," but he believed in a broader public principle: "When one analyzes the situation, it becomes apparent that public interest really lies in the consideration of dwellings, and their environments, as instrumentalities of family functioning and not in the sentimental attachments growing out of long association with a certain physical environment. Cutting family ties to a particular dwelling does not necessarily do an injury to the life of that family. It may be a very healthy operation!"[129]

Perry's healthy operation aimed to excise urban cancer, not only for the benefit of the patient but for the good of the body politic. By replacing a "whole section" of blighted cells, this surgery would be radical enough to send the disease into permanent remission. Perry promised "a new neighborhood, so attractive in appearance and so rich in service facilities that its residents would be entirely independent, psychically and commercially, of disagreeable surroundings." He framed the goals of slum clearance in terms of "the health of the district," and justified each redevelopment proposal on the basis of its "safety, health, moral and general welfare effects." "It promotes not only 'community prosperity' (the welfare of the property owners) but it contributes to public health (better light, air, and play space), public safety (less risk from street accidents), public morals (through community environment), and public convenience (better located shopping districts, among other things)."[130] In these ways, Perry fit his objectives into the language of the traditional "police power" formula, so that the necessary large parcels could be assembled by eminent domain.

Even in 1933, however, business leaders and the general public had not yet fully accepted this rationale for government-aided slum clearance, let alone the idea of federally sponsored housing projects. Still, Perry's work signaled a much broader willingness to confront the old fiscal and ideological arguments against slum clearance and public housing, part of a gradual shift that had been underway since the end of World War I. Led by reformers who documented European precedents (and American housing achievements during the war) and who argued that government-sponsored housing need not hurt private enterprise, the pragmatic needs of a nation in economic crisis eventually overcame the political constraints to federal action.

Moving Toward Public Housing

Public housing emerged as one small part of a larger federal concern over the fate of individual homes during troubled economic times. The coming of the Great Depression revealed the limitations of private markets, as residential construction declined by as much as 90 percent from the boom year peak of 1925, exacerbating the shortage of low-rent housing in cities. In this context, the national shame over slum conditions stood more starkly revealed than ever, particularly in comparison to more progressive European efforts to build housing for workers. Most visible of all, however, the Depression created massive unemployment in the building trades. Public housing thus emerged out of an uneasy alliance among housing reformers, settlement workers, architects, labor unions, and construction companies who could all agree that the first priority was putting the nation back to work. However much the "housers" within this coalition emphasized the positive value of better housing conditions, the imperative of job creation would become the driving force behind both slum clearance and housing project construction.

The National Public Housing Conference (NPHC), formed in 1931 and centered in New York, was the first pressure group to lobby actively on Capitol Hill for public housing and to propose legislation. Led by settlement worker Mary Simkhovich along with others, including Edith Elmer Wood, Loula Lasker, and Louis Pink, the NPHC fought for a housing law that would be a permanent part of public policy, irrespective of the economic fortunes of the country. In her widely circulated *Recent Trends in American Housing* (1931), Wood stated, "a substantial portion of the population cannot pay a commercial rent, much less a commercial purchase price, for a home fulfilling the minimum health and decency requirements"—an economic condition that she considered "universal and permanent."

The NPHC was soon joined by two other pressure groups, the National Association of Housing Officials (NAHO) and the Labor Housing Conference (LHC). Based in Chicago and headed by Ernest Bohn and Coleman Woodbury, NAHO was initially more of a government service organization than a pressure group, seeking to "facilitate the exchange of ideas and information among housing officials and other interested persons." The third major group, the LHC, grew out of the activities of various Philadelphia unions and was by far the most radical. Directed by Catherine Bauer, whose book *Modern Housing* did much to alert policymakers to the possibilities for government-subsidized dwellings, the LHC's first purpose was to educate labor unions about the benefits of public housing. Before the LHC, the American Federation of Labor had been opposed to public housing as "counter to our ideals of individual initiative and rights"; under LHC leadership it came to support subsidized housing legislation. Beyond the union connection, however, Bauer and the LHC stood for a fundamental realignment of the American housing industry: the creation of a substantial noncommercial housing sector targeted at the broad middle of American society as well as its poor.[131] In this, her activism challenged a hardening divide in American housing policy between reward packages aimed at the upper two-thirds of the population and coping mechanisms intended to manage public obligation to the remainder.

PUBLIC NEIGHBORHOODS WITHOUT PUBLIC NEIGHBORS

The three-hundred-year prehistory of public housing reveals two conspicuous trends. From the Puritans onward, Americans have both exalted the importance of the single-family home and distrusted the poor. With poverty seen as linked to the moral quality of home life, attitudes about housing and neighborhoods were inevitably tied to attitudes about the poor. Comfortably situated Americans viewed poverty primarily as a result of poor morals rather than poor wages, and coupled it to a variety of other prejudices—first religious intolerance, then xenophobia, then racism and gender bias. The result could only be ongoing ambivalence about serving the needs of the poor, and an understanding that any government-sponsored efforts on their behalf would be limited to those deemed most deserving.

Low-income housing in Boston, due to the circumstances of the city's early foundation, exemplifies both the full extent of the trends as well as their underlying tenets. Early Bostonians accepted responsibility to care for the local poor, but resisted the settlement of strangers and denigrated the able-bodied unemployed. Instead, they developed a wide variety of reformatory institutions, located at increasing distance from the centers of affluence.

Beyond New England's borders, one hundred fifty years of national public lands policy—with its bounty lands for veterans and homesteads for hardy yeomen—confirmed and symbolized the deeply rooted individualism of the Protestant work ethic, inculcating into the national mythology the belief that a good home must be an owned home, and must be the reward for hard work. Public housing, so long to emerge in name, was long present in deeds.

By the middle of the nineteenth century, as immigration began to flood the central city, upwardly mobile Bostonians took advantage of new suburban opportunities, both to escape the poor and, more positively, to enjoy some compromised vestige of a peaceful country homestead existence. At the same time, Brahmin leaders undertook to study, document, and remedy the worst excesses of tenement house construction, passing sanitary legislation intended to improve the public health and economic well-being of the larger metropolis. Working through charitable organizations and limited-dividend corporations, other philanthropically minded developers attempted a wide array of small initiatives to use housing as a means of moral uplift. By the turn of the century, Boston's settle-

157

ment house leaders embarked on even more concerted efforts to use housing and neighborhood institutions to Americanize the immigrant poor, educating them in "standard" civic and domestic behaviors. Constrained by their group-based stereotypes and by their inability to comprehend the economic roots of poverty, most reformers either turned low-income families and individuals into objects of resentment or subjected them to very selective recruitment.

In the 1910s and 1920s, tenement reform and tenant reform proceeded apace, confined to city districts, while new community design efforts rewarded worthy workers in the war industries and the suburbs. Throughout it all, Boston's Brahmin economic decisionmakers struggled to come to terms with the dependent poor. With an ambivalence born of empathy, duty, fear, contempt, and lingering guilt, the heirs to the Puritan conscience tried to solve the problem of the slum by passing judgment on the comparative worth of its denizens.

Looking back, the politics of ambivalence can be seen to have been played out in diverse but utterly consistent terms. As the more privileged gained urban houses, frontier homesteads, or suburban plots, those public neighbors judged least deserving were warned out, walled-in, and left behind. Relegated to their tenements, they were regulated, inspected, modeled, domesticated, and zoned. Ultimately, even when reformers proposed public-subsidized neighborhoods to serve workers, these were built to remove public neighbors rather than to house them. Given such a history, it is hardly surprising that the premise and the promise of the New Deal public housing projects was so familiar and so fraught with contradiction: these, too, were to be public neighborhoods without public neighbors.

PUBLIC HOUSING IN BOSTON

THREE

Building Selective Collectives, 1934–1954

ALL WHO HAVE attempted to introduce and imple-
ment subsidized low-income housing in the United States have struggled with a
central problem: how to reconcile it with America's market-driven individualist
ethos, the ideological preference expressed most directly through the American
Dream of owning a single-family home. The story of public housing is largely the
outcome of the compromises necessary to allow this anomaly to be tolerated. The
complexity of the tale is rooted in the persistent plurality of rationales for the institution called public housing, rationales that sometimes have little to do with
providing decent and affordable housing for low-income Americans. As Alvin
Schorr implied as early as 1963, the range of rationales for public housing may be
considered so extreme as to call into question the appropriateness of a single
term to describe it. "Public housing," he wrote, "is not a single program, historically; it is a single vessel that has been used for diverse public purposes."[1] Although the name *public housing* has remained consistent since the 1930s, the
meanings attached to it have shifted with every landmark piece of housing legislation (Table 3).

Each of the first four major turning points—establishment of the Housing Division of the Public Works Administration in 1933, passage of the Wagner-
Steagall Housing Act of 1937, enactment of the "defense housing" legislation of
World War II, and passage of the Housing Act of 1949—entailed not just reitera-
tion of need but reinvention of purpose. Programs to reward worthy workers

Table 3 Major Public Housing Legislation and Policy Developments

Year	National	Massachusetts
1933	National Industrial Recovery Act (establishes Housing Division of Public Works Administration) Home Owners Loan Corporation	Massachusetts State Board of Housing established
1934	National Housing Act (Federal Housing Administration)	
1935		Boston Housing Authority established
1937	Housing Act of 1937 (Wagner-Steagall bill, establishing United States Housing Authority)	
1938–1942		First BHA projects open
1940	Lanham Act and defense housing	
1946		Massachusetts City-State Program (Chapter 372)
1948		Massachusetts Veterans' Housing (Chapter 200)
1949	Housing Act of 1949 (Taft-Ellender-Wagner bill, urban redevelopment emphasis)	
1949–1954		Second round of BHA projects open
1950		Massachusetts prohibits housing discrimination and segregation

Year	National	Massachusetts
1954	Housing Act of 1954 ("Workable Program" for urban renewal)	
1956	Housing Act of 1956 (allows public housing for single elderly)	
1958		Boston's West End demolished
1959	Housing Act of 1959 (Sec. 202 loan subsidies for elderly housing)	
1961	Housing Act of 1961 (Sec. 221 (d)(3) moderate-income housing subsidies)	
1962	Executive Order prohibiting racial discrimination in housing	First BHA housing for elderly
		NAACP complaint against BHA for racial segregation
1963		Advisory Committee on Minority Housing to monitor BHA
		BHA Dept. of Tenant and Community Relations established
1965	Civil Rights Act of 1965 Housing Act of 1965 (Sec. 23 leased private housing development)	
1968	Housing and Urban Development Act of 1968 (Sec. 235 mortgage subsidies; Sec. 236 rent supplements)	Tenant Task Forces established

Table 3 *(continued)*

YEAR	NATIONAL	MASSACHUSETTS
1969	First Brooke Amendment (limits rents to 25% of income)	
1970		"Tenant-oriented Majority" on BHA Board Tenant lawsuits against BHA begin
1973	Nixon Housing Moratorium	
1974	Housing and Community Development Act of 1974 (Section 8 rental assistance)	
1975		BHA loses Perez case (Court appoints Master to run BHA)
1975–76		Anti-busing turmoil peaks
1979–	Federal housing preferences target public housing to least-advantaged	
1980		BHA enters receivership BHA redevelopment efforts begin
1984	Project Self-Sufficiency	BHA receivership ends
1988		BHA consent decree with HUD on racial discrimination
1989	Operation Bootstrap	
1990	National Affordable Housing Act of 1990 (Family Self-Sufficiency program)	
1992	National Commission on Severely Distressed Public Housing	

Year	National	Massachusetts
1993	HOPE VI program (comprehensive project redevelopment or demolition) commences	New BHA redevelopment efforts through HOPE VI
1996	"One Strike and You're Out" Welfare reform (Temporary Assistance to Needy Families)	
1998	Quality Housing and Work Responsibility Act	

(whether as builders of housing or as tenants in it) were transmuted, over the course of twenty years, into new mechanisms for coping with the urban poor.

BOSTON'S SELECTIVE COLLECTIVES

The federal, state, and city agencies that administered the twenty-five family public housing projects completed in Boston between 1938 and 1954 conceived of them as selective collectives. They intended the selectivity to be social, physical, and economic. Socially, they saw public housing like earlier forms of land bounties and housing reforms, both as a reward system for the most worthy poor, and as a means of dispersing the less worthy from areas thought viable for redevelopment. Physically, they believed the new public neighborhoods would serve to gather families into superblocks of solid modern construction—new healthy tissue to ward off blight and slums. Through their emphasis on open space they attempted to bring the presumed virtues of country living into the heart of cities, even in the absence of single-family homes. Finally, by promoting employment in the construction trades and by eliminating the costs of slums to their municipalities, housing authorities expected public housing projects at once to provide broad financial advantages to their cities and to protect private real estate interests by limiting tenancy to those whom private markets chose not to serve with decent habitation. Influenced by shifting federal, state, and local priorities, the history of public housing construction in Boston can be divided into four distinct phases: public works (1934–1938), slum reform (1937–1942), war production (1940–1945), and veterans' assistance (1946–1954).

The first phase, occurring under the auspices of the federal Public Works Administration (PWA), consisted of Old Harbor Village, the city's first public housing project. In the brief period between passage of the Wagner-Steagall Housing Act of 1937 and U.S. involvement in World War II, plans were advanced to replace unprofitable municipal areas with new designed communities. This campaign brought seven more public housing projects to Boston. From October 1940 through 1945, action on government-sponsored housing shifted to defense needs. New public housing appropriations stopped, and war workers gained priority for admission to existing projects. This third incarnation of federal housing policy influenced the image of public housing by further skewing occupancy toward those judged to be patriotically and occupationally worthy. After the war, decentralized public housing construction revived under the umbrella of federal, state, and city Veterans Assistance programs. From 1949 to 1954, the Boston Housing Authority completed ten state-funded public housing projects and seven federally financed developments. At the same time as the BHA made its last pitches for worthy tenants, however, the improving opportunity structure for working-class whites and the urban renewal provisions of the new housing legislation irreversibly began to shift public housing occupancy toward the increasingly needy.

The flurry of postwar activity marked the end of large-scale public housing project construction in Boston (Fig. 3.1). After 1954, available federal dollars were targeted to broad redevelopment and renewal purposes only tangentially related to the needs of low-income families, and the remaining energy and resources of the Boston Housing Authority increasingly flowed toward the task of managing what had already been built.

This chapter explores the twenty years when the Boston Housing Authority exercised firm control over its public neighborhoods and the tenants selected to dwell in them. These twenty-five public neighborhoods—like their counterparts in other American cities—were both architectural and ideological constructs, the compromised products of shifting and contentious debates at all levels of government.

166

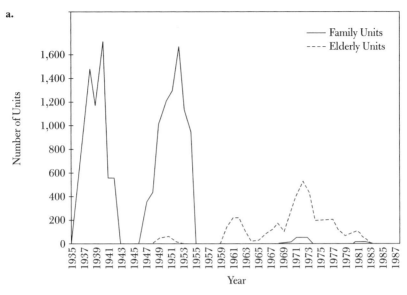

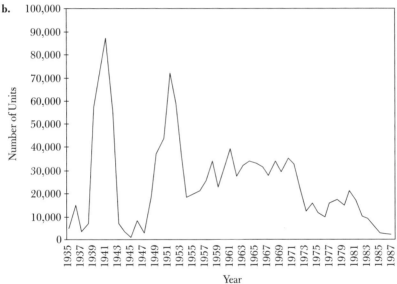

FIGURE 3.1 Public housing project construction in Boston (above) and in the United States (below) since 1935. In Boston, virtually all of the city's family public housing constructed by the BHA was completed in two waves—between 1938–1942 and between 1949–1954. A modest amount of public housing for the elderly was completed later on, but the heyday of public neighborhood construction ended in 1954. Boston's pattern is similar to the peaks of public housing construction nationwide, although much more was built in other cities after 1955.

PUBLIC WORKS AND PRIVATE MARKETS

From the beginning, nearly all discussion of public housing acknowledged the primacy of the private homeownership ideology. Detractors objected to the cost-liness and intrusiveness of big government and warned of socialist encroachment, while supporters of public housing frequently defended it in terms of its contri-butions to the private building industry and its long-term municipal cost-effec-tiveness. Although all public housing legislation made reference to the plight of the ill-housed and to the humanitarian urgency to build "decent, safe, and sani-tary" alternative accommodation, the underlying rationales bespoke far more than benevolence.

The initial legal basis for federally sponsored public housing appeared incon-spicuously in a subsection of the National Industrial Recovery Act of 1933. As part of the plan for unemployment relief and industrial recovery, the PWA was to oversee "construction, reconstruction, alteration, or repair under public regula-tion or control of low rent housing and slum clearance projects."[2] In this way, the first federal public housing legislation found its articulation buried within a broader plan for unemployment relief and industrial recovery. New Deal officials were less interested in the dwellings that would be built or the kinds of people they would house than they were in who would build them: their overriding goal was to put the construction industry back to work doing useful public projects.[3] Moreover, the new Housing Division of the PWA initially wished to leave con-struction entirely in private hands, preferring to concentrate on limited-dividend projects that would not require the federal government to enter the housing mar-ket directly. This agenda failed, in part because nearly all states lacked the proper enabling legislation, in part because of interagency feuds over the release of funds, and in part because PWA administrator Harold Ickes recognized that lim-ited-dividend companies would never be able to reach those with the lowest in-comes and still generate a modest profit to investors. Only after exhausting the possibilities of private-sector projects did the PWA turn to more complete public involvement in housing.[4]

FEDERAL SUPPORT FOR PRIVATE HOUSING

Even after the federal government accepted direct responsibility for construction of low-rent housing, these initiatives were dwarfed by others promoting the pri-macy of private markets and individual homes. These individualist initiatives

shaped the primary social aspects of federal housing policy by attempting to ensure the selectivity of private neighborhoods.

The National Housing Act of 1934 established the Federal Housing Administration (FHA) not to promote low-rent public housing but to assist private
builders by insuring mortgages for construction. In conjunction with the Home
Owners Loan Corporation (HOLC), established the year before to protect lenders from drops in the values of mortgages, the FHA was intended to make savings
institutions more willing to lend on real estate by transferring the risks associated
with nonpayment and foreclosure to the federal government. The FHA quickly
became the largest component of the federal housing program, and its administrators and underwriters worked hard to minimize the impact of its risks.[5]
Charles Abrams observed, "From its inception FHA set itself up as the protector
of the all-white neighborhood. It sent its agents into the field to keep Negroes
and other minorities from buying homes in white neighborhoods. It exerted pressure against builders who dared to build for minorities, and against lenders willing to lend on mortgages." The FHA's official underwriting manuals specified
methods for enforcing the homogeneity of neighborhoods through mandating
the exclusion of "undesirable" categories of people. "If a neighborhood is to retain stability," the FHA asserted in 1938, "it is necessary that its properties shall
continue to be occupied by the same social and racial classes." In its concern for
the "prevention of infiltration of inharmonious racial or nationality groups," the
FHA advocated both deed restrictions and restrictive covenants, "since these
provide the surest protection against undesirable encroachment and inharmonious use." In its catalogue of "adverse" neighborhood influences, the FHA repeatedly listed "inharmonious racial or nationality groups" right alongside such ills as
"smoke, odors, and fog." For a neighborhood to be considered worthy of mortgage investment, the FHA required that it be occupied in perpetuity by "substantial, law-abiding, sober-acting, sane-thinking people of acceptable ethical standards." As race and class merged into the concept of "racial class," and as
personality and behavior came to be seen as both morally and ethnically encoded, FHA practice gave federal sanction to a long history of spatially grounded
prejudice. What had appeared as an undercurrent of bias in the tracts of tenement reformers and settlement workers during the preceding half-century now
took the form of federally mandated restrictions affecting the majority of new
homes.

Although the FHA substantially revised its underwriting manuals in the late

1940s, following continued protests by the National Association for the Advancement of Colored People (NAACP) and a Supreme Court decision holding restrictive covenants unenforceable, its racially discriminatory practices continued largely unchecked. As of 1952, more than 98 percent of the 3 million dwellings insured by the FHA were available only to whites. This federally supported promotion of class and racial segregation in publicly assisted private housing formed the backdrop for the creation of a large class of what Abrams aptly called "forbidden neighbors," removed from American homeownership ideals just as thoroughly as if they had been warned out of town by the Puritans.[6]

Although the FHA remained the most powerful ideological weapon in the growing arsenal of federal housing programs, there were other efforts to keep federal involvement in housing clearly in accord with long-standing American traditions. Roosevelt himself had little interest in urban housing and, according to one biographer, "responded with much greater warmth to chimerical plans to remove slum dwellers to the countryside than he did to schemes for urban renewal."[7] To advance this idea, the president insisted that an appropriation for "subsistence homesteads" be written into the National Industrial Recovery Act. As one New York congressman argued, there was no "rhyme or reason" to continue building houses in New York City "when we do not have employment for those who are already there." Instead, government should "buy up tracts of good land outside the cities" upon which ex-urbanites "can raise a good share of their living on an acre or two of land, keep some hens, a pig, some goats, or a cow, and be almost independent." In Boston, the City Council discussed the desirability of building "low-cost housing for our poor people out in the noncongested areas," but did no more than authorize a study.[8] All told, the Subsistence Homestead Division built only a hundred or so colonies, and had no impact on urban poverty. In 1935, Rexford Guy Tugwell, in charge of newly established Resettlement Administration, scuttled support for the Subsistence Homestead projects in favor of efforts to promote new greenbelt towns, which Tugwell viewed as less anachronistic than isolated homesteads. Even these greenbelt towns faced attacks, both from surrounding communities, who were suspicious of new neighbors and fearful of lost revenues, and from legislators such as Senator Harry Byrd of Virginia, who insisted that such projects exuded the "stench" of "gross inefficiency and Russian communism."[9] Thus, even before passage of the Housing Act of 1937, the ideological atmosphere surrounding public housing had been stirred with superheated rhetoric about what was American and what was not. The FHA and the Resettlement Administration reiterated the old ideals about the linkage between individual homes and good citizenship, and even the PWA Housing Division sought ways to reconcile the provision of public neighborhoods with American traditions.

PWA Housing for Boston

Although Boston's Irish, who had dominated the city's politics and government since 1910, were early and wholehearted supporters of Roosevelt and the New Deal, Boston received a disproportionately small share of federal money. James Michael Curley, the first big-city mayor to embrace FDR, was an outspoken advocate of federal aid to cities, but PWA officials distrusted his ability to use federal funds effectively for their intended purposes. Partly as a result of this distrust of Curley (who was elected governor in 1934), and partly due to infighting among other Massachusetts politicians, the city lost thousands of Civil Works Administration jobs and experienced delays and restrictions in implementing most federal programs, including public housing.[10]

Even so, as federal subsidies became available, many Boston housing activists struggled to get the city and state positioned to take maximum advantage of the subsidies. The Boston Housing Association, under its director John Ihlder, played a leading role.[11] Founded in 1919, the Housing Association had initially concerned itself with tenement regulation issues and the formation of limited-dividend corporations. In 1932, Ihlder served on a committee charged with advising Mayor Curley on housing matters. Seeking to take advantage of federal support for limited-dividend corporations through Hoover's Reconstruction Finance Corporation, the committee worked with the Boston City Planning Board on legislation that established the Massachusetts State Board of Housing in July 1933, a month after the new Roosevelt administration had signed the National Industrial Recovery Act into law. The State Board was empowered to provide small homesteads for "mechanics, laborers, wage earners and for other citizens of the Commonwealth" along the lines of the Lowell Homesteads experiment, to accept grants of federal funds, and to supervise limited dividend housing corporations authorized by the PWA. By now Ihlder, long a promoter of private-sector ventures, hailed the PWA's emergency housing program as a tool for job creation and economic recovery. Not only would it "convert our greatest municipal liability—

the slums and decadent areas—into an asset"; it would also "create a demand for capital goods . . . and give employment to those groups in which there is the greatest proportion of unemployment."[12]

The State Board of Housing immediately began assessing applications for limited-dividend projects. In October 1933 it approved a twenty-five-acre redevelopment plan for a section of South Boston. Known as Columbia Gardens, the $5 million project was to house 4,300 people in 952 apartments, but it was soon rejected by the PWA after speculators drove up the price of land beyond program limits. During the same months another limited-dividend venture, the Neptune Gardens project, was planned in great secrecy by its sponsors, who enlisted the support of Mayor Curley but bypassed the State Board of Housing completely, preferring to negotiate directly with the PWA. Prepared in consultation with John Nolen, a well-known planner, the plans for Neptune Gardens called for 760 moderate-rental residential units, gardens, a library, and a school to be built on forty-four vacant acres in East Boston. This time federal officials approved the $4 million project, but objections by the Boston City Council, the Massachusetts Real Estate Owners Association, and East Boston residents aroused such controversy about this "gigantic steal of public money" that PWA support was withdrawn in early 1934. The failure of these early ventures did not endear Boston to federal housing officials seeking a responsible business partner.[13]

By the end of 1934 the State Board of Housing had forwarded approvals of six projects to Washington, and all were stymied. The PWA had abandoned support of limited-dividend ventures and now required participation by local municipal housing authorities. Approval for the creation of those authorities was delayed by the Massachusetts legislature. Nevertheless, intent on initiating work in Boston, PWA administrator Ickes authorized peremptory action from Washington.

On January 30, 1935, the PWA stunned 300 local landowners with the announcement that condemnation proceedings would begin on their properties in an eleven-block area of South Boston adjacent to the abortive site of the Columbia Gardens project. Ickes defended the secrecy by referring to previous problems with land speculation and told Bostonians, "If we find any attempt to force exorbitant prices, or that the land will cost too much to produce true low-rent housing, we will drop the project and go elsewhere." He described the site as having been "at one time . . . a fine old residential area" that was "now blighted, with many buildings in bad shape." At present, the PWA administrator noted, the neighborhood "is occupied principally by old three-story, frame, two-family houses." It was also occupied, however, by several thousand people, a factory employing 900, and the Slavonic Club, which had long served as a principal meeting place for Slavs from all over greater Boston. Businessmen of South Boston, the *Boston Globe* reported, were "elated" over the news of the federal plans, and the site had been strongly recommended to the PWA by a disparate variety of groups, including a citizens coordinating committee chaired by Dean William Emerson of MIT, the State Housing Board, the housing committee of the Boston City Planning Board, the Women's Industrial Union, the Boston Council of Social Agencies, the Boston Housing Association, and the Little House (a welfare organization).[14]

As formal notices went out to the owners and their tenants, however, local protests erupted. Despite federal assurances that the new project would "compare favorably with what residents of the section are now paying," many feared they would never be able to afford to live there. Owners and renters alike resented the designation of their neighborhood as a slum and pointed to areas in the "lower end" of South Boston where conditions were much worse. On February 15, the South Boston Home Owners' Association organized a rally attended by 500 people. Speakers addressed the crowd in both English and Lithuanian to assail the takings, and launched a mass-mailing of postcards to the president and Congress in an attempt to stop the plan. They pledged that the district's residents would "hold as tenaciously to their homes as did the harassed farmers of another day to the sanctity of Lexington and Concord." One man shouted: "They call it a slum district. Well, it's good enough for me and it has been good enough for you. Why didn't they find out what the people of the district thought before they decided to throw people out of their homes and out of small businesses they have taken years to build up? They kept quiet about it until the last minute because they knew there would be a roar of protest which would balk at the land grab . . . This move . . . smacks of plain communism." The Massachusetts Real Estate Owners Association organized further rallies at State House municipal finance hearings held in February and March, to condemn federal use of eminent domain for this kind of purpose. At one of these, the Association's Hannah M. Connors described plans to clear the section of South Boston as "merely a Bolshevik move to deprive people of the right to own their own homes."[15] In this way, opposition to the project referred to as Old Harbor Village became an ideological lightning rod for related matters. Displaced local residents and real estate professionals who resisted the intrusion of public housing into private markets joined forces with those—like the Boston Chamber of Commerce, the Boston Real Estate Exchange, and the Municipal Research Bureau—who viewed long-term borrowing for such purposes as fiscally irresponsible. For the residents themselves, the ideological undertones were clearly secondary to their own pending evictions.

On March 12, the final day set for filing answers or claims in response to the government's eminent-domain petitions, more than 300 property owners and residents "stormed the federal building" and congregated in the fifteenth-floor office of the clerk of the federal district court. More than fifty different land owners initiated legal complaints in what the *Boston Herald* described as a "continuous babble"; the government was forced to extend the filing deadline for ten more days just to process all the claims. United-Carr Fastener Corporation, the site's largest landholder, filed a suit charging that the taking violated its owner's Fifth Amendment rights and claiming "just compensation" of $500,000 to cover the cost of relocation.[16]

Undaunted by an adverse federal court ruling in a Louisville case that had already cast a pall over federal eminent-domain takings for slum clearance,[17] the federal government moved forward on the South Boston condemnation proceedings. In late July, however, after an appellate court decision upheld the Louisville ruling, the PWA caved to pressures from landholders and announced plans to shift the project to a nearby vacant site. Property owners on the original site reacted by complaining that their rental income had declined by 40 percent in the months since their neighborhood had been federally labeled a "slum"; good tenants had left in anticipation of forced eviction, and slum designation had prompted an increase in vandalism. Boston's mayor Frederick Mansfield (in office from 1934–1938) sided with the outraged landowners, observing that "developing vacant land is an entirely different project and will not accomplish the result originally sought." Moreover, he claimed, "new buildings erected on vacant land offer direct competition with real estate owners in the district who already have difficulty in renting their property."[18]

In the wake of the new round of protests, the PWA reversed its course again a week later and announced that the project would go forward on the original site, as long as eighteen remaining complaints pending in the federal district court could be resolved. The very next day, however, President Roosevelt—frustrated by delays throughout the PWA Housing Division—complicated matters further by announcing a plan to withdraw funds from all projects that had not commenced construction by December 15. Two days later, to cover his bets, Ickes announced that *both* South Boston projects would go forward, one on the original slum-clearance site and the other on a largely vacant adjacent parcel. By mid-September, while legal battles stalled progress on the original site, the PWA completed land purchase arrangements for the new site, only to be blamed for having paid almost twice the assessed value.[19]

On September 26—less than three weeks after affirming his commitment to the original project location—Ickes declared that the old site would be abandoned, and that the project on vacant land would supersede it. Once again, South Boston residents were left incredulous. South Boston City Councilor John E. Kerrigan called the abandonment "the worst blow ever given to the community," explaining that "at least a third of the people who lived in the houses in the first project area have moved elsewhere, some of the houses have been partially demolished and others have been boarded up. The property owners will be left holding the bag." Another South Bostonian sarcastically questioned: "Is this the reward the people of South Boston receive for being loyal Democrats?" The South Boston Citizens' Association promised take the matter up with all relevant government officials, going "even to the President if necessary."[20] From a neighborhood perspective, it is difficult to say whether the slum-clearance project sparked more controversy when it was first proposed or when it was abandoned; either way, it signaled social and financial disruption.

In any case, the saga was not over. Congressman John McCormack of South Boston, by then considered a loyal New Dealer, fought for the best interests of his district in Washington and received assurances from Roosevelt that a project on the original site would indeed eventually go forward, once the legal challenges were resolved and more money could be appropriated.[21] Eventually, the wholly cleared original site (plus several additional blocks) did become home to the Old Colony project, which opened in 1941. In the meantime, local Boston officials traded blame for the ongoing fiasco, and work on the vacant site faced additional delays and uncertainties through 1936 and 1937.[22] After five years of false starts and delays, the project known as Old Harbor Village opened on May 1, 1938. The project was a mere five-minute walk from the Vinton Street house where McCormack had grown up, and the construction deal went to one of Governor Curley's favored contractors.[23]

The tortuous advent of public housing in South Boston nurtured a fundamental ambivalence in that district, one that only increased in subsequent decades. On the one hand, South Boston residents could legitimately feel put upon by the heavy-handed and unpredictable machinations of a distant federal government; on the other hand, the district had much to gain from its position as a favored destination for government largesse. Whatever the complaints of property owners about lost revenues and social disruption, construction of the city's first public housing project brought jobs for an estimated 800 to 1,000 men.[24] By 1949, South Boston would garner nearly 3,000 public housing apartments in three large projects, a vastly disproportionate share of the city's total allocation, achieved at a time when public housing was widely considered to be a highly desirable housing resource.

Old Harbor Village: Boston's First Public Neighborhood

Contemplated and built during a fractious period of contending rationales, Boston's first public housing project did nothing to achieve slum clearance, and made only modest and mostly temporary contributions to the stated goal of job creation. As arguments about the constitutionality of federal eminent-domain powers to clear slums for public housing made their way through federal and Massachusetts courts, Old Harbor Village opened on its pleasant waterfront site, and the adjacent areas most urgently targeted for slum clearance and redevelopment remained untouched (Fig. 3.2). In its name, the project attempted to recall the small coastal New England towns of the colonial era, and many charged that its cultivated quaintness did little to serve the needs of South Boston's plenitude of low-income families. As one local commentator put it in the *South Boston Tribune,* "The same amount of money that was spent in South Boston for the housing project would have modernized every home in South Boston, so that all the 70,000 people [there], not a chosen few, could have enjoyed better living conditions then they ever knew." In this view, the public housing concept nullified the widespread benefits of private-sector building practice and fostered greedy alliances among architects, contractors, and materials suppliers, in cahoots with politicians who know how to "take care of the boys." Instead of one large public project, this early critic contended, a broader rehabilitation effort "would have given business to many contractors, not one; employed many real estate agents, many insurance agents, and there would be benefits to many landlords, and the property thus improved would not be tax exempt and a further burden upon the taxpayers."[25]

Other objections focused not on the manipulation and monopolization of building practices but on the related iniquities of tenant selection. Not only did

Old Harbor fall short of meeting the demand for high-quality low-rent housing, but the rents were set well beyond the means of any but those with a full-time job and steady income. The project also exhibited an unseemly exclusivity in its chosen tenants. By the time it opened, more than 10,000 families had applied for its 1,016 apartments, yielding a rate of acceptance considerably more stringent than that then prevailing at Harvard College. Applications from welfare recipients (with the exception of those getting mothers' aid) were actively discouraged. Prospective tenants were required to have permanent employment, so that even those who held jobs through the Works Progress Administration (WPA) were exempted from consideration. At a time when the number of people on city welfare rolls and WPA employment totaled more than 50,000, such restrictions were significant. As a key local housing official told the Boston City Council: "We don't feel we should add subsidy to subsidy. If the city is already assisting a family, in the form of welfare, that family of course should not be further subsidized."[26]

Old Harbor was also exclusively white, predominantly occupied by people from McCormack's congressional district, and overwhelmingly Irish; even the project's new street names—Monsignor Dennis F. O'Callaghan Way, Colonel Michael J. McDonough Way, Doctor Michael Gavin Way, and General Lawrence J. Logan Way—conveyed the intended ethnicity of the clientele in a city that had an Irish mayor and an Irish-dominated city council from the late 1920s to the mid-1990s.[27] As a result of concerted selection efforts, the new public neighborhood of Old Harbor Village became one of South Boston's best-off areas. Its tenants had the highest median education level in that district and were well above the

FIGURE 3.2 Newly planted courtyard at Old Harbor Village, ca. 1940.

median citywide. In 1940, when nearly 30 percent of South Boston's labor force was either seeking work or on work relief, only 8.8 percent of those living in Old Harbor Village were so affected; only five other neighborhoods in the entire city of Boston had a lower proportion of unemployed. In 1940, the tenants of Old Harbor Village paid a median monthly rent of $25.52, the highest median in South Boston—nearly double that of its least expensive areas, and only about three dollars below the median citywide.[28] Old Harbor Village, consistent with a century of rationales for government intervention in housing, served as a mechanism for rewarding the barely poor.

OLD HARBOR VILLAGE AND THE BOSTON HOUSING AUTHORITY

Old Harbor Village was launched as a federal initiative, yet by the time it was completed Boston had gained its own local housing authority, eager to lease it and manage it. State legislation, followed by Boston City Council approval, created the Boston Housing Authority (BHA) in late 1935. Seen as a necessary channel for obtaining and overseeing federal housing funds, it gained the early support of Mayor Mansfield and the vast majority of the City Council. It was organized as a five-man board (with four members appointed by the mayor and one by the governor) but, until Old Harbor was ready, the Authority had little to do except plan and urge the federal government to pass housing legislation (Fig. 3.3).[29] Once Old Harbor was up and running, however, this project became the testing ground for all aspects of BHA policies, from tenant selection to project maintenance. In 1940 alone, ninety-seven groups—from institutions including universities, settlement houses, hospitals, municipalities, and real estate firms— toured the project to learn more about public housing. Because of its prime water-facing location, its many architectural amenities (including 152 rowhouses), and the political connectedness of many of its residents, Old Harbor Village was not only first chronologically among BHA projects, but also remained "first in many hearts."

From the outset, the BHA tried to protect the Old Harbor enclave by rezoning its environs. Two months after taking over the project, the Authority convinced the Board of Zoning Adjustment to convert the project area from industrial to multifamily residential use; this zone was then extended to the nearby railroad tracks to encourage construction of a future domestic buffer. The rezoning plan designated the major street abutting Old Harbor Village for local business, in anticipation of increased trade following the opening of the project. Shortly afterwards, construction on several new stores did begin, including a supermarket, displacing some old stables.[30]

In a long report on its first five years of operations, the BHA devoted an entire section to extolling the quality of life at Old Harbor Village, noting the rapid development of great community commitment. The project had twelve softball teams, an eight-team bowling league, two Girl Scout and three Boy Scout troops, twelve indoor children's playrooms, and numerous other clubs and societies dedicated not only to social and recreational needs, but also to financial assistance programs for the needy, health care services for the ill, and programs for neighboring children. Old Harbor boasted the lowest rate of juvenile delinquency in the city, while adjacent neighborhoods had rates that were as much as forty times higher. In these early years, Old Harbor residents banded together to purchase a movie projector for twice-weekly film screenings; they also established their own newspaper, a credit union, and a symphony orchestra, aided by a federal music project providing instruction in piano and string instruments.[31]

MEMBERS OF THE BOSTON HOUSING AUTHORITY

FIGURE 3.3 The Boston Housing Authority board, 1941. Chairman John A. Breen (center) is flanked by Bradbury Cushing, Rev. Thomas R. Reynolds, Harold Field Kellogg, and John Carroll.

The BHA took special note of residents' ability to organize for the cooperative maintenance of shared common areas. In 1940 the residents implemented a plan to clean the walls, stairs, and landings "in the public areas adjacent to their apartments." Tenants also showed concern for the appearance of outdoor areas: they "displayed a keen interest in building fences around lawn areas and in maintaining flower gardens." The BHA's report included eight photographs attesting to the quality of "tenant maintenance," adding that these alterations to the environment had been undertaken with "the full approval and encouragement of the housing authority." Writing in 1944, national housing leader Nathan Straus called Old Harbor Village "one of the beauty spots of Boston" (Fig. 3.4). Its busily employed and civically engaged cohort of barely poor and upwardly mobile residents paid rent on time and in-full; in Old Harbor's first two-and-a-half years of operation, only $143 remained "apparently uncollectible." The revenue from rents covered all expenses and operating costs, and enabled a modest annual "service payment" of $15,000 to the City of Boston in lieu of taxes.[32]

In these first years, the BHA's biggest financial headaches regarding Old Harbor concerned complaints about the maximum legal income limit for continued occupancy. Those who could not get in complained that the project served a privileged clientele, while those who did resented the rent increases that came with each subsequent increase in reported income. The latter issue clearly disturbed Calvin Yuill, the executive director of the Housing Association of Metropolitan Boston, who wondered in 1940:

> What will happen . . . when a privately employed worker, living in a subsidized housing project, is offered a raise in pay or a better job? Will he joyfully accept the opportunity or reluctantly refuse it rather than move back to the "cold-water flat"? How would the boy or girl, fresh from school, react to a chance for a job if by accepting it, the family would have to leave their home? In other words, will public subsidized housing tend to "fix" low wages, dull the worker's initiative and ambition and encourage subterfuge? Such eventualities are more than imaginary, for tenants at Old Harbor Village are reported to have faced such decisions, and to be still living in the project.[33]

Thus, tenant composition remained a highly charged subject not just at the time of admission, but at every subsequent recertification of income eligibility. From the Housing Authority's perspective, the mandate to serve low-income applicants was in perpetual conflict with the desirability of retaining a stable base of fiscally and socially responsible tenants. While the income ceilings and homeownership ideology beckoned financially successful residents into private-sector alternatives, strict enforcement of evictions for excess income was never in the BHA's fiscal best interest, and the same political ties that had helped people to gain admission to Old Harbor could often be counted on to secure continued occupancy. As a

FIGURE 3.4 "Examples of Tenant Maintenance Which Have the Full Approval and Encouragement of the Housing Authority," Old Harbor Village, ca. 1940.

zone of privilege, a well-maintained enclave, and a source of municipal revenue, Boston's first public neighborhood had quickly become the kind of selective collective its proponents had long envisioned. Like the New Deal social security program, which exempted the employers of agricultural labor from participation, Roosevelt-era public housing did little to serve the bottom segment of the working poor. Public housing, in Boston as elsewhere, had been launched at the precise moment in American history when poverty extended far enough into the core of society to permit creation of a mainstream program, yet, precisely because the poverty was so widespread, policymakers had the luxury to choose tenants entirely from within the broad subcategory of "deserving poor."

PUBLIC HOUSING AS SLUM REFORM

With passage of the Wagner-Steagall Housing Act of 1937, public housing metamorphosed into a decentralized program of slum clearance, unemployment relief, and low-rent housing construction, coordinated by the United States Housing Authority (USHA). Yet in Boston as in other cities, the fundamental commitment to close scrutiny of prospective tenants remained unaltered.

Supporters of the Wagner-Steagall legislation understood that the pressures for public housing came not from the abject poor but from those who Lawrence Friedman has called the "submerged and potential middle class," families kept temporarily poor by the Depression and forced into substandard housing; thus, "the ideal housing act . . . would shut the doors on those with the ability to get housing privately, but would not open the doors to people on the dole and likely to stay there." As New York's Robert Wagner put it during the Senate debate, "there are some people we cannot possibly reach; I mean those who have no means to pay the rent . . . obviously this bill cannot provide housing for those who cannot pay the rent minus the subsidy allowed." Public housing was premised on the assumption that income from rents would cover current operating expenses. This approach would permit financial stability while allowing tenants to feel that they were "paying their own way" instead of receiving charity.[34]

The rent structure thereby excluded all but the working poor. As Friedman comments, "The projects would mainly be filled with deserving but underpaid workers—innocent victims of economic reverses, who needed a 'break' to tide them over the lean years." Many housing experts advocated targeting the housing only to "self-supporting families" and sought an outright ban on households dependent on income from relief programs. Though this ban was not federally imposed, many housing authorities did resist housing welfare-dependent families throughout the 1930s and 1940s. Although admitting a few "problem" families— those judged to be excessively large, in poor health, or to have fallen short of "a designated standard of cleanliness"—could be regarded as something of a noble experiment, most public housing authorities sought only the most "deserving" from the potential pool of public neighbors.[35] A USHA pamphlet, *What the Housing Act Can Do for Your City*, noted that the program was designed "to raise the living standards of typical *employed* families of very low income, who are independent and self-supporting, but who have not been able to afford the kinds of homes in which independent and self-supporting Americans should live."[36]

Other groups representing the building industries preferred to leave any such homebuilding to the private sector, and lobbied Congress incessantly. G. M. Stout, president of the Atlanta Real Estate Board, cast the public housing question in familiar ideological terms of individualism, self-reliance, and frontier manhood: "The working classes of this country will rue the day when they are housed in Government-owned, Government built, and Government-regulated houses. Masters house their slaves, but free men house themselves. Those who are descendants of pioneer American stock will not regard as 'Home' a unit in a fine building, built at taxpayers' expense, in a slum clearance project."[37] The U.S. Chamber of Commerce was intent on ensuring that whatever legislation passed would permit local control of the projects. The National Retail Lumber Dealers' Association was distressed at the prospect of mass construction that would not employ wood. For the lumber industry lobby, wood was no mere building material; the fireproof bricks of public housing presented a symbolic challenge to the homeownership ideology. An article in *Lumber and Building Materials Digest* stated, "It is in the American home, not in the bureaus and legislative halls of politicians, not in the tub-thumping and flag-waving organizations, that we have our real vital defense against foreign isms, subversive movements and revolutionary propaganda . . . Let's defend America. Let's combat crime. LET'S BUILD HOMES!"[38]

Private property interests molded the evolving shape of the public housing program in many important ways. Most fundamentally, the Wagner-Steagall bill targeted public housing access to low-income families through a formula that tied low rents to low incomes. By limiting eligibility to families earning no more than five times the fixed rent (six times the rent in the case of large families), the legislation thereby intended that any significant rise in income would spur their departure into private market-rate housing. The bill also appeased private homebuilders and congressional conservatives with provisions stipulating dollar limits on per-room and per-dwelling construction costs, intended to minimize the chance that public housing would compete with privately supplied housing. Further reducing competitive threats were stipulations that federal money would go only to projects that were without "elaborate or expensive design or materials" and which cost less than the "average construction cost of dwelling units currently provided by private enterprise, in the locality." Most important, the Housing Act of 1937 linked all new low-rent housing to slum clearance by mandating an "equivalent elimination agreement": public housing construction must be accompanied by the "elimination by demolition, condemnation, and effective closing, or the compulsory repair and improvement of unsafe or insanitary dwellings situated in the locality or metropolitan area, substantially equal in number to the number of newly constructed dwellings provided by the project." This provision effectively ensured that public housing would not contribute to any significant gains in the low-rent housing stock, since even if "elimination" was accomplished through rehabilitation rather than demolition, the resultant improved properties would probably demand substantially higher monthly rentals. The required link to slum-clearance efforts also encouraged public housing construction in inner-city neighborhoods, rather than in more affluent peripheral areas.[39] Such efforts to curtail costs and eligibility could not curtail controversy. Straus noted the paradoxical result: "At the same time that the USHA program was condemned by some people because the homes erected were too good, it was criticized with equal bitterness by others who, pointing to the omission of closet doors and other economies, alleged that the homes were not good enough."[40] In Boston, neighborhood reaction ran the full gamut, but support from City Hall and state officials remained powerful and constant, enabling the BHA to initiate one of the nation's earliest and largest slum-clearance public housing programs.

ECONOMIC RATIONALES FOR SLUM CLEARANCE

Just as the exigencies of the Great Depression prompted the federal job creation programs that included the first PWA public housing, so too this economic collapse gave new impetus to advocates of slum clearance. At a time when many policymakers disparaged the "social liability" of slums, they also sought to redress what they termed the "economic liability" of blighted areas, places where increases in property values lagged behind the rest of the city. In theory, the concept of blight allowed housing officials to discredit whole districts without impugning the people who lived in them, yet in practice the distinction between slums and blighted areas did not hold firm; many, like Clarence Perry, saw blighted areas simply as incipient slums. Still, the idea of blight carried the long-simmering debate over slum clearance in a new direction, since it challenged municipalities to calculate the economic costs of inaction. Slums were not just a threat to public health; they were a threat to the fiscal health of the municipality. Especially as once-dense central areas began to lose population, reformers questioned the high cost of maintaining their streets, schools, and services. As Edith Elmer Wood concluded in 1935, "The partly abandoned blighted district . . . does not and cannot pay its share of the economic burden." Unless such areas could be cleared and rebuilt to higher standards, cities would face "death from dry rot at the center" as well as bankruptcy, because other areas would be forced into paying excessively high property taxes to compensate for the laggard districts.[41] Many large American cities, beginning with Indianapolis and Cleveland, sponsored studies in the 1930s and 1940s intended to measure the comparative cost-effectiveness of various districts. The studies were intended to demonstrate that disproportionate resources flowed into blighted areas. Among such efforts, Boston's seems typical.

In the four years before passage of the Wagner-Steagall bill, the Massachusetts State Board of Housing laid the groundwork for subsequent federally funded efforts to clear slums and build public housing. The board identified a set of priority sites for slum removal and loudly proclaimed the economic rationale that made clearance desirable. In its first annual report for 1933–34, the board printed a map of Boston and Cambridge "Showing Sections in which are Blighted Areas that may be Considered for Rehousing Projects." The Board pointed out that all of these areas were within two miles of the State House, implying that their decline was an affront to the prestige of the Commonwealth itself. At the same time, the report noted that these sites were "within walking distance of active industrial enterprises which afford a wide degree of employment" and therefore quite desirable (Fig. 3.5). Over the next twenty years, many of these "First Choice" and "Second Choice" areas "most in need of rehousing" did become sites for public housing; others were subsequently redeveloped into more lucrative uses.[42]

In pushing for slum clearance, the State Board expressed the prevailing eco-

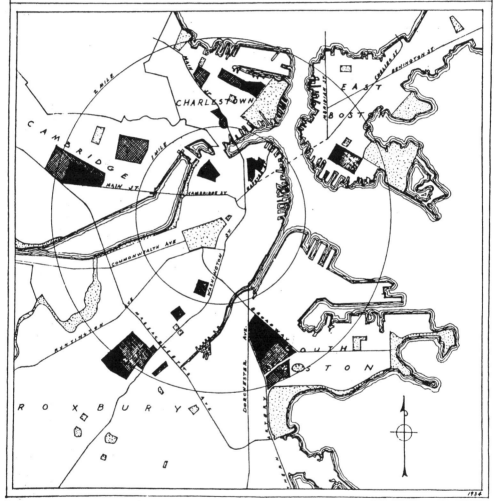

MAP OF BOSTON AND CAMBRIDGE
SHOWING SECTIONS IN WHICH ARE BLIGHTED AREAS THAT MAY
BE CONSIDERED FOR REHOUSING PROJECTS

FIGURE 3.5 "Blighted" areas in need of "rehousing," 1934. The State Board of Housing's map
helped set the agenda for public housing.

nomic rationale for public housing in Boston in no uncertain terms. Its annual report for 1936 explained that an "unbalanced policy of city growth" had "brought about decay in sub-standard areas" and argued that it would be "not only wiser but more profitable" if such areas could be cleared and rebuilt. Although the report mentioned the prevalence of disease and "social liability" in such places, its stated goal was to "restore the capital investment of the city and produce more income, thus relieving the taxpayer of an undue burden." Eliminating the "social, moral and health conditions" that characterized these substandard areas promised "inestimable social value to the community"; however, it was far from clear that this community had much to do with those who would be displaced. Rather, the professed social welfare objectives provided the legal "justification for federal, state, and municipal participation in a housing program" that could eliminate social instability and replenish dwindling municipal coffers.[43]

In its 1933–34 report, the State Board justified the need for slum clearance and new housing by analyzing "the cost to the community of maintaining a sub-standard area," using the specific example of Census Tract M-3 in South Boston. Their method of analysis is instructive. The board itemized land and building values, then compared the income from real estate and water taxes to the district's share of direct public expenditures needed to support its schools, library, hospital, parks, infrastructure, police and fire stations, and relief roll. It added to these the less significant prorated cost of thirty-five other city departments whose service to the district was more indirect. The bottom line was this: Census Tract M-3 brought the city $27,000 in income, while absorbing $275,000 in city expenses, so this slum cost the city $248,000 a year. The board's conclusion, following a logic that would have been utterly incomprehensible to the residents of the neighborhood, was that "Sub-standard areas of this character are indeed a luxury for the City to maintain."[44] The entirety of tract M-3 was leveled in 1941 to make way for the eventual construction of the West Broadway public housing development.

The Boston Housing Authority reiterated the State Housing Board's assertions that "slums cost money," but critics charged that public housing itself, having replaced hundreds of individual tax-paying landowners with a single tax-exempt property requiring the full panoply of city services, was a drag on public coffers. In 1944 one fiscal watchdog agency, the Boston Municipal Research Bureau, devoted an entire report to the subject of public housing taxes, charging that paltry payments in lieu of taxes (including what it termed Old Harbor's "trifling 'service charge'") existed merely to "quiet criticism" and provided "inconsequential revenue" to the city. From the bureau's perspective, all public housing should pay the equivalent of full taxes on the locally assessed value of the new projects; at the very least, these "token payments" could be increased by relating them to the former tax revenues from the slums they replaced.[45]

Other critics blamed slum clearance and public housing for disrupting private real estate markets. Instead of a system whereby the presence of thousands of rent-payers enabled hundreds of property owners to pay taxes to the city, the slum-clearance approach often yielded long periods of vacancies, leaving landlords without income to pay taxes on their unoccupied property. When the land was actually transferred to the government, the owners were often undercompensated.

The BHA countered such assertions at every opportunity. With the added leverage of federal dollars and pressure, it argued, the City of Boston would finally receive delinquent back taxes on many properties in the cleared slums (either from the property owners or from the BHA itself), as well as profits from the sale to the BHA of unwanted foreclosed properties that had fallen into city hands. Moreover, the BHA claimed, the annual in-lieu-of-taxes payments for its low-rent projects (based on 4.75 percent of the tenants' rent) would yield about one-sixth of the fully taxed potential return, and titles to the projects would revert to the city after sixty years.

Other economic benefits accrued even before the projects were occupied, the BHA noted, since fully one-third of their costs went to pay on-site construction personnel, yielding a "readily apparent" contribution to the economic health of the building trades, and a concomitant reduction in the need to pay out relief. At a regional planning level, the BHA administration touted the projects as a means to "prevent the decentralization of cities," by providing "decent dwelling units" within the city itself and thereby retaining a ready market for downtown and local business services. In general, the Authority claimed, the new projects would contribute to a reduction of municipal expenses for waste disposal (because of new project-based incinerators) and streets (because of the discontinued interior city roadways) and would indirectly reduce "numerous other municipal costs, such as those connected with health and institutional activities, police, courts, [and] juvenile delinquency."[46]

Implicit in this last claim was yet another iteration of the old environmental determinism; eliminating the slums would eliminate the costs of slum dwellers to

the city. Left out of this logic, however, were the socioeconomics of the tenant selection system. Far from a mechanism to reform juvenile delinquents by raising
them in a morally uplifting and recreationally rich environment, the system was
predicated on weeding out such people from consideration in the first place.
Slum clearance, in almost all cases, did not put the displaced slum dwellers into
public housing, but simply forced them to move to other slums. The negative
fiscal consequences associated with blight could more convincingly be attributed
to poverty and high-density living; removing blight could do no more than displace these underlying problems. To the extent that slum dwellers themselves
represented a municipal expense, this public charge was dispersed rather than
eliminated. Nonetheless, the economic arguments for slum clearance remained
politically appealing.

Selecting Clearable Slums

In 1935 the Boston City Planning Department conducted its own study of "Substandard Areas in Boston," which yielded a rather different map than the one just
produced by the State Housing Board. Drawn to highlight census tracts that
showed not only unusually high instances of older structures experiencing ill-re-
pair and high vacancy but also areas where land values exceeded the "value of
the improvements," this map—presumably because of artificially high land values adjacent to downtown—showed a collar of blight strangling the central business district (Fig. 3.6).[47] The Planning Board also concluded that the fifty-two
low-rent census tracts in the city—containing a population of approximately
292,000—cost the city about $10 million more annually to maintain than was re-
ceived from them in taxes and fees.[48]

Even these highly contestable numbers were not enough to make many of
these places candidates for clearance and new public housing, however. Federal
guidelines about site selection stipulated that no local housing authority could
pay more than an average of $1.50 per square foot for buildings and land (unless
supplemented by local contributions), which meant that the BHA could not
feasibly plan large slum-clearance efforts in some of the city's "most highly congested and worst housing areas," including some on the State Board's map (Fig.
3.5) and most of those shown to be choking the downtown in Fig. 3.6. In the
West End, for example, land prices averaged more than twice the federal ceiling,
and North End land prices ranged as high as five times the USHA limit. Faced
with this constraint, and initially unwilling to build on vacant land (and thereby

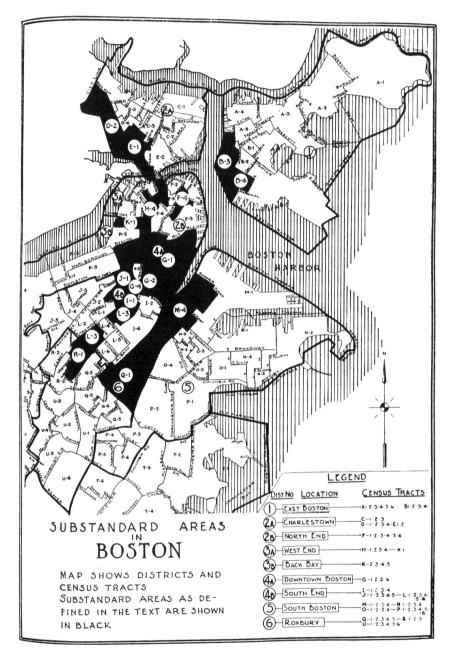

FIGURE 3.6 "Substandard" areas of Boston, 1935. The Boston City Planning Board feared that blighted areas could strangle downtown development.

face the legal necessity of eliminating an equivalent number of off-site substandard dwellings), the BHA undertook slum clearance in lower-priced neighborhoods, located somewhat farther from downtown.[49]

In addition to the cost of site acquisition, the BHA considered a wide variety of other factors, including topography, land-use patterns, traffic patterns, population trends, proximity of transportation, and ease of relocation of "site families." At the same time, the Authority balanced what it called "sectional influences"—presumably referring to the political need to distribute the housing among various neighborhoods—and "consideration of racial groups." In every case, the goal was to find sites in neighborhoods that were likely to remain residential for the foreseeable future. At the same time, the Authority sought sites that had clear "protective" edges (in one case, the immediate adjacency of a proposed crosstown highway was judged "a splendid boundary for the project").[50] This goal of "protected boundaries" most explicitly took the form of superblock construction, and the BHA selected sites that were amenable to complete street closure within the project. To contain and reverse the incursions of blight, the BHA preferred to introduce a noncontiguous street and parking system that prevented through traffic.

THE EIGHT PREWAR HOUSING DEVELOPMENTS

In addition to its ongoing management of Old Harbor Village, the BHA undertook seven projects of its own, constructed under the terms of the 1937 Housing Act (Figs. 3.7 and 3.8). All seven were erected on slum-clearance sites, and all opened between 1940 and 1942. Altogether, they added nearly 5,000 new apartments, displacing 4,722 dwelling units (83 percent of which had been occupied). In the effort to accomplish both slum clearance and public housing construction on the same site, while meeting the legislative requirement for equivalent elimination, the prewar projects built in Boston under the terms of the Wagner-Steagall Act, on average, almost exactly approximated the densities of the neighborhoods they replaced (31 to 55 units per acre).

Four projects moved in advance of the others. In September 1939 the 1,149-unit Charlestown development was the first to break ground. This was closely followed by the 1,023-unit Mission Hill project in Roxbury. Soon afterward, with its legal challenges finally under control, the BHA commenced work on South Boston's 873-unit Old Colony development, located on the hotly contested territory near Old Harbor Village. Also among the initial quartet was a second

Roxbury development, Lenox Street, with 306 apartments intended exclusively for "Negro" tenants. The BHA described it as located "in the heart of an area now predominantly occupied by negroes." Putting a project there, the BHA maintained (in its best settlement-house tone), "made it possible for the Authority to gain first-hand knowledge of the problems involved, as well as to supply

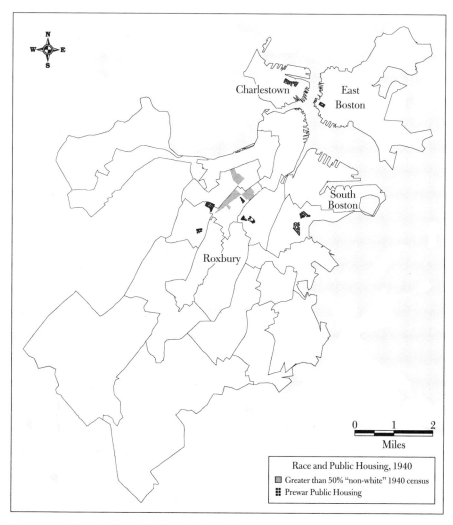

FIGURE 3.7 Boston's first public housing, located in white neighborhoods. None of Boston's prewar public housing was built in the city's few nonwhite-majority neighborhoods, although the Lenox Street project, intended for blacks, was conveniently adjacent.

adequate dwellings in an area that was rapidly deteriorating."[51] As Figure 3.7 suggests, it also enabled the Authority to "upgrade" the city's small black community without forcing it to deconcentrate from areas nearest to railway yards and industries.

In each of these first four cases, as with Old Harbor Village, the BHA worked successfully through the Board of Zoning Adjustment to shift land uses on project sites and abutting parcels from business to general residential.[52] Though the efforts were little more than token gestures, given the complexity of the existing land use surrounding these sites, the action symbolized Authority concern with buffering its social, architectural, and economic investment. That said, the BHA

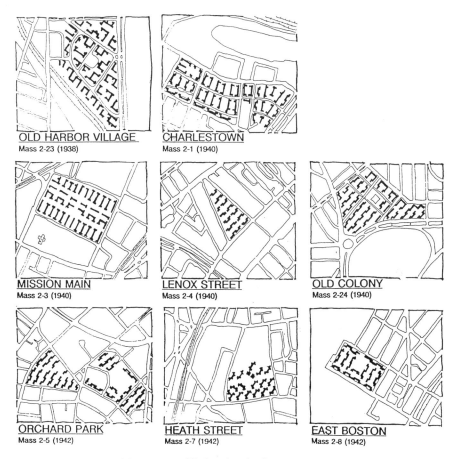

FIGURE 3.8 Boston's eight prewar public housing developments.

did not request zoning changes for the three other slum-clearance projects that quickly followed, presumably because the land in these areas did not require new zoning before construction could commence. The 414 apartments in East Boston (near the site of the abortive Neptune Gardens venture) and the 420 units known as Heath Street, located in the city's Jamaica Plain district, were built for white occupancy; the 774-unit Orchard Park development, located in a racially mixed area of Roxbury, was "bi-racially segregated," with four contiguous buildings in the bowtie-shaped project reserved for "Negro" occupancy, and the rest reserved for whites. All told, the first eight Boston projects, as built, housed a segregated tenant population that was about 93 percent white—hardly surprising in a city whose total nonwhite population in 1940 was only 3 percent. Thus, the BHA provided housing for nonwhites at approximately two-and-a-half times their share, yet nonwhites also occupied a vastly disproportionate share of the city's substandard apartments. Moreover, nonwhites with the lowest incomes were much more likely than low-income whites to be paying more than a third of their income for rent. In the 1940s, as in subsequent decades, Boston's nonwhites could still credibly claim to be underserved by public housing and private housing alike.[53]

Boston's public housing mirrored prevailing ethnic patterns as well as racial ones (Fig. 3.9), with construction as a whole skewed to favor locations desirable to the Irish, who occupied a majority of apartments right from the start. Although the early projects were spread across several wards, in general the distinctly Irish enclaves of South Boston and Charlestown attracted Irish applicants; Italians headed toward the East Boston project; and Jews waited for the two projects that opened up after the war in Dorchester. The Chinese remained in their Chinatown tenements (and seem to have been completely absent from the projects), and the Brahmin elite either suburbanized or stayed put in the Back Bay and Beacon Hill, magnetically drawn by what Walter Firey called "symbolic qualities"[54] to central districts where they remained undisturbed by any nearby evidence of public housing. Meanwhile, the mostly Irish politicians and overwhelmingly Irish BHA staff downtown assiduously tenanted the projects throughout the city.

SELECTING TENANTS

In the first four-and-a-half months of accepting applications for tenancy in its new projects, the BHA received more than 12,000 applications for 3,291 apartments. In the last two months of 1940 alone, the Authority estimated that 16,000 people toured the model apartments at the all-white Charlestown project and the all-black Lenox Street project, the latter outfitted with furniture repaired through the goodwill of the nearby Robert Gould Shaw House. With the pool of techni-cally eligible Boston families estimated at about 30,000, BHA officials—con-vinced of the marked superiority of their product—anticipated that as many as 25,000 would eventually apply. Conceding that "there is no equivalent of the slide rule for calculating the relative merit" of these first 12,000 applicants, the

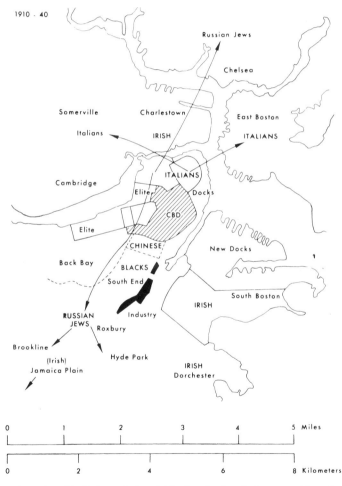

FIGURE 3.9 In a city with distinct ethnic neighborhoods, the ethnic composition of public hous-ing followed larger neighborhood trends and preferences established between 1910 and 1940.

BHA nonetheless claimed to have taken firm steps to "avoid favoritism and to cut down to an irreducible minimum the possibility of error." The BHA was bound by the terms of federal law and its agreements with the United States Housing Authority, as well as by the terms of the Massachusetts Housing Authority Law, which in some aspects was even more stringent. Taken together, these terms stipulated four major requirements for eligibility:

> Family income could not exceed five times the rent (or six times the rent for a family with three or more minor dependents);
>
> The family must have been living under substandard conditions detrimental to health, safety, and morals for six months immediately before filing of the application;
>
> The family must have resided in the City of Boston for at least one year immediately before filing of the application;
>
> The head of the family must be a U.S. citizen.

If eligible under these terms, the BHA agreed to give preference to former site tenants whose homes had been demolished to make way for the new projects.

In these earliest years of the program, the Authority emphasized the intensity of its scrutiny of every application—including "a thorough investigation of the applicant" accompanied by written assessment by "several members of the staff." The Authority claimed to "hold the scale so evenly that the only test shall be the housing conditions and the incomes of the families," and maintained that rent and income allowances were set to allow occupancy by families of all sizes from "the very lowest income groups." Not content to rely on the thousands of applications already on hand, in April 1941 the BHA used 160,000 Boston schoolchildren as messengers, distributing letters and housing applications to them to bring home to their parents. In these early years, the BHA claimed, it was the housing authority's wish to reach "the neediest cases in Boston." At the same time, however, its staff continued to sift through the accumulating applications in search of "even more worthy cases," "persons of inherent dignity and character" who, if provided with public housing, "can lift themselves to a higher level of self-esteem and achieve a measure of contentment, community pride and civic responsibility that is impossible of attainment in the bleak, insanitary dwellings which comprise the worst housing districts."[55] As in the centuries before public housing, neediness and worthiness remained less than wholly equivalent.

The Authority assumed that blight could be arrested not only by surgical replacement with housing projects, but also by the legal eviction of "blighted persons" and their replacement by families of greater social and economic stability, even if those people had also formerly resided in blighted areas. In turn, though the Authority never stated this publicly, the importation of families with greater purchasing power could be expected to result in higher expenditure of disposable income in the businesses surrounding the new project, which would encourage neighbors to invest in upgrading their own facilities. Whatever the criteria for site selection and the economic justifications for clearance and redevelopment, however, the BHA inevitably faced protests from those who failed to comprehend why their homes and businesses had to be taken for such purposes.

Displacement and "Rehousing"

Involuntary displacement always yields outrage, and court records, changing socioeconomics of occupancy patterns revealed in census reports, city directories, "police lists," and surviving accounts in local newspapers all suggest that Boston's slum-clearance efforts of the late 1930s and early 1940s were no exception.[56]

The first major hurdle for the BHA slum-clearance efforts remained a legal one. The Massachusetts Housing Authority Law had been brought into compliance with federal legislation in 1938, allowing the BHA to take over management of the federally controlled Old Harbor Village and to commence plans to construct the seven new USHA projects, yet other legal challenges persisted. Like the federal law, the amended Massachusetts Housing Authority Law emphasized the dangers of "sub-standard areas," calling them "a menace to the health, safety, morals, welfare, and comfort of the inhabitants of the Commonwealth" and "detrimental to property values therein." Sounding the old alarm about potential infection from both tenements and their tenants, the state law justified slum clearance as a "public necessity" and "a public use for which private property may be acquired by eminent domain and public funds raised by taxation may be expended."

Owners of property in the threatened areas launched lawsuits based on two major arguments. The first was a challenge to the constitutionality of using eminent-domain powers to facilitate the construction of public housing. The somewhat narrower second challenge rested on the claim that the BHA had exceeded its authority by attempting to take the premises of the plaintiffs. In late 1939 the Massachusetts Supreme Judicial Court addressed these arguments in two major decisions.

In the first case, *Allydonn Realty Corp. v. Holyoke Housing Authority,* the court held that the "expenditure of public funds in a reasonable manner to rid a community of slums" did indeed constitute a valid public purpose. The court justified the erection of public housing by contending that this was clearly a second order of business, a building venture made necessary by the need to replace razed low-rent housing units. Public housing was required to "avert hardship to those whose homes have been razed," since it "would prevent overcrowding into other slums."[57] The court could hardly have affirmed the then-prevailing rationales more strongly. Public housing was no more than the residual necessity of the prior commitment to slum clearance. Whereas the 1937 Housing Act required that public housing construction entail an "equivalent elimination" of substandard dwellings, the Massachusetts Supreme Judicial Court implicitly reversed the emphasis. Although the court argued that public housing would constitute a resource for the displaced, from a legal standpoint it did not matter that those who lost their homes would have no guarantee of rehousing in the new projects.

A second case, *Stockus v. Boston Housing Authority,* affirmed the power of the BHA to determine "substandard areas" for the purpose of such takings. This case marked the resolution of many years of wrangling over the South Boston slum-clearance site originally proposed for Old Harbor Village. The decision to resite this venture on substantially vacant land had done nothing to halt legal challenges to the proposed taking of properties on the original site. Baltramieus and Annie M. Stockus, two South Boston Lithuanians who were not U.S. citizens, repeatedly sought to stop the Authority from taking their three-story Vale Street home for the Old Colony project, and the case became another head-on challenge to the validity of the Authority's right of eminent domain. In rejecting the constitutional challenge in *Stockus,* the court cited *Allydonn* as a precedent. The only other adjudicable claim, the court held, was whether the BHA could legitimately overrule the plaintiffs' claim that their property was not located in a substandard area. The Stockus' attorney, Alexander Lincoln, argued that the Stockus property and that of another plaintiff met all relevant standards for acceptable buildings, provided evidence that such standards were met elsewhere in the district, and alleged that there was an adequate supply of decent, safe, and sanitary dwellings in Boston even without the proposed public housing construction. Moreover, he contended, the new public housing project would "require a rental beyond the reach of families of low income and will increase the burden of taxation on property owners."[58]

The court declined to enter into arguments regarding questions of housing need and ruled against Stockus chiefly on the basis of a finding that the BHA properly held the power "to determine what areas within its jurisdiction constitute sub-standard areas." In short, the BHA could overrule the claims of local owners who insisted conditions were sound. At its heart, the case turned on the question of professional judgment. Dismissing the significance of facts presented by the plaintiffs, Justice James Ronan (writing on behalf of the court) argued that assessment of the "predominating and distinctive traits of a neighborhood" is "frequently and largely a matter of opinion" depending on "practical judgment, common sense and sound discretion." The court wished to do nothing to undermine the BHA's role to act as arbitrator. Noting that the plaintiffs had neither challenged the BHA's "good faith" nor alleged "arbitrary or capricious action," he concluded that "every presumption must be indulged in as to the integrity and impartiality of their conduct." The eviction of the Stockus family was thereby upheld.[59]

The *South Boston Tribune* denounced the decision bitterly. "The statement that a local Housing Authority can declare a well-kept modern house a slum dwelling sounds to us very much like stating black is white."[60] From the perspective of the BHA, however, the legal result was wholly satisfactory. Taken together, *Allydonn* and *Stockus* affirmed not only the constitutionality of a slum-clearance approach to public housing provision, but also the Authority's judgment in designating "substandard" areas. The other six slum-clearance projects faced far less arduous and protracted litigation. The more difficult problem concerned arrangements to rehouse the 3,761 families who lost their homes as a result of these actions.

The mass rehousing efforts marked yet another area of triumph for the BHA. More than 90 percent of the displaced households, the BHA claimed, accepted the Authority's assistance in finding alternative accommodation. In the effort to determine the availability of low-rent alternatives, the BHA reviewed the available housing statistics for January 1939 and found that there were 17,149 vacant dwellings in the city, including "a considerable number of apartments at rents which site tenants could afford to pay." Representatives of the Authority then investigated more than 10,000 vacant low-rent dwellings across the city and concluded that 80 percent could be considered "fit for human habitation." With this in mind, the BHA offered to help. Included in its mass mailing of thirty-day eviction notices sent on May 20, 1939 (written in a largely impenetrable legal jargon), was an address where the "tenant or tenants at sufferance of the above premises" could go to pay their remaining one month's rent before vacating, and "where employees of the Authority will try to be of service to you in finding the location of a new home."[61] In most of the cases, the BHA provided little more than lists of vacancies. In a 1941 report the BHA announced that a survey of 3,660 displaced families showed that 95 percent held views "favorable to public housing" and that only 72 respondents could be characterized as "antagonistic toward projects." Though taking heart in "the number of families declaring their intention to apply for apartments in the new projects," the same report failed to say just how many did so. The reason for this omission seems quite straightforward: the vast majority of displaced families either could not afford or did not qualify for an apartment in the new projects. Overall, the BHA's own figures reveal, the average family in the slum-clearance areas had paid $15.88 per month in rent, on annual income averaging $1,149. The rent for a BHA apartment would be $23 per month for a family of the same average size and income, nearly 50 percent more.[62] BHA documents did not report these two rental figures in the same place.

From the BHA's perspective, the chief measure of success in the "rehousing" effort had nothing to do with getting displaced families into public housing. What mattered most was simply getting them out of the substandard areas where they had previously lived. The Housing Authority provided two kinds of humanitarian assistance—removing pernicious slum conditions and aiding worthy families—and it did not seem to matter if these objectives were met separately. According to the BHA, site surveys of the areas cleared for the first eight projects fully supported the Authority's "previous conclusion" that the dwellings "were so deficient in one or more of the accepted American standards of structural soundness, room arrangement, sanitation, ventilation and bathing and toilet facilities, that they required immediate demolition." The surveys found that 21 percent lacked a toilet within the dwelling unit, 47 percent lacked hot water, 62 percent lacked a tub or shower, and 93 percent lacked central heat. In a follow-up investigation of some of the "former site tenants" whose new addresses were known, the BHA concluded that 69 percent "were living in better homes than those which they had vacated." It did not report whether this improvement (however measured) had been accomplished without a substantial increase in outlay for rent. What mattered most was that these tenants had accepted their fate. "Throughout the rehousing period," the BHA report concluded, "the Authority found a spirit of complete cooperation. What had commenced as a serious problem was consummated as a speedy and successful program."[63]

Other statistics cast doubt upon the Authority's classification of the project areas as "slums." Data collected from BHA files in 1941 by an enterprising graduate student (which were not subsequently archived by the Authority) indicate that large parts of the first four districts targeted for clearance contained much acceptable housing.[64] In terms of rehousing arrangements too, the BHA's public announcements may be called into question. When BHA data about the large number of requests from displaced tenants for new apartments in the projects are analyzed along with city directory and police-list data showing who actually got in, the discrepancies are extreme. In Charlestown, South Boston, and Roxbury, thousands were displaced from viable low-rent living quarters and denied a place in the public housing projects that replaced their former homes.[65]

Charlestown

In Charlestown, on the very site where British troops had landed for the Battle of Bunker Hill nearly 165 years before, the BHA cleared 460 structures on eighteen acres to make room for 1,149 units of public housing (Fig. 3.10). A 1939 house-to-house BHA survey judged that 84 percent of the 781 displaced families had been living in "good" conditions of cleanliness (as opposed to "fair" or "poor"), and that 87 percent had taken "good care" of their property. On a room-by-room basis, fewer than one-third failed to meet Authority standards for size, light, and ventilation. Despite such findings, the Authority retroactively justified its decision to clear the area by arguing that its "physical aspects reflected dreariness and depression." The accounts of depression, of course, were not clinical judgments of environmental effects on residents but, rather, simply the negative assessments of BHA staff, seeking justification for Authority action. A majority of families had lived in their homes for more than five years, and more than a third for at least ten.[66] More than 20 percent owned the homes from which they were evicted, and many of these complained about delays in obtaining the money from the sales. As one homeowner put it, "We have something over here . . . that a lot of millionaires haven't got. We have got peace and contentment and happiness in American homes, and we don't want to lose them."[67]

Though the BHA claimed that most homeowners subsequently used the pro-

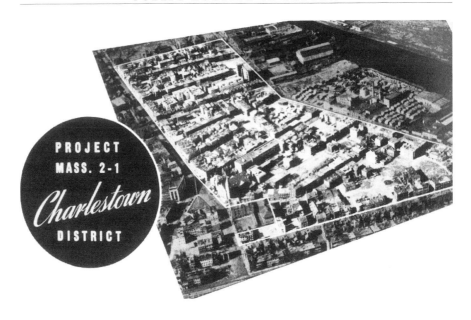

FIGURE 3.10 Charlestown, before public housing and after.

ceeds from sale of their property to purchase another home elsewhere, others faced less auspicious alternatives. In Charlestown as elsewhere, the BHA promised them preference for rehousing in public housing, and more than 70 percent applied to enter it, yet police-list data suggest that only about 8 percent of those displaced gained homes in the new project. Although it is possible that many were offered public housing apartments but chose not to accept them, it seems more likely that many were never offered the choice and that, even if they were, many could never have afforded the rent. In Charlestown, more than one-third of the households on the cleared site were categorized by the BHA as less than "wholly self-supporting" because of their reliance on relief or WPA employment; even the local Charlestown newspaper matter-of-factly pointed out to its readers that "those who have not a fixed income stated in the [rent] schedule prepared by the Authority will be barred." Also excluded were dozens of families headed by noncitizens and all those whose prior residences had not been deemed substandard.[68] Clearly, the BHA poll documenting the overwhelmingly positive attitudes of displaced households toward the idea of public housing was taken before the vast majority of such respondents discovered they would not get to live in it.

Meanwhile, Charlestown's representative William J. Galvin told his Boston City Council colleagues that "Charlestown will take three or four more of these projects if [we] can get them."[69]

Old Colony

The Charlestown experience was echoed in the twelve-acre section of South Boston razed for the 873 apartments of the Old Colony project (Fig. 3.11). According to the unpublished results of its own survey, the BHA judged that more than 80 percent of residents had been living in clean conditions and had taken "good" care of their property; only about half of the rooms were judged "substandard." Two-thirds of residents had lived in their homes for more than three years, half of these for more than ten.[70] According to BHA records, at least 276 displaced families, nearly 80 percent of those for whom the Authority held records, applied for apartments in the new project. Yet police lists and Boston city-directory data suggest that fewer than a dozen of these families actually gained a place at Old Colony. Here the usual problems of eligibility (including the presence of 235 noncitizens) were compounded by the salient fact that in 1941, shortly before the project was due to open, it was taken over by the federal government

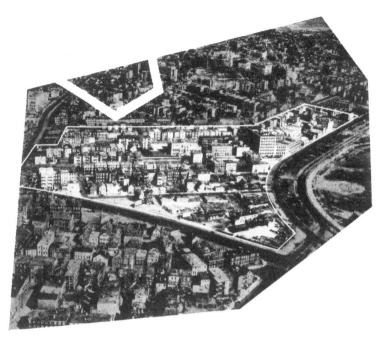

FIGURE 3.11 Old Colony (South Boston) before public housing and after.

for use by defense and war workers. As a result, the usual BHA procedures were bypassed, and housing was awarded on the basis of job qualifications rather than on other criteria. The project remained under federal jurisdiction for more than fifteen years. Less than 10 percent of the original tenants moved there from else-where in South Boston. More actually came from out of state, and nearly two-thirds came from outside Boston, encouraged by a federal preference for appli-cants who would otherwise face a long commute to city-based war industries.[71] Not surprisingly, the changed priorities for admission resulted in a socioeco-nomic profile that bore little resemblance to the one prevailing on the site before the project was built.

Mission Hill

There is also good reason to question BHA claims about slum conditions and re-housing arrangements at the third slum-clearance venture, Mission Hill (Fig. 3.12). In its assessment of the nineteen-acre section of Roxbury leveled to build the 1,023-unit development, the BHA survey again found that more than 80 per-cent of residents had been living in clean conditions and had taken "good" care of their property. Only about half of the rooms in the cleared neighborhood were judged "substandard." More than one hundred families had lived in their homes for at least ten years. Although BHA records suggest that at least 540 families out of the 679 known to have been displaced applied for admission to the new pro-ject, police-list data suggest that only about 12 percent of these gained apart-ments. One local newspaper reported that "general dissatisfaction" was "preva-lent throughout the . . . district among those who have filed applications for apartments." The bitterness was especially strong among families who were forced to lose their homes. Another local newspaper sympathized: "People are waking up, we believe, to the fact that there is NO Santa Claus, and all money supposedly spent by the bewhiskered gentleman is in reality taken from you and you and you."[72]

In April 1941, well after the clearance had been completed and as the Mission Hill project was readied to accept its first tenants, Councilor William A. Carey re-ported to the Boston City Council that some of his displaced constituents ("who were of fine, yet very simple, stock") had been rejected for consideration of an apartment in the new project because their incomes were as little as fifty cents a week above the ceilings stipulated by the Authority, while others had been re-jected because they had already relocated to homes that the Authority did not judge to be substandard, even though this relocation had been intended as no more than a temporary move made "at great sacrifice" in anticipation of admission to the Mission Hill project. Many others had been rejected because they were noncitizens, had too many children, or were considered to be too dependent on relief.

Like other city councilors, Carey wrote many letters on behalf of constituents seeking admission, but feared that his past lukewarm endorsement of public housing had turned the BHA against him. Authority Chairman John A. Breen, he complained, told him that he could "not expect the same consideration for [his] friends . . . that other councilors would get who had always, without any hesitation, gone down the line for housing." Breen was "playing politics" and Carey

FIGURE 3.12 Mission Hill (Roxbury) before public housing . . .

viewed the failure of former site residents to obtain housing as a personal affront. For his constituents, there was sad irony: "Many homeowners who have otherwise been able to struggle along and retain their little home will be forced to resort to public welfare, yet not one family now on welfare will be permitted to live in these housing projects."[73]

Lenox Street

In the Lenox Street area of Roxbury, the neighborhood targeted for Boston's first all-black housing project, only about one-third of the 1,500 rooms surveyed were judged to be substandard in terms of size, light, and ventilation (Fig. 3.13). Yet, having pronounced the physical conditions mostly sound, the BHA survey judged that only 19 percent of apartments were in "good" repair and less than one-third exhibited "good" standards of cleanliness. Taken together, these statistics would seem yet another instance of the tendency to blame slum dwellers for the conditions of the slums. The BHA survey also showed, however, that on average the Lenox Street residents were markedly less well off than those in the other

. . . and after.

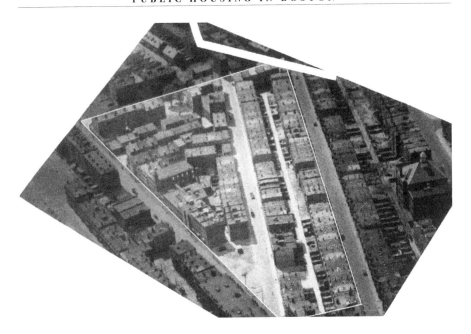

FIGURE 3.13 Lenox Street (Roxbury) before public housing and after.

"slum" districts, with nearly a third receiving relief and another 17 percent dependent on the uncertain future of WPA employment. In all, only 40 percent of the families displaced by BHA slum-clearance efforts in the Lenox Street area were classified as "wholly self-supporting."

Under the usual BHA policy, this fact alone guaranteed that the majority of residents would be denied access to public housing. The more immediate problem for the BHA, however, was getting them out of the way of the Lenox Street project. In June 1939, 152 families who had been ordered to vacate the Lenox Street site went on record as being unable to find alternative affordable accommodation. Having paid monthly rents of twelve to sixteen dollars in the buildings about to be razed, they found that it would cost them 25 to 35 percent more to live elsewhere. Moreover, many claimed, these alternatives were frequently less desirable than the accommodations that were about to be torn down. The BHA temporarily extended the deadline for eviction while these families continued their search for viable alternatives. Part of the problem was that many of these economically trapped families were on relief, and the welfare department—already trying to cope with relocating relief families from project sites in Charlestown, South Boston, and elsewhere—did not want to pay moving expenses or want the families to move to higher-rent apartments. One exasperated local commentator, observing the impasse, concluded that "These so-called 'slum-clearances' as far as many people can see are . . . 'a lot of hokum.' The people the clearances are supposed to benefit get left out in the cold, as the rent is too high for them to meet."[74]

In the summer of 1939 the Housing Association of Metropolitan Boston undertook a survey of the 314 former site tenants in an effort to compare systematically the difference between their past and present housing conditions. By the first week of July, when the survey work began, all but twenty-six families had moved off the project site, and BHA files contained new addresses for about 80 percent of those who had relocated. By visiting displaced families in their new homes, four college student volunteers obtained comparable housing conditions for 171 of the 233 relocated families for whom addresses were available. They concluded that three-quarters had moved to "better homes than they formerly occupied" but that more than two-thirds of these were also paying higher rent. In about half of these cases the increase in monthly rent was between three and five dollars, and another one-third faced increases of five to seventeen dollars, thereby confirming the earlier claim that many forced evacuations entailed rent increases of at least 25 percent, in some cases approaching 100 percent. Even more disturb-ing, two-thirds of those who moved into "worse conditions" also faced higher rents, though the amount of increase was usually less substantial. The authors of the survey declined to interpret the effects of such rent increases, since "informa-tion on incomes was not available" and it was "therefore impossible to estimate whether expenditures for housing form a disproportionately large item in the family budgets of this group or whether increases in the cost of shelter will cause sacrifices of other necessities." Conceding that this "forced migration" may have resulted in "difficult budgetary adjustments for many families," the authors also speculated that some families may have previously paid a "relatively small part of their income for rent," and that some of the rent increase was due to temporary "profiteering by landlords" seeking to take advantage of the small market of rent-als available for black occupancy. The report couched its allusion to pervasive housing discrimination against nonwhites in an economist's euphemism—"the inelasticity of supply of homes for these families"—but this could not hide the additional hardships that forced displacement had brought. From the perspective of the Housing Association and the BHA, however, any such hardships paled in significance before one central demonstrable fact: slum clearance had meant that at least 134 of the original 314 site tenants now lived in "better dwellings than those formerly occupied."[75]

Yet even this major conclusion of the study raises questions. The Housing As-sociation measured "improvement" according to a scorecard that rated "neigh-borhood environment, condition of building, repair and size of apartment, equip-ment, amount of light and air, crowding, and privacy." The gains, where apparent at all, were mostly in the realms of improved repair and "better location" of dwellings, with the quality of location judged not by anything the tenants said about convenience, but by some other "objective" criteria. As for the other fac-tors, the report acknowledged that both dwelling size and privacy had, in most cases, been "adversely affected" by the moves, since most families had been forced to choose smaller quarters. On average, there was no improvement in plumbing facilities; for example, more than 25 percent of the displaced house-holds still had no bathtub in their new apartments, and more than 99 percent of households were still without central heat. Of the twelve families in the sample who had previously owned their own homes on the Lenox Street site, the survey proudly noted that all "moved into better quarters," yet a footnote acknowledged that eleven of these former owners were now renters. No effort was made to calculate the meaning of this lost autonomy.[76]

Significantly, only about 10 percent of the displaced families told Housing Association interviewers that they had been "aided by private real estate agents or took advantage of the vacancy listings of the Boston Housing Authority in finding new dwellings." This finding stands in marked contrast to subsequently published BHA claims that its outreach efforts had assisted 90 percent of the families it displaced, and is all the more noteworthy since this particular group of respondents were the ones whose forwarding addresses the Authority had on file, thereby indicating some ongoing relationship. Presumably the others were even less likely to have received much BHA assistance. Similarly, in contrast to the BHA claim that 95 percent of all its "rehoused" tenants were "favorable to public housing" and that 94 percent of Lenox Street site tenants had been "cooperative," the Housing Association survey found that less than half of those displaced from the Lenox Street site "expressed a favorable opinion of the activity of the Housing Authority."[77]

For the Lenox Street project, which experienced considerable trouble in finding eligible black tenants, the BHA agreed that families receiving temporary aid, mother's aid, and old age assistance would be eligible, as would displaced tenants who were WPA employees. This concession, however, did little for the families of the sixty-five noncitizens living on the site, who were not likely to get into public housing unless they married an American. Also barred from consideration for future public housing were both very large families and the seventy-eight households (constituting more than a quarter of the total) that consisted of a single person living alone, since BHA apartments were designed for "occupancy of between two and nine persons."[78] Taken overall, BHA definitions of "family" public housing did not make for a very good fit with the families displaced to build the Lenox Street project.

Of all the households living on the Lenox Street site in 1939, only about one-third included a spousal pair. The majority of households were comprised of single people, unrelated individuals, and multigenerational families. The average age of household adults was forty-seven. Thus very few households resembled the BHA-favored model of hard-working young parents and their offspring. Observing this, the 1939 Housing Association survey noted that "the development of a project in this section has displaced many who will not be eligible to obtain homes in the new buildings." This did not stop at least 154 families from applying for places in the new project, though the application rate from Lenox Street displacees was markedly lower than that prevailing in the other early slum-clearance sites, perhaps—one observer remarked at the time—because "relief families realize that the projects are not for them." Most of the displaced families seem to have reconciled themselves to their fate; about half stated that they liked their new apartment better than the one they had left behind, and more than two-thirds "considered their new locations permanent," a clear indication that they harbored little expectation of gaining entry to public housing. Despite evidence of BHA efforts to accommodate some elderly tenants (presumably together with their grandchildren), police-list data show that only about 12 percent of families displaced in 1939 reappeared as tenants in the new public housing three years later. Although the new project, like the old neighborhood, accommodated predominantly unskilled and semiskilled blacks, the two populations differed markedly in social composition. In contrast to the highly disparate households of the preproject neighborhood, nearly two-thirds of the applicants selected for initial occupancy in the Lenox Street project included married couples, and 80 percent of the female adults described their occupation as "housewife." In contrast to the displaced cohort, the adults in the project were on average thirteen years younger, a clear by-product of the Housing Authority preference for families with children. Even though half of the men displaced from the project site in 1939 and half of those living in the project in 1942 described their employment as "laborer," the two groups bore little social resemblance to each another. Only 40 percent of the old neighborhood's laborers were listed as living with their wives, whereas 94 percent of the laborers living in the project in 1942 seem to have arrived as a dual-spouse socioeconomic package. Moreover, it may well be that many more of those who listed their employment as "laborer" in 1942 actually had stable employment than the laborers of 1939.[79] Clearly, even though the BHA made some greater accommodation for non-nuclear families at this project, the Authority selected its tenants to maximize the presence of traditional family structures.

The local Roxbury newspaper greeted the arrival of the Lenox Street project optimistically, yet subtly conveyed its concerns over the shift of neighborhood identity. In a district once settled by Irish immigrants, many streets named after "Ireland's stalwart men" disappeared under the wrecker's ball; the new divisions of the project would be named after new heroes, such as William Munroe Trotter, founder of the *Boston Guardian,* a black newspaper. The *Gazette* faced up to the prospect of changes in this district with unmistakable ambivalence: "What the make up of the persons will be who come here to live in the project, after it is built with government funds, remains to be seen. They cannot be more loyal to America than the people that have gone before them. We hope they are Americans. Need more be said."[80] With American citizenship already a clearly stated prerequisite for admission to public housing in Massachusetts, the underlying concern was necessarily something else. The nervous anticipation of the new all-black project, so it would seem, had once again united a concern over "American standards" with wariness about the domestic proximity of public neighbors, even as the BHA did all it could to ensure that it served only the most "reputable" of the poor.

THE DIVERSITY OF NEIGHBORHOOD REACTION

Neighborhood reaction to the coming of the early projects seems to have been mixed. Local politicians regarded public housing as a form of community service; displaced homeowners often resisted and sued; construction workers and their unions coveted the jobs; real estate organizations railed about socialism; new project residents were grateful; and those forced out of low-rent neighborhoods and denied access to public housing continued their struggles elsewhere. Most of the debates in neighborhood newspapers and in the Boston City Council turned on issues of equity and expense. Several councilors grumbled that too many non-Bostonians and noncitizens were getting construction jobs; a few others consistently protested that public housing "virtually ignored" the poor and the destitute.[81] Local residents (especially those who were homeowners) charged that the new projects had evicted people from viable neighborhoods, only to replace their homes with extravagant housing they could not afford. Others protested that they were caught in the middle, earning too much for public housing eligibility but not enough to afford suitable alternatives. Indignant homeowners in the South End, whose properties were taken at "slum prices" in anticipation of that district's first project (which was delayed until after the war), charged that the forced moves would "wipe out their savings and confront them with the necessity of adopting a lower standard of living elsewhere."[82] As job-creation measures, these early slum-clearance ventures provided plenty of employment for attorneys.

Though public housing enjoyed widespread support among local politicians, who welcomed the opportunity to bring federal money to their districts, the

South Boston Tribune remained an ardent foe of the very concept of such housing. In June 1939, just a year after Old Harbor Village had opened to great downtown acclaim, the *Tribune*'s editors asserted that "The people of Boston don't want any more federal housing projects." The editors cited the objections of property owners, who "are particularly opposed to the government going into competition with them," as well as the squawks of taxpayers, "who see no reason why they should be called upon to pay, through taxes, the rents of people who live in government-built palaces." As a business proposition, these projects represented the "height of absurdity," since rent payments "hardly equal half of the interest and maintenance costs of the project." If the problem was slum conditions, then the government should simply compel building owners to correct conditions.[83]

The diatribe continued the following week, condemning "the socialistic-communistic scheme to provide practically free rent to the favored few without actually benefiting the families they are supposed to benefit." Equally offensive was the thought that politically well-connected outsiders could reap huge profits: "It seems perfectly reasonable to suspect that somebody stands to make a lot of money out of these housing projects. Somebody is going to sell the government something, either land, lime, cement, stone, patented materials, brick, or some other commodity, a whole lot of it at a big profit to himself and those who stand in with him."[84]

In February 1941, when plans for a third South Boston public housing project were announced by Mayor Maurice J. Tobin (who held office from 1938–1944), the *Tribune* praised Tobin's "integrity" and "ability" but bemoaned his failure to listen to "the practical advice of hard-headed businessmen," and condemned his acquiescence in the "half-baked theories of social experimenters who have a notion that the ills of the poor and unfortunate people can be cured by housing them in palatial apartments, for which the public treasury pays more than half of the actual rent, adding free light, free heating, and free janitorial service and other gratuities." Moreover, the editorial charged that the presence of the projects "makes petty 'chiselers' of the families who have sufficient political drag or influence to get themselves installed in these apartments," a practice which had the additional consequence of concentrating "a powerful political block which, on account of half or two-thirds free rent, may well control any election unfairly." Instead of such "obviously socialistic or communistic" practices, the editorial concluded, it would be better to rely on well-regulated private enterprise, with tenants allowed to remain "self-respecting, liberty loving people who get a real thrill out of paying their own rent, and in not having to be subsidized from the public treasury."[85]

The rival *South Boston Gazette* was less critical of the district's public housing, and newspapers in other Boston neighborhoods provided direct and consistent support. In West Roxbury, located on Boston's southwestern middle-class fringe and well distant from any projects yet proposed, support for the BHA remained effusive. Chairman Breen of the BHA garnered kudos for his civic-mindedness. West Roxbury's *Parkway Transcript* noted that Breen "opened special offices to assist residents . . . whose homes are to be razed to make way for the construction of the housing units, to find new homes." The paper also went out of its way to praise the quality of life at Old Harbor Village, providing considerable detail about a lecture given by one of its residents, sponsored by the Boston League of Women Voters. The "sincere talk of one woman whose life was changed by the housing project," the story concluded, "won many new friends for federal housing." Regarding future public housing construction, the paper approvingly quoted Reverend Thomas R. Reynolds, a member of the BHA Board, who asserted: "If we do not avail ourselves of the money offered by the Federal Government for better housing of the working people, some other place will get it, and you will pay for it. As practical people you should secure a large allotment of these available funds to rehabilitate Boston." For West Roxbury readers, the goal was not to obtain a local project but, rather, to nurture all possible economic gain.[86]

Other local papers, while consistently extolling the benefits of the new housing for those receiving the "honor" of admission, sometimes acknowledged the presence of detractors. *The Roxbury Gazette and South End Advertiser,* for instance, gave full and approving coverage to the coming of public housing to its own neighborhoods, but also cited the disparaging views of Thomas Flynn, executive secretary of the Apartment House Owners' Association. For Flynn, public housing was "a socialistic programme of regimenting the living quarters of the citizens of Boston," with each new project "another fateful step." He decried the way that people were "rudely evicted from their homes and forced to migrate like some lost tribe to other districts," and dubbed the replacement projects "nothing more or less than 'charity wards' which are being foisted upon the citizens of Boston despite the overwhelming protests of the inhabitants of the condemned districts."[87] Here, in the attempt to defend private ownership rights, an opponent attacked public housing for replacing worthy citizens with highly questionable charity cases, even as the preponderance of evidence pointed to the BHA's wish to accomplish precisely the opposite transformation.

In these newspaper accounts, as elsewhere, the cultural complexity of the public housing issue caused critics to interweave many strands of argument, yielding little more than a Gordian knot. Public housing was indiscriminate socialized control yet targeted the "favored few"; it was "practically free" yet failed to reach the most impoverished; it was an affront to business, yet many businesses stood "to make a lot of money." At base, the arguments turned and twisted over questions of fairness and individual initiative, over questions of federal action and local control. Public housing raised hackles because its premise challenged the basic underlying tenets of American liberal democracy. As Alexander Lincoln, the attorney representing Baltramieus Stockus, argued while unsuccessfully attempting to overturn the Massachusetts Housing Authority Law:

> No doubt bad housing conditions are an evil, and so is an insufficiency of food and clothing. All result from the ever present curse of poverty. But it does not follow that it is the function of government to attempt to remedy these evils by the expenditure of public money raised from the people by taxation and by the taking of private property. The doctrine is a dangerous one that everyone is entitled to be well fed, well clothed, and well housed, and if one by reason of misfortune, incompetence or sloth cannot achieve that end by his own efforts the public will pay the bill. No permanent improvement to mankind can result from the attempt by government to remove the necessity of the struggle for existence.[88]

Embedded in those last two sentences is the conflicted three-centuries-long history of public poor relief in America. In this view, the problem with public housing is that it fails to distinguish among types of public neighbors. It is one thing to aid the poor and disabled who have come to penury through no fault of their own, but quite another matter to "remove the necessity of the struggle for existence" from those whose poverty stems only from their own sloth. Though this argument failed to convince the Massachusetts Supreme Judicial Court in the Stockus case of 1939, its underlying principles of classification permeated the public housing program that did prevail, ensuring that any ideologically palatable system of government-sponsored housing would serve only the most worthy.

Public Housing as Neighborhood Design

The classification process that justified the creation of public neighborhoods did so by providing worthy people with a modern living environment intended to demonstrate and enhance their worthiness. While some supporters accepted the public housing project as a by-product of the economic necessity to clear the slums, others emphasized its positive function as a designed community. As a BHA report put it in 1941, "The building of a housing project should not only clear away the greatest number of sub-standard dwellings possible, but it should help to rehabilitate the neighborhood by virtue of its plan, by virtue of its open spaces, landscaping, play areas and juxtaposition of its modern buildings. In size, a project should be sufficient in itself to withstand encroaching blight from all sides."[89] In this view, openness itself was a moral virtue, yet simultaneously the projects were expected to be able to defend themselves as self-sufficient islands. To a great extent, the moral uplift attributed to the site plan—symbolized by letting in more light—was actually a function of the tenant selection process, but supporters of public housing insisted that the form of the project reinforced its social purposes.

Having asserted that its tenants should be "independent and self-supporting," public housing's most ardent backers sought ways to make the architecture and urbanism of public housing consistent with established American domestic traditions and values. USHA administrator Nathan Straus saw public housing as the closest fulfillment of the American Dream for low-income people. Giving each family a private place of its own would foster a sense of "turf" and a sense of belonging. He stressed the need to individualize the entry to each dwelling and to allow each family have its own plot of ground to permit cultivation of a garden; even in public housing, it should be possible for "a man and his family" to "work at the day's end to produce fruit, vegetables, flowers, and above all to produce human contentment." In a 1939 USHA publication, Straus linked possession of a garden to self-reliance and efficiency: "While the extent to which families may be expected to [cultivate a garden] will vary widely with climate, racial background, types and location of project, and management policy, the allocation of open space to the tenants for their own care is in accord with American tradition, and will aid in keeping down the cost of maintenance." In advocating voluntary tenant labor in common areas (including "stairhall cleaning, painting, and litter patrol"), Straus remained clearly in the American tradition of self-help, a tradition harkening back to the idea that land value is linked to the quality of hard work put into improving it.[90]

In a related manner, Straus fought to keep USHA projects at low densities. Accordingly, he advocated building projects on vacant land outside of existing slum areas.[91] Given the legal requirements regarding equivalent elimination and the relatively high land values in many slum areas, building a project on the razed site of an overcrowded slum would tend to redistribute the tenant populations into new buildings at a similar density. Such high-density projects might bring an improvement in safety and sanitation, but would fall well short of the broader goals of designed communities. Straus's strong preference was for "individual houses at the rate of twelve families to the acre," assuring each family "breathing space, play space, room for a small garden," although as a concession to land costs he was willing to settle for "row houses or two- or three-story apartments at a density of twenty-five to sixty families to the acre."[92] In practice, almost every prewar USHA project was built in this latter form.

Straus's ideal of twelve families to the acre came directly from the English Garden City practice espoused by Sir Raymond Unwin, and adapted to America at even lower densities in Clarence Stein and Henry Wright's plan for Radburn, New Jersey. Garden City environments also drew praise from other design-oriented public housing advocates. In a booklet produced for the USHA in 1939, Edith Elmer Wood discussed "Thirty Present-Day Health Requirements for Housing" and concluded that neighborhoods must be protected from the hazards of automobile traffic. Praising the solution of "the Radburn superblock, with its interior park safe for children and other pedestrians," she asserted: "If urban life is to endure, it must find a way to recapture some of the nerve-relaxing security of the countryside."[93] For Straus, Wood, and other major public housing proponents such as Lewis Mumford and Catherine Bauer, the overriding goal of community design entailed a retrograde pursuit of an American pastoral ideal. They saw wholesome housing in terms of self-contained communities that could mimic small-town social interactions.

Chief among the critics of this decentrist view was Harvard's Joseph Hudnut, who argued as early as 1943 that "you can have good housing without eliminating the street." Hudnut, anticipating the later critiques of Jane Jacobs and others, called the street "the most active channel of human intercourse" and the "oldest theatre of democracy," and ridiculed architects and authors who "take it for granted that no one in the lower income-group would live in Chicago if he could help it, that only a lack of funds prevents that group from moving *en masse* to Concord, Massachusetts." Yet while Hudnut and some like-minded others defended "a preference for crowds and streets, for the drama of business, for neon lights and the adventure of shop windows," many public housing designers and planners deliberately sought ways to ignore or subvert urban lifestyles.[94]

Straus's image of public housing was modeled upon the ideal of the New England village. In his advocacy of the town common, Straus charged architects, engineers, and landscape architects with translating this earliest Anglo-American form of community into physical reality. In the USHA booklet *Housing and Recreation,* he argued that "These early American communities, with daily life centering about the village green, can teach us much in the design and planning of public housing projects." In *The Seven Myths of Housing* he elaborated on this notion that the site design of public housing projects could be a repository of cultural memory: "Old and young alike find that the center of life is the open play area of the housing project as it once was the village green. There, children play in safety, mothers sew and gossip as neighborliness is awakened and civic pride grows apace. There, pageants are held. Something new is kindled in the hearts of people who experience for the first time the comfort of clean and livable homes. Perhaps it is rather that something long forgotten is recaptured."[95]

Whatever the power of vestigial collective memories of the colonial town common, asserting the analogy did little to reproduce the social relations that once gave rise to such physical environments. Once again, it was Hudnut who saw through the inadequacy of "open space" designs, even as he accepted much of their environmental determinist logic. "What I miss most of all in your housing schemes is a spire," he wrote in 1943. "You must make room for that symbol, if only to relieve the monotony of your roof lines. Next to the spire I miss the promise of the schoolhouse, the relaxation of the clubhouse and the gymnasium, the invitation of the theatre; and, to tell the truth, I am not long in a project before I begin to miss the barroom also."[96] In Hudnut's view, the housing project failed to provide either the visual and social stimulus of the city, or the spatial and institutional qualities of the old New England town center. As the initial conception of Clarence Perry's mixed-use neighborhood unit gave way to a single-use residential environment lacking either commercial or civic facilities, and as the initial ideas of low-density developments with private entrances and private yards gave way to apartment blocks surrounded by ill-defined "open space," what remained in public housing was the town common without the town.

Boston's municipal leaders touted the projects not only as bastions of fire protection and public health, but also as places of enhanced public safety and as settings for good citizenship. In 1941 G. Lynde Gately, Boston Health Commissioner, credited to public housing what his predecessors had long claimed for model tenements: "Housing projects with their well-planned areas, sanitary and heating facilities, and open spaces allowing plenty of air, light, and sunshine are sure to decrease the work load of the Health and other departments, and result in a healthier, sturdier manhood and womanhood." Emphasizing the difference between the healthy open ball-playing possible on dedicated project courts and the cramped collusion of aimless huddles on dark stoops, the BHA glibly called for a goal of "Hi-Courts Instead of Juvenile Courts" (Fig 3.14). Boston Police Commissioner Joseph F. Timilty argued that the physical environment of the housing projects—no less than the social one—would "result in a healthier and happier growing boyhood and a deterrent to crime." For Timilty, the layout of the projects, with their multiple outdoor recreation areas, offered "the opportunity for supervised play." The key was not just more recreation, but the supposed enhancement of its supervision. Presumably, this supervision was to be largely the function of parents, but Timilty stressed the ways that a "well-planned development" aided police supervision as well, by making patrols "easier and quicker but not less efficient" (Fig. 3.15).[97] The Boston police and the BHA believed that the openness of modern housing project planning deprived crime of its "breeding places." Since a project had "no hiding places and alleys," it seemed the perfect architectural companion to police surveillance by automobile. With long and penetrating vistas visible from the street, and with private vehicles forbidden from passing through, both trespassers and their trespasses could be exposed. In contrast to the multiple dark warrens of potential escape routes in the city's older neighborhoods, the new spatial order of the projects allowed both the Housing Authority and the Police to patrol easily, quickly, and efficiently. As one BHA annual report stated, "There are no back alleys in public housing" (Fig. 3.16).[98] Just as the spacing of buildings let in sunlight during the day, so too the open spaces of the projects let in headlights at night. In contrast to the panopticons of Bentham-inspired penitentiaries where control radiated from an all-seeing center, the surveillance by patrol car of the projects operated from the edges inward. With principal concern directed at protecting the selective collective within while

FIGURE 3.14 "Hi-Courts Instead of Juvenile Courts."

FIGURE 3.15 With no hiding places and alleys, the Mission Hill public housing project *(below)*, unlike its tenement house precursors *(above)*, could be supervised easily from a patrol car.

rebuffing the incursions of outsiders, securing the perimeter made programmatic as well as automotive sense.

The BHA believed that pedestrian-friendly project design promoted public safety. In 1945 the Authority asserted as a "conclusively proved" fact that the streets and ways of its developments were "far safer for pedestrian traffic than the average City street." Noting that "it is no accident that accidents seldom occur on the Development grounds," the Authority extolled the benefits of "careful planning" in superblocks, just as Clarence Perry had done a decade earlier.[99]

In addition to the much-touted health and safety advantages of open spaces, BHA planners and designers also advanced more aesthetic and symbolic interpretations of the legal requirement that prohibited local authorities from building on more than one-third of the area acquired for their developments. Fundamental to the moral redemption of the slums, in this view, was the reinvention of a more rural idyll in the heart of the city. Like the earlier promoters of the parks movement, many public housing advocates initially saw the projects as offering the opportunity to create urban oases—sudden and expansive areas of nurturant green. Although landscape maintenance suffered under the constraints of wartime austerity and under the heels of thousands of eager children, the BHA continued to plant trees. In 1945, the BHA's annual report proclaimed that "if [Joyce] Kilmer's spirit were to visit our Developments, it would find no cause for complaint."[100]

These open spaces were designed, photographed, and promoted by the BHA as programmed vestiges of the lost New England town common. In the elaborate annual reports of the early 1940s, a flagpole towers over the Charlestown project, setting off the distant view of the Bunker Hill Monument; the Mission Hill development is depicted as though its namesake church stands on the edge of its green space; and the girls of Old Harbor dance around a Maypole, giving the lie to criticisms of the "communistic" projects (Figs. 3.17 and 3.18). The consolidated presence of such images, so repeatedly and so pointedly juxtaposed against the malingering backdrops of suffocating tenement street scenes, attest to a persistent longing for an alternative urbanism, one thoroughly rooted in a nostalgia for a small-town past. Public housing was more than an attempt to destroy the slums; it was also a concomitant effort to rebuild the village. Even as the buildings moved toward large brick apartment structures, the landscape attempted to recall a picket-fence enclave where it was both safe and possible to stage a fifty-doll carriage parade. Even at this apex of modernist planning, the tenants of public hous-

FIGURE 3.16a "There are no back alleys in public housing."

FIGURE 3.16b Instead of back alleys, public housing promised parade routes for doll carriages (Old Colony).

FIGURE 3.17 Church and town common, Mission Hill. In contrast to filthy streets lined with three-deckers, the grassy mall of the Mission Hill project seemed to reach out toward its neighboring church.

FIGURE 3.18 May Day in Old Harbor Village: A time to recall dancing, not revolution.

ing demonstrated their unwillingness to abandon their last links to the pastoral ideals of house and garden.

PUBLIC HOUSING AS A MORAL IMPERATIVE

Well into the mid-twentieth century, the official language of the BHA remained rooted in the melodramatic metaphors of nineteenth-century tenement reform. To build public housing was to embark on a spiritual transformation, delivering huddled masses "out of the shadows" and "into the sun" (Fig. 3.19). Official BHA assessments of housing conditions still invoked the polar opposites of darkness and light, filth and cleanliness, despair and hope, and transformation was always wholesale and completely realized. In the mid-1940s the BHA publicly phrased its mission in religious terms: public housing was a "crusade to rid the city of substandard areas" and a "mandate from destiny" to prove that Boston was not "past redemption." Preventing "the octopus of the slum" from reaching out to "defile all of our city" would require both "good morality" and "good business," and the BHA firmly believed it had made a start: "eight clean, shining Developments rising fresh to the sun where once in dreary, dirt-filled dilapidation slum dwellings had shambled in contaminating hopelessness against a gray and somber sky."[101]

Such statements, of course, remained firmly in the category of public relations gestures. Yet public relations, then as now, was always an intrinsic component of the changing mission. The dance of rationales for public housing had to remain a step ahead of skeptics all too willing to put a foot down to quash it, and it is hardly surprising that the Housing Authority prepared its annual reports and other brochures with such enthusiasm, care, and craft. The underlying excitement may always have been grounded in more prosaic matters of economic development that primarily served the needs of the best-off among the city's low-income citizens, but the rhetoric remained tinged with an all-encompassing moralism that promised no less than the redemption of urban society. During the 1940s, even as the rationales for public housing shifted twice—from slum clearance to war housing to veterans' housing—BHA officials believed they had orchestrated a groundswell of public trust. What began in "vociferous antagonism" had yielded first to "silent reproach," then changed from "grudging acquiescence into final open approval."[102] Although such approval remained considerably less than universal, the BHA's public relations task was greatly eased once the cause of public housing became inseparable from the prosecution of World War II.

*Out
of the
Shadows...*

ON YESTERYEAR...

The Authority looked briefly over its shoulder with the passing of the year, and then swiftly went on into the future.

It saw in that one quick backward glance the heartening and everlasting results of nine long, hard pioneering years.

It beheld eight clean, shining Developments rising fresh to the sun where once in dreary, dirt-filled dilapidation slum dwellings had shambled in contaminating hopelessness against a gray and somber sky.

FIGURE 3.19 "Out of the Shadows . . . Into the Sun."

It saw red brick, green grass and sunlight reflecting on shining window panes where once was rotted, cracked, unpainted wood, cinders and dust and glass, grey-filmed. It saw energy and eagerness for the hope of tomorrow where only yesterday drudgery and despair held sway.

It saw vociferous antagonism yield to silent reproach and watched as this changed too from grudging acquiescence into final open approval.

It heard the strident voice of the doubter fade into thunderous silence. It heard the challenge of tomorrow but knew the achievements of the past were good and strong and would endure forever.

It looked back no more but with confident courage went on into tomorrow.

... Into
The Sun

PUBLIC HOUSING AS WAR PRODUCTION (1940–1945)

The slum-reform impetus of Boston's first phase of public housing construction necessarily receded during the exigency of the war years. Yet World War II not only curtailed public housing construction, it also drastically altered its purpose. Instead of a program to put unemployed construction workers back to work building projects to replace slums, the wartime public housing program was premised on providing housing first for "defense workers" and, as U.S. involvement in the hostilities deepened, for "war workers." In this third incarnation, the public purpose of public housing could be measured not by its eradication of public health hazards and unemployment but by its patriotic contribution to the war effort.

HOUSING WAR WORKERS IN BOSTON

In Boston, war workers and the families of servicemen gained priority for admission to all developments, and the projects bristled with victory gardens. Old Harbor Village, Charlestown, Mission Hill, and Lenox Street gave priority to the families of servicemen who were eligible for low-rent housing. The four other projects—Orchard Park, Heath Street, East Boston, and Old Colony—gave priority to war workers and members of the armed forces even if their incomes were above the peacetime ceilings for admission. Not surprisingly, many of the projects soon began running a surplus (most of which, to the frustration of city officials, was then turned back to the federal government).[103]

Old Colony differed from the other three projects initially operated as war housing. Under the terms of the Lanham Act, it was sold to the Federal Works Authority and subsequently transferred to the Federal Public Housing Authority to serve chiefly "in-migrant" war workers—non-Bostonians who came to work at the Quincy shipyards south of the city. The announcement of this revised wartime role came just before Old Colony was due to open for low-income occupancy. Local politicians were outraged to lose the housing resource, even for what they probably expected would be a short period, and were especially upset that it would be used to house people from outside South Boston. Ignoring such protests, BHA Chairman Breen worked out a deal in Washington whereby the federal government agreed to send Boston more than triple the usual "payment in lieu of taxes" during the time Old Colony was occupied by federal workers. Expressing his own satisfaction with this arrangement, Mayor Tobin commented that the resulting 15 percent payment would "yield approximately $43,000 to the city each year, or more revenue than the area yielded when it was occupied by substandard dwellings prior to the taking by the Boston Housing Authority."[104]

The political fallout continued, however. As the project opened for occupancy in early 1941, workers from Quincy's Fore River Shipyard demonstrated little interest in commuting twenty miles each day from South Boston, and federal officials were "forced to throw it open to others." By January 1942 the project was more than 93 percent occupied, and Old Colony's households worked for a wide array of war-related industries. Ironically, fully one-eighth of the project's households had moved there from Quincy, yet needed to commute back to jobs at the Fore River shipyard. The project was dominated by skilled and semiskilled industrial workers, with occupations like shipfitter, electrician, rigger, welder, machinist, metalsmith, boilermaker, pipefitter, galvanizer, ropemaker, and riveter. At the same time, 96 percent of its adult women described themselves as housewives. Thus, through upgrading the occupational classifications of residents and opening the project to domination by non-Bostonians, the shift to federally mandated requirements for tenancy promoted the BHA preference for traditional nuclear families. As a lost resource for low-income South Bostonians, the project remained controversial, yet from the perspective of Boston officials, the Old Colony project continued to generate substantial annual revenues for the city. In 1956, shortly before the project was finally transferred back to the BHA for use as low-rent housing, annual tax revenues to the city reached $231,000, more than half as much as the *total* in-lieu-of-taxes payments for the rest of the other twenty-four BHA projects.[105] It therefore satisfied city government even when it failed to serve many low-income families.

HOUSING FOR WORKING PATRIOTS

As late as 1945, more than a third of applications for BHA housing came from workers in the war production industries, and many of the rest came from the families of the 50,000 servicemen living in Boston. Applications from these servicemen, the BHA acknowledged, were "of course, given special and immediate consideration," and it quickly became possible to view admission to public housing as a reward for ongoing service to one's country.

This infusion of worthy patriots into the upper ranks of the BHA applicant pool set the program on a course reminiscent of the nineteenth-century bounty land disbursements to veterans. In the case of public housing, however, the new frontier was an urban wilderness of cleared slums, and the economic promise was affordable proximity to downtown and waterfront employment. Now worthiness could be externally validated by the National Housing Authority on the basis of "contribution to the war effort." This new means test both altered and clarified the mission of public housing. For the Boston Housing Authority, it was a chance to wrap the controversial program in the mantle of patriotism and to engage in an all-out campaign to convince a still-skeptical public that public housing—far from a socialist conspiracy—should be seen as a significant source of national pride.

The intensity of this sentiment was clearly expressed in the cover collage of the Boston Housing Authority's 1944–45 annual report (Fig. 3.20). Here, in graphic form, public housing was given a place among the major monuments and historic achievements of the city: the Boston Tea Party, Paul Revere's famous ride, the naval exploits of the U.S.S. *Constitution,* the Bunker Hill Memorial, Faneuil Hall, the Old State House, the New State House, and even the swan boats of the Public Garden were juxtaposed with sturdy housing projects, captioned "In Which We Live." Without conscious irony, the BHA asserted its standing in a proud tradition of brick and stone construction, affirmed its role as a guarantor of civil liberties, and cast public housing firmly into the mainstream of the American heritage.

In its prose as well, the BHA not only justified the need for public housing but also championed its contribution to American democracy: "Certain it is, that the providing of good and decent homes for families of men at war is equal in importance to the construction of ships, guns, tanks and planes." The BHA took full credit for enabling the city to avoid "the chaos that might have come in war-busy Boston had not the Authority's eight Developments been erected," and argued that its "war record" alone demonstrated the enduring importance of public housing: "Indeed, if it served no useful purpose beyond that of helping to bring the war to a speedier and more successful conclusion, then it is forever justified."[106]

During the war years, the BHA noted with pride that public housing tenants took on increased responsibility for maintenance of common areas. The 1944–45 annual report praised their willingness to shovel snow from walkways and to step around newly seeded areas of grass. Inside the buildings, too, there was an "almost total absence of conflict between tenants," and the general "good will" was expressed through "the waxing of floors and the washing of windows in common stairhalls, as well as the curtaining of common entrance doors." Even though care for common areas was in those days written into the lease, the BHA maintained that enforcement was nearly trouble-free and that "in fact, most tenants vie with each other in their efforts to out-wax and out-work their neighbors."[107] Despite these effusions, however, some middle-class areas of the city grew increasingly apprehensive about low-rent housing of any kind.

Defending against "Defense Houses"

In 1942, residents of the Woodland Hill section of predominantly Irish West Roxbury banded together in the most widely discussed effort to prevent government-subsidized housing from infiltrating a neighborhood of owned homes. Uniting as the Woodland Hill Improvement Association, the 123 homeowners fought off not a large BHA public housing project but a proposal for twenty-nine FHA-approved single-family "defense houses." Believing that these low-cost houses would undermine their own property values, they registered a protest appeal with the chairman of the War Production Board. In trying to keep the small houses out of their neighborhood, they gained the full support of Senator David Walsh and two Massachusetts congressmen (including John W. McCormack). Mayor Tobin, another supporter, vowed never to issue the necessary building permits. Escorting federal War Production Board officials around the site, Tobin pointed out that the Woodland Hill property was "one of the remotest sections of Boston from the waterfront and war industries," at least seven miles from the nearest defense plant. Since this middle-class neighborhood was clearly "not a defense housing area," the mayor concluded, there was not "the slightest justification for granting priorities for this project." Six weeks later the War Production Board canceled the project, claiming that the decision turned on "the increasingly critical shortage of materials" and the "marginal necessity" of the houses. West Roxbury's *Parkway Transcript* interpreted the decision differently: in contrast to "the official public explanation," the paper noted that the approval of the War Production Board was withdrawn as a result of "sharp complaints by West Roxbury residents and civic leaders."[108]

Juxtaposed with public housing's newfound status as a bastion of patriotism, the Woodland Hill controversy revealed that even patriotism had its limits when it clashed with economic self-interest. To nervous neighbors, government-sponsored housing—however worthy the intended beneficiaries—still meant coping with the economic uncertainties of a public neighborhood. These homeowners, whose own mortgage arrangements also presumably benefited from FHA-deliv-

FIGURE 3.20 Public housing as a civic monument. The BHA's cover collage from its 1944–1945 *Annual Report* juxtaposes the projects (shown on the left and right) with the high points of Boston's architectural and historical past.

In which we live

ered government assistance, may not have been consciously hypocritical. When the BHA tried to move public housing outward into areas that were more disparate (and less desperate), its projects not surprisingly faced an even more uncertain welcome. To maximize receptivity, public housing supporters turned to America's veterans as the most likely source of worthy tenants.

PUBLIC HOUSING AS VETERANS' ASSISTANCE (1946–1954)

World War II put a halt to all new construction of public housing, but not to the demand for more of it. With the war's end, the return of veterans precipitated a massive housing shortage in the private sector as well. The 700,000 units of temporary housing built for war workers could have been used for future public housing, but the Lanham Act—a dramatic indication of the power of the real estate lobby and the underlying homeownership ideal that gave it strength—stipulated that all such housing must, at the conclusion of the war, be either demolished or sold to private individuals. Much of it was of such poor quality that only the first option was possible; in Massachusetts, most units were turned over to the cities and towns in 1950 or 1951, and 90 percent of these were demolished or scheduled for demolition by 1954.[109]

In the meantime, despite the objections of many in the real estate industry, Massachusetts launched its own Veterans' Housing Program in 1948, and the federal government gave public housing yet another new lease on life with passage of the Housing Act of 1949, which authorized construction of 810,000 low-income housing units. The Massachusetts program explicitly targeted its public housing to veterans, while the federal program merely gave veterans a preference, yet both of these legislative breakthroughs sought ways to continue targeting public housing to citizens judged both needy and worthy. Raymond Foley, head of the Truman administration's Housing and Home Finance Agency (within which public housing programs then resided), emphasized during congressional testimony in April 1949 that public housing would still be targeted to those judged capable of paying the rent; it would "not . . . be used as a program of relief."[110] Although the final bill prohibited housing authorities from discriminating against "families, otherwise eligible for admission . . . because their incomes are derived in whole or in part from public assistance," this provision was not closely enforced.[111] With postwar housing initiatives enabling a large percentage of the "submerged middle class" to surface into single-family homes on the urban periphery both in Massachusetts and nationwide, local public housing authorities sought ways to ensure that the next round of tenants remaining in the cities would be as worthy of public subsidy as the first one. At the same time, all supporters of public housing were forced into direct confrontation with a resurgent real estate lobby.

PUBLIC HOUSING VERSUS PRIVATE HOMES

After the war as before, low-rent public housing remained subordinate to other federal efforts to promote and extend homeownership opportunities to middle-income Americans. During the war, while public housing advocacy groups such as the National Public Housing Conference geared up for the five-year fight that would culminate in passage of the 1949 Housing Act,[112] many periodicals gave advance promotion to the surge in private construction that would occur as soon as "G.I. Joe" returned and the ban was lifted on private use of construction materials. *Fortune*'s nationwide survey of December 1943 was the most widely cited account of the impending housing boom. When asked "What one or two things will you buy when peacetime comes?" 13.3 percent of the respondents answered, "a home." Subdivided by economic groups, the survey estimated that demand would be greatest among those of lower incomes (and greatest of all among "Negroes," whom the survey tabulation listed separately):

Upper class	6.8%
Upper middle class	13.4%
Lower middle class	13.4%
Lower class	14.0%
Negro	16.2%

Fortune estimated this "first choice" demand to be more than six times greater than in 1941, itself a fairly prosperous year. A special report issued in 1946 by *Better Homes and Gardens* sounded the call to buy more directly: "Two new home-building booms are coming. In the first, thousands of new homes will be built to meet the present crisis in lack of housing. In the second, millions of families will build the homes which they've dreamed and planned for years. The two will merge as an all-time high in new-home construction. This much is inevitable." Though the periodical press certainly did not invent the housing shortage, it did much to articulate a strategy for alleviating it. In Truman's goal of "A decent home and a suitable living environment for every American family," public housing was simply a small part of a more comprehensive housing program premised on massive but nonstigmatized government subsidies to support private housing ownership for the middle class.[113]

The Housing Act of 1949, known on the congressional battleground as the Taft-Ellender-Wagner bill, drew the full and wrathful attention of the real estate interests both before its passage and for many years afterward. In attacking the bill, critics consistently referred to it as a piece of public housing legislation, though as Nathan Straus pointed out at the time, "it would provide nine times as many private as public housing units." Morton Fitch, president of the National Association of Real Estate Boards (NAREB), insisted that public housing was "the cutting edge of the Communist front," and his successor, T. H. Maenner—who was president at the time the 1949 Housing Act passed—declared that the bill was "pure socialism" and a step toward the nationalization of all housing. "Surely," he argued, "if there is one thing clear about socialism, it is that it has never gained ascendance in one full blow. It always moves in bit by bit, eating away one area of free effort at a time until finally the people wake up and find that everything is controlled at a central political headquarters."[114]

Adept at the art of rhetorical excess, NAREB's leaders fancied themselves as directing the outcome of congressional housing proposals. The Association's newsletters were an essential component of the lobby against public housing. They disseminated the propaganda to the local boards, which in turn organized opposition to public housing at the level of the congressional district, where they believed they could best influence each vote. Through nationwide radio appeals, newspaper advertisements, canned editorials, pamphlets, speeches, and mass letter-writing and telephone appeals to individual members of Congress, the real estate lobby launched an all-out campaign to thwart public housing, and congressional committees gave them ample floor time during key debates. On May 5, 1949, as the congressional vote on the bill drew near, the Public Relations Department of the National Association of Home Builders (NAHB) sent a memorandum to all local affiliates. The memo was accompanied by four prepared editorials, radio scripts, fact sheets, and an advertisement warning about the high costs of the program to taxpayers. It concluded with a call to "Accuse your housing authority of squandering funds, of being inefficient and failing to live up to promise. Deride failure to clear slums and to house the poor." Other real estate lobbyists suggested that their supporters should "expose public housing" by photographing television aerials in projects—"when ordinary citizens without television see that people being publicly supported have television, it will make them mad, and when they get mad you will have them on your side." In June Truman himself issued a scathing criticism of the lobby and its tactics. "I do not recall ever having witnessed a more deliberate campaign of misrepresentation and distortion against legislation of such crucial importance to the public welfare," the president complained. "These attempts to mislead and frighten the public and their representatives in the Congress—these false claims designed to prejudice some groups of the people against others—these malicious and willful appeals to ignorance and selfishness—are examples of selfish propaganda at its worst."[115] A year later, the U.S. House Select Committee on Lobbying Activities held hearings to investigate the realtors' tactics.

Despite the use of such pervasive and often outlandish methods, Harry Bredemeier has argued that the economic interests of NAREB and NAHB were not at all threatened by the Housing Act of 1949. The true basis for the sustained vehemence of their opposition was more symbolic than economic: they wished to preserve a picture of themselves as "*the* suppliers of the nation's homes." The disproportionate expenditure of time and rhetorical energy spent fighting public housing seems best explained as part of a broader effort of the business community to regain a more secure role after the blows of the Depression. The real estate lobby was concerned less with actual fears about socialist encroachment in public housing than with its own viability as an industry (or collection of industries) in a post–laissez-faire economy. The attack upon public housing was simply the most expedient way of expressing its fears. The entire housing industry, both public and private, had become increasingly regulated by government intervention, whether through mortgage and loan guarantees or through direct subsidy. An industry that had sought to cultivate in its clients the values of self-reliance and individual initiative found that, as an industry, it lacked those qualities itself. The implication of all the new government programs was clear and unpalatable: the crippled housing industry required a permanent governmental crutch to prevent another fall. The inevitable result was ambivalence toward government programs, even those quite supportive of private interests. Consequently, the housing industry labeled most governmental programs as "aids to private enterprise," singling out only public housing as a program of "bureaucratic interference."[116]

With housing and ideology resolutely linked, a Cold War mentality colored the attack on public housing, even as the postwar version of such housing moved into ever greater partnership with private industry. Advocacy of the individually owned home became part of a crusade against the spread of communism, even as public housing advocates and home builders alike argued for a system grounded in traditional Jeffersonian assumptions. Public housing's proponents had long emphasized the necessity for a decentralized program, with a minimum of federal control. Public housing was regarded as a way station along the road to private ownership, not as a permanent alternative to private housing. To demonstrate this point, the National Association of Housing Officials compiled data from the late 1940s showing that up to 90 percent of those who had been forced to vacate public housing because of excess income had moved on to homeownership.[117]

In 1938 Nathan Straus had written that "in an incredibly short time, the charges that public housing is 'communistic' or 'class legislation' or 'extravagant' will sound strangely antiquated . . . We shall come to look upon slum destruction and rehousing of slum dwellers as a great national good—as a war on the very source of disease and crime and discontent—as a campaign for implanting the American standard in every American home." Six years later, Straus noted:

> public housing throughout every phase of its production is actually private business . . . The sites are appraised by qualified private appraisers. The buildings are designed by private architectural firms. The projects are constructed by private building contractors chosen on a competitive bid basis. The labor employed works under normal conditions of private business . . . The products of mine, mill, and factory all go into the construction of a housing project. Iron mines and asbestos mines, copper smelters and brick kilns, the lumber camp in the forest and the mill in the town experience increased demand for their products. The makers of bathroom fixtures and of plumbing equipment, of heating and lighting apparatus, the producers of coal, oil, gas, and electricity find that public housing opens up new markets.

Even after completion of the project, Straus argued, the stimulus to private industry continued: "Not only do new stores, new food markets, new motion picture theaters, new garages spring up in the vicinity of a public housing project, but a boom in private construction is usually touched off by the ground-breaking ceremonies."[118] Despite such assurances, the Taft-Ellender-Wagner bill barely survived a 209–204 vote that would have completely eliminated its provisions for public housing.

The interests of the private realtors were well guarded in the Housing Act of

1949, especially by the requirement of a 20 percent gap "between the upper rental limits for admission to the proposed low-rent housing and the lowest rents at which private enterprise unaided by public subsidy is providing . . . a substantial supply of decent, safe, and sanitary housing." Even so, for the next decade the NAHB, NAREB, and other groups did their best to thwart public housing construction locally. The NAHB identified key junctures at which opponents could attempt sabotage: "If you know these steps—if you watch for them—if you take action when they are about to occur—you will have an excellent chance to stop socialized public housing projects in their inception . . . Hit the public housing program in your city at each of these steps."[119]

In Boston, where a few projects were indeed altered or forestalled, the next several years nonetheless marked the high point of the BHA's construction efforts.

HOUSES AND HOUSING FOR BOSTON'S VETERANS

After the war, the Boston Housing Authority, the Massachusetts legislature, and the U.S. Congress sought to ensure that public housing would continue to serve worthy citizens while also supporting the local construction industry. At a time of intense housing shortage when rental vacancies sometimes fell below 1 percent, local officials sought all possible ways to assist returning veterans and their families. In 1946 a resurgent Mayor Curley, in his role as chairman of the Veterans' Emergency Housing Committee, established a local referral service to make sure that veterans received first news of all new rental vacancies. The BHA took over management of 765 temporary dwelling units built for war workers under the Lanham Act and used these structures as temporary housing for veterans. The Massachusetts legislature amended the state's Housing Authority Law to expand its local housing authorities into designated redevelopment agencies. This move was intended to permit the earliest possible use of anticipated federal funds for such purposes, purposes that would eventually alter the nature and intent of government involvement in city renewal and urban housing in fundamental ways.

While federal legislation languished, however, the state established its own public housing admissions preferences for the families of servicemen and veterans and moved forward on two new veterans' housing programs of its own. The first, known as the City-State Program, was implemented under Chapter 372 of the Acts of 1946 and provided homes for "moderate-income" white veterans and their families. In contrast to previous public housing practice, which at least claimed to serve only those of lowest incomes, this program explicitly targeted veterans whose incomes "were immediately above that category," and demonstrated that "separate homes are possible at higher rents." Intended as a "stop-gap" measure to be implemented over six years (later extended to eight), the City-State program built 1,306 homes on vacant land in Boston. Three-quarters of these were one- and two-family houses, and all were for rental to veterans with an option to buy; the program required that the houses be sold after five years, thereby returning them to private ownership and full taxation.[120]

In addition to this program, which clearly supported the broader homeownership ideology, Chapter 200 of the Massachusetts legislature's Acts and Resolves of 1948 established a major program of new public housing projects for veterans with lower incomes. Patterned after federal public housing legislation, it provided for state guarantees of local housing authority credit, and for annual contributions by the state—totaling not more than 2.5 percent of development costs—to subsidize the rents. At the same time, it differed from the federal program in that the Massachusetts Veterans' Housing program required no equivalent elimination of substandard areas. Rather than a slum-clearance program, this incarnation of public housing was clearly intended as a reward system for veterans. As a special commission established by the Massachusetts legislature in 1947 to review the subject concluded, there were at least 50,000 families of veterans "in desperate need of housing," and the "Commonwealth of Massachusetts has a positive obligation to such veterans." Taking note of the past willingness to provide housing for war workers, the commission argued that the government "should be equally ready to take care of the veteran who responded to the call of his government" and that such people should be "now entitled to every possible assistance within the command of the State to provide. This is no time for short memories." Among such veterans, the commission focused on the majority who could not yet afford to "purchase a home at a cost of $10,000 or more," and proposed several ways to assist them.[121] The Chapter 200 program emerged substantially unaltered from the commission's recommendations and passed both houses in 1948.[122] Legislator John F. Collins made clear that the success of the program depended on the willingness of large private banks and insurance companies to play a "vigorous part in combating the dire housing shortage." Anticipating the massive public-private building programs he would help lead while mayor of Boston during the 1960s, Collins made clear that his reliance on government assistance was secondary to his "faith in the ability of private capital to solve our economic needs."[123]

The Chapter 200 program was a major commitment of state resources to public housing, and was passed with some reluctance. The Boston Municipal Research Bureau joined many other fiscally conservative groups who questioned any legislation that might further erode the city's tax base. In 1944, following a long Depression-era decline in Boston's aggregate real estate assessments, a slide exacerbated by increased numbers of tax-exempt properties, the bureau had warned that public housing forced the city into an annual tax loss of about $1 million, and that an "additional loss of $164,000 would be incurred for each thousand families rehoused under an expanded program." To carry out the program "much beyond existing limits" (meaning the first eight projects) would "certainly necessitate violent readjustment in the use and taxable valuation of land in Boston." Emphasizing the emergency nature of the housing shortage, the state legislation tried to appease the real estate industry by stipulating that if the board of a local housing authority should determine, any time after 1953, that "an acute housing shortage no longer exists," that board was empowered to sell off the projects, provided that it received fair market value and "not less than the total of the outstanding obligations of the housing authority with respect to such project." At the same time, many in the legislature also felt that public housing for veterans was properly a federal responsibility, and the act included a provision stipulating that if the federal government should pass its own legislation for this purpose, the local Massachusetts housing authorities should "immediately enter into negotiation with the federal government to arrange for federal financial assistance . . . and for the termination, in whole or in part, of state financial assistance."[124] With these two escape clauses, the Massachusetts Veterans' Housing program moved forward.

Intended as a statewide program, about one-quarter of the initial $200 million guarantee of local bond issues by the state was earmarked for the City of Boston, though intrastate competition was intense. Within forty-eight hours after the Veterans' Housing Act was signed by Governor Robert Bradford, the State Board of Housing received written requests involving one-third of all available credit allocations.[125]

PUBLIC NEIGHBORHOODS ON VACANT LAND

Whereas all prewar Boston public housing except Old Harbor Village was built on slum-clearance sites rather than on vacant land, thirteen of the seventeen large state and federal projects built between 1949 and 1954 were built on city-owned or city-acquired land that was mostly or entirely vacant. Two others, in South Boston and in the South End, were built on sites that had been cleared before the war and remained empty.[126] Thus, only two postwar project sites involved substantial postwar clearance, and even these did not run the risk of targeting new neighborhoods. Instead, they were built immediately adjacent to the Mission Hill and Heath Street projects and were intended to function as their extensions. Though many communitarian-minded housing activists had long argued in favor of building on vacant land as a way to steer public housing construction toward peripheral areas where it could be built according to garden city principles, the sources for the BHA shift were rooted in politics and practicality.

In January 1946 the BHA formally abandoned what John A. Carroll, the new chairman of the BHA Board, called its "long established policy of building new developments only in areas that had been previously cleared of sub-standard dwellings." Squeezed by the tight rental market of the immediate postwar period, the Authority believed that it would prove impossible to find sufficient available vacancies to rehouse the large number of people expected to be displaced if further slum-clearance projects were to go forward. Noting that the Boston papers were running advertisements from people offering substantial rewards for procurement of an apartment, Carroll claimed that the BHA undertook the policy shift "with extreme reluctance," since "the very essence of the public housing program was the elimination of sub-standard areas." In particular, he lamented that this policy change would effectively prevent the Authority from razing parts of the North and West Ends. What he did not say was that the move away from slum clearance also opened up future possibilities for redeveloping such central city areas for more lucrative uses than public housing. In the meantime, the BHA Chairman observed that the acute housing shortage effectively split the housing problem into two pieces, one being the established BHA mission to provide long-term permanent housing and the other prompted by the immediate need to supply temporary housing for veterans and their families.[127]

In 1946 this meant emphasizing programs to convert Lanham Act housing into temporary postwar accommodation, while pressing for new legislation. Soon afterward, however, the "split" in the housing program began to heal, carefully drawn together by state and federal programs that sought to serve veterans by whatever methods would provide permanent housing most expediently.

In the three years following the end of the war, 25,000 families applied to the

Boston Housing Authority for tenancy in its developments. This, in turn, created an "untenable" problem for members of the Boston City Council, who were deluged with requests to assist constituents. BHA officials quietly admitted that they were allowing a huge pool of pending applications to build up as a way to show Washington that the city needed more funds for housing, but this did not help councilors: "When we inquire . . . into the status of cases, we are told that the walls are not made of rubber, that each of these developments can accommodate just so many and no more, although the applicant is led to believe . . . that in a reasonably short time he will be among the elect." These councilors wanted the BHA to cease collecting applications from "people they know they cannot house," since this would "alleviate a bad condition for us and for them." Others worried that "the boys coming back" would be outraged if they were unable even to file an application. The public housing shortage also prompted renewed complaints against the prevalence of high-salaried "outsiders" who had moved to Boston as war workers, but lingered on in public housing at war's end. Several councilors used language reminiscent of the earliest settlement laws, claiming that these people would become a public charge once "we get into unfortunate times" and they "have to go on welfare." They wished to "throw out" those migrants who came "to usurp and pirate a splendid development" and were "living on the fat of the land of Boston" while "keeping the Boston veteran serviceman out of a home, and driving him into a packing case." Thomas Linehan, a councilor who had served on the BHA board for a year, was more conciliatory: "If there is no available housing" in the greater Boston area, "the Boston Housing Authority has not got the power to move people out, for the sole reason that they come from Oskaloosa, or Kansas."[128] In October 1948 the BHA ceased taking new applications entirely until more new housing could be built and made available.[129]

While federal legislation to meet this housing shortage remained under debate, Massachusetts pressed ahead on its own. From the state's perspective, under Chapter 200 legislation the mandate was to serve veterans, not to clear slums, and the ten postwar state-sponsored public neighborhoods moved forward quickly on this premise.[130]

STATE HOUSING FOR WORTHY VETERANS

The state's first two developments in Boston built under Chapter 200 opened in 1949, and the eight others were well into the planning stages before passage of the

Housing Act of 1949. First to open was South Boston's third public housing project, West Broadway, intended for occupancy by white veterans and their families. Paradoxically, this 972-unit public neighborhood was also the longest in gestation. Contemplated since an abortive limited-dividend scheme in 1934, the site (Tract M-3) was cleared in 1941 in anticipation of its inclusion in the federal program. After the war the project was revived under the state's Chapter 200 program. As a result of this complex history, West Broadway was the only state-financed development built on slum-clearance land.

The other development to open in 1949 was the state's smallest, the 72-unit Camden Street project. Located on Boston School Committee land adjacent to the federal Lenox Street project, this too was targeted for exclusively black occupancy. In 1950, Boston's nonwhites still comprised only 5 percent of the population, and the Massachusetts Veterans' Housing Program saw no reason to do more than build a system that was both separate and equal to the black proportion of the city's population. It was not long before civil rights advocates provided documentation to show that even this modest level of commitment had not been sustained.

The rest of the Chapter 200 program reached out into highly dispersed white neighborhoods. In 1950 and 1951 the BHA completed 258-unit Faneuil and 648-unit Commonwealth in the city's Allston-Brighton district, a northwestern arm that cradled the more affluent Brookline. Soon afterward, the BHA constructed state-financed homes for veterans in other outlying areas: 202 units in Hyde Park's Fairmount at the city's extreme southern border and 354 units in East Boston's Orient Heights, located on several tax-foreclosed parcels near the city's northernmost point. To the west, the BHA constructed 288 apartments at Archdale in Roslindale, and 132 at South Street in Jamaica Plain. Finally, in the southeast, Chapter 200 gathered together veterans at Mattapan's 251-unit Gallivan Boulevard project and Dorchester's 504-unit complex at Franklin Field. Thus, the state component of the BHA's family public housing program formed its outermost ring (Figs. 3.21 and 3.22).

In building the state-sponsored Veterans' Housing projects, the BHA had no corresponding mandate to eliminate substandard housing and so, it claimed, could instead select its sites on the basis of the quality of neighborhood amenities. The State Housing Board asked local authorities to consider such factors as the presence of convenient and affordable public transportation located between

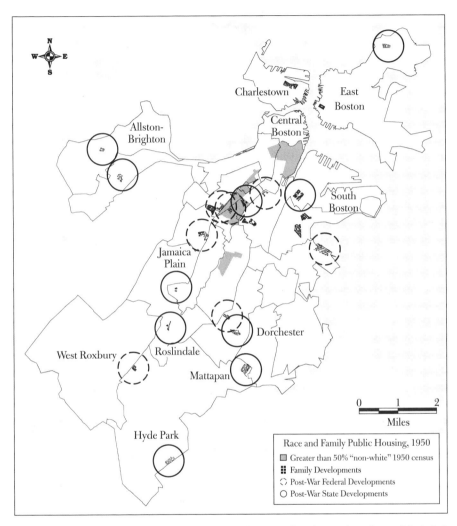

FIGURE 3.21 Many of Boston's ten state-sponsored postwar housing projects (see solid circles) were located in peripheral areas, as were some of the seven postwar federal developments (see dotted circles). Of the twenty-five family projects completed by 1954, all but the Lenox Street, Camden Street, and Whittier Street projects (intended for black occupancy) were located in white-majority neighborhoods.

WEST BROADWAY
Boston 200-1 (1949)

CAMDEN STREET
Boston 200-2 (1949)

COMMONWEALTH
Boston 200-3 (1951)

FANEUIL STREET
Boston 200-4 (1950)

FAIRMOUNT
Boston 200-5 (1951)

ARCHDALE ROAD
Boston 200-7 (1951)

ORIENT HEIGHTS
Boston 200-8 (1952)

GALLIVAN BOULEVARD
Boston 200-10 (1953)

SOUTH STREET
Boston 200-12 (1953)

FRANKLIN FIELD
Boston 200-11 (1954)

FIGURE 3.22 Site diagrams of the ten "Chapter 200" housing projects for Massachusetts veterans.

one quarter and three-quarters of a mile from the site; the availability of employment "within safe walking distance" and "within 1/2 hour travel time by public transportation"; the presence of a "neighborhood shopping center" within one quarter to half a mile; and the availability of schools, recreation areas, churches, theaters, libraries, and clinics "within easy reach." With careful site selection, it would be possible to make use of preexisting "community facilities."[131] The state's charge, in short, was to find ways to build "neighborhood units" while paying only for their residential components.

In general, the new state program followed well-established standards for site design, insisting that interior streets "must be minimized or completely eliminated" in order to save service and utilities costs, and asking local authorities to limit building coverage to 20 percent of the site's ground area. As built, the ten Boston state-aided developments averaged 22 percent lot coverage (compared to 27 percent in the city's federally aided projects), ranging from 11 percent to 30 percent depending on the site and building type. In its 1948 *Primer for Use of Local Housing Authorities,* the State Housing Board did not mandate any particular building type but touted the "advantages of the row house" over apartment buildings. Citing both cost considerations and aesthetic issues, the board stressed that "row houses give the privacy and livability of a single family home" and would "provide the tenants front and back yards," highly desirable since "families with children require . . . access to a yard" and nearly all families admitted were expected to have children.[132] Ideal public housing for Massachusetts veterans was supposed to resemble private single-family housing; the call for "open space" was in the service of a familiar social agenda. In the State Housing Board's 1948 booklet *Massachusetts Housing for Veterans,* the rendering of the kind of "group housing" possible under Chapter 200 resembled nothing so much as a large neocolonial single-family home (Fig. 3.23). As built in Boston, however, most of the state housing projects were visually indistinguishable from their federal counterparts—not rowhouses or single-family homes but three-story brick walk-up apartment buildings with shared entryways and stairwells. The lower land acquisition costs of some of the outlying sites in the state program did sometimes encourage a markedly lower density than contemporaneous federal projects: Orient Heights, Franklin Field, and South Street all averaged twenty to twenty-five units per acre, and both Fairmount and Gallivan Boulevard actually met the vaunted twelve units-per-acre ideal. The other five Chapter 200 projects approximated the forty- to fifty-five-unit-per-acre density of most of Boston's federally aided developments.

BOSTON'S FEDERAL DEVELOPMENTS AFTER 1949

The five-year flurry of large project construction in the state-aided program was matched almost exactly by a parallel spate under the terms of federal legislation. Of the 8,000 new family public housing units built in Boston from 1949 to 1954, approximately half were built under the federal program and half under the auspices of the state's Veterans' Housing Program. Though federal legislation still encouraged equivalent elimination of substandard areas, it allowed such measures to be delayed. In making decisions about where to build, the BHA took full advantage of this new flexibility. In 1952 BHA officials affirmed that "as a general policy the Authority is committed to slum clearance, with the greater portion of equivalent elimination being on site." However, the BHA Board acknowledged that "some developments building or being planned under the Housing Act of 1949 are on vacant sites," a decision it said was based on "relocation and land cost problems."[133] In postwar Boston, to build rapidly meant seeking out the least expensive and least contentious sites (Fig. 3.24).

GROUP HOUSING GIVES LOWEST RENT

FIGURE 3.23 This prototypical "group housing," proposed by the Massachusetts State Housing Board, was rendered to resemble a pair of neo-colonial detached single-family houses, though the site plan more accurately suggests the multifamily superblock arrangement that actually prevailed.

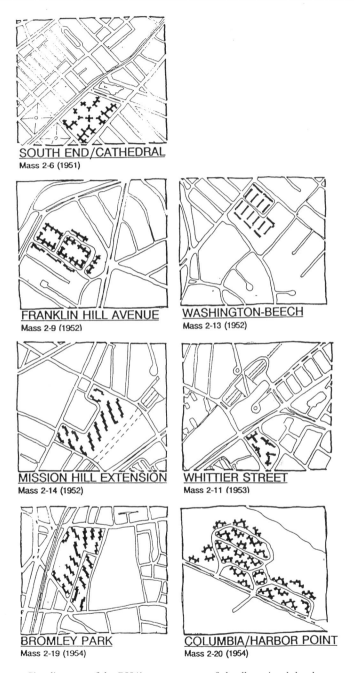

SOUTH END/CATHEDRAL
Mass 2-6 (1951)

FRANKLIN HILL AVENUE
Mass 2-9 (1952)

WASHINGTON-BEECH
Mass 2-13 (1952)

MISSION HILL EXTENSION
Mass 2-14 (1952)

WHITTIER STREET
Mass 2-11 (1953)

BROMLEY PARK
Mass 2-19 (1954)

COLUMBIA/HARBOR POINT
Mass 2-20 (1954)

FIGURE 3.24 Site diagrams of the BHA's seven postwar federally assisted developments.

The federal share of the 1949–1954 Boston public housing surge took the form of seven projects. Five combined lowrise and midrise buildings, and two retained the BHA's characteristic three-story walk-up pattern. Two of the mixed, mostly midrise projects were additions to existing slum-clearance developments: Bromley Park, a 732-unit extension to the Heath Street project (which was eventually administratively fused into the complex known as Bromley-Heath); and the 588-unit Mission Hill Extension. Very close to Mission Hill Extension, the BHA built Roxbury's similarly configured 200-unit Whittier Street project. These three midrise developments provided a new way for the BHA to channel black public housing applicants into increasingly black neighborhoods without disrupting racial occupancy patterns in adjacent white developments. By 1956, 115 nonwhite families had moved into Bromley Park, while only six such families lived next to them in Heath Street; 222 more nonwhite households had moved into Mission Hill Extension, while Mission Hill Main remained exclusively white.[134] Thus, the term "extension" was little more than a euphemism for segregation. Nor was the housing separate but equal: the postwar BHA did extend more public housing offers to black families, but disproportionately these placements required them to live in elevator highrises.

Also centrally located and targeted for black occupancy was a fourth new federal project, known as Cathedral. Like the West Broadway project in South Boston, this site in the South End had been disruptively cleared before the war only to lie fallow for nearly a decade. Mayor Curley compared the interim result to an "ugly shell-hole in a bomb-wrecked European city," and deplored the treatment of former site tenants who "were simply turned out into the streets" by a previous mayoral administration. Within a week after passage of the Housing Act of 1949, the mayor (who had been restored to his office after a stint in federal prison) applied for federal funds to build Cathedral.[135] Though the 508-unit project was named after its adjacent church, its distinctive cruciform thirteen-story central tower, flanked by progressively lower structures toward the periphery, led further (if rather ironic) credence to the choice of name.

The other three federal projects were built on vacant land in outlying areas: Roslindale's 274-unit Washington-Beech project in the far southwest; Dorchester's 375-unit Franklin Hill development, constructed nearly opposite the state-sponsored Franklin Field project; and, last and largest, the massive 1,504-unit Columbia Point project. Built on thirty-five acres of a then-desolate Dorchester peninsula, on a site adjacent to a sewage pumping station and an incinerator for the disposal of commercial waste, Columbia Point was the biggest housing project constructed in New England and would soon become its most notorious.

THE PROJECT STOPS HERE

When the postwar BHA building program first got underway, local politicians in peripheral white neighborhoods still actively campaigned to get housing projects onto vacant sites in their areas, though the rumbles of dissent were not far off. In 1949 Representative Frederick C. Hailer Jr. met with the State Housing Board chair and wrote to the BHA Board to push for two sites in his Jamaica Plain/ Roslindale district, noting that "our ward has not had a housing project" and that he had "talked to several people who own houses in the area and they are extremely favorable to such a worthy project." Two years later, Hailer's efforts paid off and Roslindale's Archdale project was ready for occupancy. Similarly, City Councilor Philip A. Tracy of Jamaica Plain pledged a "fight to have a veterans housing project built in this section" and, during a groundbreaking ceremony, took full credit for convincing the City Council and BHA Board to site South Street, his ward's first housing development.[136]

In many cases, local lawmakers worked hard to attract new public housing to their districts, but immediate neighbors raised objections. With sites now selected to minimize the need for clearance of existing structures, most objections came from abutters concerned about future residential property values. Of the twenty-five successfully completed BHA family public housing projects, only one, the all-white Fairmount veterans project, was located in area that was zoned "residential" on all sides. Here, to appease local sentiment and blend more with the neighborhood, instead of the usual red-brick walk-ups, the BHA built two-story duplex houses and even used wood framing. Everywhere else the residential projects abutted nonresidential uses, at least on one side. In nine cases, these public neighborhoods were entirely surrounded by nonresidential areas.

Whereas the prewar BHA sought ways to protect its slum-clearance projects from the threat of encroaching blight, now it was the neighbors who attempted to protect themselves from the threat of an encroaching BHA. Before the war the BHA repeatedly tried to upgrade the zoning of project peripheries, but after the war the Authority turned to the Board of Zoning Adjustment chiefly to secure changes necessary to build large multifamily housing projects in zones that would not otherwise have permitted them. At Whittier Street and Bromley Park, the

BHA obtained zoning variances to build midrise structures that went above the locally zoned sixty-five-foot height limit. To obtain increased height limits at Faneuil and Cathedral, the Authority convinced the Zoning Board to eliminate certain existing *residential* zoning designations, and to classify both sites as entirely and contiguously "local business zones." The business designation increased height limit on the South End site to 155 feet, and gave the Authority the flexibility to construct the Cathedral tower, thereby increasing the project's residential density to cover the more expensive site-development costs.[137] By the time of this second major incarnation of public neighborhood construction, then, BHA concerns about zoning had become wholly internalized within the projects.

Although the BHA was successful in the majority of its efforts to site public housing, its track record was far from perfect. Many areas failed to be developed or redeveloped as public housing for a variety of reasons. Some fell short on technical grounds, found to require excessive fill or extensive use of pilings. In other cases, technical reasons seem to have been excuses to withdraw from an area seen by competing real estate interests as likely to attract private development. Twice the BHA was dissuaded by the prospect of long delays in assembling necessary parcels because of existing religious and school use of desired property. Two vacant sites in Dorchester approved by the BHA were rejected by federal officials, though one of these was eventually accepted in revised form. Closer to downtown—despite multiple attempts and plans for small projects—high acquisition costs kept proposed projects from going forward on Salem Street and Hanover Street in the North End, on Dover Street in the South End, and on Leverett Street in the West End (once home to the early nineteenth-century almshouse, and a street that eventually would be swept away by developments of a decidedly more upscale nature). Finally, five projects on vacant land in outlying areas were stalled at various stages by the BHA's inability to obtain necessary zoning changes.

In one hard-fought case in Jamaica Plain, the BHA made the mistake of challenging not only local homeowners, but also park lovers and Harvard University attorneys. Seeking to take by eminent domain a section of the Harvard-owned Arnold Arboretum and the adjacent city-owned Joyce Kilmer Park, the BHA first attempted to secure a change of zoning from single-family residential to "multiple residence, forty feet high." Predictably, the response from all relevant parties caused this petition to be dismissed.[138] Despite earlier BHA published assurances to the contrary, these Kilmer neighbors did not think projects so lovely as a tree.

In what was perceived as another challenge to homeowners in outlying residential districts, the BHA attempted to build three-story multifamily apartment buildings in a middle-class section of Brighton, very close to the border of affluent Chestnut Hill. This time, though the Zoning Board did grant a necessary zoning change, nearby property owners took the Authority to court and won their appeal.[139]

The few planned projects that were permanently stalled tended to be smaller ventures, and never seriously threatened the ability of the BHA to carry out its construction program. What the various challenges accomplished was to make the BHA more careful about the sites it proposed for development. This meant not only keeping projects out of certain types of areas, but also steering some of them toward less than optimal sites.

PUBLIC NEIGHBORHOODS AND THE NEIGHBORHOODS BEYOND THEM

Despite the high-minded rhetoric about provision of proximate services to residents, the twenty-five projects provided these services very unevenly. In some cases, the effort to find vacant land yielded sites that were not only peripheral but utterly detached. In 1957, a graduate student who mapped all retail facilities near Boston public housing projects found that the Orient Heights development— home to more than 1,000 people—lacked even a single store within a quarter-mile of its periphery, and that the distance was further accentuated by steep topography. Columbia Point arguably marked an even more extreme case; the city's largest project was served by the smallest number of nearby amenities. In 1957, three years after the project opened, there were only three retail facilities within a short walk of the edge of the massive project, and families generally had to take a taxi to get to the nearest supermarket; among 7,000 project tenants, there were only about 200 cars.[140]

Columbia Point's isolation was exceptional, however: in 1957, twenty-one of twenty-five projects had a supermarket within 600 feet of a project boundary, a far better level of service than that prevailing forty years later. Most projects, especially those built on the slum-clearance sites closer to the city center, benefited from extremely dense concentrations of retail facilities at close range. At one extreme, the Orchard Park development, adjacent to bustling Dudley Square, had

153 retail establishments within 600 feet of its edges in 1957. Included among these were thirty-three places to buy food, fourteen restaurants, fifteen drinking places, five drug stores, twenty-four clothing stores, six barbers and two beauty parlors, four laundries, eight general merchandise stores, ten places to purchase furniture or appliances, four shops selling used items, and eighteen repair shops. More ominously, there were also forty-nine vacant stores.[141]

In its publications the BHA always stressed the availability of neighborhood services. Yet for every case of an amenity-rich environment there was another site that was excessively isolated. Moreover, the direct abutment of industrial areas to ten projects augured poorly for long-term residential stability. In the 1940s and 1950s, however, the leaders of the BHA still believed that stability in public neighborhoods could be achieved and sustained through the mechanisms of the Authority itself: its tenant selection staff, its attorneys, its political patrons, and its own reservoir of paternalist faith.

THE AUTHORITY IS WATCHING

From the 1930s through the 1950s, the Boston Housing Authority acted in a variety of ways as the adjudicator of its tenants' moral worth. This occurred most explicitly at the time of initial selection, although the Authority's site managers kept close watch on their tenants' household habits and behaviors, and the BHA's legal staff used its wide powers of eviction with singular efficacy.

Into the 1950s, the BHA applicant pool remained wholly skewed toward two-parent families of working-class veterans. In 1950 and 1951 fully 90 percent of all BHA applicants were veterans and 95 percent were employed, a clear indication that applicants were a self-selected lot even before the BHA applied its own scrutiny. In those same two years, the "investigators" of the Authority's "Tenant Relations Section" made 9,308 visits to the homes of applicants in an effort to sort out which among them most deserved to be housed. These investigators came armed not just with a set of formal eligibility standards; they also, much more subjectively, were empowered to pass judgment on acceptability.

The distinction between eligibility and acceptability is elegantly illustrated in Irwin Deutscher's classic analysis of "the gatekeeper in public housing," detailing the value-laden decisionmaking methods of the woman in charge of tenant selection at a small city public housing authority during the late 1950s. Using ethnographic methods, he shows how a single individual (with tacit management approval) could steer an entire public housing program toward a system of racially segregated occupancy that excluded unwed mothers and those found to exhibit an undesirable demeanor. Deutscher observed that "the law" did not permit families to be excluded from public housing on the basis of family constellation, but "the filing system" did. As for judgments about an applicant's demeanor—what Erving Goffman called "front"—Deutscher observed that decisions about desirability were based entirely on middle-class criteria of "cleanliness, clarity of speech, appropriate clothing, self-assurance, integrity, and the like." In other words, however complete the formal record on an application blank, a highly discretionary system allowed for much reliance on "the memory of the gatekeeper," able to pass over the folders of formally eligible but otherwise undesirable applicants for years on end.[142]

In Boston during the 1950s the gatekeepers were not one but many, and the gatekeeping functions were even more far-reaching. Until the challenges of civil rights activists compelled a formal change of policy during the mid-1960s, BHA tenant selection staff could reject an applicant for any one of fifteen different listed reasons. These social prohibitions included excessive use of alcohol, use of drugs, cohabitation without marriage, out-of-wedlock children (except under certain specified conditions), "unsanitary housekeeping," and "obnoxious conduct or behavior in connection with processing of application."[143] Though this list was certainly not publicly circulated, the BHA promulgated its underlying ideals in a variety of other subtle and not-so-subtle ways. In a 1953 report the Authority reaffirmed its priorities: public housing was intended for "certain qualified citizens, previously living under improper housing conditions." Its developments were "not charitable institutions for people who cannot or will not work." Nor were they places where tenants would be allowed to forgo their rent payments: "It must be paid," the Authority intoned; "there are no charge accounts."[144]

Having labored hard to find a cohort of tenants who would be socially and financially stable enough to afford the rent, the Authority did not take kindly to those who fell behind in their payments. It also dealt harshly with those whose behaviors fell short of current standards. In a sociolegal climate in which the landlord reigned supreme, the Authority's judgments were rarely challenged successfully. In 1945 alone the Housing Authority went to court in 334 cases, most of which involved evictions. Eighty percent of the eviction cases involved nonpayment of rent; the others centered on a variety of nuisances, including such matters as "constant traffic of servicemen and others; late parties; quarreling and fighting with neighboring tenants; drunken brawls; and filthy condition of apartments." All but two of the eviction cases argued in the district court were resolved in favor of the BHA, and the Authority won the remaining two on appeal. In the 1940s and 1950s, housing projects were treated as communities rather than simply as collections of individuals, and disruption of neighborhood well-being—whether measured by financial stability or evening peace—itself could count as grounds for eviction. Internal memoranda suggest that some BHA staff worried about the futures of those they chose to evict. One BHA attorney noted that "if people cannot pay their rent in a public housing development, then one might well ask how they can pay it in the private market."[145]

In the 1940s and 1950s, however, the Authority's major tenant problem was not one of rent delinquency or undesirable behavior, but of excess income. In 1947 BHA Acting Executive Director Jeremiah Sullivan estimated that one-third of its tenants—about 2,000 families—were "receiving annual income in excess of that permitted by law." Some 400 of these had incomes up to three times the ceiling, at a time when the Authority had "approximately 9,000 applications from veterans and others of low income who are seeking and deserve the assistance which this Authority was established to provide." Sullivan complained that restrictions imposed by the local Office of Price Administration (OPA), which was under federal obligation to ensure that evictions were carried out only after documentation of locally available alternative accommodation, prevented the Authority from swift action to evict over-income tenants. In March 1947 the OPA agreed to let the BHA commence a staggered program of over-income tenant evictions, with approximately twelve to fifteen notices sent each month. As Sullivan commented, this program "would not only serve to notify the specific tenants but would also have the salutary effect of putting all of the others on notice that they would have to make plans to find other accommodations."[146] During the war, the incomes of project occupants had been skewed upward by more lucrative forms of war-related employment. With the return of peace, there was a push to return public housing to its more wholly low-income clientele, but the lingering presence of higher-income and higher-status tenants also appealed.

By the 1950s, the urgent wish to see tenants get up and out was already tempered by a concern that those left behind were increasingly less desirable. Facing (and acting on) political pressure not only to get specific tenants in but to enable them to stay, and equally concerned with retaining a core of maximum-income tenants who could regularly and responsibly pay the highest category of assignable rent, it was firmly in the BHA's best interest to find ways to keep more of its better-off tenants in its developments. Therefore, the Authority kept an assiduous watch over its tenants' incomes.

In the tight rental market of Boston in the early 1950s, BHA apartments were a real bargain—maximum Authority rents were not just 20 percent below what was readily available in the private sector (as stipulated by law), but usually less than half of what would otherwise be paid. Yet under prevailing ceilings for income eligibility, about half of those judged to be living in substandard housing in 1950 earned too much to qualify for public housing. The lowest-earning construction laborer in full-time employ, receiving hourly union wages of $1.75 over a forty-hour week for fifty weeks, would earn $3,500 annually, well over the limit for admission or continued occupancy in public housing (even for a large family with no other source of income). The income limits restricted access to all but the "lowest 20%" of blue-collar and service workers, whose earnings were as little as $1.20 per hour. Even their annual income of about $2,500 was near the uppermost end for public housing eligibility in 1951. On average, according to this threshold, Boston city garbage collectors, printer's assistants, punch-press operators, and piano movers would be eligible, but subway security guards, newspaper deliverymen, drill press operators, and bricklayers would not.[147]

Though the BHA did not officially specify a minimum income for admission, it was always clear that the Authority expected nearly every household head to be employed and to earn sufficient income to pay the rent. Given the statutory necessity to enforce income ceilings, the fiscal future of the Authority depended on the ability of its tenants to maintain a steady (or rising) income floor. In 1951 the Authority attempted to quantify the income level needed to sustain a minimum standard of life while paying 20 percent of that income as rent. In determining this, the BHA cited an "Estimated Minimum Adequate Budget" drawn from standards established by the Massachusetts Department of Public Welfare. These minimum standards, described by the BHA as "based upon a typical four-person family consisting of a male wage earner, his wife who stays at home, and two children," served simultaneously to set an economic standard and to epitomize a social one. Socially, these standards worked to affirm the BHA's strong bias toward married couples with children, and economically they worked out to an annual budget of $2,384.21. With this "minimum standard of life" budget, however, families seeking public housing would be squeezed on two sides: 20 percent of income would be insufficient to cover monthly BHA rent of $46 for a two-bedroom apartment, yet this same annual income would also be only $15.79 short of the maximum income of $2,400 for a family of four seeking admission. To be eligible for the BHA's bargain rents, then, families were expected to stretch their finances in other areas more than the Department of Public Welfare judged wise. To say the very least, the BHA sought to tenant its developments with a very narrow range of families.[148]

Boston public housing in the 1950s was a place for two-parent, one-earner, low-income, blue-collar families whose earnings—if they were to be able to afford the rent at all—hovered near the maximum-allowable ceilings, and constantly forced the Authority to try to raise these limits to maintain the BHA's own economic viability.[149] Targeted to a very narrow stratum—a layer below the bulk of blue-collar employees but above that of the unemployed, the irregularly employed, and the welfare-dependent—public housing excluded not only the most economically desperate but also many other low-income working people whose incomes edged just above Authority threshold or whose citizenship, veterans' status, or family structure were not up to BHA standards and preferences.

Patronage and Paternalism

With such intense competition for admission, it is hardly surprising that many outsiders sought to influence the BHA's choice of tenants. A wide array of city and religious officials sought to advance the claims of their protégés. As patronage fused with paternalism, especially in certain perennially favored projects like Old Harbor Village, the clublike operations of the early BHA stood fully revealed.

Allegations of patronage are often difficult to assess. First, patronage may operate at the subtle level of a casual remark, a brief telephone call, or a scribbled note, leaving little or no paper trail. Second, even an explicit written request for favorable treatment may not survive a selective archival process. Moreover, even when letters survive, it is not always certain what actions, if any, were taken to meet the request. That said, the archives of the Boston Housing Authority are laced with such attempts at influence, and the diverse pleas of elected and appointed officials appear beneath a wide variety of letterheads. Even though Boston—which has not elected a Protestant or a Republican as mayor since 1925—was a one-party town ruled by a series of conciliatory Irish bureaucrats (interspersed with several incarnations of the irrepressible Curley), the city had no shortage of competing patrons, and public housing resources served them well. Although Curley's last term in office (1946–1950) expired before most of the postwar projects were ready, his tenure marked the extreme of neighborhood-focused involvement. As Thomas O'Connor observes, Curley "left the upper-class residents of the downtown to wallow in Puritan self-righteousness while he turned his attention and his municipal favors to those 'other' Bostonians who never failed to give him their loyalty—and their votes." Curley's more sober immediate successors initiated a slow thaw in relations between the Irish-Catholic Democrats who dominated municipal politics and the Yankee-Protestant Republicans who controlled the banks and most businesses,[150] but distribution of public housing largesse remained very much a matter of local ward and parish politics.

A former chairman of the BHA Board admitted to the *Boston Globe* in 1951 that the Authority had received "literally thousands of requests from people in public, private, and religious life asking for consideration for certain families for housing and pointing out conditions surrounding these families." Although he insisted that such testimonials were "not the determining factor in whether the family is rehoused or not," interviews of BHA employees in the Authority's earliest decades indicate that political patronage was "a way of life at the BHA." One priest who had led the effort to get a project built in his own parish reported that "Boston politicians were being allotted thirty apartments apiece for which they could 'name' the future tenants" and, oblivious to the impropriety, resented the fact that his own list had been ignored. This pattern of political meddling was accompanied by allegations (also later confirmed by interviews of veteran employees) that tenants had been asked to make illegal payments in order to obtain public housing apartments. As one city councilor put it, "It is obvious people have been for many years getting into these housing projects through just plain politics" (by which he meant the interference of *federal* elected officials, of course).[151]

Whatever the actual extent and pattern of influence, the BHA clearly managed to house many families whose desirability as tenants outweighed the fact of their relative prosperity. Through the 1950s and well beyond, for instance, the developments housed hundreds of Boston policemen and firefighters. In 1959, when income limits for continued occupancy were again scaled upward to preserve solvency by retaining higher-income tenants, revised ceilings allowed 304 families of Boston policemen and firefighters to remain. These kinds of city workers were the sorts of tenants that the BHA wanted to continue to accommodate.[152]

In the 1940s and 1950s the Authority used its tenant selection prerogatives to resist becoming a social welfare agency. But even with a limited intake of relief families, increasing numbers of households threatened to fall out of economic self-sufficiency as a result of separation and divorce. To the extent that the BHA provided social assistance to needy tenants, it did so with an eye to stabilizing families to save them from charitable dependency. By the early 1950s the Authority had a counseling program for tenants. In 1952 alone BHA "social service consultants" made nearly 10,000 visits to tenant apartments and addressed 2,000 separate cases. In addition to these home visits—sparked by "unfortunate circumstances" such as "sickness" or "death of the head of the family"—400 families attended office-based conferences. The BHA consultants regarded themselves very much in the old tradition of settlement workers, as sources of "help and advice," and as liaisons to a wide variety of health, education, welfare, and correctional organizations. The BHA took special pride in its marriage-counseling efforts. In a 1957 report its Economics Section claimed that "Hundreds of broken families have been reestablished as family units."[153] From the perspective of the city's largest landlord, "broken families" were a serious economic liability.

TEMPERANCE AND TEMPTATION

The moral policing function of the early BHA also extended beyond the boundaries of the projects, as part of a broad search for measures to reduce the potential for future social problems and economic instability. Having recognized the limits of directing desirable neighborhood change through zoning negotiation, the Authority sought other ways to influence the edges of its public neighborhoods. Beginning in the late 1930s and continuing after the war, the BHA endeavored not only to secure its own premises but also to protect its tenants from victimization in surrounding neighborhoods. Most directly, the BHA repeatedly attempted to prevent the Boston Licensing Board from granting liquor licenses to establishments within 500 feet of its housing developments. The BHA went so far as to file maps indicating the perimeter within which the Authority would object to the presence of establishments serving alcohol. As Paul Liston, General Counsel for the BHA, put it in a letter to Mary Driscoll, chairman of the Licensing Board, "what savings in rent are made as a result of occupancy of an apartment of this Authority should go toward better food and clothing rather than liquor." Noting that the BHA's housing developments "have a higher ratio of minor children than any other area in the City," and that "the future citizens of our community will be just what we make of them today," Liston concluded that "it is the opinion of the Authority that the proximity of liquor stores, cafes and taverns to its developments is inimical to the welfare and future of the great number of children in its Developments."[154] In all this, the paternalist concern for the welfare of residents seemed triggered not by fears of incursions by disreputable inebriates from outside the public neighborhood, but by lingering doubts about the temperance and temperaments of the tenants themselves.

Despite such concerns in the early years of the program, by 1957 twenty-one of twenty-five projects had at least one liquor store within 600 feet, and there were eighty drinking establishments within the same distance, serving all but seven of the project neighborhoods.[155] Whatever the Authority's moral stance on the matter, for better or worse, the mosaic of zoning inclusions surrounding most projects legitimated and sustained all manner of amenity and temptation.

CLEANING UP THE TENANTS

Within the projects, the Authority attempted to be not only a vigilant landlord but also a municipal housekeeper. Those coming into public housing had been rescued from the "spawning spots for juvenile and adult delinquency" and "Such people and places" suffered "from a minimum of public supervision and a maximum of public apathy." The BHA expected the physical and social environment of the projects to facilitate any necessary behavioral changes. The 1953 annual report concluded, "the job of the Boston Housing Authority hardly ends with the contribution of bricks and mortar . . . The care and attention and the rehabilitation of the families is really the goal of its work." On top of the federal language of "decent, safe and sanitary housing," then, the BHA grafted on its own paternalist agenda of tenant rehabilitation. Built to reward meritorious families, the projects were also coming to be seen as reformatories.

BHA efforts to cope with the behaviors of its tenants took several forms and were justified with a variety of rationales. Sometimes the Authority tried to ease its own maintenance burden by invoking the cause of public safety. In 1952 the BHA installed blacktop in "all seating and play areas" in its federally funded developments, claiming that this would eliminate "dust and serious accidents."[156] The shift away from grass was a tacit admission that tenant cooperation with "newly seeded areas," much-touted in the 1940s, had begun to erode. Blacktop was a way not only to protect tenants from themselves but also to cut costs and eliminate a perennial source of frustration.

Every tenant's lease contained a twenty-nine-item list entitled, "Conditions of Occupancy." Its prescriptions and proscriptions went well beyond what most private-sector landlords would attempt to specify. Some of these involved the apartments themselves, but many others centered on efforts to establish control over the public areas just beyond the confines of each family's individual unit. The Authority reserved the right to "enter the Tenant's premises during all reasonable hours," not only for the purposes of repairs, but also to "examine" or "exhibit" the apartment and to remove "placards, signs, fixtures, alterations, or additions in the premises which are in violation of the Tenant's lease or of these conditions of occupancy." Outside their apartments, tenants were required to "comply with reasonable directions of the Authority" in all matters concerning "the maintenance in a clean and orderly manner" of the public halls, stairways, and yards. To this end, "the tenant shall not permit his children to play in public halls, stairways, walks, or areas," since "convenient play areas have been provided for this purpose." Tenants were permitted access to "interior community facilities in the project" only with "written permission" from the Authority. All pets were forbidden. Moreover, the Authority reserved "in all cases the right to control and prevent access" into the buildings or grounds of any visitors "whom it considers undesirable." Finally, "any case of infectious or contagious disease occurring in the premises" must be reported immediately to the project's management office.[157] Even as the Authority struggled to ensure that it housed only the cream of Boston's poor, its conditions of occupancy were premised on a view of tenants as dirty, disruptive, and diseased.

Into the 1950s, though the heyday of the prewar reform impulse was long since past, the BHA continued to claim that public housing "produces better citizens, happier families, and enhances the pride of its men, women, and children, who enjoy its benefits endowing them with a greater sense of responsibility to their government and fellow men."[158] In this last phrase, a fundamental impulse behind the whole public housing enterprise stood revealed. Public housing—on the one hand a reward for exemplary service and character under conditions of hardship—could also be viewed by its beneficiaries as a form of public indebtedness. In the early 1950s it was still possible for a housing authority to view public housing as a way to bring the least-advantaged into grateful partnership with the government. Just as the dominant homeownership ideology was forged in the social certification resulting from the economic agreement between a prospective home-owner and a banker, so the selection for a subsidy could imply a similar set of mutual long-term responsibilities. The analogy crumbled, however, once the partnership ceased to confer an unambiguous increase in status.

As the last of the large family projects opened, public criticism of the tenants began to mount. In contrast to the early years of the program, when "survey after survey showed there was less delinquency in the projects than in the areas they replaced," a series of investigative reports in the Boston-based *Christian Science Monitor* concluded that the situation was now "sharply reversed," and "rather than curing social ills, projects have appeared to concentrate them." According to the *Monitor*, "the impression has gained ground that housing projects are 'focal points for crime,'" plagued by disorders including "vandalism, delinquency, murder, and assaults on children," all because "public housing has entered a new and unexpected era which revolves around a new type of tenant." Careful not to blame all tenants and all projects equally, the *Monitor*'s series warned of "a potentially explosive situation," since the citywide average for welfare families in Boston public housing projects had crept up to 13 percent, and the "rate of broken and problem families" stood as high as 30 percent in some of the newest midrise projects located in nonwhite or isolated areas.[159]

During the 1950s, as the most upwardly mobile residents exited Boston's public housing projects, the status of those who remained continued to decline. As Charles Abrams wrote in 1955,

> The policy of restricting eligibility to fixed maximum income has given an institutional character to the projects. The occupants are tagged as people who earn less than a specified income, so that a tenant feels more like the inmate of a poorhouse than a rent-payer . . . A rise in income due to increased earnings, which should be a cause for joy, may result in a family's eviction . . . The policy of evicting those who do improve their status drives out the more exemplary tenants, leaving a less successful residuum.[160]

It was still possible to draw sharp contrasts between public housing environments and their substandard alternatives, but the BHA's own internal ambivalence regarding the "less successful residuum" among its chosen public charges was deepening. Gradually, the Authority began to regard more and more of its tenants not as worthy workers but as public neighbors.

THE END OF AN ERA

With the completion of Columbia Point in 1954, the Boston Housing Authority stopped building large public neighborhoods for Boston's low-income families. In all of the largest neighborhood skirmishes the cause of public housing had won out, whether that cause was job creation, slum clearance, or the creation of affordable homes for worthy citizens. The BHA stopped building large public housing projects for families not just because it had become harder to find politically viable and physically desirable tracts of vacant land but, more fundamentally, because the supporters of housing and redevelopment initiatives moved on to three other priorities: housing the elderly, curbing decentralization, and rebuilding the tax base of the central city. Not coincidentally, this upsurge of interest in the elderly and in the urban middle class occurred just as the client base of family public housing shifted toward nonwhite occupancy. For the public neighborhoods already constructed, recognition of this transformation came too late. With most of the city's largest public housing projects ensconced in districts that were overwhelmingly white, to serve the changing public housing waiting list would entail changing both neighborhoods and attitudes. As it turned out, the fast and easy part of the BHA's job was building its public neighborhoods; the slow and painful part was learning how to manage the consequences.

FOUR

Managing Poverty and Race, 1955–1980

IN ITS FIRST twenty years, the Boston Housing Authority oversaw construction of the nation's fourth-largest collection of housing projects, and its Board stocked them, separately and more or less equally, with worthy tenants both black and white. In the decades that followed, however, the full import of the Housing Act of 1949 became clear: the federal government shifted its priorities toward urban renewal ventures aimed at curbing decentralization, and public housing and its tenants became increasingly marginalized. The Boston Housing Authority, like others in major American cities, underwent a protracted identity crisis as demand for its housing shifted toward clients who were poorer and darker-skinned than any group the early proponents of selective collectives could ever have imagined. What follows is the story of how the BHA managed—and mismanaged—the issues of poverty and race.

THE GEOPOLITICS OF PUBLIC HOUSING

Boston was an overwhelmingly white city at the time its family public housing was constructed. As late as 1960, the self-proclaimed "Hub of the Universe" remained 91 percent white.[1] Its twenty-five family housing projects, built in two short bursts between 1938 and 1954, arose in widely scattered neighborhoods at a time when local politicians could court such housing without having to face the challenges of a pluralist society (Fig. 4.1). Intended to serve the carefully screened white working poor of the city, while also accommodating a few hundred non-white families in separate projects or in projects where they could be safely and overwhelmingly outnumbered, the selective collectives of Boston public housing could be touted as a stabilizing force on neighborhoods, economically as well as racially. Only three projects—Lenox Street, Camden Street, and Whittier Street—were constructed in census tracts that had a nonwhite majority in 1950 (see Fig.

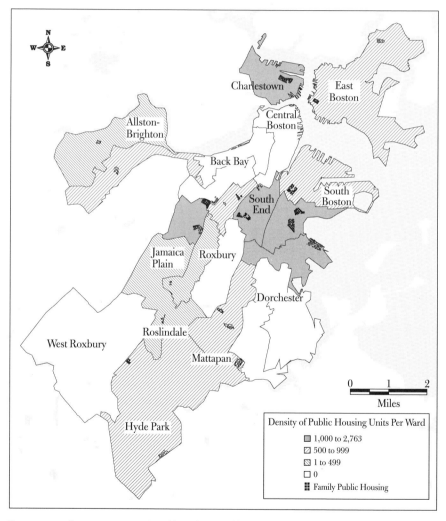

FIGURE 4.1 In contrast to many cities where public housing was concentrated in a few areas, Boston's family projects found favor with local politicians and were built in all but a few of the city's wards.

3.19), and only two of the twenty-five were built in an area of concentrated poverty (Fig. 4.2). By the mid-1950s, however, incomes of public housing residents had already commenced their long decline, and it became increasingly difficult for city leaders to discharge their obligation to take care of Boston's poor chiefly through inclusion of the long-preferred two-parent white families whose low in-

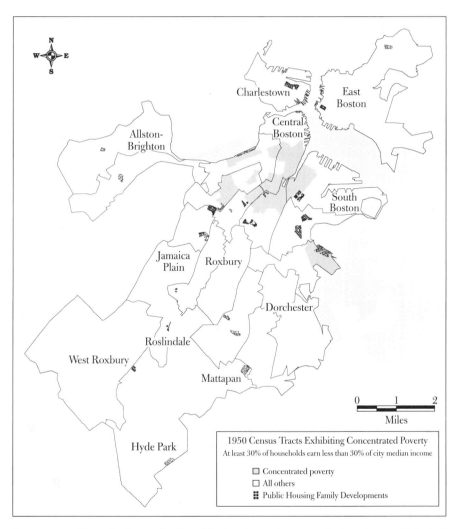

FIGURE 4.2 When the Boston family public housing projects were built, only two, Cathedral/South End and Columbia Point, were built in areas of concentrated poverty, and the latter was situated well away from population of any kind. Concentrated poverty census tracts are defined as those where at least 30 percent of households had incomes below 30 percent of the city median.

comes could be reliably judged to be accompanied by a strong work ethic. Even before the Boston Housing Authority was forced to confront the demands for wholesale racial integration in the 1960s, public housing had lost its cachet. Whereas the first generation of project tenants embodied the BHA's idea of the worthiest cases among the poor, by the late 1950s, some Boston public housing projects were already seen as domiciles of last resort. Increasingly, the "worthy" white working poor simply chose not to apply.

As the initial postwar cohorts of residents moved out of the projects, those who remained or newly sought entrance were those with the fewest housing alternatives. Once seen as a place to separate deserving families from the less-reputable slumdwellers surrounding them, the image of public housing plummeted in the eyes of the working class it was originally intended to serve. Once the projects were up and running, Boston city officials gradually lost interest in them, except as avenues for patronage. Federal incentives for urban renewal now encouraged other mechanisms for propping up the middle class and replenishing the city's tax base, and new public housing construction for low-income families—since it served neither of those objectives—ceased to be a priority. Unlike some cities, where public housing became a major relocation resource for urban renewal efforts and where further new project construction in the late 1950s and 1960s could be seen as a useful tool for ghetto reinforcement,[2] in Boston the central political challenge was to preserve public housing projects in white neighborhoods for white occupancy. While city leaders in places such as Chicago, St. Louis, and Philadelphia struggled to come to terms with the vast migration of impoverished southern blacks, in Boston this challenge remained smaller and was managed—or at least forestalled—by doing nothing.

In Boston, two-thirds of the projects (including several of the largest ones) were scattered well away from black ghetto areas and, as late as 1962, public housing occupancy remained about 85 percent white.[3] This meant that when racial pressures arose during the 1960s and 1970s, tensions were played out not just in some single consolidated ghetto, but neighborhood by neighborhood across the city.

Beginning in the 1950s, Boston's housing and development officials adopted two avoidance strategies in response to the growing problem of public neighbors in the city's low-rent projects. The first strategy was to interpret federal urban renewal programs in ways that provided little role for public housing of any kind, except as an auxiliary resource for rehousing families displaced from those central areas of the city where low-income people were no longer welcomed. The other was to shift priorities away from family projects and into programs designed to house the elderly, an ideologically more palatable form of subsidy that could also be seen to have long-term appeal to whites. Together these new priorities marginalized the importance of Boston's existing public housing projects and undoubtedly hastened their already-visible socioeconomic decline.

Urban Renewal: Redistributing Public Neighbors

The Housing Act of 1949 and its successors cloaked public housing in the larger mantle of urban redevelopment efforts, and dramatically altered the course of American subsidized housing. Although the preamble of the Act still spoke in terms of "the goal of a decent home and a suitable living environment for every American family," Title I focused on urban redevelopment goals and did not require developers to re-use cleared sites to build housing. The federal legislation left it up to local authorities to determine which areas were considered slums or blighted, and cities could request federal aid for urban redevelopment without also requesting aid for public housing. The legislation appealed to many groups for different reasons: downtown business leaders hoped it would promote orderly expansion of the central business district into previously derelict areas; retail merchants favored the re-centralization of higher-income shoppers; organized labor again saw opportunities for construction jobs; municipal officials coveted opportunities to have more areas that generated a revenue surplus; and city planners saw it as promoting greater efficiency and curbing sprawl. In Boston, this unlikely confluence of interests quickly led to a focus on clearance and redevelopment that had little to do with providing new low-income housing for anyone. The earlier hope that good citizenship could be fostered in and by public housing gave way to using public policy to nurture private investment.

The central problem, as Mayor Curley saw it in 1949, was that public housing projects in themselves were not sufficient to arrest the spread of blight, since private developers had failed to "take heart and continue to rebuild around the old core."[4] From the perspective of city hall and downtown business interests, Boston's poor economic health outweighed concern over the social costs of bad housing, and city leaders who contemplated federally subsidized alternatives to blighted areas saw little reason to limit themselves to the creation of low-income housing. In the early 1950s, under the new and more-restrained mayoral leadership of John B. Hynes, Boston's housing policy was soon subordinated to broader redevelopment efforts.

As Hynes sought to direct available federal money to other fiscal priorities, the BHA—designated as the city's local public authority for redevelopment purposes under the terms of the 1949 Housing Act—struggled to redefine its identity. Still in the midst of its second construction boom during the early 1950s and committed to large-scale housing opportunities for Massachusetts veterans, the Authority was also empowered to define residential districts as blighted and to designate them for redevelopment as business or industrial areas rather than for public housing. Under the 1949 urban redevelopment regulations, the federal government would pay two-thirds of the costs of purchasing slum property, which would then be cleared and sold off to a private developer at an appealingly reduced price. In 1950, partly in response to the 1949 Housing Act's requirement that all housing and redevelopment projects be carried out in conjunction with an overall municipal master plan, the Boston Planning Board issued its General Plan for Boston, which proposed redevelopment projects covering about 20 percent of the city's land area over the next twenty-five years.[5] Contemplating this ambitious redevelopment agenda, a 1953 BHA report called the Housing Act of 1949 "the most liberal and yet most conservative measure ever adopted by the U.S. Congress." Its liberality inhered in its willingness to hand local government "the responsibility of wiping out the slum areas of a nation," while its conservatism lay in giving private enterprise "the mandate of rebuilding the areas made available by slum clearance." Lost in the attribution of political labels was any remaining trace of the earlier commitment to better housing for low-income families. As 8,000 new public housing units rose across the city, the Authority declared that "the housing shortage, at least in its acute stage, is slowly but surely approaching its end," and that it did "not anticipate a great deal of future construction." Mayor Hynes concluded, "We have all the low-rental housing projects we need." Another kind of venture seemed more necessary: in the Authority's words, "a vast slum clearance and urban redevelopment program which will 'face lift' Old Dame Boston to such an extent that even her youngest inhabitants will have difficulty in recognizing her." Most postwar public housing projects had been built well away from the downtown areas on city-owned vacant land. For redevelopable areas closer in to downtown, Hynes and his successors had more lucrative uses in mind.[6]

The Housing Acts of 1954 and 1956 allowed cities to use public housing as part of a "Workable Program" for the elimination and prevention of slums and blight, but gave it secondary emphasis. To be considered "Workable," a city's program had to contain seven basic elements: code enforcement, a master plan, neighborhood inventories of blight, an effective administrative organization, financial capacity, "full-fledged, community-wide citizen participation and support," and a rehousing plan. In the attempt to encourage private investment, public housing was relegated to the category of "other aids that can be used for urban renewal purposes," and the Housing and Home Finance Agency explained that federal support for it would come only "where wanted and needed."[7]

Once private enterprise gained a solid foothold in the public development business, the Boston Housing Authority quickly found itself without a leading role. In December 1957 the urban renewal efforts that since 1949 had come under the umbrella of the BHA were transferred to the newly created Boston Redevelopment Authority (BRA). With this transfer of power, the BHA was increasingly relegated to managing past housing commitments, while the BRA forged ahead with bold ideas about what Mayor Hynes famously called the "New Boston."[8] Although most of the actual building and rebuilding of the New Boston occurred in the 1960s under Hynes's successor John Collins, the marginalization of the Boston Housing Authority was well under way much sooner. With each annual report, the BHA's self-image declined: by the end of the 1950s the photograph-enhanced annals of a proselytizing reform movement had shrunk to mimeographed statutory necessities of a floundering bureaucracy.

The End of the West End

The tortured saga of attempts to redevelop Boston's West End during the 1950s illustrates the changing role of urban public housing in the face of higher-priority commitments. Boston's first major experience with urban renewal was marked not by an upsurge of new public housing construction, but by the construction of upper-middle-class highrise housing on the site of what planners injudiciously termed "an obsolete neighborhood" (Fig. 4.3). At one level, the decision to redevelop the working-class West End into an enclave of luxury housing made clear that the most desirable sites for housing in the New Boston would not be used for rehousing low-income people. At the same time, this redevelopment effort revealed the extent to which the BHA's existing family public housing projects already failed to represent an acceptable option for the vast majority of displaced families, especially if they were white. By the end of the 1950s, large family public housing projects were neither needed nor wanted either by the stable white working-class families they had been built to house nor by the local politicians who had championed them.

The redevelopment of the West End differed in a fundamental way from the earlier slum-clearance efforts of the 1930s. The West End was home to the Massachusetts General Hospital, and several researchers armed with funding from the National Institute of Mental Health made sure that Bostonians, and indeed the entire nation, would never forget the human impact of this sort of wholesale clearance and displacement of a still-viable neighborhood. In a now-classic ethnographic work, Herbert Gans examined the living conditions in the West

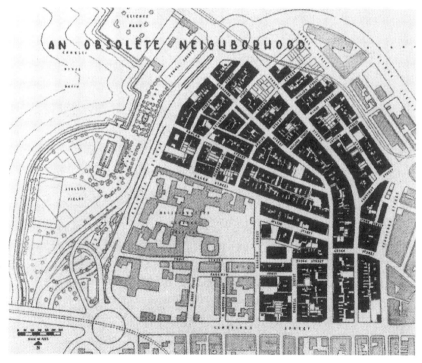

FIGURE 4.3a "An Obsolete Neighborhood and a New Plan," Boston's West End. In 1950, the Boston City Planning Board's *General Plan for Boston* anticipated the wholesale demolition of much of the city's West End and its replacement by modern highrise housing.

End neighborhood before its demolition. Other scholarly writing, by Marc Fried, a psychologist, and by Chester Hartman, a planner, described the grieving process undergone by residents who had lost their homes, and analyzed their subsequent relocation and adjustment to new locales. Taken together, these studies have left an indelible portrait of the ways in which a tax base–driven definition of a slum could result in the demolition of a working-class neighborhood that for its residents remained, to the end, "a good place to live." Since, as Hartman has convincingly argued, most of the decline in the West End housing stock occurred during the six years between the announcement of the plan in 1953 and the commencement of demolition, the West End redevelopment conclusively demonstrated that mere anticipation of urban renewal could precipitate ex-

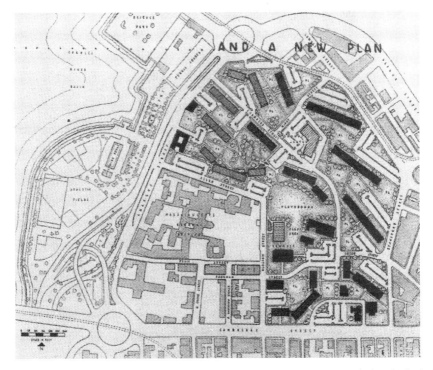

FIGURE 4.3b Instead of an environment that "undoubtedly impairs the mental and physical health of its inhabitants," the Planning Board proposed "an environment of good physical and mental health" which "should be less of a financial burden to the city."

actly the kind of decline that renewal proponents needed to justify their calls for clearance.[9]

In any event, the West End redevelopment made clear that preservation and provision of low-income housing was clearly secondary to the pursuit of municipal fiscal stability. Boston was the only large city in the country where the tax base actually *declined* during the 1950s, due in large part to housing deterioration. Mayor Hynes believed that redevelopment would "increase employment [in the construction trades], increase our tax base, enhance peripheral realty values, and provide increased tax revenues to the city." Urban renewal continued what public housing had begun: the targeting of federal subsidy to neighborhoods that could be made to serve the worthiest and most economically dependable of citizens. In the BHA view, the West End had just this potential: "Existing schools and recreation, churches, library, stores and hospital in the area will combine to form the nucleus of a good neighborhood when the existing slum housing is cleared and proper redevelopment is effectuated." The West End district had all the institutional amenities and proximities of a well-planned Neighborhood Unit—if only the tenements and the tenement dwellers could be removed. The new West End, like many other subsequent downtown redevelopment efforts, could be wholeheartedly championed by city hall, the city's major newspapers, and the Boston business community as "a strategic way of bringing middle-income families—'quality shoppers'—back to the heart of the city." The BRA held that all but the most objectionable displaced West End families could find alternative housing through the private market, and that the rest could be exported to the peripheral islands of public housing projects—just as had been accomplished by erection of the Deer Island institutions a century earlier. With nonproductive people marginalized, the center city could be both rebuilt and repopulated, turned into "a bright shiny new environment for the type of people who would patronize downtown department stores, dine at expensive restaurants, and make purchases at fashionable boutiques." As the Chairman of the Boston Finance Commission put it, Boston must "provide pleasant accommodations for the great American middle class, or perish."[10]

Rehousing West Enders

In April 1953, when Mayor Hynes publicly announced the BHA's plan for a West End project, the *Boston Globe* reported that it would include low-rent housing for 1,175 families, 200 middle-income apartments, and just 640 high-rent apartments.

The *Globe* correctly explained that thousands of families would be displaced, but asserted that "many of these persons will find new quarters in the new low rent housing units."[11] What the paper neglected to mention was that the promised units of low-rent housing would be found not in the redesigned West End but in public housing projects scattered across the city.

The BHA itself was more forthcoming: "If this project were to go through as now planned," an early report conceded, "there would be only about 1,000 apartments in an area where there are nearly 2,300 families and 900 single persons now. Even if every apartment in the new project could be used for present residents of the area, there would be room for only one family in three. Unfortunately the present high cost of construction means that many of the new apartments would be too expensive for most of the people who now live in the West End." In a preliminary study published in March, 1953, prepared weeks before the story was revealed to the press, the BHA called for redeveloping the West End with "new housing for both high- and low-income groups," but acknowledged that there would be only 200 units to serve the less affluent. The BHA "tentatively set aside" a five-acre tract for public housing, "located well-inland from the more highly marketable riverfront property," but judged it "preferable" to rebuild the West End entirely without subsidized tenants. While one arm of the BHA struggled to select veterans and other worthy families for its array of postwar projects, another arm, the Urban Redevelopment Division, pursued selectivity through the mechanisms of the market; a neighborhood where apartments rented for nearly 50 percent less than the citywide average would be replaced by one catering to wealthier taxpayers. Although the Authority distributed pamphlets to West End residents tactfully reassuring them that "it is not the people who are substandard, but their neighborhood,"[12] the message was at best ambiguous.

From the beginning, the Authority's "rehousing" message stressed that it was doing a favor to those who were being involuntarily displaced. The West End, with its "worn out buildings," "too small lots," "too narrow and crooked streets," suffered (and induced further suffering) because its "whole layout is out of date." Reiterating a century of language about tenement reform, the BHA observed that the buildings "are so close together that there is less sunlight and air in many dwellings than is needed for healthy living." Redevelopment in accordance with a modern plan would therefore be not only "better for the city" but also better "for the people living there." As the BHA put it, "The most important reason for redevelopment of the West End is to get rid of existing bad conditions—to improve the living conditions of people who now live there, and relieve the City of the tax burden of extra expenses for fire protection and the like which go with substandard areas. Redevelopment is not undertaken for the benefit of new residents and new investors but for the benefit of all the people of Boston." The BHA seems to have expected West Enders to embrace the logic of the scheme, circulating another pamphlet in 1956 to inform any remaining doubters that "The majority of the people in the area are anxious for the project to go through as soon as possible [since] areas like the West End . . . are undesirable places to live." Such professional judgments were not open to legitimate challenge: "To people who have lived there for a long time," the BHA intoned, "the West End may not seem 'substandard.' But the preliminary studies made by the Housing Authority show that it is."[13]

As it had done in the 1930s and 1940s, the BHA touted public housing as the alternative to substandard accommodations. In the case of the West End, however, no on-site public housing was needed because the site itself was so well-located as to be able to attract unsubsidized tenants. With private development interest returning to the central business district and its environs, the city's obligation to its public neighbors could again be shifted to more marginal locales.

Ignoring the clear implications of its own history of clearing low-rent areas to site housing projects, the BHA repeatedly sought ways to reassure the families who would soon lose their entire neighborhood. In every sporadically produced pamphlet, the message was a variation on the same paternalist theme: "Don't worry, the Housing Authority will find you a new place to live"; "Before anything is done, before any building is torn down, before any one has to move, the Authority will tell you what is going to happen"; "Don't move unless you planned to anyhow. You will be informed well before you have to move and helped to find a new and better home"; "The Authority has made plans to rehouse every family that would have to move"; "Don't spread rumors; keep the facts straight"; "You can help the redevelopment program, your city and your family by cooperating"; "The best advice we can give you is to 'sit tight.' There is no cause for worry"; "You do *not* have to worry about finding a new place to live. It is the responsibility of the Authority to do this for you, when and if it becomes time for you to move. The Federal law requires that you must be relocated in a decent, safe, sanitary apartment at a price you can afford to pay, or there can be no project"; "No one has to worry; everyone will be rehoused, most of you in much better apartments than you have now."[14]

These "much better apartments," the BHA assumed, would be found through normal turnover in the existing stock of the city's public housing. The Authority's surveys showed that six of every ten families to be displaced from the West End would be eligible for public housing. Every BHA report simply assumed that virtually all those offered a project apartment would jump at the chance. Ten thousand copies of a March 1954 flyer distributed directly to West Enders shamelessly announced: "Every resident of the area will be rehoused in good housing . . . For most of you who live in the West End Project Area, this means that you will be given an apartment in a low-rent public housing project run by the Housing Authority."[15] No longer something to be offered as the result of an intensive and competitive screening process, public housing units had become something to be "assigned" or—worse still in the minds of charity-averse recipients—simply "given." And, if they were to be given at all, they were to be given well away from those parts of the city, like the new West End, that could support lucrative uses of land and attract people with higher incomes.

The initial idea of some limited on-site low-rent public housing in the West End gradually disappeared from private plans and public debate. In 1956 West Enders were told to expect "rental housing . . . built by private developers," and the revised plan showed that most parts of the site had been rezoned to allow highrise luxury apartments not just along the river, but well inland as well. By the time residents—many of whom believed that the project would never happen—received official eviction notices in the spring of 1958, the BRA made no mention of on-site public housing, and the rentals for the proposed Charles River Park apartments, like the buildings themselves, towered well beyond the means of the West Enders they displaced. As subsequent studies by Chester Hartman showed, denied the option of living in public housing in their own razed neighborhood, very few West Enders moved on to public housing anywhere else in the city. Ultimately, Hartman's careful research demonstrated, this low reliance on public housing should be interpreted less as an indictment of public housing's availability than as an index of its diminished desirability among those who could plausibly find affordable alternatives.[16]

RESISTANCE TO PUBLIC HOUSING

As the West End was reduced to forty-eight acres of rubble in 1958–59, 1,731 families and 824 individuals were forced to look for new homes. Although two-thirds of these households were apparently eligible for public housing, only about one

in ten ultimately chose to relocate to a project. In probing the reasons for this reluctance to seek public housing, Hartman and his colleagues interviewed a random sample of nearly 500 of these households, both before and after they relocated.

Prior to relocation, the researchers asked: "Do you think you would like to live
in a public housing project?" Three-quarters of the respondents said no, and
only 11 percent wholly embraced the idea. The interviews revealed a variety of
negative factors associated with public housing. The objection voiced by a majority of the 369 respondents who cited specific concerns had to do with perceptions about "the quantity or density of population" in the projects. Hartman's
West Enders offered up a litany of complaints: "'Too many people; it's like being
cooped up with people on a boat.' 'Too many families close together. Each family
would know what the others were doing and saying.' 'Because they look and
smell like insane asylums. Too many families.' 'It's too congested. The West End
was congested, but not like the projects.'" Given that the West End itself was
"probably the most densely populated neighborhood in the city, in terms of land
coverage and persons per gross acre," such comments initially seemed both surprising and ironic.[17] Probing further, Hartman found that the complaints about
density were inextricably bound up with perceptions about public housing residents and the "institutional quality" of public housing regulations. The West
Enders' resistance was not to high-density living per se, but to the perceived high
density of strangers, full of unwanted and unpredictable behaviors. In contrast to
the intimate scale of the West End tenements—which usually contained one or
two apartments per floor and allowed for "the clustering of related and friendly
households"—the vast projects, with their hallways and stairwells, created zones
of anonymity where "adjacent tenants . . . are perceived, not as neighbors, but as
an undifferentiated crowd." To reject public housing was to resist becoming a
public neighbor in a dual sense. At one level, the white working class viewed
public housing as "too public"—too large, open, congested, and unmanageable.
At another level, their resistance bespoke an unwillingness to see themselves as
objects of public charity, housed together with those whose motives they distrusted, and delivered there by a process that severely limited the freedom of
choice long associated with the process of selecting desirable homes and neighborhoods. In Hartman's words:

> Housing projects were perceived as places lacking stable family life,
> social controls, and integrated social networks; as places where all

manner of anti-social behavior runs rampant, a bad environment for bringing up children, a receptacle for the very lowest elements of society. These characteristics were especially repulsive to members of the working class whose life and neighborhood represented a far more structured, acceptable, and respectable *modus vivendi*, both to themselves and to the public at large; and this was considered far more important than the superior physical facilities and lower rents available in public housing.[18]

Hartman's nuanced interviews revealed a psychologically complex conflation of architectural form and social status among displaced West Enders.

Those who ultimately went to public housing often saw it as something less than a freely chosen option. More than half expressed "feelings that they had no choice." A disproportionate number of these households had arrived in the West End only recently, had a minimal interpersonal network in the neighborhood, and thus were more dependent on assistance in relocating. More of them consisted of old people, large families, and "incomplete households" than did the portion of the low-income population that found new homes in private housing. The few other families who relocated to the projects but did not fit this demographic profile could be "characterized by special problems that would predispose them to accept public housing, such as exceedingly low income or the recurrence of forced relocation." In fact, in Hartman's sample of fifty-two households that moved out of the West End and into public housing, only three could be described as "upwardly mobile," families who were "moving to public housing as a temporary dwelling on their way either to home-ownership or to some other form of residential improvement." "*Public Housing*," Hartman concluded, "*at least among displaced families, thus appears to be largely the province of the deprived and the incapacitated*—those families with some social or personal impairment or disadvantage which limits their resources, or their home-seeking capacities, and often creates landlord reluctance to rent them apartments."[19] Boston's twenty-five family public housing projects had been built to keep such people out. Yet by the end of the 1950s the initial cachet of the projects had been replaced by stigma.

The West Enders who were eligible for public housing but rejected it as an option were not deterred by issues of race or ethnicity. Rather, they saw it as marking a loss of status and individual control over their domestic lives. Hartman's interviews revealed a deeply rooted sense that relocation to public housing represented downward mobility, even though the apartments themselves were—by all objective measures—better constructed, better outfitted, less densely grouped, and often better priced than the tenements of the West End. For those who did move to public housing, Hartman noted that three-quarters of those interviewed indicated "a feeling of estrangement and alienation, with such comments as: 'I just feel lost. I don't know anybody.' 'Nowheres to go around here. It just doesn't feel like a neighborhood; people are all strangers.' 'I can't confide in anyone here.' 'It's not friendly here like the West End; too many people in one building to get to know and be friendly to any.'"[20]

The projects failed to sustain the social arrangements that had made working-class areas like the West End so desirable. As perceptions about the social decline of the projects gained credence among the white working class, such views became a self-fulfilling prophecy. "For those who do relocate in public housing," Hartman observed, "the grouping of the disadvantaged, the stigmatization of projects, and the feeling of resentment at limited choice serve to exacerbate existing social and personal problems. Neither the objectively superior housing nor the subsidized rents sufficiently compensate for these disadvantages of status and sociability." Given the troubled history and declining image of public housing, Hartman issued a stark prediction: "social and economic realities make it almost inevitable that projects will increasingly turn into islands of poverty, segregation, deprivation and despair."[21]

AFTER THE WEST END

Hartman's concerns about the fate of Boston public housing in an era of urban renewal proved prescient. In the aftermath of the West End redevelopment, urban renewal in Boston underwent a massive expansion. Under the leadership of Mayor John F. Collins, elected in 1959, the BRA greatly increased its powers and ambitions. Led by Edward Logue, Collins's development czar, Boston embarked on a remarkably successful drive to obtain federal urban renewal funds. In terms of total redevelopment dollars approved from 1957 through 1971, Boston trailed only New York and Philadelphia, and on a per-capita basis, it far outranked all other large cities.[22] In the meantime, construction of public housing stalled, and its reputation deteriorated further.

In 1962, to assess the likely role of public housing as a relocation resource, the BRA hired Elizabeth Wood, who wrote "A Comprehensive Program for Family Relocation." Wood, who had served as executive secretary of the Chicago

Housing Authority from 1937 until 1954 (when she was ousted by the CHA Board largely because of her support of racial integration), was clearly one of the nation's most prominent experts on public housing, and her report reflected her disillusionment. "Public housing," she said, "offers the best answer to the housing problem of many more families than move in," yet few of the "good solid citizens" among those displaced by urban renewal had any desire to move into public housing. The problem was that the system had been compelled, under the 1949 Housing Act, to give priority of access to the neediest families, those displaced by urban redevelopment, at the expense of maintaining socially desirable communities. Income to fund operations had already entered "a slow downward trend," and Wood feared that accommodation of more economically troubled families portended financial disaster for the Authority and social disaster for the projects. Despite efforts to increase maximum income limits in order to secure greater rent receipts, higher-income families chose not to apply, and the average incomes of families remained well below the allowable maximum. More disturbing to Wood than the fact that average incomes of project families had declined was a decline in "cultural level." The new population lacked "the expectations or actualities of rising income." In 1961, only about half of BHA households reported receiving income from employment, and 45 percent received income from public assistance, chiefly Aid to Dependent Children (ADC) and Old Age Assistance. Under welfare rules, these families were charged artificially low rents, resulting in what Wood called "a double subsidy" that adversely affected the economics of BHA operations.[23]

Wood's findings paralleled those of the United South End Settlements (USES)—the successor institution to Robert Woods's South End House. In 1960, as one attempt to cope with "an increasing concentration of multi-problem families," the BHA had entered into a joint venture with USES to staff a community service center at the South End/Cathedral development. The first annual evaluation report noted the loss of "small families who are on the economic climb" and "residents who have assumed leadership responsibilities," as well as the fact that nearly half of those who remained were dependent on public assistance (well before the expansion of welfare programs in the mid-1960s). The report also warned that families expected service providers and housing authority managers "to make the most simple decisions for them," and that "policies do not really provide an incentive to leave this vicious circle of dependency." Within the development itself, the USES report noted, "Many residents have expressed the opinion that this Project is becoming the reception center for 'all the problems in the city of Boston.'" Moreover, at a development with a growing nonwhite majority, racial tensions were on the rise: "Many of the white tenants and some of the Negro tenants of long standing, feel that Negroes are moving into the Housing Project in large numbers and that they are to blame for many of its problems."[24]

Unable to stave off the economic decline of public housing as a whole, BHA officials sought to protect certain favored projects. In her report Wood spelled out a litany of negative public perceptions: "According to its image, public housing has inferior architecture; looks institutional; is inhabited by people who are inferior by virtue of their residence or because they are all on public assistance, or because the projects are rife with crime and muggings, or because they are spied on by management which makes them turn out their lights by ten o'clock but allows crime to rampage." In contrast, Wood pointed out that

> there are sections of projects, if not whole projects, that display none of the negative factors that make up the image. There is a section of Old Harbor Village that has no physical characteristics in common with, say, Columbia Point or South End. It has excellent architecture and site plan. The trees and shrubs have flourished over the years and there is plenty of evidence that the tenants not only have cared for the project's trees and shrubs, but have added flowers and shrubs of their own . . . The image of public housing does not recognize the existence of that kind of public housing.[25]

What Wood failed to point out was that Old Harbor Village was the only Boston project built under the more lavish standards of the initial PWA housing program, and that admission to it had long been monitored carefully and reserved exclusively for well-connected whites. In the climate of enhanced civil rights awareness that would soon follow Wood's report, "that kind of public housing" would itself come under attack.

In the meantime, however, Wood focused not on racial discrimination, but on the broader social and economic consequences of "the present trend in tenancy," a trend that "will inevitably—though slowly—bring bankruptcy to the program and destroy its usefulness to urban renewal." She castigated the BHA for treating public housing only as "a real estate operation" and called for fundamental changes in its attitude toward management. Only if the BHA adopted a "planning

with people" spirit and devoted concerted effort to changing the "physical appearance of existing projects" could the BHA eliminate the negative images of
public housing held by current and prospective residents. At present, "Everything is impersonal and public," intended "to protect the projects from the people." Wherever projects continue to "look institutional," she concluded, "the
public tends to think of them as institutions; and of their tenants, by that fact, as
different from and inferior to the people who live outside, because an institution
is where people go who can't take care of themselves."[26] Wood believed Boston's
public housing, like its nineteenth-century institutions constructed to provide indoor relief for the indigent, had become a kind of status-demeaning containment
vehicle for the poor.

REWARDING THE ELDERLY

In the twentieth century as in the seventeenth, Boston's local officials found it impossible to remove the stigma attached to the receipt of any direct public provision of domestic accommodation for the indigent. With only minor exceptions,
all construction of BHA-owned family public housing projects ceased in 1954.
Instead of trying to salvage existing programs, federal and local officials (joined
and encouraged by neighborhood residents) preferred to support a completely
new incarnation of public housing, intended to serve a socially and politically
more acceptable constituency: the elderly.

Massachusetts preceded the federal government in supporting housing for
the elderly, passing legislation in 1953 and 1954 to provide for it. In March 1954,
to elicit greater interest among architects, the State Housing Board announced
a markedly increased schedule of fees for designers and, in cooperation with
the Housing Association of Metropolitan Boston, issued an illustrated booklet,
Housing for the Elderly: Standards of Design. The State Board emphasized the
desirability of smaller interventions, on the grounds that "older people dislike being segregated in large numbers." On the one hand, the Board claimed that "experience elsewhere suggests that projects for the elderly can be too big," causing
"individual identities to be lost in a sea of alien faces." At the other extreme, however, the State Board warned that "where the number of people is too small certain individuals become isolated, their problems increase and must finally be
solved with public or charitable help." In other words, to keep the elderly from

becoming an undesirable social burden, it would be necessary to control the size of their communities. Again on the basis of unspecified "experience elsewhere," the Board concluded that "projects of from twenty-five to forty-five dwelling units are the most successful."[27] Despite such assertions, when public housing for the elderly finally did get built in Boston, thirty-seven of the forty projects contained more than this recommended maximum, and most more than doubled it.

More important than the issue of scale, the decision to focus on the elderly signaled a desire to build public housing where it was most wanted. Massachusetts law stated that this housing "shall, when practicable, be established near the neighborhoods where elderly persons reside." In many cases—by the 1970s at least—this criterion implied adjacency to the family projects where many long-term tenants had aged in place. In other cases, however, it meant new construction in highly scattered locations, allowing public housing to serve many neighborhoods that would never have permitted a large family public housing project. In 1954, the State Housing Board explicitly acknowledged the primacy of attachments within neighborhoods. "The elderly who move into these projects will have given up their own homes. Their neighborhood, with all this implies in terms of friends and associations, may be about all they have left. To have given up their own homes is bad enough. To have to give up their neighborhood too, is worse."[28] The implication was that public housing for the elderly would serve a clientele that had previously achieved their "own homes." To a middle class growing weary and wary of charitable housing handouts to public neighbors of questionable pedigree, public housing for the elderly offered a golden opportunity to bypass the guilt-ridden path of nursing homes for aging and weakened parents no longer able to work. In Lawrence Friedman's terms, shifting the orientation of new public housing to the elderly was simply the latest method for rewarding a "submerged middle class." In this sense, the rationale for public housing retained a clear consistency: housing once targeted to those depressed by economic circumstance or waylaid by wartime service now could go to those whose reduced status was the result of natural decline after a lifetime of hard work and proper homes.

With the Housing Act of 1956, the federal government redefined low-income families to include single elderly people. Despite the federal legislation and corresponding amendments to state housing laws, actual planning and realization of elderly housing projects in Boston took several years, with the first flurry of developments completed only in 1962 and 1963.

In the intervening years, the Boston City Council repeatedly expressed interest in the issue.[29] In May 1958 a council committee issued a report urging the city to go forward with a request for 1,000 units of elderly housing, and to withhold any further authorization for new low-rent family projects. The BHA had earlier sent out a letter to 18,000 elderly recipients of Old Age Assistance stating that the Authority was considering construction of new units for the elderly and inquiring about their interest in such units; 2,000 households had returned the BHA's self-addressed cards. The BHA then calculated the operating costs of 1,000 units and concluded that such projects would be financially feasible only if 200 could be reserved for "tenants who could pay a higher rent." A later study by the Welfare Department to determine how many of its Old Age Assistance clients lived in substandard housing and how many were paying excessive rents to remain in standard housing found that only 3 percent (518 households out of 16,939) lived in substandard conditions, and that an additional 6 percent were paying excessive rents that caused forced curtailment of "other necessities of life." The social workers concluded that although public housing would be desirable for those living in substandard conditions, most of those paying excessive rents would "prefer not to occupy public housing facilities."[30] The City Council thereupon inquired into the "reason why [the] elderly group paying more than it can afford for standard housing have such a dislike of public housing." If public housing for the elderly was to go forward, the councilors implied, it was going to need to interest this group of potential public neighbors, not just those living in substandard conditions. Drawing on the Welfare Department's survey of the geographical distribution of those Old Age Assistance recipients paying excessive rent for standard accommodations (and ignoring the very different geographical distribution of those living in substandard housing), city councilors emphasized that any new public housing must be constructed in neighborhoods where the elderly desired to live.[31] In August 1958, a Boston City Planning Department report estimated that there would be sufficient demand for public housing among Boston's eligible elderly to justify "an additional 300 to 1,000 units," as long as these were relatively small projects located in neighborhoods that already had substantial elderly populations. Most important to the elderly, the planners noted, these locations must provide "a familiar and stable environment and nearness to relatives and the same ethnic group."[32] Public housing, in this prevailing view, was to be a vehicle for reinforcing existing ethnic and racial ties; otherwise, it would fail to attract the desired constituency. With such guidelines in mind, in September the

City Council cautiously authorized the BHA to apply for a preliminary loan to permit construction of 400 units of housing for the elderly.[33]

Not content to let the BHA operate on its own, the City Council appointed a Committee on Public Housing to keep the Council apprised of BHA site-selection plans, and Mayor Hynes appointed an Advisory Committee on Housing for the Elderly. Despite all the structures for oversight, there was still little going on to oversee. Nearly two years later, in May 1960, with no new elderly housing yet in sight, the BHA asked the City Council to authorize application for up to 1,000 additional dwelling units. The matter was referred to the Committee on Public Housing where it remained dormant for a year. In May 1961, the committee recommended approval of the order, stipulating that the units should be built as small, lowrise projects "scattered in as many communities as possible." City and federal approvals took until September, at which time the BHA's elderly housing program finally moved toward implementation. In November 1963, with several elderly projects up and running, the BHA asked for an additional 1,000 units of public housing; once again, loan approvals took a full two years. Eventually, despite delays in all jurisdictions, the BHA gained approval to construct its desired 2,000 units. More than 80 percent of these were to be "located in developments designed and constructed exclusively for elderly occupancy."[34]

As Eugene Meehan has pointed out, public housing for the elderly carried not only a moral appeal but also a financial bonus to both builders and housing authorities. "The Housing Act of 1956 allowed a special premium of $500 per room for the construction of housing for the elderly; the Housing Act of 1961 provided [local housing authorities] with an additional $120 per year for each elderly family housed in the developments. In combination, the two subsidies made the elderly poor into the favored darlings of the public housing program; their numbers increased spectacularly in the 1960s and 1970s."[35]

The real estate industry remained a powerful enemy of public housing. Every time the BHA discussed plans to request more units, groups such as the Greater Boston Real Estate Board responded with statements denouncing "our housing competitor." One article from *The Realtor,* forwarded directly to the mayor, lambasted the BHA ("the largest landlord in the city's history") as an unfair competitor, working against "every owner of private housing in our area":

> Our competitor does not have to show a profit, does not have to make ends meet nor even pay real estate taxes. This competitor also

agrees that nineteen or twenty percent of an occupant's income shall determine the rent to be charged for a unit regardless of its size. This shelter rent furthermore includes payment for all utilities used by the tenant. How, then, do we as owners expect to compete? Why should anyone choose to live in one of our buildings when he can live in a publicly subsidized one? Many answers may be given for any of these questions. Suffice it to say that more of our citizens desire independence without the social stigma attached to living in this type of "welfare housing" as it is called in some circles.[36]

As before, the strongest challenge to public housing was phrased in ideological terms—it would collapse of its own accord because it was un-American.

From this perspective, the real estate board's worst scenario was a large program of less-stigmatized smaller projects, which "would put new units next door to privately owned buildings" and "might well bring into an area those who usually look for a free handout or those in a wage category that could well afford to rent private housing." With the objection that tax-paying property owners should not be "contributing to, and picking up the tab for our own competition" and renewed alarms about the "socialization of private property," the realtors again struck blows against the entire concept of public neighbors, making it all the more likely that new construction would serve the most obviously worthy constituencies.[37]

Although even housing for the elderly aroused controversy in targeted neighborhoods, its popularity among potential recipients outweighed all opposition. In 1960 and 1961, with construction of the first projects under way, housing applications from eligible households skyrocketed. In May 1961, the BHA trumpeted the results of a special citywide survey by the U.S. Bureau of the Census that contradicted earlier studies and showed that 8,625 of Boston's elderly families (nearly one in five) were living in substandard housing. In a press release, Edward Hassan, chairman of the BHA, emphasized that the elderly were more poorly housed than other Bostonians, and often faced excessive rent burdens in order to obtain standard housing. By contrast, the BHA claimed to deliver high-quality housing specifically designed for the elderly at rents only half of those charged by the private sector for new construction. Capitalizing on this very real housing need, the BHA sought to alter its constituency in order to improve its image. "While continuing to serve the housing needs of low-income families generally," the BHA stated, the Authority would continue to "focus particular attention" on the "pressing problems" of the elderly. In support of this reoriented image, later that month the City Council passed a resolution changing the name of the BHA's flagship project—Old Harbor Village—to Mary Ellen McCormack, to honor the mother of South Boston's own Congressman John W. McCormack, Speaker of the House, in the family's home neighborhood.[38]

Thereafter housing for the elderly gained even greater appeal. By 1963, 2,500 elderly households had placed themselves on the BHA waiting list. Of the 4,827 new applications received by the BHA in 1964, the majority came from the elderly. A pair of eighty-unit state-funded elderly housing developments opened adjacent to the Franklin Field project in 1962 and 1963, and applications from the elderly immediately outnumbered those newly seeking apartments in the Massachusetts Chapter 200 projects for families. Even with a rule prohibiting existing BHA tenants from obtaining apartments in the new projects for the elderly, applications dramatically exceeded the available number of units. A thousand applied for 81 apartments at the Washington Street development in Brighton; 875 applied for 53 spots at Ashmont; and more than 2,000 sought entry to the 64 units at the Chestnut Hill project.[39] The result was a level of selectivity (and room for political intervention) not seen since the prewar heyday of the original family projects.

Such heady signs of renewed demand and desirability among this new constituency, however, could not forestall the larger questions over which public neighbors the rest of the BHA inventory should house. As the specter of civil rights enforcement hovered over the still largely segregated program, the Authority grappled with what its 1962–63 annual report called "the complicated problems of tenancy."[40] In choosing to build accommodation targeted chiefly to elderly whites, the Authority embraced its least problematic tenants. Everywhere else, it struggled to cope with the human displacement caused by urban renewal, which carried with it the growing realization that family public housing no longer constituted a desirable option for the white working class.

THE MECHANISMS OF PATRONAGE

Even as many family projects acquired increasingly negative reputations, the Boston Housing Authority continued to reign supreme as a source of patronage. In the hands of a politically astute mayor who could control the BHA Board,

Boston's public housing system proved doubly useful. At one level, its 15,000 subsidized apartments could be managed as an unparalleled reservoir of favors to bestow upon more-or-less low-income citizens, with the choicest accommodations going to the politically faithful. At a second level, public housing continued to provide the opportunity to distribute hundreds of management and maintenance jobs and promotions on the basis of connections rather than merit.

Although patronage systems exist in cities regardless of the dominant ethnicity of their political culture, the practice of the Boston Irish had its own particular flavor and style. In a city previously managed by Puritan-inflected Yankees, Thomas O'Connor observes, politics used to be "a serious business, a civic responsibility that a member of the more fortunate classes assumed with sober reflection and objective concern for the general welfare." The typical Yankee, heir to the Puritan conscience, was "shocked by the idea that government should be used for the benefit of particular individuals, that an exception should be made for a relative or a close friend." To the Irish who permeated all levels of Boston's municipal government in the twentieth century, however, it would be equally shocking for "a humane official [to] overlook the plight of a constituent or the needs of a friend." In an era when many benefits such as social security, unemployment insurance, workman's compensation, and the G.I. Bill offered unparalleled sources of direct federal assistance, public housing was one of the best remaining vehicles for ward- and parish-based local intervention. The public housing bureaucracy found itself caught between the increasingly rational politics of most post-Curley mayors seeking identification of the "public interest" and conciliation with the downtown business community, and a still-powerful ethnic politics of neighborhood leaders who cared principally about the personal interests of individuals, families, and groups.[41] Both kinds of politics were now dominated by Irish Democrats; and both kinds accepted obligation to the poor, but continued to do so for different reasons.

Those in charge of dispensing the societal obligation to public neighbors still struggled over how (and where) to sort them. The perennial concerns over jurisdictional responsibility and behavioral standards remained powerful even among non-Puritans, yet came into irreconcilable conflict with other powerful impulses toward justice and civil rights. The friction between narrow personal interests and broad societal principles came to a head over questions of patronage, especially once patronage became interpreted in terms of race.

Although patronage had undoubtedly been endemic since the inception of the

BHA, John F. Collins was the first Boston mayor to preserve and make available enough of his administration's papers to permit a firsthand glimpse of its tenor and mechanisms. Immediately after taking office, Collins moved to fill two Board vacancies, appointing Edward Hassan as chairman.[42] A few months later, an aide prepared a scathing memo reviewing the salaries and capabilities of fifty-two "employees, so called" at the BHA, to help determine which senior staff should be promoted, retained, demoted, or dismissed so as to advance the interests of the Collins administration. In its opening salvos, the author reminded Collins that the BHA should be treated as enemy territory: "As you well know, about 99% of them were against you in your recent fight. Many of them were viciously so." There followed a highly intimate assessment "gained from long observation and at close range," amounting to an indictment of each person's abilities.

The hit list attempted to trace the lineage of every employee's political loyalties and, most often, to pair evidence of inappropriate sponsorship with evidence of occupational incompetence. The Authority's assistant director of management was dismissed as an "'A.A.' bosom pal" of a BHA board member who went "jumping around developments" with him to "brow beat the workers" to vote for State Senator Johnny Powers against Collins in the 1959 election. This employee was "as dense a bum as you'd ever want to meet" who retained his job only because his boss saw him as no threat.

Others in more senior positions fared no better. The chief of finance ("as gutless as anybody I've ever met," a "sweet-talking school teacher type . . . who'd knife you as soon as you turned around," and who "never went to Accounting School"); the chief of planning ("strictly beholden to [former BHA Chairman] John Carroll," "was Powers a mile a minute," "is supposed to be an Engineer [but] his records don't show it," and "has nothing to do but chin by the hour" since there's "no construction going on"); the director of tenant relations ("one of the 'master' frauds at Housing" who "plays the 'pols' (all of them) up to the hilt," and who "ran a mammoth house party for Powers that lasted until 3 A.M. at his home")—nearly everyone faced withering, one-sided, incontroverted scrutiny. The memo blasted one area management supervisor as "a 'stool pigeon' for John Carroll" who met him each Sunday outside St. Columbkille's Church to provide a "'weekly report' of housing happenings."

Others had their prominent positions traced to membership in Carroll's Cement Finisher's Union ("glorified laborers"), while still others had lingered on since the days of Curley. A few gained grudging marks for "experience," but others were dismissed as "half-baked most of the time" or as "fond of the jug." The report pegged one assistant manager as "a snarly sort of guy" who couldn't be trusted as far as he could be thrown, while a maintenance superintendent in Italian East Boston got labeled as "A real North End 'Sharpie,' with more mouth than performance," and another superintendent warranted the label "Lousy with Drag."

Having so thoroughly skewered more than four dozen BHA employees, the aide apparently thought it wise to reassure young Mayor Collins about the sincerity and necessity of the venture: "You perhaps think I'm exaggerating these statements, but you'll never know what a network of intrigue existed and still exists at Housing. Because of this system, I swear that many of the employees were given High positions without even the least capacity, but instead for their 'reporting' and 'informing' ability and allegiance to Carroll and others like him, who placed no weight on ability, but all on 'pigeon' ability." Instead, the mayor's own BHA informant called for "infusing the agency with some vigorous, intelligent, and loyal Collins appointees in Key positions and getting rid of the 'deadwood,' who, nearly to a man, vigorously opposed your election as Mayor."

Although annotated BHA personnel lists in the Collins files suggest that the mayor relied on many sources to make personnel decisions, no one seems to have questioned that these were the mayor's decisions to make. Ultimately he retained many key long-term players, as long as they demonstrated an ability to shift political loyalties from older brands of Irish Democrats to his own. At the same time, Collins valiantly hired a scattering of more competent bureaucrats.

When it came to tenant selection, Collins and the BHA Board he controlled also sought ways to fill the most coveted BHA apartments with well-connected citizens, and to ensure that some public housing projects continued to be occupied by wage-earners at a time when the welfare-dependent poor were starting to place unprecedented demands on its resources.

Like his predecessors, Collins received dozens of requests every week to intercede in the tenant selection process. Appeals came from fellow polio victims, from campaign workers proffering evidence of repeated service at the polls, from Catholics alluding to their common cultural heritage, and from religious, city, state, and federal officials seeking favors. In nearly every case, the mayor informed the Housing Authority that he "would like to be helpful." In the early years of his administration, Alice Cantwell in the mayor's office forwarded annotated lists to Ruth Oppenheim in the BHA Board chairman's office on a weekly, and sometimes even daily, basis. Nearly every case included the surname of its sponsoring politician, and the two women worked as a team to maximize the chance of a positive outcome, especially for those cases annotated with such imperatives as "A must," "Vet," "Gold Star Mother," "Police Officer," or "Very Special . . . *from the Mayor.*" Sometimes, though, there were fewer fine-grain distinctions to be made: one seventeen-person list was sent off with the plea, "These are all special." At other times, however, Cantwell's annotations expressed editorial suspicion: "3 children—A.D.C.—not married—?????????????????????" The twenty-three question marks seemed to signal not only the moral disdain of the patronage gatekeeper but actual surprise that such a request should travel through the channels usually filled by the politically faithful.

Cantwell and Oppenheim turned their task into a playful game, and the various lists were sent off with casual comments like "Spring must be here—everyone wants to move"; "You've been real good lately, so this is very mild"; "They are all yelling so please help a desperate woman, me"; "This is quite a list, but the calls are coming fast and furious"; "They're really ganging up on me, afraid of the cold weather"; "I must be crazy about you—this is the second letter today"; and "There must be an easier way to make an honest buck." In all, this direct line between Mayor Collins and the BHA Board channeled hundreds of applicants past the official tenant selection procedures during the peak years of 1961–62.[43]

Most politically channeled applicants seem to have been both white and Catholic, and many specifically requested the all-white developments, so the BHA sought other ways to fill its less desirable projects. Faced with the federal preference afforded to those displaced by acts of urban renewal, the Authority tried to channel these people into places where the "worthy" poor would not venture. In a letter in 1963 to Edward Logue, BRA development director, Hassan stated, "Experience has shown . . . that a procedure of assignment on the basis of the applicant's choice can result in an overload at a particular development . . . The procedure therefore has been modified so that each applicant entitled to the displaced family preference is being offered an apartment suitable to its needs in whatever development it becomes first available without regard to the choice of the individual applicant."[44] Because the developments with the most available vacancies also tended to be the least desirable, this policy served as a convenient way to steer potentially less desirable public neighbors away from the most sought-after projects.

KEEPING OUT "SUBSTANDARD" FAMILIES

Through the early 1960s, the BHA explicitly resisted housing families with illegitimate children, or at least placed them in less favored projects. James Crowley, the chief of tenant relations, had first joined the BHA in 1939, and the two women who served as "final review clerks" had been with the Authority since the 1940s; all remembered the early days of public housing when selection was a privilege dependent on prior evidence of proper behavior, suitable family structure, and economic self-sufficiency.[45] Whenever possible, they sought ways to retain and enforce such standards. When faced with complaints about exclusion of mothers with "illegal children," Crowley wrote back to say that "preference is given to legitimate families who are living under distressed conditions." He told another that, if she should marry, "every consideration will be extended to you." Faced with such moral surveillance, many desperate people wrote the mayor to apologize for out-of-wedlock children or youthful arrests for drunkenness, in the hope that they could still be rewarded with public housing. Usually the verdict was stingingly straightforward: "After a careful check, the records show that you do not meet minimum requirements."[46]

Sometimes, the mere mention of ADC status was enough to keep an applicant out, even if the application had been channeled through the mayor's office. In these cases, the basis of judgment was that of financial watchdog as well as moral guardian, since ADC families paid only a preset minimum rent that did not generate sufficient revenue for the Authority: "in the interest of solvency," Crowley asserted unambiguously, "applicants having the highest incomes for rentals, in excess of the minimum, are receiving preference."[47] Despite such efforts, by 1962 at least 20 percent of the households in four large projects—Columbia Point (which beginning in 1963 had its own on-site welfare office), Bromley-Heath, Mission Hill Extension, and South End/Cathedral—were receiving ADC. This was four or five times the rate of those in all-white projects such as Old Harbor, Old Colony, and Mission Hill.[48]

In 1963, the Boston chapter of the Congress of Racial Equality (CORE) confronted the BHA with allegations of discrimination on the basis of family composition and source of income. Chairman Alan Gartner wrote Hassan:

> It has recently come to our attention that applicants for public
> housing have been turned down for various reasons connected with

their family status. In particular, we have heard that unmarried mothers have been refused. While we all recognize the broad social problem that such families present, we believe that the provision of adequate housing—by public authorities where necessary—is a crucial element of meeting this problem. The large number of families being displaced by urban renewal, and the high proportion of these families who cannot afford housing on the open market, make the question of eligibility all the more pressing. We would very much appreciate your comments on this matter.[49]

Hassan rejected Gartner's argument that public housing—because it was public—had an obligation to assist such people. The BHA, he explained, had "established certain standards that govern the admission of families" with "the objective of creating and maintaining for its tenants an environment that is conducive to sound family and community relations, family stability, healthful living and proper rearing of children." These standards were intended to "exclude applicants whose admission would endanger the health, safety or morals of neighbors or be inimical to the proper operation of the low-rent program." Hassan's view of the public neighbor question remained wholly consistent, whether he was responding to civil rights activists or to the mayor who had appointed him. Fully imbued with the nineteenth-century notion of housing as an agent of moral development, he wrote Collins to affirm how he would continue to give "every effort to not only take care of the physical side but also the moral side of housing." Hassan assured the mayor that "95% of our tenants are fine, upstanding God-fearing citizens whose only fault is that they are poor."[50] In Hassan's view, integration efforts and other attempts by outsiders to manipulate the system would place such conditions in jeopardy.

The tension between housing the neediest families and housing the "worthiest" among the needy came to a head over the tortuous questions of urban renewal relocation and racial integration. Because these two pressures, though coming from different sources and directions, coincided during the early and middle 1960s, race and relocation inevitably came to be seen as a single issue. Both the reform-minded challenges of the civil rights groups and the redevelopment-minded challenges of Logue's BRA posed threats to the way the BHA Board had conducted its business for the previous twenty-five years. Although state and federal legislation had long specified a preference in public housing for those displaced by urban renewal ventures, Hassan continued to resist any attempt to constrain what he viewed as the Board's "prerogative as to the location of tenants." Specifically, he feared that the Authority (by which he meant the Board) would "no longer be able to take care of worthy applicants for both low-rent and elderly housing without approval" by the BRA and other agencies, which could lead to "a lower or double standard of acceptability."[51] The power struggle involved both patronage rights and the kind of tenant that public money ought to be used to support. With Hassan interested in preserving the power of patronage for the Board and the mayor, civil rights leaders interested in promoting fair housing measures, and Logue interested in smoothing the way for redevelopment, public housing was caught in the crossfire of clashing public purposes.

Public Housing and Relocation

As the BRA expanded its urban renewal efforts across the city, Logue's frustration mounted over the quality of the family public housing that already existed and the BHA Board's patronage-based control over assignment to the best projects. When he asked Hassan for a greater share of BHA openings to be used for families displaced by BRA actions, he was told, "you're third on my list," behind John McCormack and State Senate president Johnny Powers, who retained jurisdiction for the majority of all tenant placements.[52] At base, however, the problem with using public housing for relocation was not one of too little supply, but one of too little demand. Each BRA planning report affirmed that "sufficient units of public housing" existed to meet "the needs of eligible families displaced" from project areas, yet also revealed that few of those eligible families chose to exercise this option.[53] The New York Streets project of 1958—in which 368 families were evicted from an "area [that] had little, if any, community spirit or civic pride"—was the first example of the lack of interest in public housing expressed by eligible families. Only 15 percent were relocated into public housing, although 58 percent had been eligible. In 1962–63, when Boston's BRA embarked on its sixty-acre clearance project to create the new downtown Government Center, it evicted 440 families and individuals. Although two-thirds of these all-white households were officially eligible for public housing, only 7 percent expressed a preference for such housing, and only 10 percent actually relocated into the projects (Fig. 4.4).[54]

In 1964, faced with relocating residents of a largely white South End neighbor-

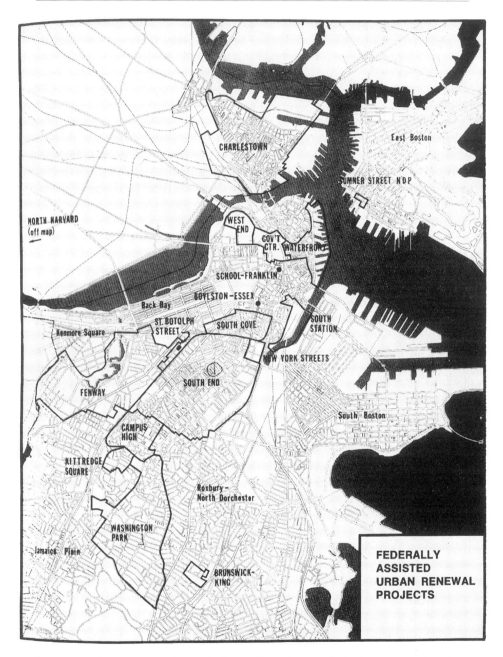

FIGURE 4.4 Between 1957 and 1972, the Boston Redevelopment Authority commenced work on sixteen federally assisted renewal projects, scattered across much of the inner city.

hood to make way for the Castle Square renewal project, the BRA hired United South End Settlements to promote public housing as a resource. In the initial USES "Site-Occupant Survey" of August 1962, only 49 of 675 households indicated that they would "prefer or accept" public housing when they moved, although half were eligible. The reasons they gave echoed Hartman's observations about West Enders. As the USES report put it:

> Relocation families and individuals seemed to have gone along with the image (as frequently conveyed in the Boston press) of the large, poorly designed institutions with all manner of behavior taking place. They had no idea of the variety of public housing developments in Boston. They seemed reluctant to accept the controls exerted by public housing management. Other families with marginal behavior problems had a feeling that living in public housing would expose them to community view and to subsequent trouble with the authorities.[55]

To combat this resistance, USES prepared a *Public Housing Notebook* as part of a campaign to dispel misconceptions and convince more displacees to apply. They arranged "look-and-see tours" in cars and buses; they tried to work closely with the BHA Board, with development site managers, and with the BHA Tenant Selection chief; they arranged interviews for Castle Square displacees with tenant selection personnel, and they assisted with eligibility paperwork. The result: 150 families applied for public housing, triple the number that had previously expressed interest.[56]

As it turned out, though, only about a quarter of these households actually moved into public housing, and most of these were elderly. USES angrily blamed the BHA for the attrition. First, the BHA tried to bar noncitizens receiving Old Age Assistance from eligibility, causing USES to spearhead a four-month legal battle. Although BHA counsel eventually ruled that such people were admissible, many applicants were dissuaded by the delay and found private housing elsewhere. Others were deterred by the BHA regulations against pets and by the ways the BHA conducted home visits and "determinations of social desirability for public housing." At base, however, USES blamed the BHA for steering displacees away from the best apartments and the best projects: "on several occasions, Relocation Workers were shown desirable first and second floor vacancies in some of the better projects, but were informed that these were not available to applicants from the relocation caseload." Instead, "families were offered vacancies in projects or in neighborhoods which they did not want."[57]

In the early 1960s, racked by interagency struggles over which of the economically eligible public neighbors it ought to house, the BHA undertook all manner of rearguard actions intended to keep at least some projects reserved for "socially desirable" people. Such actions encountered many obstacles. Households facing displacement overwhelmingly evinced a preference for replacement apartments in the private rental housing stock, and those who chose to exercise their priority status for public housing tended to be those with fewest choices. Among the elderly, the newly constructed projects distributed across many desirable neighborhoods held understandable appeal. But for families too large (or too troubled) to find large enough apartments or landlords willing to accept them, public housing had become little more than a default option. The problem was greatly exacerbated for nonwhite households. The Castle Square relocation effort, whatever its other problems, was made markedly easier because—like many of the earliest BRA projects—80 percent of those displaced were white. The USES report drew italicized attention to the problem: "*Had the ratio of non-white families been the reverse, relocation could have been considerably more difficult.* For even with this small number of non-white families there was a problem of finding good housing in desirable neighborhoods."[58] Here, as would soon be the case elsewhere across the city, nonwhite displacees were sometimes disproportionately willing to seek refuge in public housing, even as many forces both inside and outside the BHA valiantly fought to keep them out of certain projects.

In the larger South End urban renewal project (of which Castle Square was an early component), a sample survey of 500 households found that 91 percent of the Puerto Rican respondents (who accounted for 18 percent of the sample) would prefer being rehoused in public housing, largely because of a need for large, affordable apartments. In the predominantly nonwhite Washington Park urban renewal area, however, only 89 of 428 households initially judged eligible expressed a preference to relocate to public housing. Ultimately the Washington Park project displaced more than 1,000 households eligible for public housing, but no family public housing was proposed for the area. Boston officials continued to assume they would readily accept placement in other vacant public housing across the city. As the civil rights movement gained legislative strength during the 1960s, any discussion of "neighborhood choice" became conflated with the burning issue of racial segregation. The USES report recognized the dilemma quite explicitly: "There is not a clear-cut solution to this problem since the residents' preferences tend to increase the existing racial imbalance of present housing projects."[59]

RACIAL DISCRIMINATION AND THE BHA

In November 1962, President Kennedy signed Executive Order 11063, directing all executive agencies to "take all action necessary and appropriate" to prevent racial discrimination in the renting of residential property financed or supported by the federal government. The federal Public Housing Administration followed this with a regulation of its own, stipulating equal opportunity in public housing. Long before, in 1950, Massachusetts lawmakers had acted to prohibit "any dis-

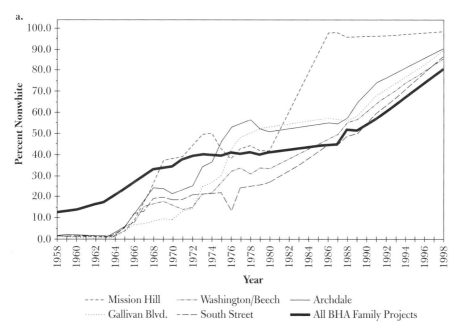

FIGURE 4.5 Although the racial composition of Boston family public housing shifted dramatically toward nonwhite occupancy, especially in the 1990s, the racial change was by no means experienced evenly or equally. Instead, the pattern of racial change took four forms as follows.

(a) The gradual progression of these five projects toward nonwhite occupancy closely resembled that of the Authority as a whole (Washington/Beech, South Street, Gallivan, Archdale, and Mission Hill).

crimination or segregation" in public housing tenant selection "because of race, color, creed or religion." Like other early civil rights legislation, though, strong language was followed by weak enforcement. At first, the BHA tried to convince the State Housing Board to omit the "or segregation" part of the anti-discrimination clause. Failing that, the BHA attempted no more than token integration of its new projects, though even such modest efforts drew local and national praise during the early 1950s.[60] Others remained much more suspicious.

By the mid-1950s, the Massachusetts Commission against Discrimination (MCAD) noted extreme disparities in project-by-project racial distribution. As long as the number of nonwhites on BHA waiting lists remained relatively small and pressures from civil rights activists remained muted, however, change was unlikely. Under PHA regulations, a housing authority could designate a project as integrated if it contained just one nonwhite and even if there was "racial separation or segregation by area within the project, a separate building or buildings, a separate floor within a building, or separate stairwell within a building."[61]

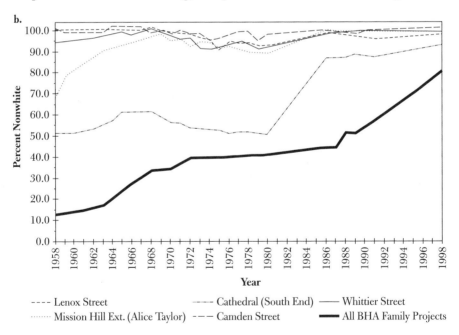

FIGURE 4.5b These four projects were intended for minority occupancy right from the start (Lenox Street, Camden Street, Whittier Street, and Mission Hill Extension). South End/Cathedral, where a high level of integration was present in the early years, is also included in this group.

In Boston, housing segregation faced its first serious challenge in 1962 in response to an NAACP and CORE analysis of BHA public housing occupancy. In May of that year, Melnea Cass, president of the Boston branch of the NAACP, filed a formal complaint with MCAD alleging "an apparent pattern of discrimination in Public Housing in Boston." Most damning was the situation prevailing in all-white Mission Hill and the adjacent Mission Hill Extension: "of the 572 housing units in the Mission Hill Extension Project as of 1961, 492 units were occupied by non-white families. The number of non-white occupants in this project has increased from 314 families in 1957, to the present number of 492 in 1961, while the Mission Hill Project across the street from the Mission Hill Extension has admitted no non-white occupants from 1957 to 1961."[62]

Stung by the negative publicity attending these charges, the BHA "integrated" Mission Hill eighteen days later by quietly renting an apartment to a lone elderly black woman. Even before she finished moving in, however, her apartment was stoned on two successive nights, resulting in twenty-four broken windowpanes. A major institutional embarrassment was made worse by the site manager's offer to

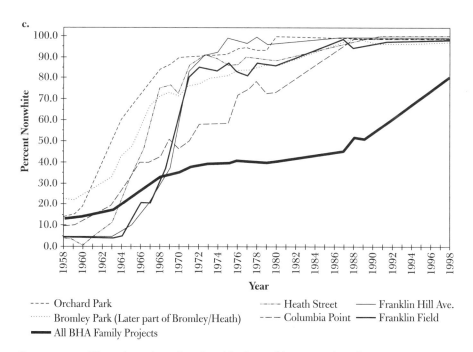

FIGURE 4.5c These six projects tipped rapidly from white to nonwhite during the 1960s (Orchard Park, Heath Street, Bromley Park, Columbia Point, Franklin Field, and Franklin Hill).

move the woman to another development where nonwhites would be more welcome. Mayoral aides and a local church leader quashed an attempt by the Massachusetts attorney general to launch a high-profile probe, and convinced the editors of *Boston Globe* and the *Boston Herald* to get "the press room boys to forget the meeting." Aides congratulated each other for having minimized "harmful publicity to the Mayor," noting that "if the press hadn't been curbed—we would have been involved in a national disgrace."[63]

In the meantime, tensions at Columbia Point, located adjacent to two municipal dumps, had escalated since April, when a six-year-old girl was run over and killed by a dump truck driven by a negligent city employee. Large-scale protest marches at the site mounted by summer into what mayoral staff called "interracial riots," leading to the eviction of several black families. The NAACP prepared discrimination charges against the Authority but dropped these following negotiations

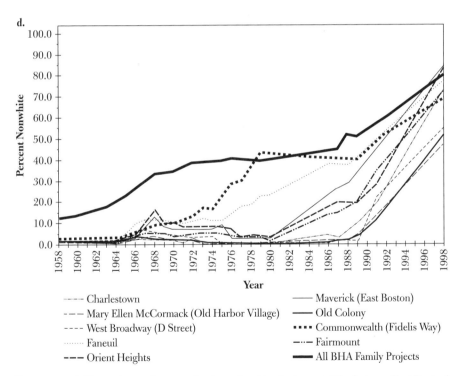

FIGURE 4.5d These nine projects remained mostly white the longest (Charlestown, East Boston/ Maverick, Old Harbor/Mary Ellen McCormack, Old Colony, West Broadway, Commonwealth, Faneuil, Fairmount, and Orient Heights). All of these remained largely white into the 1990s, despite a waiting list that had become overwhelmingly nonwhite.

with the mayor's office.[64] Nevertheless, the BHA and the mayor faced other highly damaging investigations into their efforts to sustain segregation.

If anything, the NAACP charges seem understated. As of September 1962, seventeen of the twenty-five BHA family developments and all of the five elderly developments had no more than a token nonwhite occupancy; collectively, these were 99 percent white. Conversely, in four of the eight projects where nonwhites were accepted, their collective presence was 93 percent, and the other four—Orchard Park, South End/Cathedral, Bromley Park, and Columbia Point—were becoming increasingly nonwhite. Although the federally sponsored developments were themselves highly segregated, the state's Chapter 200 projects were more so. Of the 3,686 Massachusetts-sponsored units, all but 129 were occupied by whites, and more than two-thirds of the nonwhites were concentrated in the all-black Camden Street development, constructed adjacent to the earlier all-black Lenox Street federal project (Figs. 4.5–4.6).[65]

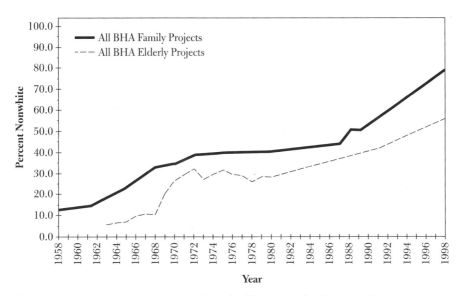

FIGURE 4.6 From the moment construction of public housing for the elderly began in the early 1960s it housed a markedly higher percentage of whites than did BHA family public housing. Though the disparity continued, both kinds of developments moved toward nonwhite-majority occupancy.

When the BHA went into receivership in 1980, white households occupied 60 percent of its family public housing and 72 percent of its housing for the elderly. By 1998, however, only 20 percent of residents of family public housing were white, and whites constituted a minority of those living in public housing for the elderly.

The Authority's Defense

Edward Hassan rejected the charge of willful segregation, arguing that the distribution of tenants in public housing was driven largely by the tenants' own choices and preferences. He told a *Boston Globe* reporter: "I personally have never had a complaint from anyone claiming they were being discriminated against. If [the NAACP] has any specific cases in mind, I know nothing about them. You must remember people choose their projects. They make application and usually state the projects they prefer to go into. We try to house them where they want to go." He added that because "the applications make no reference to color," even "the most searching investigation will fail to disclose any pattern of discrimination." In subsequent statements before MCAD, the Authority marshaled racial occupancy statistics to demonstrate both progress and nondiscrimination. Pointing to a 21 percent increase in overall nonwhite occupancy from 1959 to 1962, the Board noted that nonwhites resided in more than 15 percent of BHA apartments, a ratio more than 50 percent higher than nonwhite occupancy for the city as a whole. Moreover, the rate of admission for nonwhites had been steadily increasing and currently constituted one-fourth of all new admissions. Finally, countering the argument that nonwhites needed public housing more than whites, the Authority observed that nonwhites occupied only about 17 percent of the city's substandard housing units. In this view, far from evidence of discrimination, nonwhites could be seen as getting their "fair share." As for the segregation charge, the BHA expressed concern about "the slow rate of non-white family admissions in some developments and . . . imbalance of ethnic relationships in other developments," but argued that "the non-white occupancy ratio in public housing generally exceeds the racial pattern in private housing in the neighborhood surrounding the development." If there was a racially dichotomous pattern of residence, it was because "applicants, white and non-white, have demonstrated an overwhelming preference for developments in neighborhoods that are familiar to them through present or prior residence." The Board concluded that "any significant extension of its open occupancy policy" not only depended on its own actions but also "must involve general community enlightenment and acceptance."[66]

Even as it sought to shift blame for racial segregation to society as a whole, by the spring of 1963 the BHA was under siege by a variety of groups intent on reform. The Massachusetts Commission on Discrimination in Housing (MCDH) served as an umbrella organization for twenty different civil rights groups (including both the NAACP and CORE); a variety of social agencies cooperated to form the United Community Services committee on Public Housing; and tenants from several predominantly black housing projects expressed their own views through the Tenant Association Council (TAC). All these groups, bolstered by the efforts of CORE and the NAACP to collect further evidence of discrimination, insisted that the Boston Housing Authority make fundamental changes. Most directly, they placed pressure on Collins to appoint a strong new administrator who could wrest control away from the Board.

SEEKING AN ABOVE-BOARD LEADER

To a degree unequaled elsewhere in the country, the Boston Housing Authority of the early 1960s was a public housing agency entirely operated by its Board. From 1938 until his death in 1960, Francis X. Lane, who had been progressively stripped of power, formally directed the BHA. For the next three years, neither the Board nor the mayor made any conclusive move to replace him. With four members loyal to Collins, and the fifth a long-serving gubernatorial appointment, the Board acted as both administrators and policymaking body, "making all day-to-day decisions and running the program without interference." Each member had an office and private secretary at BHA headquarters; as chairman, Hassan got two secretaries and a chauffeured limousine. During this time, changes in state law allowed each Board member to receive per diem compensation totaling up to $10,000 annually ($12,500 for the chairman). One contemporary investigation estimated that overall annual expenses to support the Board totaled nearly $100,000. Although they were not housing professionals and were entitled to retain their other occupations, their annual remuneration was second only to the salary no longer being paid to the administrator.[67]

At a time when the federal public housing program prohibited compensation to housing authority board members, and when only five states allowed this practice, BHA exploitation of the Massachusetts law permitted payments that were five to ten times higher than those prevailing in any other city in the country, reimbursement that had to be paid out of the rental receipts from the State's Chapter 200 program. In the eyes of critics, the system caused "men whose job it is to make policy [to] put in daily appearances in order to collect their per diem payment," and put Board appointments into "the category of desirable 'plums,'" preventing the positions from going to "more dedicated or qualified men, who would need to meet only weekly or bi-weekly to perform their basic policy-making function."[68]

In early 1963, with the MCAD complaint still unresolved, the civil rights groups focused on the need for a new administrator who would make a formal commitment to desegregate the projects. Attempting to fill the long-vacant post in the least disruptive manner, Hassan (who, at age seventy-three, had recently been appointed to another five-year term) nominated Jeremiah Sullivan, superintendent of maintenance at the Mission Hill project. Although the Board kept to its usual policy of not providing reporters or outside groups with advance indication of its agenda, Victor Bynoe, a black man nominated for the Board in the waning days of the Hynes Administration, apparently tipped off the civil rights leaders about the plan. At the meeting where Sullivan was proposed, CORE member James Bishop read a statement on behalf of nine civic groups indicating their dissatisfaction: "There has been no public indication that the Mayor has done anything to stimulate an intensive search for the best qualified candidate. [The BHA chairman] has apparently refused to submit any names—except the man he favors—to others for their consideration." In the context of large-scale displacement of low-income families, anticipated to include many blacks, the groups doubted that "the candidate has the background necessary for the job." They called for an open and through public search for a new administrator, and charged that "If a new director is appointed without a firm public commitment [to end] isolated racial and economic ghettos, second-ratism will have become further established in a significant sector of the community."[69] With this well-publicized statement of outrage, the urgency of the situation stood revealed. Still, the Board continued to table the matter from week to week through its spring meetings without public discussion.

Mayor Collins knew he had to act or face continued political embarrassment. In mid-May, he usurped the Board's role and appointed Ellis Ash as acting administrator. Ash, who was Ed Logue's deputy at the Boston Redevelopment Authority and who had held senior housing posts in Baltimore and Seattle, had close ties to civil rights groups and housing reformers, and proved to be an acceptable choice both to the Board and to the various pressure groups.[70] Desperate to move the BHA toward a more rational basis of public accountability, an Irish Catholic mayor bravely—if half-heartedly—bucked three decades of precedent and installed a Yankee reformer in the BHA's midst.

REFORM AND ITS LIMITS

Almost immediately upon taking office, Ash wrote a letter to MCAD commissioner Ben Shapiro asking him to defer a finding on the year-old NAACP complaint until the two of them could speak, implying that he would try to wrest control of this issue from the BHA Board.[71] Armed only with the title of acting administrator, Ash tried to move swiftly and sincerely to meet Mayor Collins's challenge to "take care of that NAACP business."[72] Collins, Ash later recalled, was "not in favor" of integration but was "a very politically sensitive individual, and he understood quite well the social forces going on during this period, and that integration was inevitable." Ash and Collins both saw the BHA administrator position as a chance to "transform some of the hostility" directed at the BHA into praise for the mayor's "willingness to adopt a reform attitude."[73] A month later, on the basis of Ash's recommendations, the BHA Board issued a "Policy Statement on Tenancy," promising to ensure the BHA's "obligation to be non-discriminatory in all of its practices and to achieve and to maintain integrated housing developments." The statement substantially prefigured the conditions of the actual agreement later reached with the NAACP and CORE. The *Boston Globe* printed the BHA statement in full and heralded the event with the rather premature headline "Hub Adopts Fair Housing."[74]

The BHA statement acknowledged that "public housing is public business," and was expected to be "part of the arsenal of public resources devised to cope with the problems and complexities of urban living." That said, the Board made it clear that it would not consent to be the repository of all such problems and complexities. The Authority promised to abide by a reformed tenant selection system designed to permit greater identification of relative need, consented to seek affirmative ways "to achieve and maintain integrated housing projects," and agreed to prohibit applicants from targeting their application to a particular project on the basis of "reasons suggesting prejudice." At the same time, however, the statement included what amounted to a public neighbor clause. Admission and assignment of households could be modified to ensure "the economic stability of the housing projects (a legal and practical requirement)" and "to avoid serious jeopardy to the general welfare of a tenant body by referring a household with aggravated cultural deficiencies and social problems that cannot be serviced adequately by a combination of BHA and community resources. (This circumstance refers to the serious multiple social problem household.)"[75] This clause proved too inflammatory and discretionary to be included in the framework of the final agreement with the NAACP. Instead of language warning of "aggravated cultural deficiencies and social problems," the final stipulation—signed by the BHA Board, CORE, and the NAACP in November—stated that tenant placement should "promote the general welfare of the inhabitants of the project or the applicant" in ways consistent with the agreement.[76]

While the Board remained concerned that action to promote racial integration would accelerate the economic and moral decline of the projects, the agreements signed in 1963 set the BHA on a contentious new course, one characterized both by unprecedented public oversight and by internal turmoil over basic mission. As part of the stipulations accepted to reach resolution of the MCAD complaint, the BHA agreed to an independent Advisory Committee on Minority Housing that would provide guidance on race relations matters and monitor BHA progress in implementing desegregation goals. The Advisory Committee was to be chaired by Reverend Robert Drinan, S.J., then the dean of Boston College Law School, who—like Ash—had already been instrumental in negotiating resolution of the MCAD complaint.

Within the housing authority itself, the Board agreed to establish a new Department of Tenant and Community Relations staffed with an "intergroup relations officer" and other "tenant relations aides." Ash and the Advisory Committee expected the new department to help the races "interpret" one another and to provide referrals to community social agencies, much in the manner of the old settlement houses. Staffing the department proved highly contentious, revealing a deep-seated ambivalence in City Hall. Ash and the Advisory Committee hoped to install Richard Scobie, a social worker, as head, but one top mayoral aide warned Collins that "we will be in serious trouble" unless the mayor could "prevent Scobie from getting the race job or any responsible job in BHA." Scobie, together with Ash and the civil rights leaders they supported, constituted a "combine" that "means business." "We have not got much time left to halt them," he appealed to Collins. "This group can cause more trouble, more headlines and real bloodshed so easily, they will make [the NAACP] look like amateurs." Adding sectarian strife to the mix, he charged that "Ash and Scobie are out to put the Catholics in their place and this attitude will cause nothing but trouble."[77] Another Collins aide asked police department staffer Thomas Francis to conduct an informal investigation of Scobie, which pegged him as "a most vocal member of the Mass. Committee for [*sic*] Discrimination in Housing," and as "young, in-experienced, starry-eyed, and a close associate of extremists."[78] The thirty-year-old Scobie eventually did get "the race job," but the mayor's office made sure that the post of intergroup relations officer went to Francis, regarded as a loyal spy who could be counted on to observe and curtail any excess of civil rights activism.

With City Hall offering little more than cautious acquiescence to the whole venture of integration, Ash tried to provide BHA staff with guidance on coping with the changing clientele of the projects. In July 1963, he obtained funds to send forty-six development managers and central office staff to one of two three-day "Intergroup Relations Orientation Institutes." These retreats, held outside Boston and conducted by university faculty, focused on racial sensitivity and aimed to help participants understand such concepts as "Who am I" and "With whom am I dealing." As one participant put it, "This was a chance for all Managers and Assistant Managers and other personnel to sort of let their hair down in the huge problem of segregation." Daily exit evaluations of these retreats, submitted anonymously, were quite positive, yet also revealed the growing cultural chasm between a management and maintenance staff that was more than 95 percent white and a tenant population that was becoming increasingly racially diverse. One staffer claimed to have gained a better approach to "the correct handling of Negro persons that we are to deal with"; another reported having learned "that the Negro must be accepted into our community and society." Others were more self-critical, acknowledging that it was improper "to project my personal feelings and attitudes in dealing with tenants" or that "I would have to change my way of thinking." Most respondents stressed that three days was not enough time to come to terms with the complexity of the issues.[79]

Despite the new initiatives, rearguard actions by the Board and other recalcitrant BHA staff continued to frustrate Ash's efforts at reform. Until 1965 the Board conducted all its substantive business in closed executive sessions and continued to hire key personnel without Ash's knowledge, much less his recommendation. Hassan, whom Ash considered to be "militantly, even viciously" against integration, led other members in resisting efforts to implement the publicly stipulated changes in policy and operation. Meanwhile, with the Board's blessing, many development managers also continued to exercise "heavy authority." In opposition to stated policy, they would regularly collect available vacancies in waiting list "pools," awaiting patronage-based placements rather than reporting the openings to BHA headquarters. This practice kept the vast majority of projects closed to the "relocation families" that the BRA wished to place.[80]

The efforts to sustain spatial distinctions among public neighbors subverted the efforts at integration by consolidating a kind of two-class system of projects, one with clear racial overtones. As a memo from the Advisory Committee on Minority Housing complained to Collins in 1964, many projects "have become the houses for lower income problem families," and the social environment "is little better than the slums these projects replaced"; at the same time, Advisory Committee chairman Drinan noted, other BHA projects "provide model living conditions" but exclude "white families with problems and all but a few Negroes." To demonstrate the point, Drinan provided the mayor with the following annotated tables:[81]

Some of the better projects are listed below:

	TOTAL UNITS	# NON-WHITE TENANTS
Mary E. McCormack	1,000	0
Mission Hill	1,010	1
Old Colony	852	0
Gallivan Blvd.	251	0
Franklin Field	500	16
Washington/Beech	272	3
TOTAL	*3,892*	*20*

Other less attractive projects that have been reserved for problem families and Negroes are as follows:

	TOTAL UNITS	# NON-WHITE TENANTS
Mission Hill Ext.	580	509
Columbia Point	1,392	220
Lenox St.	300	300
Bromley Park	694	203
TOTAL	*2,966*	*1,222*

In this way, Drinan linked racial issues to the other factors that had made coping with the new wave of public neighbors so contentious. Significantly, even in the mind of this civil rights champion, "problem families and Negroes" could be construed as a single category. Drinan's categorization of problem people could also resonate with Board members who believed that Ash's reforms promoted moral decay by allowing more projects to slip from the first category into the second.

Ash's attempts to reform the Chapter 200 public housing program proved most daunting of all. With its budget controlled by state officials who held "very rigid opinions in favor of white occupancy," Ash struggled with what he called "resistance to any kind of integration." In late 1964, in a speech to the commonwealth's Special Commission on Low-Income Housing, he complained that the state deliberately resisted serving "lower income Negro households" by setting its minimum rents too high. Noting that the state also refused to help cover the budget of the BHA's new Tenant and Community Relations department, he concluded that such decisions "seem to reflect a lack of concern about the social and human implications of a public housing program in a general welfare context."[82] Ash had a prominent ally in Washington, Robert Weaver, then the administrator of the Housing and Home Finance Agency (and later to become the first head of the Department of Housing and Urban Development). But ultimately Ash needed allies within the BHA itself, whose staff as he viewed as "fundamentally incompetent" to make public housing into "a compatible and accommodating resource for urban renewal."[83] With nearly all of this staff eligible for lifetime tenure under the terms of a 1962 state law, the situation was not likely to change any time soon.

In the bureaucratic purgatory of his position as acting administrator, Ash felt stymied at every turn. In March 1964 he pleaded with Collins to take a stand on his behalf, since only the mayor could "tell the Chairman the rules of the game." Instead of telling Hassan what to do, however, Collins asked for his opinion. The chairman urged the mayor to let the BHA Board (what he called "the Authority") retain its control over the "hiring and firing of employees" and continue to have the "last word in tenant selection." He conceded that Ash as administrator could be allowed to "administer the program," but contended that "this administration should be done under the supervision of the Authority." Only Victor Bynoe gave Collins a more complex view of the implications for BHA administration, if it were to implement the agreement reached with the NAACP and CORE. Echoing the findings of the Elizabeth Wood report, Bynoe noted that "socio-economic problem families . . . now represent almost one-half of our public housing population," and admitted that "we seem to be lost as babes in the woods trying to find the answers." The only solution, in Bynoe's view, was to "accept responsibility for the rehabilitation of many of our tenants and their children," by providing enough affordable accommodation for large low-income families. Bynoe blamed private real estate interests, which since 1929 "have not built one apartment that could be said was available for families with three or more children at a price they could afford." Bynoe acknowledged that recasting the Authority's relationship to its tenants would require changes in the BHA bureaucracy. "Cognizant of the political implication," he pointed out the necessity of upgrading the level of competence among BHA staff. "I acknowledge that herein lies the only area where political patronage is available in the City, and I am confident that a formula can be worked out where we may establish a framework of competent personnel which would be able to carry in a large degree the less competent, so that the overall operation will not suffer and we could then show some progress in this area."[84] Even Bynoe, however, stopped short of asking Collins to strengthen the position of Ellis Ash.

Ash's nebulous status as acting administrator continued into 1965, when, buffeted by complaints from a variety of civic groups, Collins finally replaced Hassan with Jacob Brier as Board chairman. Although this move paved the way for Ash to become administrator in name as well as in deed a few months later, Brier continued the "longtime practice of using his position and the Board generally to provide concessions and favors for friends and related interests."[85]

In November 1965, despite procrastination by the Board and ongoing problems with many staff, Ash finally succeeded in steering through a new tenant selection and assignment procedure. Richard Scobie and the other liberal reformers replaced the fifteen criteria previously used to justify exclusion, charging that these had fostered "capricious decisions on the basis of personal philosophy, temperament or bias." The new "Occupancy Standards," which formally applied only to federally aided developments, eliminated specific prohibitions against accepting tenants with illegitimate children, drug and alcohol problems, unsanitary housekeeping practices, arrest records, poor rent payment histories, and the like. The BHA now defined an unacceptable family as one whose composition or behavior constituted "a danger to the health, safety, or morals of other tenants; a seriously adverse influence upon sound family and community life; a source of danger or damage to the property of the Authority; a source of danger to the peace and comfort of other families; or in any other sense, a nuisance." Although these proscriptions, too, allowed considerable leeway to the BHA in defining morals and sound family and community life, the resolution explicitly prohibited "discrimination against families, otherwise eligible for admission, because their incomes are derived in whole or in part from public assistance," and disallowed "quotas or other devices" intended to limit the number of tenants receiving such aid.[86]

The new screening system made it harder to declare an applicant flatly ineligible for public housing, but continued to allow the BHA to invoke many of the fifteen old proscriptions through use of a "tentative eligibility" category. Applicants found to exhibit evidence of "lack of family stability, inadequate housekeeping standards, anti-social behavior, lack of parental control over children, or other situations that require study and evaluation" were referred to the social workers at the new Tenant and Community Relations Department for further scrutiny. According to a study produced by the department, the majority of such referrals were occasioned by the presence of "children out-of-wedlock." Other sources of concern included a Board of Probation record, a previous poor record of BHA rent payment, as well as "poor housekeeping, questionable control of children, age of applicant, medical problems, and rejection by [a] housing manager." The key difference between the new system and the old one was that these borderline cases were now adjudicated not by the tenant selection staff and the Board, but by the new Department of Tenant and Community Relations. Faced with such questionable public neighbors, the new system behaved very differently: of the first 297 referrals it evaluated, only fourteen (less than 5 percent) were returned to the Tenant Selection Department with a recommendation of "ineligible." As Jon Pynoos put it, the new gatekeepers were now "welfare professionals . . . committed to serving applicants rather than excluding them."[87]

The shift in attitude at the BHA, however incomplete and however contentious, paralleled efforts in most other large American cities. Across the country, housing authorities abandoned minimum-income requirements for admission, and by 1966 nearly half of the households being admitted to public housing lacked an employed member, and half were headed by a single parent. As a nationwide study prepared for the National Commission on Urban Problems concluded, "The statistical data show that public housing is reaching the lowest income families among those who apply. If anything, public housing developments are becoming isolated colonies of the poorest, least competitive elements of society."[88] Every large urban public housing authority faced the same struggle, caught

315

between one set of critics who charged that housing authorities still discriminated against the least advantaged and another set who complained that these agencies catered excessively to such people.

SERVING PUBLIC NEIGHBORS

In setting its own policies, the BHA significantly and explicitly recast its public mission, declaring: "The Authority recognizes that not only its statutory responsibility but its moral, public responsibility to accommodate low-income families in need of housing limit its freedom to reject the potentially unacceptable tenant." Further, "families whose standards make them unacceptable are a responsibility of the community and, so far as their need for low-rent housing is concerned, of the Authority." Such a statement, grounded in an ethic of public obligation, was a far cry indeed from the original narrow system of selective collectives. Public neighbors were now wholly welcomed in public housing.

In the brave new world of 1965, public housing was expected to supply the battlefield hospitals for the War on Poverty. The perennial concern for solvency did not disappear, of course, but the Board now sought to assure it through reliance on tenant selection predicated on a "two-range" system of rent. The "lower range" included families able to pay less than "the rental average required to meet routine operating expenses" (including those paying the "minimum welfare rent"); the "upper range" embraced those able to pay more than the average rent needed to meet operating costs. The BHA planned to select families alternately from the two ranges or in such other way as to guarantee that operating expenses could be met, while thereby producing "a desirable economic mix." Moreover, the BHA stated that this system, which established an implicit ceiling of 50 percent on overall accommodation of welfare families, would be used to correct "existing imbalances" among projects in terms of "race, number of broken families, over-crowding, [or] economic stratification." More specifically, the BHA stated that its "positive policy of integration and racial balance" would be used to make each development eventually "reflect the racial balance of the total racial ratio existing throughout all the developments maintained by the Authority."[89] In other words, all developments in the city were theoretically to be integrated to the same extent, regardless of the racial composition of their surrounding neighborhoods or the preferences of their residents.

For Ash and his allies at the BHA, driven by overarching principles of fairness and general welfare rather than by personal responses to the particular claims of individual citizens, broad-based integration of the developments remained the overriding goal. This meant that tenant assignments would immediately depend less on the preference of the applicants than on the needs to advance integration and racial balance. The plan had two key components: "promotional efforts" to "arrest or reverse 'tipping' trends" once a project had 25–30 percent black residents and, where integration had not yet been achieved, initiating it through "careful selection of 'pioneer' families." In an odd twist to the language used to describe the nineteenth-century Western homesteaders, the BHA regularly used the term "pioneer" to describe those "whole family units with a good work background" who agreed to be sent off to settle the interracial wilderness.[90] Their pioneer status, of course, lay in their presumed willingness to endure a harsh climate and unfriendly natives, but offered none of the ideological supports associated with the earlier house form and tenure. Unlike other public housing applicants, however, these pioneers could at least have some say about which development they were to integrate.

Otherwise, the new policy now forbade the Authority to honor "preference for accommodation in any particular development" or to accede to any request that seemed "based on like or dislike of the racial composition of a development." Applicants could, if they wished, express preferences for "areas" of the city. In this frontal attack on the principle of tenant residential preference, the new BHA system seemed a direct response to challenges raised a few months earlier by Drinan's Advisory Committee on Minority Housing, which contended that "as long as tenants were allowed to choose their project, they will *choose locations on the basis of ethnic group identification,* although they may be careful to state more acceptable reasons for their choice." In the case of public housing, a tenant assignment policy that bowed to preference "encourages intimidating behavior on the part of individuals and groups who do not want 'outsiders.'" To combat this tendency, Drinan argued that in a democracy personal preference must be seen as a "qualified right," and that a "public institution" such as a housing authority must "balance the rights, dangers and responsibilities of a community" in setting policies aimed at "over-all welfare."

> So long as the Authority responds primarily to personal preference they will be encouraging people to continue to live in the segregated ways they have been trained to employ in the past. Negroes have been taught to accept the worst; they are shown by behavior of

the community that their presence is not desired, and they have been trained to keep their places and not make trouble.

If the Authority permits the fear of demonstrations, incidents, or riots to keep them from responsibly assigning significant numbers of Negroes to units where they feel white tenants will rebel, they are then, in a sense, permitting a kind of mob rule and submitting to fear. It is comparable to not giving Negroes the opportunity to vote in Mississippi so long as white persons object to it strongly enough.

Like Ash, the Advisory Committee was committed to public housing integration not just because it was the law, but because—if it could be made to occur on a significant rather than a token basis—it would result in a genuinely healthier society. Once members of differing ethnic groups "live together and identify with one another," Drinan claimed, "history shows" that their "irrational and damaging" attitudes and behaviors are transformed. Only with "sufficient maturity of the individual and of his society" would housing applicants "feel more free to make choices on a realistic basis instead of through attachments to an ethnic group."[91]

In the view of reformers, the obligation of a public agency—and, by extension, the special responsibility of the public neighbors that it assisted—was to suppress urges for ethnic solidarity in the name of societal peace. Taken on its own, this saddled the poorest with a broad civic duty in exchange for their subsidy, a responsibility that the more affluent of 1965 could systematically evade through purchase of monoracial peace in suburbia or in other white neighborhood enclaves in Boston itself. Moreover, by coupling this forced suppression of "ethnic group identification" with restrictions on "individual preference" for dwelling and neighborhood, the reformers were asking low-income tenants to counteract three centuries of ideological ties between residential choice and moral worth. Even some progressives cast doubt on the advisability of the venture. Writing in 1966, Chester Hartman warned:

> By positing the goal of racial integration above all others, a key element of personal decision is taken away from public housing tenants, [and] a further invidious (and possibly unacceptable) distinction placed between those who are and are not recipients of government welfare benefits. If one of the key elements of a satisfactory living arrangement is location, neighbors, surroundings, convenience, etc., single-minded pursuit of racial integration as the

criterion for tenant placement and selection may prove counterpro-
ductive . . . It may be that until such time as there is "no hiding
place," when open occupancy housing is achieved throughout all
sectors, we cannot and should not expect a significant level of racial
integration in public housing.[92]

Rather than waiting for society to change first, however, the BHA sought to set a
model for society. Just as public housing itself had been seen as a provocative
challenge to the operation of private real estate markets, now public housing
tenants—already constrained in their choice of private neighborhood by economics and racial animus—were asked to let a government agency also limit their
choice of a public neighborhood in order to promote a public purpose that, in
the short run at least, could prove detrimental to their mental health and physical
safety. Once again, "rational politics" and "ethnic politics" had converged in the
projects.

At a time of rapidly increasing black migration to the city, the BHA's 1965 resolution promised to scatter "Negro and problem families," rather than let blacks
concentrate in certain projects to the point where developments "tipped" and all
the remaining whites ran out.[93] The BHA Board implicitly took the view that
public housing residents—and the city as a whole—would be better off without
more all-black projects, since these could in turn promote the expansion of the
black ghetto. In this view, the safest city was one in which whites could safely
outnumber nonwhites in almost every neighborhood.

For others, however, the risks of integration seemed too high. Despite the
broad review powers granted to the social welfare staffers of the Tenant and
Community Relations Department, the old institutional politics persisted. Although Ash gave the new department control over managing integration efforts,
he could not prevent the site managers from continuing to deliver news of vacancies directly to the Board chairman, thereby bypassing all official tenant selection
procedures. According to Ash, until at least 1968 "the actual assignment of tenants to units, or who got what, was done in the Chairman's office" in an attempt
to satisfy "the wishes of the Mayor, City Council members, certain legislators and
each Authority [Board] member." As the BHA's "thoroughly exasperated" Advisory Committee phrased it in 1966, the "performance gap" between rhetoric and
reality remained "of alarming and disheartening proportion." Instead of steady
progress, "One senses the continued functioning of a 'system within the system'

which tends to resist, if not defy, direction from the Office of the Administrator." According to a report by the Boston Municipal Research Bureau,

> The Housing Authority's major problem can be summed up as control. Authority Board members do not delegate powers. As a result, there are no guidelines on who can make what decisions or supervise whom; and there is no decision-making power assumed by anyone that cannot be recalled by the Board at any time for any reason, dealing with any one. The Administrator has no power to supervise the department heads—or lower level employees. There are some who have the courtesy to deal with the Board only through the Administrator and some who do not.

Lewis Popper, a Harvard undergraduate who spent several months as Ash's administrative assistant, concluded that "the constant criticism" of the administrator had little to do with "personal dislikes and personality clashes," but rested more fundamentally on "the nature of the policy demands that Ash imposes on the rest of the organization." "At staff meetings," he noted, "when Ash argues for new policies on which there is deep disagreement, some of the staff members stare at the table and ignore him altogether." Moreover, at an organization formally headed by a Yankee reformer and prodded by a Tenant and Community Relations department led by a black and a Jew, but where the eleven top nonprofessional BHA staff were either Irish (nine) or Italian (two)—as were most of the managers—unspoken ethnic tensions within the BHA itself may well have contributed to the policy impasse.[94]

Whatever the forces undergirding the BHA's dysfunctional bureaucracy, the staff perpetuated the racial and ethnic discrimination faced by prospective tenants. Advisory Committee investigations of Tenant Selection office procedures in 1966 confirmed that "Negroes are furnished with only a limited range of selection—mainly Orchard Park, Columbia Point, Bromley Park [and] Mission Hill Extension" and "have no way of knowing" about other vacancies. In his efforts to integrate white developments, Ash had to solicit a parallel system of vacancy reports, relying on tenant informants and depending on the NAACP to help recruit the "pioneer" black families willing to move into white projects. Many of these white projects were in areas where no blacks lived in the private-sector housing or attended the local schools.[95]

Despite such efforts, Ash acknowledged that "neighborhood hostility" led to "strong reluctance" among most blacks to be "pioneer" families. This held true especially in "predominantly Roman Catholic areas," such as South Boston, Charlestown, and East Boston, where potential applicants themselves often became "hostile and adamant in their opposition" to placement. Moreover, as Pynoos has noted, "When many of the original 'pioneers' requested transfers to projects in black areas, civil rights groups became disenchanted with the strategy and hesitant to recruit new applicants." Reformers had called for quotas of 25 percent blacks in the white projects to lessen the social problems associated with tokenism and isolation, but Boston's political leaders, from Mayor Collins on down, resisted such a move, and were especially unwilling to try to move whites into predominantly black projects.[96] Despite the difficulties, the staff of the Tenant and Community Relations Department spent "hours, days and even weeks" with individual nonwhite families, attempting to "evaluate their strengths and abilities to cope with possible anti-Negro attitudes and pressures that could possibly arise when they moved into all white or nearly all white projects" and to "convince them of the importance of integration and the benefits and opportunities available to their families, especially their children." But with BHA staff still 93 percent white as late as 1967, the Authority did little to create a racially mixed management structure to facilitate integration.[97]

Despite the impediments, by 1967 some black, Puerto Rican, or Asian families had moved into nearly every development. However, eight projects remained more than 95 percent white, and five others were still 90 percent white. With nonwhites making up the majority of the waiting list, they could still legitimately claim to be underrepresented.[98]

On the equally contentious issue of halting racial "tipping," Advisory Committee members pressured the BHA to make all tenant assignments on the basis of integration goals, and particularly disparaged the rapid racial turnover occurring at Orchard Park (12 percent black in 1957, 23 percent black in 1961, and 59 percent black in 1964). In June 1964, 335 Orchard Park tenants sent a petition to the BHA: "We, the tenants of the Orchard Park Housing Development, would like to make it known that we feel that Negro and White people can live together harmoniously. We have demonstrated that people of good will, regardless of race or cultural background, can and will work with one another to achieve a decent neighborhood. Therefore, we are asking for co-operation from the Boston Housing Authority to help maintain a racial balance in this development." The BHA said it would try to arrest the accelerating imbalance through a variety of means. The

Board agreed to let all transfer requests be personally approved by the administrator, who would disallow moves based on racial animus, but warned the mayor's office that such scrutiny would prevent it from "aiding in the many requested transfers" received from City Hall.[99] The Board also said it would encourage black families needing larger apartments to transfer to predominantly white developments, invite whites displaced by urban renewal to move to majority-black projects, and ask nearby Catholic churches to identify local white parishioners in need of housing. In response, the Advisory Committee called for more radical measures, arguing that the backlog of vacancies should be filled according to a simple rule: "process the entire 'white' backlog through Orchard Park and other predominantly Negro projects. Process the entire 'colored' backlog for predominantly 'white' projects." Needless to say, the Authority resisted, noting that "the imposition of a 'benign quota system' is clearly illegal under the state and federal fair housing laws." By 1969 Orchard Park was 89 percent nonwhite.[100] Several other BHA projects "tipped" just as precipitously during these years (see Fig. 4.5).

NATIONAL PRESSURES FOR DESEGREGATION

While Boston-area civil rights groups were pressuring the BHA for reform, national civil rights legislation was creating federal pressure for public housing desegregation. These efforts encouraged the Housing and Home Finance Agency (and later the new Department of Housing and Urban Development) to set uniform federal standards. Those standards, promulgated in 1965, ushered in the idea of a "Free Choice Plan," under which applicants for public housing were to be able to apply for housing in any public housing development they wished, a move ostensibly intended to allow nonwhites to gain entry into previously closed projects. However, such a system could also have the effect of encouraging racial separation, and civil rights groups soon charged that it did nothing more than promote "amiable apartheid."[101]

In February 1967 the coalition of religious, labor, and civic reform organizations that made up the National Committee against Discrimination in Housing (NCDH) released a scathing report, titled *How the Federal Government Builds Ghettos.* "'Free choice' in public housing," the coalition contended, "as every local authority knows, really means that each Negro is free to live in the dark ghetto of his choice, and each white is free to live in the white ghetto of his choice." The report singled out the BHA for special disdain, noting that "three years after 'total integration' had come to Boston, Mission Hill was still 96 percent white and Mission Hill Extension was 87 percent Negro." The only solution, the civil rights groups charged, was for the federal government to exercise its "affirmative obligation . . . to *compel* the Authority" to shift families from one side of the development to the other.[102]

This attack, coupled with other evidence that the "Free Choice Plan" was doing little to promote desegregation, convinced Robert Weaver, secretary of HUD, to propose a new system, intended to reduce the discretion available to both applicants and bureaucrats. The new plan required housing authorities to offer applicants three choices, limited to projects where vacancy rates were highest. Many local public housing authorities objected to the "1-2-3 Plan." Ash contended that although the 1-2-3 policy might desegregate southern projects, where the highest vacancies existed in desirable white-occupied developments that were unfairly closed to nonwhites, "in Boston it would only cause whites to flee projects, leaving more vacancies and creating black ghettoes that wouldn't appeal to either white or black families."[103] Ash argued that Boston's own desegregation plan would be more likely to promote a more effective local solution than the federal mandate, but HUD determined that the plans developed in Boston contravened federal guidelines, and rejected them. Since the Civil Rights Act of 1965 allowed the federal government to withhold funds from agencies found to be in violation of its desegregation procedures, and since the BHA could not afford to let this happen, the agency capitulated. In December 1968 the BHA agreed to abide by HUD's 1-2-3 plan, and to assign applicants only to those projects with the highest vacancies.[104]

As before, however, stated BHA policy bore little relation to practice. Both staff and applicants knew that the places with the most vacancies also had the worst reputations. Moreover, most applicants expressed a strong desire to live in a project located in their current neighborhood, except in the cases of some whites whose neighborhoods were undergoing rapid racial transformation. Such concerns help explain why more than half of those offered only the three choices refused them, even if doing so meant forfeiting their chance to obtain public housing for the foreseeable future. According to one staff member, "The 1-2-3 projects were always in black areas. While white families definitely didn't want those projects, about 50 percent of black families didn't want to go either."[105]

With white applicants more than three times as likely as nonwhites to reject their public housing options, the tenant assignment system concentrated nonwhites in Boston's family public housing and exacerbated its segregation. This racial and spatial concentration seems to have occurred for a variety of interconnected reasons. Since the projects with the highest vacancies were also those in the worst physical shape, many whites (whose current housing conditions tended to be better on average than those of black applicants) simply did not see public housing as yielding an improvement over their current circumstances. Moreover, since the vacancy counts that determined the 1-2-3 rankings included many apartments that were not only vacant but vandalized and uninhabitable, and since reclaiming such apartments for renewed occupancy occurred very slowly if at all, — the same three developments (Columbia Point, Bromley-Heath, and Mission Hill Extension) remained at the top of the list for years on end. As a consequence, the desegregation plan "never progressed to the point that black applicants were routinely offered assignments at predominantly white projects."[106] Thus, continued vacancies in three heavily black projects insulated the white projects from participation in the plan. Deferring maintenance became a mechanism for deferring integration.

To the extent that they believed that the only public housing available was in projects that were distant, decrepit, and black, many whites whose low incomes and poor housing conditions would have made them eligible for public housing no longer even bothered to apply. By 1967, though whites still occupied about three-quarters of BHA apartments, they constituted only 41 percent of the applicant pool.[107] Moreover, many whites who did apply knew how to seek entry into the particular project they wanted by exploiting the "system within the system."

BEYOND 1-2-3: MAKING PUBLIC HOUSING COUNT FOR WHITES

With all official attention ostensibly focused on filling the vacancies in the three emptiest projects, the 1-2-3 system allowed vacancies to accumulate in the projects not included as priorities, which site managers filled by more informal means. One study of 3,280 applicants who were offered assignments from June 1969 to September 1970 found that only 22 percent (most of them nonwhites) accepted regular assignments consistent with the 1-2-3 rule. An additional 28 percent (most of them whites) were offered but refused assignment to one of the three high-vacancy developments, and went to the bottom of the waiting list. The rest—fully half of the total and most of them white—obtained BHA housing even though they had declined to accept the units offered to them under the terms of the 1-2-3 rule.[108]

Pynoos, who analyzed the tenant selection process from inside the BHA during the early 1970s, concluded that "political advocacy usually occurred for working class white families or elderly who desired prime family or elderly developments." The result was a sustainable symbiosis: politicians helped their friends, relatives, and supporters while BHA staff were given license to target more of their housing to 'good, solid citizens' who exemplified the screening criteria of the earliest years of the program. Moreover, Pynoos observed that many BHA staff believed that, despite the job securities of the tenure system, their survival at the Authority "depended partly on the actions of politicians who could be influential in promotions, demotions, firings, or even job assignments."[109] In any case, the Authority was dependent not only on sustained federal financial commitments to public housing, but also on perennial support by Boston-based state legislators for the Massachusetts-funded portion of the stock. More locally, the BHA senior staff realized they needed to cultivate the full support of other city agencies, such as the Boston police department and sanitation departments, whose assistance was crucial in the most troubled developments.

With such a pervasive political consciousness, the "system within the system" continued to count many options beyond the official 1-2-3. Pressures to manipulate the project assignment system had internal as well as external sources. Central management staff resisted the idea of accumulating vacancies at other developments until these would qualify for tenant assignment under the 1-2-3 rule, since doing so failed to keep developments filled with rent-paying tenants at a time when the Authority desperately needed funds. Site managers themselves felt that their job performance would be judged, in large part, on their own ability to deliver a healthy rent roll. And, since they were at the developments on a daily basis, they were the most likely contact point for people wishing to join friends and family already living at that development.[110]

BATTLES WITHIN THE BUREAUCRACY

Among BHA staff, the nature and direction of advocacy varied greatly as the Authority experienced a profound struggle for control between those Pynoos calls "traditionalists" and "reformers." The traditionalists, who tended to be long-term BHA employees appointed through political connections, "longed for the 'happy years' when clients were working- and middle-class and projects were attractive and easy to maintain," and favored a return to stricter screening.[111] Acting out of this mindset, the traditionalists sought ways to ensure that those families judged to be good would get sufficient advice and assistance to get them into the best projects.

Traditionalists operated in the projects as well as in BHA headquarters. May Hipshman interviewed all BHA development managers in 1967 and presented a collective portrait: "white (there is only one Negro manager [appointed in 1963]), male . . . 52 years of age, and of Irish descent." The managers, she concluded, worried first about rent collection and second about maintenance of buildings and grounds, with tenant relations taking "a poor third place."[112] Pynoos reached much the same conclusion a few years later: "Generally, the staff, because of both tradition and their personal ideologies, believed that racial integration would lead to ruin." Even after reform efforts reduced site-based discretion over admissions, some managers exercised a full repertoire of techniques to try to hold the line against admitting tenants deemed undesirable. Managers, who were responsible for arranging interviews with prospective tenants after first viewing their files, would frequently neglect to do so, or would use the occasion of a missed meeting to eliminate that applicant from consideration for an apartment. Another strategy was to report a unit as "vacant but leased," a tactic that allowed the manager to reserve the unit in advance for a more desirable applicant. Alternatively, during an interview a manager could try to dissuade an unwanted applicant by stressing the high crime rate at the development or by steering her toward a unit that was in a high state of disrepair.[113]

Traditionalist managers faced new pressures once tenant-organizing efforts got underway in 1968. Elaine Werby, an Ash appointee who served as the BHA's director of social planning, initiated the idea of tenant task forces at individual developments as a way of increasing tenant input citywide. With the task force structure established, she later recalled,

> Minority (particularly black) residents became very vocal. It created an opportunity for leadership that didn't exist before. It was a strident advocacy, and that bothered the hell out of the traditional managers who were used to running their developments like a plantation. [They] gave out favors to tenants based on their behavior, with behavior goals set by the local manager. If he didn't like kids running around on the grass and your kids did, you were punished in a variety of small ways. So, suddenly, these managers who had

been ruling their developments like a fiefdom, saw their powers begin to erode and be curtailed, both by tenants who now spoke out
against them and weren't afraid, and by regulations that were coming from reformers in the housing authority.[114]

By the end of the 1960s, the traditionalists faced increased pressures from
younger, reform-minded employees recruited by Ash. The reformers wanted
public housing to be available as a last resort for poor families and sought ways to
house the neediest applicants. They saw such families not as the source of problems, but as people who had problems that needed to be addressed by additional
targeted social services. They sought to teach people how to manipulate the system and were willing to send nonwhites to the better projects rather than insist
that the 1-2-3 ones were all that was available. Those traditionalists unable to
cope with countervailing internal and external politics eventually moved on, or
were moved out. Even James Crowley—tenant selection chief for thirty years and
a vociferous advocate for the "good" families—was transferred elsewhere and replaced by his black reform-minded assistant.

The turnover of three seats on the five-member Board between 1968 and
1970 offered an unprecedented opportunity for reform. In 1968 newly elected
mayor Kevin White appointed Julius Bernstein, a civil rights and housing activist;
in 1969, Governor Frank Sargent tapped John Connolly, a white tenant from
Mary Ellen McCormack; and in 1970—pressured by the Citizens Housing and
Planning Association (CHPA) and other groups—White appointed Doris Bunte,
a black Orchard Park tenant. Until CHPA filed legislation to allow it, public
housing residents had been prohibited from serving on the Board, presumably
because no one who accepted the per diem Board pay would then be income-eligible to remain in public housing. The new trio soon described itself as "the tenant-oriented majority." In April 1971, the tenant-oriented majority issued a statement of objectives, which included a broad promise to centralize maintenance
tasks so that they would be performed more equitably across developments, and
a plan to implement a personnel policy based on merit, one that involved hiring
more tenants and giving them a greater role in management. Regarding tenant selection, the trio declared that the age of BHA patronage was over.[115] This announcement proved premature.

Even before Kevin White helped create the tenant-oriented Board, he set limits
on its power by taking control of the administrator's post. To defuse change, he
replaced Ellis Ash, who in 1969 had suffered a serious stroke and resigned as ad-

ministrator, with Daniel Finn, whose previous municipal experience was limited to code enforcement and civil defense.[116] Soon afterward, the BHA enacted new by-laws that greatly expanded the administrator's power, giving him "the authority to determine administrative procedures, organizational structure and staff requirements" and the jurisdiction to "hire and fire employees." Thus, even after reformers for tenant rights gained their majority, most new Board policies were thwarted. As Bunte put it, "we didn't own the Executive Director—Dan Finn was the Mayor's Man." Finn sought to rein in the progressive tendencies of the Board, especially regarding the limits placed on patronage. Bernstein and Bunte complained to White but were rebuffed. Finally, in frustration, Bunte used the occasion of a televised Board meeting to fire Finn. An irate Kevin White responded by charging Bunte with several trumped-up counts of "misconduct in office." A thirteen-day "trial" by the mayor and City Council found her guilty of three charges. She was removed from the Board in July 1971, only to be reinstated by a court. The case continued on appeal all the way to the Massachusetts Supreme Judicial Court. Once the court exonerated Bunte, the Boston City Council at first refused to reinstate her, backing down only to avoid a contempt of court charge. After Bunte rejoined the Board in March 1972, the relationship between the mayor and the BHA continued to deteriorate. Nearly three decades later a still-incredulous Bunte recalled, "He refused to meet with the Board, and withdrew a number of city services from all of the developments, from public housing as a whole. He cut them completely—we had to *pay* for them. We didn't get them back until . . . the 1980s."[117]

According to J. Anthony Lukas, the actions against Bunte and the BHA symbolized a "new Kevin White." In this same mode of retrenchment, White "downplayed his Office of Human Rights, Model Cities, and other programs designed to aid the black community, while talking tough on crime and drugs, beefing up the police, and promising to hold the line on taxes." Faced by critics who felt he coddled blacks, the mayor sought to assert control. "The Mayor said Mrs. Bunte had been dismissed because 'she didn't bring about reform,'" Lukas observed, "but others saw the episode as a clear signal that henceforth the Mayor would adopt a more skeptical attitude toward the black and the poor."[118]

PLAYING IT BY THE LETTER

While the Board sought to remove politics from public housing, and while Kevin White used hardball politics to disassemble the Board, the "system within the system" at the BHA continued to operate. Many applicants evaded the 1-2-3 rule by persuading those in charge to grant them an "exception." These exceptions officially depended on demonstration of hardship unrelated to race, color, or national origin, and Pynoos found that "the staff permissively interpreted those conditions so as to increase the number of people affected." Most of these exceptions involved the need to be near particular medical facilities or were applied in cases of emergency housing needs. The presence of the large state-funded public housing program, where federal guidelines did not apply, significantly augmented the BHA's discretion. Ultimately, BHA staff controlled access to information about the application process, could determine the priority for housing, and could control where applicants would be sent. Board member Bunte recalled that tenant assignments were based on "'the letter system': As you weighed who got what, you'd say, 'Let's see, this person has two medical letters, three clergy letters, and one boy scout reference, and this one has four medical letters but only one clergy.' It was like playing God, but only certain populations were told about that possibility. [Those that weren't told to bring letters] were the ones that went to the three places with the largest numbers of vacancies."[119]

Initially, the letter system—in contrast to the official number system—operated quietly and served the same well-connected whites in South Boston and Charlestown who had previously relied on elected officials for special assistance. But eventually, Bunte recalled, word of this procedure filtered through "to the service agencies who then *told* you to go get those letters." In 1970 the three official 1-2-3 choices remained Columbia Point, Bromley-Heath, and Mission Hill; "Not to go to one of those developments meant that you had to have your letters in order." Since about two-thirds of those offered apartments at these locations refused the assignment, Finn concluded in 1970 that "integration efforts have had to be abandoned." Only if HUD changed its policies could the BHA reverse the "separatist roles" of its black and white residents.[120]

The 1-2-3 tenant assignment plan not only failed to make progress toward integrating public housing; it also fostered antagonisms between applicants and BHA staff, encouraging all concerned to seek both old and new ways to get around a system that worked well for no one. In 1972 HUD acknowledged that the 1-2-3 rule did not work in Boston, and federal enforcement of it "simply died quietly."[121]

CLIENT-DRIVEN PATRONAGE AND EMERGENCY NEEDS

Prompted by the gains of the civil rights movement, political influence on the behavior of the Housing Authority in the late 1960s and early 1970s began to diversify. Whereas traditional forms of patronage had depended on exchanges of favors—whether tacit or explicit, immediate or deferred—the civil rights movement brought about a less reciprocally self-serving form of advocacy. Championed by a wide variety of service organizations, the new patronage was client-driven rather than constituent-based, though it had the same effect of skewing—or even skewering—the official priorities and mechanisms of the system. Beginning in the mid-1960s, as more and more economically desperate families pressed for admission to public housing, service agencies sought ways to place their clients, and local politicians relinquished whatever monopoly on advocacy they had once held. As early as 1964, the Welfare Department itself regularly sent letters attempting to intercede on behalf of its clients.[122]

By the end of the 1960s more than two-thirds of households in Boston public housing reported they had no employed member; at Columbia Point, Bromley-Heath, Orchard Park, and Franklin Field, three-quarters were without jobs. Nearly half of the nonelderly households were headed by a single parent. At Columbia Point there were 450 single-parent families, and 159 of these had five or more children. At some developments, there were more than ten children for every nonelderly adult male. Between 1962 and 1969, the share of BHA families receiving Aid to Families with Dependent Children (AFDC) nearly doubled, to an average of 27 percent, with much higher concentrations at several overwhelmingly black projects. Elsewhere, older households grew in number; fully 40 percent of the households in BHA family projects had a household head over age sixty. In 1970 whites still occupied two-thirds of BHA apartments, but nonwhites formed an increasing majority of those wishing to get in, and the economic status of both white and nonwhite applicants continued to decline.[123]

By 1970, with the BHA waiting list at 6,000 and still rising, social service agencies vied with one another to find placements for clients seen to be in the most desperate need of housing. Many Tenant Selection personnel greeted their efforts with some sympathy, and cultivated ongoing personal relationships with agency staff. Such relationships often proved more effective for obtaining housing than did letters from politicians that lacked personal follow-up.[124]

On top of the advocacy systems employed by social agencies and politicians, the BHA increasingly bypassed the official procedure by selecting and assigning tenants on the basis of emergency need. In 1972 the chief of Tenant Selection expanded the classifications for emergency transfers to include not just the homeless and the about-to-be-homeless but also those who were exposed to lead paint, living in overcrowded conditions, or inhabiting buildings with code violations. This policy shift dramatically increased the number of emergency cases admitted and since these were not subject to a home visit, the result was that more households entered BHA projects with little prior scrutiny. In the late 1960s, emergency assignments had constituted only about 10 percent of BHA placements, but a HUD audit found that by 1972 the Authority made "comparatively few assignments from the long-standing waiting list," and instead housed "most families" on an "emergency or exceptional basis without formally defining these special circumstances or informing all applicants of their availability."[125]

The cumbersome yet highly idiosyncratic methods for tenant assignment led to what Pynoos called "confusion" and low morale in the Authority; "staff members seemed more interested in minimizing their own workloads than in efficiently fulfilling the Department's purpose of processing applicants." Interviews with BHA staff at the time revealed that many long-term employees increasingly distrusted the applicants they were there to serve and complained about the rules that limited more comprehensive screening. The result, according to Pynoos, was "a processing of cases with little regard for date of housing application or housing need, except in the case of emergencies." As one staffer put it, "The waiting list is all bottom."[126]

A study conducted in 1967 by BHA Tenant and Community Relations staff tried to counter such attitudes with evidence showing that most families judged to be problems at the time they were admitted subsequently presented no such difficulties. However, the study also found that in the first six months of occupancy, one-third of these families exhibited problems paying the rent and one-quarter were judged unable "to maintain basic housekeeping, basic childcare standards, and basic workable relationships with neighbors with or without help and supervision." Richard Scobie, the head of the department, later completed a dissertation on the subject, in which he concluded that "the entire group of identified problem tenants represent a much smaller proportion of the total population of all developments than the literature might have led us to expect." Even at Columbia Point, site of the greatest problems, he asserted, they accounted for no more than 5 percent of households. But at both "high-reputation" and "low-reputation" developments, coping with problem tenants took up fully half of a manager's time.[127]

Scobie's central point was that the presence of such problem families bore no easily adducible relationship to the *categories* of families (such as welfare-dependent single-parent households) so often thought likely to pose problems. He found "no evidence" that conflict among tenants was associated with differences rooted in such factors as "age, size of family, sex of head of household, source of income, or age of children." Moreover, in contrast to what he perceived to be the prevailing wisdom, he found no sign of any "deep-seated irritation on the part of the working poor toward their economically dependent neighbors, particularly when they are headed by black females on AFDC." As a policy matter, he concluded, all of this meant that it would be impossible to obtain stable developments simply by attempts to "screen out problem families or dependent families, or any other general category." In the context of sweeping condemnations of "the culture of poverty" and "lower-class lifestyles," Scobie's liberal defense of BHA tenants carried little weight, especially since it was mounted by the same person who had attempted to loosen BHA standards. Moreover, even as Scobie championed the cause of the least advantaged, a fellow doctoral candidate studying the Boston projects reached completely contradictory conclusions; in a survey of residents from all twenty-five BHA family developments, Gerald Taube found that the "social dissatisfaction" of older families increased with "the presence of young, dependent families." He surmised that "the appearance of lower status families, with the attendant stigma of AFDC status, may threaten the tenuous hold the more advantaged families may feel they have on working-class identity."[128]

In 1973 members of the Boston City Council argued that the declining status of public housing was exacerbated by the term "projects": in contrast to the "elegant" names of private apartment complexes such as "Harbor Towers, Prudential Apartments, [and] Church Park," the BHA project names "steal dignity from residents" because they "not only identify residents as tenants of public housing but also stigmatize them as low-income persons."[129]

THE DECLINE AND FALL OF THE BHA

Scholars, housing officials, and tenants have been debating the causes of decline in American public housing since at least the 1950s. For some, the central cause of problems is the arrival of too many tenants who, in socioeconomic terms, were "all bottom." Others have blamed the architecture and urban design of the projects, seen as excessively large and institutional, isolated from neighborhoods, ill-maintained, and designed in ways that discourage tenants from taking responsibility for surveillance of shared facilities. For still others, the sources of problems have inhered in the management structure of housing authorities, organizations so dependent on patronage and so bereft of mechanisms for quality control that they cannot behave efficiently. Finally, some hold that housing authorities, buildings, and tenants alike have been joint victims of a built-in financial disaster—the inability of public housing's financial structure to generate the funds necessary for long-term operation and maintenance. Each of these factors has considerable explanatory power, but it is their complex interaction and their collective embeddedness in the sustained ideological ambivalence toward public neighbors that has made the decline of public housing, in Boston and elsewhere, such a tragic and distinctively American saga.

Ultimately, the problems with tenants, buildings, managers, and funding are products of the same underlying cultural unease. Because public housing challenged long-standing ideals about the relationship between hard work and quality homes, and because it increasingly (and for not-unrelated reasons) came to serve a less politically influential constituency, Congress has never funded public housing production commensurately with the numbers of low-income families eligible to live in it, and the system has been under constant attack from those pressing for more ideologically palatable alternatives emphasizing private-sector involvement.

Retreat from the Projects:
Private Alternatives to Public Housing

Throughout the 1960s and early 1970s, Congress passed legislation providing alternatives to conventionally developed public housing projects in an effort to align subsidized low-income housing more harmoniously with national ideals of homeownership and private initiative. One major enterprise centered on FHA efforts to extend homeownership opportunities to greater numbers of low-income families, thereby elevating them above the less-yeomanlike public neighbors who could then be relegated to public housing.

The Housing Act of 1968 introduced the Section 235 program, intended to increase homeownership by providing federally subsidized mortgage payments for people of modest income. Proponents saw this not only as a way to help stabilize urban areas at a time of maximum national unrest ("people won't burn down houses that they own") but also as a way to promote virtue. The chairman of the

House Banking and Currency Committee explained, "Pride of ownership is a subtle but powerful force. Past experience has shown us that families offered decent homes at prices they can afford have demonstrated a new dignity, a new attitude toward their jobs . . . By extending the opportunity for homeownership to low and moderate income families, we will give them a concrete incentive for striving to improve their lives." HUD's Section 235 handbook made the same points, concluding that "the program can be a vital influence in promoting personal responsibility and social stability." At a time when public housing seemed increasingly socially unstable and when critics charged that older family developments served too many people who lacked such personal responsibility, the Section 235 program (like the companion Section 236 below-market interest rate rent-supplement program) could also be seen as a means of "further skimm[ing] the 'redeemable' higher income cream from the low-income tenant pool."[130] Meanwhile, the legislative retreat from the old-style projects continued.

In the ongoing search for alternatives to conventionally developed and managed public housing, legislators also enacted a variety of programs providing direct and indirect subsidies to private developers and landlords. Even as the quality of life in many of its family projects declined, Boston housing officials made considerable use of many such new programs.

Most visibly, the BHA greatly augmented its program for the elderly by employing the "turnkey" method of development. First authorized under the Housing Act of 1965, this system enabled the Authority to enter into contracts with private developers who would build developments according to public housing specifications and then sell the completed product—turn the key over—to the BHA. This development process, though initially challenged in the courts, helped the BHA to add 2,343 units for the elderly between 1968 and 1975, and nearly 1,000 more thereafter. In the 1970s, as earlier, the politically expedient emphasis on elderly housing enabled the Authority to associate itself with a less-problematic constituency while continuing to expand the city's much-needed low-income housing stock. Moreover, since the staff of the BHA Planning and Development Department was paid out of a percentage of development contracts, the department had to continue to generate new developments in order to survive.[131]

Other opportunities for publicly subsidized new construction in the private sector occurred completely outside BHA auspices. Just as earlier programs of urban redevelopment and urban renewal had rewarded savvy developers for tackling inner-city sites, Congress continued to devise new roles for the private sector in an attempt to make development of low-income housing commercially profitable. This growing privatization movement began with a program providing private nonprofit developers with direct below-market interest-rate loans intended to spur construction of housing for the elderly (Section 202 of the Housing Act of 1959), and continued with other programs (in 1961, 1968, and 1974) inviting sponsorship of multifamily subsidized housing by private for-profit groups. More locally, the Massachusetts Housing Finance Agency (MHFA) funded numerous mixed-income developments using private-sector design and development teams, and eventually a variety of neighborhood community development corporations (CDCs) also initiated programs to expand the supply of Boston's affordable housing. Critics charged, however, that subsidizing the private market in such ways produced "not only too little housing, but housing invariably aimed at the not-so-poor"—just as the housing philanthropists of a century earlier had also discovered.[132]

Taking advantage of a provision in the Housing Act of 1965 (Section 23), the BHA expanded low-income housing programs through increased reliance on leased housing. By 1973, with tenants of the Authority occupying nearly 3,000 leased units, it had one of the largest such programs in the nation. Most apartments were located in the urban renewal areas of Roxbury, North Dorchester, and the South End, the heart of the black community. With landlords receiving subsidies to cover the difference between fair market rent and what tenants could pay, low-income tenants paid as little as one-fourth of the prevailing market cost. Because these "instant public housing" facilities served a population economically similar to that in the projects, the BHA was saved the impossible ordeal of undertaking new project construction. Initially, some critics charged that the Section 23 program functioned as yet another way for housing authorities to classify the poor, by reserving the best leased units for those who were "deserving" while "herding" society's least-manageable members—the ones private landlords wouldn't take—into the worst public housing projects. And indeed a 1968 study of dwelling preferences among Roxbury blacks showed that the new leased developments were far more popular than public housing and were considered preferable to any type of dwelling except a house in the suburbs. In later years, however, some leased developments became as notorious as public housing.[133]

In 1973 President Richard Nixon declared a moratorium on public housing expansion and, when it was lifted at the end of the year, allowed only the leased-housing program to resume. This concept gained full favor with passage of the Housing and Community Development Act of 1974. Section 8 of the act provided for subsidized rents not only in existing housing but also in new construction and in rehabilitated buildings. It dramatically expanded the ability of local housing authorities to administer a system of housing allowances, and also enabled tenants to go out and identify the units they wished to rent instead of being assigned to particular properties. With all earlier leased-housing subsidies converted into Section 8 subsidies, by the end of the 1990s the BHA leased housing department managed more than six thousand vouchers and certificates.[134]

Thus, a public housing program that had been initiated over the staunch opposition of private real estate interests underwent a gradual privatizing transformation, first by the inclusion of private developers in urban renewal ventures and subsequently by three decades of programs that spurred the homebuilding industry and provided many new investment opportunities. In Boston as elsewhere the housing constructed or leased under such programs supplied significant waves of affordable dwellings. Still, despite the various new options, the BHA's twenty-five older family projects continued numerically, visually, and psychologically to dominate local perceptions of "public housing." These projects, located in so many neighborhoods and beset by such widely publicized problems, repeatedly provided Bostonians (and suburbanites) with striking evidence of the combined effects of concentrated poverty and governmental failure.

THE SOCIAL CONSEQUENCES OF FINANCIAL COLLAPSE

The fiscal status of the BHA had been a contentious issue since the founding of the Authority, but only in the late 1960s did its declining financial viability become a widely acknowledged crisis. Under the terms of the Housing Act of 1937, the federal government paid for the development and construction costs of its portion of the BHA's housing stock, and made annual payments to cover most of the debt service on notes and bonds issued by the BHA; the BHA, in turn, would cover operating expenses out of tenant rent receipts. The Authority assumed that this relief from debt service would enable it to keep rents low and still pay for wages, salaries, and maintenance. As long as public housing was a program to serve the temporarily submerged middle class, the financing plan made some sense; indeed, until the early 1950s many local housing authorities could even afford to return some portion of their substantial rent surplus to the federal government as partial reimbursement of mortgage costs.[135]

In the 1960s, however, inflation drove operating expenses higher, even as average tenant incomes declined. Nationally, between 1961 and 1970, the median family income of nonelderly public housing tenants declined from 47.1 percent to 36.9 percent of the U.S. median family income, and continued to plummet thereafter.[136] In Boston, an impoverished clientele increasingly comprised of the elderly, families receiving welfare, and low-wage workers who had not shared in the benefits of the expanding economy could not possibly generate sufficient rent receipts for the Authority to keep pace with inflated operating costs. The state-financed veterans' housing developments confronted an even more dire financial squeeze, since in these cases the state contribution covered much less of the full debt service. Here, too, with a majority of tenants relying solely on public assistance or social security payments that were not increasing as fast as inflation, rent receipts fell well short.

At all its developments, the Authority had to cut back on essential maintenance and much-needed services: expenditures for such things as new boilers, replacement of aging refrigerators, and repair of sidewalks and play areas were all deferred. Unable to raise rents, since many tenants were already paying more than one-third of their income for rent, and unable to reduce expenditures, since salaries and utility costs were so sensitive to inflation, the BHA, like most other large housing authorities across the country, desperately needed further subsidy. In 1968, according to a HUD survey, half of the nation's eighty major housing authorities were operating at a deficit, and seven of the ten largest ones were near bankruptcy.[137]

To stave off financial collapse, starting in the mid-1960s the federal government attempted a variety of ad hoc subsidy schemes, providing "modernization" funds and special allowances for the elderly, the displaced, the unusually poor, and for extra-large families. But as one contemporary critic put it, "these patchwork additions have only partially ameliorated . . . a terrific financial squeeze." In 1969, under the first of the so-called Brooke Amendments, Congress limited rents in public housing to no more than 25 percent of tenant income, thereby keeping public housing affordable to those of lowest incomes, but exacerbating the shortfall of rent receipts. Recognizing this shortfall, Congress added legislation to allow increased annual federal contributions to offset the loss of rental income and provide an operating subsidy, and the Massachusetts legislature followed with parallel legislation to cover its state-sponsored developments. Unfortunately, both the HUD and the state subsidy formulas yielded inadequate revenue for the BHA, and the pattern of deferred maintenance in the developments continued. Nearly half of BHA tenants responded by failing to keep up with rent payments, and those who did pay resented it when rents were increased. By 1976, having amassed three cumulative operating debts, the agency was "on the edge of bankruptcy"—partly as a result of underfunding and partly as a result of failure to cut staff in order to bring expenses into line with revenue.[138]

MASTERING THE BUREAUCRACY:
THE TENANTS AND THE COURTS STRIKE BACK

BHA tenants themselves took the lead in efforts to stem the BHA's decline. Assisted by legal services attorneys, they launched numerous individual criminal and civil complaints against the BHA, and initiated a series of class action suits against the Authority and various state and federal officials. The suits against the state claimed that conditions in BHA apartments and buildings violated the Massachusetts Sanitary Code, and that the Commonwealth should be responsible for providing funds to rectify the situation. A federal suit sought HUD action to require the BHA to provide decent housing. Both the Massachusetts Supreme Judicial Court and the United States District Court, however, dismissed the class action suits, urging that the plaintiffs instead make their claim to the Boston Housing Court.[139]

In February 1975, Greater Boston Legal Services (GBLS) brought the case of *Armando Perez et al. v. Boston Housing Authority* before the Boston Housing Court. In March Chief Judge Paul G. Garrity found in favor of the plaintiffs, and described in detail the level of devastation requiring remedy. At Mission Hill, for example,

> It was observed that in every building almost every pane of glass facing common area stairways was broken from the first floor to the roof, that most incinerators were erupting flames a few feet into the open air at the height level of small children, that smoke and soot from incinerators permeated the air, that sidewalks and streets were cracked with entire sections missing, that automobiles were speeding through play areas set aside for children . . . Also according to the Manager, there are scores of "hard drug drops" both at Mission Hill and at Mission Hill Extension.

The court order contained an entire litany of such stories, making it clear "beyond any doubt that countless violations of the State Sanitary Code exist in developments owned and operated by BHA," and that "those violations result from vandalism and from BHA's financial inability to conduct routine maintenance at its developments and to replace antiquated heating, plumbing, electrical and other systems." The Court found some apartment conditions "so intolerable that relocation is immediately required." Elsewhere, where vandalism of unoccupied apartments had already set in, the accumulated rubbish and garbage and uncovered incinerators constituted "a present danger of fire and disease." Throughout the system, the court concluded, "serious crime and the fear of it make the developments intolerably unsafe." Finally, making the condemnation complete, the court addressed the still-simmering integration issue, charging that "occupancy by race in BHA's developments and leased housing reinforces and exacerbates segregated housing patterns in Boston's neighborhoods."[140]

Garrity's court order called for the BHA to produce and file a plan for addressing each of these issues. By the end of May, however, the judge determined that the BHA lacked the expertise to comply and ordered the appointment of Robert B. Whittlesey as master. Garrity asked Whittlesey, a professional housing reformer in the Ellis Ash tradition, to prepare long-term and interim plans and to draft for him the court orders that would help guide the transformation of the agency. Initially the BHA seemed to pay little attention to the whole *Perez* case. Whittlesey recalled that neither the court decision nor his own appointment as master even warranted mention in the minutes of the Board; they simply regarded it as "a kind of a skirmish for more money" and "never took it seriously." In 1976, however, the Massachusetts Supreme Judicial Court dismissed the portion of the *Perez* suit directed against state officials and thereby freed the state of the obligation to provide more than $100 million of funding. The loss of prospective funding immediately forced "a shift away from planning for large-scale physical restoration of BHA developments to emphasis on improvements in the system of delivering management, maintenance, and related functions." The BHA now "became adversarial."[141]

With the tenant-oriented majority long since superseded by more conservative appointments, Mayor White and the Board continued to exercise considerable control over day-to-day operations. White, Whittlesey recalled, "didn't believe we existed," and was appalled that he could not control hirings and firings. The power struggle came to a head when the mayor appointed an underqualified twenty-nine-year-old as chief of management. At Whittlesey's prompting, Garrity intervened with an order granting the master's office final say on all senior appointments. The mayor and BHA staff subverted the order by passing on only unqualified candidates and asking Whittlesey to choose from among them. Whittlesey's appointment also faced public condemnation from minority activists (including Doris Bunte) because he was a white male. These objections were partly appeased by the appointment of Joanne Barboza Ross, a tenant-oriented Cape Verdean social worker who served as his unofficial 'co-master' and received an equal salary.[142] Still, BHA staff resented any form of outside scrutiny. As one department head put it, "They [outsiders] were intrusive. They would want to know why we were spending money on one development and not on others. They created more work. They made people justify what they were doing." BHA administrator Samuel Thompson—one of many to hold this post during the mid-1970s—joined the chorus of critics, complaining that he spent too much time preparing replies to Whittlesey's many letters. Attacked and resisted from all sides, Whittlesey and Ross valiantly tried to grapple with "the whole culture" of an agency that had faced "no accountability for forty years, except to political favors and poor people who can't say anything."[143]

Whittlesey regarded the BHA as a "second-rate business" staffed by "good, well-meaning people who had adapted to a system." The Authority was not only "basically bankrupt" but also riddled with "ineptness." It was so racked by internal mistrust that senior-level personnel "wouldn't even talk to one another." An incompetent legal staff lost all its eviction cases "so management wouldn't bother to bring them any more." The maintenance system was paralyzed by jurisdictional battles and union rules: carpenters couldn't fix broken windows because they weren't glaziers, while glaziers said they couldn't put boards up because they weren't carpenters. As Whittlesey saw it, "That's the way the whole thing worked. It was never meant to be any kind of business." In contrast to the early days of the BHA, when maintenance workers often had family living in the developments they serviced, "all the mechanics and tradespeople with their good union salaries resented having to fix up the apartments of these 'lousy, sloppy poor people.'" As a HUD audit of the BHA found, some resentment seemed understandable where maintenance staff coped with repeated instances of vandalism: "The demoralizing effect of vandalism on maintenance personnel is unmeasurable, as is the demoralizing effect on the laborers of tenant delinquency in the form of throwing of garbage and other refuse out of windows. In some areas where security is a problem, maintenance personnel will not work except in pairs."[144] Even if only a few residents behaved destructively, they were the ones whom maintenance staff would remember. In an underfunded and overpoliticized system, angry tenants and lazy personnel formed two sides of the same worn-out coin.

On top of all the problems with the buildings and the personnel, Garrity's ruling had also asked the master to confront race relations. "The complaint had been structured around sanitary code," Whittlesey noted, "But then Garrity threw in integration. We questioned whether we should deal with that, but it was an urgent need—there was flagrant discrimination." Increasingly, Whittlesey came to realize that the "race thing was all over everything. It wasn't supposed to be in the case, but it was. Everything we touched, there it was."[145]

Whittlesey's staff worked closely with the Tenant Selection Department on a new Tenant Selection and Assignment Plan (TSAP), intended to give tenants more choice than the ill-fated 1-2-3 system while promoting integration by giving priority in assignments to applicants willing to move into a project where they were racially in the minority. Most of the court's desegregation orders focused on maintaining integration in the four family developments and seven elderly developments where a substantial racial mix already existed. In itself, this proved no easy task. In many cases, the master's report observed, once previously white developments were integrated they "quickly resegregated with all minority residents." In other cases, the violent turmoil of Boston's antibusing protests of 1975-76 caused some previously integrated developments to resegregate to all-white. With violence initially directed at "pioneer" families in the 1960s and again at nonwhites in several white-dominated developments during the busing crisis, the BHA was forced to acknowledge that regardless of the requirements of Title VI of the Civil Rights Act, some of its developments were just too unsafe for minority applicants to move into. Fearing that some low-demand projects (such as the predominantly white West Broadway and the predominantly nonwhite Columbia Point) would simply "empty out" if vacancies had to be filled in ways that fostered integration, the BHA resumed its practice of allowing applicants to list specific project choices.[146]

In 1975, the master's office estimated that although whites still constituted two-thirds of the city's income-eligible households, 80 percent of those on the waiting list for Boston's family projects were nonwhite. By contrast, 92 percent of the demand for units for the elderly still came from whites. Apparently, white families had "chosen to spend a larger percentage of their income on the private market for what is often substandard housing rather than live in BHA developments," although the difference could also be explained as a response to housing discrimination. In addition to the explicit practice of nonwhite exclusion from certain properties and areas, a sophisticated study of housing market discrimination in Boston found that blacks paid a substantial mark-up over whites for identical "bundles of housing attributes," supporting theories of racial discrimination grounded in "a dual housing market, a strong white preference for segregation, and pure racial price discrimination." In any case, Whittlesey's team did little to address the disproportionately white constituency of the elderly developments, focusing instead on ways to "affirmatively market" more of the family projects to whites. Still, Whittlesey and his colleagues recognized that "if the fundamental physical, management and social problems which initially caused the developments to decline are not changed," increasing numbers of BHA developments would become exclusively black and Hispanic, while some projects would continue to generate "no effective demand" at all, yielding a dangerous cycle of vacancy and vandalism.[147]

In transforming tenant selection policies, Whittlesey believed he had an ally in John Murphy, chief of Tenant Selection, who had been appointed at the behest of Mayor White in 1973 (and who still held the post more than a quarter-century later). Although Murphy got his position as a patronage gesture, he proved himself willing and able to move on with the times. Murphy described his career thus: "When I came here I had to make a decision, whether I would basically be a tool of City Hall or I would commit myself to improve the place. That decision became easier with the appointment of the master; I saw them trying to accomplish things that I really wanted to do in the tenant selectioning . . . I never saw—as some of my colleagues did—the court-appointed master's staff as the enemy." Murphy joined a department in which tenant screening and the regulations for admission had been largely abandoned. Inspired by Whittlesey's commitment to reform, he supported computerization of the waiting list ("getting away from the shoebox") and, although faced with the usual barrage of patronage requests, "tried to keep the political stuff to a minimum."[148]

Still, some site managers continued to exercise considerable discretion, especially in classifying undesirable tenants and thus denying them housing. At the state-sponsored Gallivan Boulevard development in Dorchester—a project heavily populated by firemen, police, and other city employees—the manager informally employed his own criteria by insisting that households had to consist of two-parent families because "there had to be someone in the household who was able to cut the grass and shovel the snow." Murphy successfully lobbied Doris

Bunte to get "this obnoxious rule" changed, but after Bunte's term on the BHA Board expired, the Authority proposed a new tenant selection plan that gave explicit priority to "upper-income" applicants (that is, employed families at the upper end of low-income eligibility for public housing) and to applicant households containing two parents. In 1976 HUD rejected the plan and the master's report concurred in the decision: since any increased revenue generated by the presence of higher-income tenants would be offset by a corresponding reduction in subsidy from HUD, there was no good financial reason for the BHA to favor such applicants. Whittlesey's team concluded that the BHA should select its tenants on the basis of individual screening rather than on the basis of "broad distinctions" about family composition and class. As the Board and the master battled over the appropriate definition of public neighbors, the whole point already seemed moot, since upper-income families were already at a premium on BHA waiting lists. Recognizing this, the master urged the BHA to adopt ceiling rents that would diversify the economic mix not by tenant selection but by giving higher-income tenants a financial incentive to remain (by allowing them to pay less than 25 percent of their income for rent).[149] The issue of ceiling rents revealed just how far the occupancy ideals of public housing had shifted. Whereas public housing authorities had once assumed that the best public housing tenants would be those who most rapidly managed to get themselves 'up and out' of it, now they desperately sought to convince such upwardly mobile families to remain up and in.

Since most family developments were experiencing either rapid or protracted decline, convincing desirable families to remain would entail major efforts to improve conditions. Yet Whittlesey saw little hope for such an outcome. In his investigation of how the BHA had previously used its state and federal modernization funds, Whittlesey found there had been "major, unjustifiable delays" in doing the work and a "history of poor quality" once it was completed. Organizational bungling had made poor use of existing funds, the master's report asserted, and in the final analysis it had been the tenants who suffered: "How can anyone place a price on [the need] to climb flights of stairs because elevators need renovation, the sickness due to the dampness from leaking roofs and backed-up sewage, and the robberies and assaults and batteries which have resulted from delays in installing security screens and doors?"[150] In this climate of low funding and high distress, staff morale at the BHA continued to plummet. In August 1978 Bradley Biggs (yet another short-term administrator) circulated a memo on employee attitudes to all BHA personnel. In it he reviewed the barrage of criticism facing the agency, noting that it came from both outside and internal sources. To quiet outsiders, he suggested that employees present the facts accurately, asking them to admit that "although we are a slumlord, we are working feverishly to improve conditions." To insiders who he felt were preoccupied with "maneuvering for their own benefit," he spoke more harshly: "you will be dealt with by your colleagues who have the moral strength, guts and ability to straighten [you] out."[151] Ultimately, though, the straightening out of the BHA required further action by the courts.

In 1977, after months of negotiations, the parties to the *Perez* suit agreed to a consent decree, a 250-page compendium of plans and timetables for change in areas such as management, maintenance, tenant selection, security, and financial operations. Even with this attempt to provide Whittlesey with enhanced powers, the BHA Board continued to obstruct his efforts, another acting administrator remained largely a figurehead, and conditions at BHA projects worsened.

COURT-ORDERED RECEIVERSHIP

In January 1979, the BHA itself classified only two of its twenty-five family developments as "sound" (Fairmount and Gallivan Boulevard, both of which were smaller outlying developments financed by the state). Six (including the long-protected Mary Ellen McCormack) were judged to be "slipping," four were felt to be "in danger," and the other thirteen were "severely distressed." By contrast, sixteen of the much newer elderly developments (containing 1,950 units) were still considered "sound," although nine (855 units) were "slipping," seven more were "in danger" (531 units) and four (447 units) were already "seriously distressed."[152]

Later that year, after visiting many of these developments and listening to testimony, Judge Paul Garrity concurred with the BHA's assessment. In a 150-page ruling, he placed the Boston Housing Authority in receivership, marking the first time a court had ever taken charge of a publicly financed independent authority. In explaining his decision, Garrity blamed the BHA Board for "gross mismanagement, nonfeasance, incompetence and irresponsibility" that had led to "indescribable conditions" and "incalculable human suffering" in Boston public housing. "The conditions," he continued, "were and are indecent, unsafe and . . . in violation of almost every provision of the State Sanitary Code. If the BHA were a private landlord it surely would have been driven out of business long ago or its Board jailed or most likely both." Garrity described the conditions in the BHA's

FIGURE 4.7 Vandalized vacant Boston public housing apartment, ca. 1979.

family developments as "depressingly similar irrespective of the deterioration or absence of deterioration in the surrounding neighborhoods" and noted tenant accounts "of leaky ceilings, of frequent cessation of such basic services as heat, hot water and electricity, of windows which do not open in hot weather and which cannot be closed in cold weather, of infestation of rodents and insects, of mounds of rubbish and trash, of packs of wild dogs and of much more remind one of casualty lists in wartime" (Fig 4.7).[153]

In February 1980 the Massachusetts Supreme Judicial Court upheld Garrity's order.[154] A quarter-century after it had stopped building its large family projects, the Boston Housing Authority had reached its nadir.

The Boston Housing Authority since 1980: The Puritans Return

THE RECEIVERSHIP

IN FEBRUARY 1980, when Lewis Harwood (Harry) Spence took over as receiver of the Boston Housing Authority, he inherited a decrepit 17,000-unit real estate empire, a debt-ridden $55 million budget, and a rudderless and demoralized 700-person bureaucracy. Harry Spence also inherited responsibility for housing nearly 10 percent of Boston's population—and fully a quarter of its poor—who still clung to homes in this benighted archipelago of projects. At the nation's fourth largest housing authority, more than one-quarter of public housing apartments lay vacant and often uninhabitable, a rate of vacancy and abandonment nearly double that found in any other American city. To add insult to injury, tens of millions of dollars in previously allocated HUD modernization funds remained unspent, trapped within a disorganized and deficit-plagued system.[1]

Spence—a charismatic thirty-three-year-old Harvard Law School graduate who had already won kudos for his leadership of the Cambridge Housing Authority just across the river—remained undaunted. He had easily won over a selection committee faced with more than two hundred applications for the receiver's post (including expressions of interest from the directors of the rest of the nation's ten largest housing authorities). To his many admirers, Spence's demeanor seemed nothing short of Kennedyesque—"an attractive, magnetic public figure from a privileged background who talks passionately about economic injustice and the government's responsibility to the needy, who walks comfortably through Boston's poorest neighborhoods, and who leaves deprived people feeling that *someone* respects them and cares about their problems."[2] The *Boston Globe Magazine* put Spence on its cover, photographing him from below so that his head rose confidently above the roofscape of a troubled development. Just above Spence, the city's largest paper posed the editorial question: "Can this man save public housing?" (Fig. 5.1).

Judge Garrity's order granted the receiver "full power to direct, control, manage, administer and operate the property, funds and staff of the BHA." Spence also took over the policymaking function from the board, and was empowered to "disaffirm, reject, discontinue, amend, revise, or rescind any internal rule, regulation, bylaw, policy, custom or practice of the BHA." Kevin White, in his fourth term as Boston's mayor, regarded the BHA receivership as little more than good riddance. Although Judge Garrity's order eliminated a board dominated by White's appointees, the mayor's response was "That's all right. If they want it, they can have it."[3]

With City Hall pushed aside, Garrity charged his receiver with using his broad powers to reform the BHA bureaucracy, repair or rebuild its developments to meet all sanitary codes and regulations, and reinstate efforts to integrate all projects.[4] To the disappointment of many who saw the advent of the receivership as a means to dismantle a troubled enterprise, Spence insisted upon using his unprecedented powers to restore the BHA. As he declared only a few weeks after assuming his duties, "the task of this receivership is not the liquidation of the public housing stock and the communities it is intended to serve, but rather the restoration of the public housing stock and the poor communities which occupy public housing." He argued that the persistent desire to eliminate the projects stemmed from "an assumption that concentrations of poor people are synonymous with centers of disorder," and "a threat to the stability and well-being of the larger community."[5] Spence's explanation of public mistrust hearkened back to the same nineteenth-century ideas that first animated calls for slum clearance and model tenements. Ironically, public housing now stood accused of enhancing the very same threats its construction originally had been designed to forestall.

Moreover, Spence observed, the public housing nay-sayers implicitly assumed that "the poor are either unwilling or unable to maintain reasonable order within their communities." The real problem, however, was not the attitudes and attributes of the public neighbors, but "the failure and abdication of responsibility by

FIGURE 5.1 Can Harry Spence save public housing?

governmental authority." This occurred because "we as a society have breached the social contract between ourselves and our poor communities" since "the vast majority of public housing residents have willingly and in good faith surrendered their right to exercise force to the state—but in return have received no protection." The BHA's collapse represented a "fateful breach of faith we have committed against the poor communities in our midst."[6]

Spence's language recalled the earliest motives of his Yankee forebears, linking civic obligations to religious duties. Several colleagues and commentators in the early 1980s only half-jokingly likened Spence's role to that of an archangel and savior. Reporters invariably remarked on his daily habit of walking up all eleven flights of stairs to reach his office, and commented on his willingness to drive alone in the BHA's aging yellow Chevy Nova into hostile neighborhood settings. Although he constantly made new promises to downtrodden tenants, he stressed to them that he was "not paid to make miracles." Spence resisted developing a cult of personality by refusing interviews until after the first year of the receivership, yet this whole business venture—in part because of its deliberate elevation above the usual morass of Boston politics—retained a quasi-religious aura. *Boston Magazine* captured this duality of purpose beautifully in a glowing portrait entitled "Is Harry Spence God? Or Is He Just Damn Good?"[7] Although Spence drew his inspirations more from Rousseau, Montesquieu, and Locke than from Matthew, Mark, and Luke, his civic liberalism still seemed a true heir to the Puritan conscience.

To an even greater extent than his reform-minded predecessors—Ash and Whittlesey—Harry Spence not only managed public housing; he theorized about it. In a world of messy ethnic politics, he tried to extract a sense of public purpose for public policy. While accepting communal obligation for the care of the city's poor and a desire to keep them "in our midst," Spence also inherited the Puritan mistrust for those who abused the system. In contrast to those public neighbors who deserved the support of the state, Spence railed against "groups of persons who maintain a tyranny over the majority of residents by the threat and execution of violent reprisal." He divided these "extra-legal and illegitimate groups" into four categories—adolescents who "engage in ceaseless incivility and harassment"; criminally violent juvenile gangs; retail and wholesale dealers of hard drugs; and racists "who are determined that it is better that the poor have no place to live than that they risk the danger of living in an integrated setting." These four groups, he charged, have "never been challenged in a coherent and consistent way by the government."[8] For Spence, the sacrosanct concept of public neighbors had been systematically violated by decades of malign neglect by the BHA and other city officials. To give public housing tenants the protection they deserved, he argued for harsher, more expedient eviction proceedings (a position that greatly rankled others in the liberal legal community and proved largely unenforceable in the courts) and more elaborate systems of policing.

Spence believed that the social contract between city officials and their public neighbors had broken down because of a deep ambivalence engendered by the successes of the civil rights movement. As Spence put it, prior to the mid-1960s, site managers operated their developments according to "a system of benevolent or malevolent despotism" where "the authority of the housing manager was absolute . . . [and] subject to constant individual, class and, most of all, racial abuse."[9] "Until the civil rights revolution, housing authorities were essentially run like mom 'n' pop stores . . . The manager could walk into court and have anyone he wanted thrown out." The BHA "creamed for the 'worthy poor,'" and the rhetoric of worthiness was all too often a code word for race. Once the outcry of the civil rights movement insisted upon justice as well as order, the task of the housing authority grew vastly more complex. As the courts, the advisory committees, and the periodic presence of internal reformers subjected BHA operating procedures to increased scrutiny, Spence contends, the "stupid lawyers" of the BHA proved institutionally incapable of screening out or evicting the most problematic tenants. BHA staff struggled to bridge "the race-and-social-class gap" between themselves and the poor they were housing, and reacted angrily to the rise of tenant activism and to their own corresponding loss of authority. From the first civil rights cases to the final receivership decree, set against the backdrop of the "forced busing" turmoil, management and tenants experienced escalating confrontations that coincided with the BHA's institutional collapse. By 1980, Spence later recalled, "we were in the middle of real warfare."[10] Spence saw his role as transforming, once and for all, the governance of a mom 'n' pop store into a sophisticated institution capable of coping with the complexities of a pluralist culture.

He began, in effect, by firing mom 'n' pop, along with most of the rest of their politically appointed cousins. He replaced almost the entire BHA senior administrative staff (except for tenant selection chief Murphy) and picked new managers for two-thirds of the fifteen most troubled developments. A year after taking control, Spence asserted that "Politics has all but died in the operation of the receivership. Politicians don't call me up and threaten, cajole, or otherwise try to influence my operation . . . Who you know doesn't count, your connections don't matter, you can't end-run the receivership by making the 'right' phone call."[11] Murphy concurred that the receivership brought a "drastic change": "I was able to stay, [and] fend off the pressures that were coming to do things. I would just say—I've got people looking over my shoulder; I'm not going to jeopardize my position by sneaking one through. It was a kind of cowardly approach, I suppose, but it worked."[12] As most other old employees departed, Spence made a concerted effort to enhance the racial and gender diversity of the staff, while also attracting large numbers of younger personnel who suddenly found the BHA an exciting place to be. As one such nonwhite newcomer later recalled, "The BHA wasn't a jaded bureaucracy [anymore]. It was a new bureaucracy."[13]

In the four-and-a-half years Spence served as receiver, Garrity credited the BHA with "numerous and significant" accomplishments. The BHA retired its prereceivership deficit and produced three consecutive balanced budgets in accordance with HUD requirements and, with stricter management and maintenance efforts, Spence's staff arrested the cycle of vacancy and vandalism that threatened much of the housing stock. The BHA successfully regained the confidence of state and national funding agencies, and proved itself capable of both obtaining and expending substantial funds in an efficient manner. Spence placed special emphasis on developing meaningful tenant participation in various modernization and security programs, and markedly enhanced the hiring of tenants for BHA jobs. At some deteriorated developments, tenants took the lead in demanding redevelopment funds, and programs for architectural reconstruction served a second purpose by building community capacity through tenant organizing and service provision.[14]

Spence vowed to show tenants and the general public that it was possible to turn around some of the city's most devastated projects. Accordingly, he chose to invest disproportionate amounts of funds in the comprehensive redevelopment of three of the most troubled places: West Broadway, Franklin Field, and Commonwealth. "If we didn't do a couple of grand, glittering showcases," he explained, "the polity would have been yelling and screaming that we weren't getting anywhere, that we should just close down public housing. It was explicitly clear that we had to do these projects as a way of getting time and buying respect."[15] In addition to these three, Spence also recognized that he needed to do something about Columbia Point—where more than three-quarters of the units stood vacant, vandalized, and boarded up. Because this nationally notorious development was "dragging down" the whole program and he wanted to "get it off the books," Spence "very reluctantly" acquiesced in a plan to redevelop it as a private mixed-income community.[16] Taken together, the four redevelopment efforts begun in the early 1980s reached a scale and sophistication unmatched in the country, and have remained the most visible legacy of the receivership.

FOUR REDEVELOPMENT EFFORTS IN THE 1980S

When Spence took over as receiver, he sought to transform the public image of public housing. To pursue this, he looked for "targets of opportunity," seeking to invest redevelopment funds in those projects that enjoyed "a strong, effective tenant organization, and collaboration with the surrounding neighborhood." Aided by an internal BHA study conducted just before the receivership that ranked the redevelopment potential of the most distressed projects, and prodded by a well-organized group of tenants, Spence quickly zeroed in on Brighton's Commonwealth development as the most promising place to start. "We picked Commonwealth," he later recalled, "precisely because it seemed like it had the greatest potential to be the most successful turnaround effort, and we really wanted a flagship . . . that would begin to show what [public housing] could be at its best, and . . . get people to listen to why what was bad was bad, instead of just writing it all off as a problem." For the other three redevelopment efforts, however, Spence inherited the priorities of others. The Columbia Point plan was already politically irreversible. Redevelopment of West Broadway, too, came at the explicit behest of William Bulger, president of the State Senate. Bulger, who had been raised in a South Boston project, remained highly responsive to the persistent demands of West Broadway tenants, and arranged for appropriation of the redevelopment funds. Because West Broadway was an all-white development, however, the legislature recognized the political necessity of tackling a distressed black development as well, and chose Franklin Field, even though it would be subsequently ranked dead last in the BHA's own study of those places where redevelopment would be most likely to succeed.

Not surprisingly, the results of redevelopment efforts varied dramatically from project to project. At Commonwealth, a strong tenant organization worked with a private developer and private management team to transform this mixed-race development from a fifty-percent-vacant hellhole into a luxuriantly landscaped apartment community that is still roundly praised by tenants and management alike fifteen years after completion of the redevelopment (Fig. 5.2).[17] The design and development team that carried out the revitalization effort drew heavily on Oscar Newman's ideas about "defensible space," intended to encourage tenants to regard more of the common areas of the project as being under their own control. This architectural transformation—achieved at Commonwealth by reconfiguring many of the buildings into three-story row-houses, replete with private entrances and private yards—marked a dramatic repudiation of the usual project appearance, and a reconciliation with many of the norms associated with a middle-class condo development, if not a single-family home. When combined with the innovative privatization of its tenant-monitored management functions, Commonwealth's transformation arguably became the most celebrated effort to turn around the problems of a large public housing project anywhere in the United States.[18] Of signal importance, the BHA accomplished the upgrading of Com-

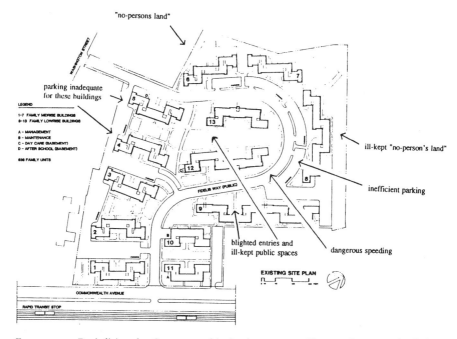

FIGURE 5.2 Revitalizing the Commonwealth development: problems and proposed solutions. Redevelopment entailed reduced density of buildings, reconfigured apartments, extensive relandscaping and roadway reorganization, new community facilities, and privatized management.

monwealth while retaining it as a resource for very low-income tenants, even though this transformation occurred in a stable mixed-income neighborhood that would have welcomed market-rate housing in lieu of the project.

At Commonwealth, success was multidimensional and sustained; at the equally devastated Franklin Field development, however, the promises of redevelopment nirvana have remained wholly unfulfilled. Undertaken at the same time as the Commonwealth redevelopment effort, the Franklin Field revitalization attempt received similar funding (well over $100,000 per unit in today's dollars), also spent primarily on the enlargement and upgrading of apartments, the reconfiguration of buildings, and the relandscaping and restructuring of the site. Here, however, the residents of the development (who were predominantly African-American) remained perpetually skeptical about the intentions of the housing au-

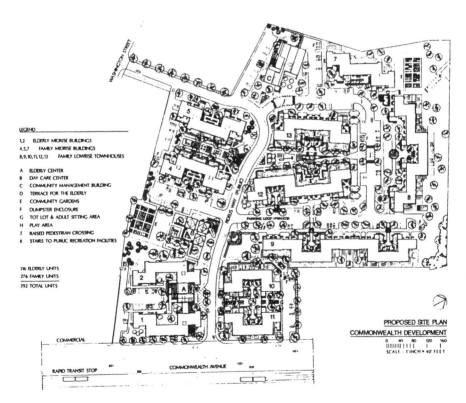

LEGEND

1,2   ELDERLY MIDRISE BUILDINGS
4,5,7   FAMILY MIDRISE BUILDINGS
8,9,10,11,12,13   FAMILY LOWRISE TOWNHOUSES

A   ELDERLY CENTER
B   DAY CARE CENTER
C   COMMUNITY MANAGEMENT BUILDING
D   TERRACE FOR THE ELDERLY
E   COMMUNITY GARDENS
F   DUMPSTER ENCLOSURE
G   TOT LOT & ADULT SITTING AREA
H   PLAY AREA
I   RAISED PEDESTRIAN CROSSING
K   STAIRS TO PUBLIC RECREATION FACILITIES

116 ELDERLY UNITS
276 FAMILY UNITS
392 TOTAL UNITS

PROPOSED SITE PLAN
COMMONWEALTH DEVELOPMENT
0   40   80   120   160
SCALE   1 INCH = 40' FEET

thority, the project retained BHA management, and the surrounding neighborhood suffered from ongoing disinvestment and drug-related crime. The BHA and its design partners again delivered "defensible space," but the residents still felt unsafe. Many long-term residents, when interviewed several years after the completion of the redevelopment, reported that they (and their apartments) were better off before the BHA spent $26 million to help them out.[19]

The third parallel BHA redevelopment effort of the 1980s, at West Broadway, falls somewhere in between the Commonwealth and Franklin Field extremes. It received multiple urban design awards for its carefully programmed courtyards, its efforts at architectural destigmatization through the inclusion of pitched roofs and other familiar residential elements, its subdivision of a 27-acre site into seven smaller "villages," and its efforts to reintroduce the South Boston street grid into an island superblock (Fig. 5.3). At West Broadway, as at Franklin Field, the BHA retained management control, but this time an active cadre of politically well-connected residents (who, prior to the racial integration efforts that immediately

FIGURE 5.3 West Broadway before and after redevelopment. Urban designers aimed to reconnect the site to South Boston and diminish the institutional look of the project.

followed the redevelopment effort, were almost exclusively white) continually exerted pressure on the Authority to improve its performance. The ambitious transformation garnered high approval from most residents, but only three-quarters of it was completed. Eventually, in 2000, with South Boston experiencing unprecedented gentrification, the BHA and the state initiated plans to redevelop the final quadrant into mixed-income housing and service facilities.[20]

The fourth transformation of the Spence era took the city's most notorious project completely out of the Authority's hands and turned it into an award-winning mixed-income privately run rental community now known as Harbor Point. By the late 1970s, only 350 out of Columbia Point's 1,502 original apartments were still legally occupied, and the project had become one of the most infamous in the country, a last resort for residents and a last priority for the housing authority. When built in 1954, it stood alone on a desolate peninsula south of the city, adjacent to two large dumps. By 1963, resident activists had succeeded in getting

the dumps to close, and other powerful institutions gradually moved onto the peninsula, including the John F. Kennedy Presidential Library and a new campus of the University of Massachusetts. In the years that followed, these were joined by the Massachusetts State Archives and a large Exposition Center. Columbia Point no longer was an isolated eyesore; it had become an odd anomaly occupying one of the most attractive large parcels of waterfront real estate on the entire northeastern seaboard.

After more than a decade of false starts and indecision on the part of the BHA and others, Columbia Point's tenants themselves took the lead in forging a viable redevelopment plan. Rather than accept piecemeal renovations or risk wholesale

IT'S THE BIGGEST YET

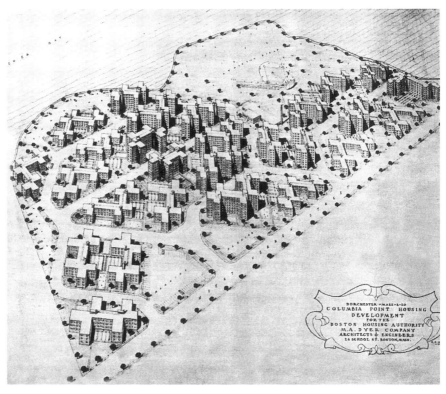

FIGURE 5.4a Touted by the BHA as "the biggest yet," Columbia Point soon became the Authority's biggest headache.

demolition, the Columbia Point Community Task Force (CPCTF), led mostly by African-American women, lobbied for a large-scale redevelopment effort that would preserve low-income housing in perpetuity. In 1983, the Massachusetts Housing Finance Agency organized a multiagency effort and solicited redevelopment proposals from developers willing to guarantee that existing residents of Columbia Point could be rehoused. With so few apartments still occupied by public housing families and such a large site, it was possible for developers to meet the political need to incorporate those families while still assembling an attractive financial model dependent on renting the majority of new apartments at prevailing market rates. In other words, the BHA and BRA had presided over sufficient attrition to allow profitable private redevelopment.

Although the redevelopment effort continued to face delays, progress eventually accelerated. In 1986, a private development team led by Corcoran, Mullins, Jennison, Inc. (CMJ) (who had been campaigning to redevelop the site since

FIGURE 5.4b During the 1980s, Columbia Point was transformed into the mixed-income apartment community known as Harbor Point.

1978) joined with the CPCTF and other developers and construction teams to form Peninsula Partners. The team assembled $250 million in public and private financing to undertake the redevelopment. The redevelopment involved the demolition of most of the buildings on the site, rehabilitation of the remainder, and construction of new grey clapboard townhouses and brick midrise buildings (Fig. 5.4). In addition, the new community included a convenience store, a community center, and a number of new recreational amenities and service facilities. The architects and urban designers thoroughly reconfigured the site plan to make better use of water views, and even scaled the central boulevard to recall Commonwealth Avenue in Boston's Back Bay. In short, architecturally and urbanistically, the designers aimed at complete dissociation from the old project image, and sought to invoke alternative images of New England, both rustic and urbane. By 1991, CMJ and its architects finished the redevelopment, and the vast majority of the stalwart holdovers from the former Columbia Point received places in the 400 subsidized apartments at Harbor Point, intermixed—economically and racially—with those paying market rents for the other 873 units.

During and after the redevelopment process, Harbor Point's critics complained that public investment in this place was excessively high, and argued that the market-rate tenants (most of whom were initially white single individuals or couples who were highly transient) and the low-income former public housing residents (most of whom were nonwhite larger families intending to remain for the long-term) would never mix. Others bemoaned the loss of subsidized units, noting that the new Harbor Point housed only about one quarter of the low-income families that Columbia Point housed when it was fully occupied.

On the whole, however, the Harbor Point experiment received lavish praise, including multiple awards. Despite its high public costs, many pointed to the inestimable societal value of transforming the single most stigmatized place in Boston into an amenity. By the end of the 1990s, having survived a recession and a major restructuring of its financing, Harbor Point achieved nearly 100 percent occupancy. Moreover, the predicted racial divide between subsidized and market-rate tenants began to dissipate. As of 1999, aided by strong demand from students at area universities, more than 40 percent of Harbor Point's *market*-rate units were occupied by nonwhite households.[21] Despite its labyrinthine financing, housing professionals discussed Harbor Point as a precedent for other mixed-income public-private housing ventures using tenant and developer partnerships, and it would become an important reference point for many housing authorities seeking to leverage funds to redevelop failed projects under the large-scale federally sponsored redevelopment initiatives of the 1990s.

Taken together, the Boston examples from the 1980s suggest two quite different approaches to transforming public housing. The first approach, most successfully accomplished at Commonwealth but also partially realized at West Broadway, is premised on making public housing work on its own terms—accepting the footprints of the existing buildings and working with the socioeconomic limitations of the existing residents. The second approach—carried out so dramatically at Harbor Point—involves major demolition and total neighborhood redesign and insists that removing the project stigma entails attracting higher-income tenants. The first approach can still be characterized as public housing renovation and revitalization, whereas the latter sounds more like public housing replacement. The first kind of redevelopment accepted fully the obligation to house public neighbors; the second approach—recalling the slum-clearance efforts of the 1930s—sought to use public housing to replace most public neighbors with more prosperous citizens.

THE POLITICS OF PUBLIC HOUSING PREFERENCES

Although he supported the efforts to restructure Columbia Point, Spence regarded the private, mixed-income model as limited to "certain unusual and specific circumstances," and warned against seeking "false comfort in illusions that we are solving the problems of the poor by displacing them; or in the ascription of magical powers to private endeavor." As Spence pointed out,

> The so-called mixed-income approach is not, in truth, a *solution* to the problem of public housing; it is largely an *elimination* of the problem of public housing. It begins by withdrawing from 75% of the task—for the redevelopment plan usually reduced to one-fourth of their original number the units available for low-income occupancy. The mixed-income alternative is roughly 25% more sophisticated than the argument of those who say to me: "Tear it all down and get rid of those people."[22]

In all his efforts to salvage public housing, however, Spence recognized that projects composed entirely of "those people"—if this meant the permanently jobless—would not be sustainable. As he declared in a speech to the Ford Hall Forum,

> No matter what programs of physical reconstruction, improved maintenance, security, recreation, and social services we introduce to public housing developments in Boston, they will remain centers of disorder and despair, so long as 80 percent of the residents are unemployed. Adequate transfer payments and service programs are essential to aid and support persons who are out of work. But no such programs can compensate for the profound alienation that afflicts those excluded from productive life in the community. Work is the fundamental badge and activity of social membership; those who are without it are exiles, castaways, and pariahs.[23]

Even as Spence spoke, however, federal legislation moved inexorably toward granting public housing preferences for the least-advantaged. To the Reagan administration, a society had an obligation to assist at least a few of its "exiles, castaways, and pariahs," and public housing seemed just the place to herd them up and rein them in.

Recognizing the danger of increasingly concentrated poverty in the projects, the Housing and Community Development Act of 1974 had tried to guard against letting public housing serve only the most desperately poor, but subsequent legislation served to target public housing to the most needy. As federal preferences were expanded in 1979 to favor the applications of families who were living in "substandard housing" (a definition that later came to include the homeless) and, starting in 1984, to give priority to those who were spending more than 50 percent of their income on rent, public housing became increasingly targeted to those with the lowest incomes. Beginning in 1981, Congress also severely constrained the number of public housing units that could go to those earning more than half of the median income. At the same time, by increasing the percentage of income that participant families would have to pay for rent from 25 to 30 percent, the legislation undercut the incentives for higher-earning families to remain in public housing. The absence of ceiling rents also discouraged working families from remaining in public housing communities as a stabilizing factor, while disruptive tenants—taking advantage of enhanced legal protection against eviction that resulted in protracted litigation—often were able to stay put.[24]

In 1983, seeking to halt and reverse the socioeconomic decline of the projects

in Boston, Spence put forward an ambitious and highly controversial plan to attract the working poor back to public housing. He proposed a "two-tier" tenant
selection system: one tier for those earning less than 25 percent of the area's median income (a maximum limit of $7,700 for a family of four)—a tier presumed to
be comprised mainly of those on public assistance; and a second tier for those at
or above 25 percent of median (up to a maximum limit of $17,400 for a family of
four)—a tier presumed to be comprised of wage-earning households. For every
tenant selected from the lower-income tier, the BHA wished to select two from
the higher tier, until the ratio at each given development reached 1:1. Although
Spence phrased the plan in terms of income tiers, he consistently argued that the
fundamental need was not "income-mixing" but infusion of public housing developments with more people engaged in gainful employment. Especially in
housing projects where informal institutions—the networks of clubs and other
voluntary organizations—had withered, Spence concluded that work had become
"the major—or only—source of connection to a larger culture." "If you want people to have some sense of efficacy and social membership," he continued, "it's
very hard to have that unless you're working . . . The reasons are not because it's
wicked for them to be on welfare but because it is fundamentally depressing and
demoralizing to be on welfare. It's very hard to feel you're living a full human life
when you're on welfare in a culture that so values work, and offers so few other
opportunities for social connection." For Spence, public housing served its tenants best by bringing them into contact with what others have increasingly referred to as *social capital.* "The social impact of not working is huge in terms of
the isolation of individuals," Spence observed. "And when you get huge numbers
of isolated individuals, you get a huge isolated community. That isolation is devastating to kids growing up in that community . . . We all know that everybody
gets their first job through knowing somebody. If you don't know anybody that
works, you ain't never gonna work."[25] In this context, the proposed preference for
finding public neighbors with jobs was not an implicit punishment of wicked
welfare mothers, but a necessary means to help the neediest achieve greater social
and economic mobility.

During the mayoral election campaign of 1983, Spence obtained support for
his economic mixing plan from both finalists, Mel King, a black activist, and Raymond Flynn, a populist city councilor and the eventual winner. He garnered approval from both state and federal authorities and, in April 1984, the *Boston Globe*
warmly endorsed this latest attempt to recalibrate the public neighbor concept,

calling the BHA plan "a bold and welcome step toward strengthening the political clout and social stability of public housing."[26]

Others, however, greeted Spence's proposal with derision. The Massachusetts Coalition for the Homeless staged a demonstration against the plan at BHA offices, and issued a position paper explaining the housing crunch faced by Boston's female-headed and minority households. One of the Coalition's coordinators responded to the *Globe*'s editorial with her own interpretation of the plan's demeaning effect: "Underlying the BHA's move to thin out the number of welfare recipients in public housing," Monica Hileman charged, "are belittling assumptions about women and the poor: that what women do in the home is not valuable, that it is not 'work,' and that the poor are responsible for their poverty." The Coalition for Basic Human Needs sent a letter to the *Globe,* later circulated to city and state officials, blasting the BHA plan as a heartless attempt to squeeze the homeless and near-homeless out of scarce affordable housing opportunities. The Coalition also lambasted the plan for its sexist assumption that only male-headed households could control their children, and sarcastically dismissed the argument that imported higher-income role models could solve the deeply rooted poverty afflicting most public housing residents: "Lack of day care, inequitable wages, discrimination, and lack of training are problems which are not going to be solved with a little 'networking.'" A recently formed public housing tenants organization—Tenants United for Public Housing Progress (TUPHP—pronounced "tough") also came out against the BHA's income-mixing plan. Faced with such grassroots opposition, Flynn reneged on his pre-election promise to Spence, and withdrew his endorsement of the idea. In July 1984, recognizing that mayoral disapproval marked a fatal blow, Spence decided not to try to implement the proposal.[27] Once again, efforts to sort out the poor and implement policy in accordance with broad principles fell victim to the highly charged claims of needy individuals.

Spence also felt thwarted in many of his efforts to improve the BHA's record on racial integration of its developments. He tried to work with residents to develop fair housing plans for the white-dominated ("powder keg") areas of East Boston, South Boston and Charlestown, but progress remained limited. In Spence's mind, the racial integration question went straight to the heart of his beliefs about the obligations of government in a pluralist democratic society. "Our theory," he later recalled, "was that if you said that public housing ought to be moderately more integrated than the surrounding neighborhood, you'd get what

always happens when public housing gets integrated. There's slowly some percolating out into the neighborhood, and the neighborhood becomes somewhat
more mixed. And that would then raise the proportion that had to be mixed in
public housing. So, over a period of time by kind of process of osmosis it would
leak out into the neighborhood."[28] Although HUD initially supported BHA efforts to act on this theory, the NAACP later successfully sued to stop the plan,
since—among other things—it implied clear upper limits for minority occupancy
in some developments. Throughout his efforts to get public housing to carry a
"larger burden" than private housing on fair housing matters, Spence remained
trapped between his critics. To some, Spence's approach simply stirred up trouble; to others, its model of attenuated neighborhood evolution seemed frustrat-
ingly gradualist.

GETTING BEYOND RECEIVERSHIP

To Judge Garrity, however, the BHA had made "remarkable progress" in many
areas during four-and-a-half years of Spence's leadership. Four months before the
receivership was due for its annual re-assessment, Garrity ended it in November
1984. With Kevin White finally out of office, Garrity believed that the BHA's
"historically abusive relationship" at the hands of the city's political leadership
no longer held sway. Whatever the disagreements over tenant selection criteria,
Ray Flynn's Boston surely seemed a much more congenial environment for public housing. With no Board of Commissioners re-established, Garrity's order
granted Flynn complete control over the BHA, subject only to the advice of a
monitoring committee.[29]

Flynn brought BHA leadership full circle by appointing Doris Bunte as his
first administrator. In contrast to past practice, however, this time the choice of
administrator was supported not only by a mayor, but by a judge and by a committee chaired by the Perez plaintiffs' lead attorney, Leslie Newman, and comprised of housing experts (including former BHA master Robert Whittlesey),
BHA staff, Barbara Mellan (president of TUPHP and a West Broadway tenant),
and two city representatives. Bunte, who had previously parlayed her Wagnerian
term on the BHA board into a decade-long stint in the state legislature, thus enjoyed a broad mandate—a mandate she would need to run an agency Garrity described as "troubled with system-wide problems."[30]

Bunte continued with efforts to modernize several BHA developments, most notably Mission Hill Extension, now known as Alice Taylor. Yet redevelopment never obtained the scale or lavishness achieved during the receivership. One leading Boston economic development official observed that whereas Harry Spence was a visionary who "raised the stakes" with a "redevelopment agenda," his successor had an agenda rooted in "maintenance and basic services." Although she and Harry Spence were long-time friends, Bunte chose not to carry out many of his priorities and resented the ways that the media compared the two leaders. As a black single parent who had raised her family at Orchard Park, Bunte sought to maximize the availability of public housing to the neediest, and resisted redevelopment plans that proposed to reduce the density of housing projects by eliminating units.[31]

By the early 1990s, policies like Bunte's, which viewed public housing as the exclusive province of public neighbors, started to come under repeated attack, both in Boston and nationally. Reviving earlier concerns, Congress called for altering admissions preferences to attract a greater mix of incomes, imposing ceiling rents to retain working families, and implementing speedier eviction procedures to rid the projects of their most problematic denizens.[32] In Boston, following Bunte's departure in 1992, the BHA quietly resuscitated Spence's ideas for a "two-tier" admissions system that favored working families, and argued against federal preferences for housing the homeless.[33] With more than 20,000 families on its waiting list, BHA officials resented the fact that nearly every public housing opening had to be filled by a family coming from a shelter. As Bunte's successor David Cortiella complained in 1992, "the homeless have social problems way beyond housing—a whole range of social problems." Cortiella wished to curtail homeless admissions drastically, concentrating instead on the next tier of federal preferences—those spending more than half of their income on rent or doubling up with another family. Throughout the early 1990s, he pointed out in 1994, efforts to house the homeless in public housing meant that not even one family in this next preference category could be housed. "Working poor families," Cortiella noted, despite being "desperately in need of safe, decent, affordable housing, never even had a chance." Unlike the homeless, he contended, the next tier of financially strapped families were "people whose only need is housing." Whereas the formerly homeless threatened "to drain all the social services revenues we have" and to damage the "quality of life" in some developments, Cortiella preferred an employed population that was "less transient" and "doesn't have service needs."[34] City Councilor James Kelly of South Boston (soon to become City Council President) put the matter even more harshly: "I don't think the homeless should be assigned to BHA developments. The vast majority of homeless are not homeless because of financial problems. Many have substance abuse problems. Twenty-five to thirty percent have mental problems. Putting people with mental problems into a public housing project, where life is tough enough, is not fair."[35]

Others, of course, saw fairness quite differently. Steve Hitov, director of the homeless project at Greater Boston Legal Services, doubted that the BHA had any evidence that the formerly homeless caused disruption. Sue Marsh, executive director of the Massachusetts Coalition for the Homeless, called BHA actions "illegal, immoral and based on a whole range of myths."[36] While advocates for the homeless, the mentally disabled, and other groups facing extremely limited housing choices continued to decry any shift away from a commitment to use public housing to house the least-advantaged, most others concluded that public housing projects nationwide had already become disastrously overconcentrated zones of poverty.

In the mid-1990s, according to HUD figures, more than 80 percent of nonelderly public housing households nationwide lived below the poverty line, and average income of public housing households was only $6,100, equal to about 17 percent of the median income for the local areas in which these developments are located. In many large developments across the country, more than 90 percent of households reported no earned income at all. In large cities, only about one-quarter of nonelderly households living in public housing reported that their major source of income came from wages.[37] The problem, in short, was neither a Boston problem nor was it limited to a few notorious "severely distressed" projects. Rather, the entire system of public housing developments across the country suffered from severely concentrated impoverishment. Nearly every public housing authority, with greater or lesser success, struggled to house a similarly distressed cohort of public neighbors. In the Boston of the 1990s, a city where family public housing projects had been built entirely outside the areas of highest poverty, many of these same projects now stood squarely within such a zone and, in fact, helped to indicate its boundaries (Fig. 5.5).

The BHA's John Murphy, having presided over tenant selection for a quarter century, remains among those who consider this willingness to house the least-advantaged to be a public duty. Because private landlords still tend to be "able to

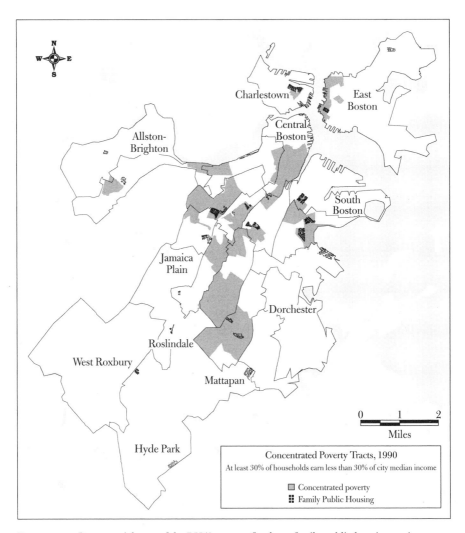

FIGURE 5.5 By 1990, eighteen of the BHA's twenty-five large family public housing projects were within or immediately adjacent to the city's areas of most concentrated poverty, whereas only two projects were within these areas when the projects were built (see Fig. 4.2). Concentrated poverty census tracts were defined as those where at least 30 percent of households had incomes below 30 percent of the city median.

exclude people for reasons that are not entirely legitimate," public housing must continue to accept the neediest: "We have an obligation to house people who would otherwise not be selected for housing elsewhere," he contends, "That's why public funds are used." To act on this belief meant that the original kinds of intensive selection processes that once filled developments had to be deliberately inverted. "Harry Spence," Murphy recalled, "always said that the public housing system is based on rejections not selections":

> What it means is that we don't really select who we want to live in our units. We can only reject people because they don't meet the eligibility criteria for one reason or another, whereas [private] landlords, and particularly subsidized landlords, can look at five families and say 'Well this one has a minor problem there, and that one has a minor problem there, so we'll select number four.' Public housing is based on rejection. If we *can't* find a reason *not* to allow you to move in, then you've got to be housed.[38]

By the 1990s, however, such cheerful championing of a system "based on rejection" garnered increasingly little support.

BOSTON PUBLIC HOUSING IN THE 1990s: SEEKING NEW PUBLIC NEIGHBORS

In the 1990s, public housing reform in Boston and elsewhere once again focused on redeveloping both projects and their tenants. In the early 1990s, HUD launched the most ambitious comprehensive redevelopment program yet undertaken. Known as the HOPE VI program (in which the HOPE acronym stands for Homeownership and Opportunity for People Everywhere), the program followed on failed attempts during the Bush administration to implement HUD secretary Jack Kemp's plan to sell off public housing to tenants. Kemp doggedly sought to reconcile public housing with the dominant American ideology of homeownership, and even believed public housing sales to be a contemporary version of the Homestead Act of 1862.[39] Ultimately, though, Congress recognized that the vast majority of public housing residents lacked the stable income stream to support the financial responsibility of homeownership and acknowledged that most large urban public housing projects—the biggest problems in the whole system—were too decrepit to seem a terribly attractive investment. Instead, Congress pushed for HOPE VI, an "Urban Revitalization Demonstration" program that was expected to improve many of the worst public housing sites and lessen their political liability. Catalyzed by the efforts of the National Commission on Severely Distressed Public Housing, which released its Final Report in 1992, HOPE VI provides public housing authorities with grants of up to $50 million for redeveloping up to 500 units of "severely distressed" public housing. By 1999, Congress had authorized HOPE VI grants totaling about $3 billion, intended to permit the redesign of scores of public housing developments nationwide.

In most HOPE VI proposals approved after 1993, redesign usually entailed plans for outright demolition of all or most of a project, and HUD proudly and repeatedly affirmed that at least 100,000 units would be razed. By the end of the first Clinton administration, HUD touted a new model for "tomorrow's public housing," one premised on "leveraging federal funds with private and public resources to build a new community of garden-style apartments; creating market-rate housing for mixed-income families; and seeking private management for the development."[40] Clearly, the precedent of Boston's Harbor Point was headed for national application.

At the same time, however, the HOPE VI legislation required initiatives aimed at shoring up the socioeconomic status of existing public housing residents. Whereas previous large-scale redevelopment efforts focused on bricks-and-mortar needs, HUD allowed HOPE VI recipients to spend up to 20 percent of their grant on social service and economic development initiatives. Seen this way, the HOPE VI initiatives offered up the possibility of unprecedented efforts to expand and coordinate physical redevelopment goals with strategies aimed at achieving greater socioeconomic "self-sufficiency" for low-income families in public housing.

Two Boston HOPEs

Building on its well-established track record of comprehensive public housing redevelopment, the Boston Housing Authority received its first two HOPE VI grants in the mid-1990s, which it used to redevelop Mission Hill Main and Orchard Park, widely regarded as among the most physically and socioeconomically distressed developments in the city.

In 1993, as part of the first round of HOPE VI grants, HUD awarded the BHA nearly $50 million to redevelop Mission Main. This development, located next to a district of prosperous medical and educational institutions, had long since become an isolated enclave of poverty, and its rich neighbors had put "pressure on the BHA to renovate it and get its social problems under control." Initially, the BHA proposed to renovate the development in the manner employed at West Broadway and elsewhere, and to keep Mission Main under Authority management. Having watched as the private management takeovers of Commonwealth and Harbor Point gained national acclaim, BHA leaders explicitly wanted to demonstrate the ability of the public sector to manage a successful turnaround of distressed public housing. To do so, BHA officials believed, entailed not just better management but better tenants.

Here, as elsewhere, the favored panacea involved creation of "a more economically diverse population." To salvage Mission Main, the BHA called for admitting half of the resident population with incomes at or above 50 percent of median; reinstating ceiling rents (pegged at 80 percent of fair market rent) to encourage higher-income residents to remain; creating an on-site screening committee to be composed of residents, management, and legal personnel with veto power over applicants; and implementing a separate waiting list for the development (as opposed to a citywide one) to insure that applicants really wanted to live at Mission Main. In addition to these efforts, the BHA proposed a variety of security reforms (centered on a community policing program), and sought other ways to meet the needs of those very low-income tenants who would initially want to be rehoused in the renovated Mission Main. To deal with this, the HOPE VI plan set aside more than $8 million for community and social services, intended to "encourage family self-sufficiency, to promote resident empowerment, and to enhance community spirit."[41]

By 1995, however, almost everything about the Mission Main plan had been called into question, and the BHA again experienced protracted instability at the top levels of its administration. Mayor Thomas Menino (who took over when Flynn left office to become ambassador to the Vatican) ousted David Cortiella as BHA administrator, leading to another period of interim leadership. At the same time, the HOPE VI program itself faced a change of director; the projected architectural costs for the Mission Main rehab came in at least $10 million over budget, requiring a total reconsideration of the design approach; and—most crucial of all—turmoil at HUD and in Congress brought not only uncertainty but also new constraints and new opportunities. Beginning in mid-1994, HUD promoted its "HOPE VI Plus" concept, encouraging housing authorities to leverage the

HOPE VI grant with other grants and investment opportunities to develop larger mixed-income neighborhoods. HUD also agreed to allow HOPE VI grantees to build new housing both on-site and in surrounding neighborhoods, even if those neighborhoods already housed high concentrations of low-income minority households. Finally, in 1995, HUD stopped requiring housing authorities to provide one-for-one replacement for lost public housing units.

In late 1995 and 1996, the BHA responded to these changes with a new approach to the redevelopment of Mission Main, one that involved phased demolition of the entire site (seen as the most cost-effective solution) and its replacement with a privately managed mixed-income community (seen as keeping with the tenor of congressional and HUD preferences).[42] Rather than a demonstration of the BHA's abilities to manage a public housing turnaround, the Authority now proposed that Mission Main be both redeveloped and managed by private-sector firms. Instead of a project-centered reinvestment, the BHA reconceptualized the Mission Main HOPE VI plan as a broader neighborhood revitalization strategy based on the development potential of the land, even including controversial plans for a land swap with a neighboring university, which the developer rejected.[43] All the various changes soured the relationship between the BHA and the Mission Main tenants, yielding a protracted impasse.

Eventually, Mission Main residents established a good working relationship with the private development team (Arthur Winn Development and Edward A. Fish Associates), and the project moved forward. By early 2000, more than 300 of the planned 545 units had opened for occupancy. The private management team (Winn/Peabody/Cruz) issued a marketing brochure called "Mission Main: A World of New Beginnings" that completely avoided the phrase *public housing*. Instead, the promotional materials pointed to "endless possibilities for recreation, culture, restaurants, shopping, education, and entertainment," noting that "residents enjoy a spacious and well-designed home located in a vibrant, diverse community that boasts world-renowned cultural, educational, and medical institutions among its neighbors." Three hundred households from the former Mission Main project were expected to return to the site, interspersed with households paying market rents of $1,400 a month for a two-bedroom unit. Although 80 percent of the townhouses and apartments were reserved for those earning less than 60 percent of median income, demand for the market-rate units was so intense that many people signed leases even while the units were still under construction. Slowly but surely, the sixty-year-old brick boxes of the old Mission Hill project gave way to a new streetscape of pastel townhouses. For the BHA, the result was a "typical family-housing neighborhood," where "the 'institutional' feel is removed."[44]

Stung by the long stalemate over Mission Main, and seeking to take full advantage of the new HUD rules and enticements, the BHA proposed a highly leveraged neighborhood-oriented strategy for its second HOPE VI site right from the start. In the case of Orchard Park, which received its HOPE VI implementation grant in 1995, the BHA stressed that the plan was about more than "rebuilding distressed public housing"; it was expected to be "truly a neighborhood revitalization strategy," one that "combines the best of urban renewal with the best of the community empowerment movement."[45] In 1996 the Housing Authority and the Orchard Park Tenants Association (OPTA) selected a private development team (Madison Trinity Ventures) in accordance with careful design guidelines that stressed eliminating all forms of stigma and called for developers to "reorganize the site to create a typical urban family housing neighborhood, one which cannot be readily recognized as public housing" (Fig. 5.6).[46] Moreover, the BHA and OPTA required the development team to pay special attention to a variety of "edge conditions" beyond Orchard Park itself, including plans for other developers to produce new and rehabilitated affordable housing in the neighborhood outside the original project boundaries. At the same time, the plan outlined strategies to "increase economic development opportunity" and provide for the "self-sufficiency of residents through job training and community service."[47]

The Orchard Park plan marked an attempt to leverage the HOPE VI funds (using private investment and Low Income Housing Tax Credits) in order to make public housing less apparent. They even renamed the development Orchard Gardens Estates. As with the examples of Boston public housing redevelopment in the 1980s, the task was made somewhat easier by a high vacancy rate in the housing project itself. With only 326 apartments occupied out of 708, once again it was possible to use a redevelopment process to reduce the density of public housing units while still maintaining the politically necessary potential to include current public housing residents in the new community. Aided by HUD's formal abandonment of the need to provide one-for-one replacement for demolished units, and assisted by relaxation of HUD standards governing the construction of new housing in "impacted" neighborhoods, this HOPE VI initiative replaced public housing with a set of privately managed mixed-income housing developments (including opportunities for homeownership). These developments were financed largely through private equity and debt, yet still relied on HUD to fund an operating subsidy to preserve long-term affordability for some public housing residents within this mix.[48]

These two Boston HOPE VI plans can only hint at the variety of approaches currently underway nationwide, yet they illustrate many of the major trends, and make clear the broader challenges that confront efforts to revitalize distressed public housing in neighborhood settings with widely differing development pressures.[49] Once housing authorities were no longer confined to rebuilding their projects on the footprints of the old structures, once they were no longer constrained by the need to provide one-for-one replacement for demolished public housing units, and once it became possible to solicit waivers for all manner of other former HUD regulations, the possibilities for innovative redevelopment schemes rapidly multiplied. Even so, it seems possible to characterize the central themes of HOPE VI public housing redevelopment efforts across the country, and to see how these plans collectively attempt to render public housing more ideologically palatable to a polity impatient with government programs that support the persistently poor.[50]

FIGURE 5.6 View of Orchard Gardens Estates, January 2000. The white fences and colorful duplexes and townhomes of the redevelopment were designed to erase all vestiges of the site's former public housing project.

Throughout the United States, most HOPE VI public housing redevelopment efforts share six common goals: first, deconcentration of very low-income residents through dispersion and reduction in the number of public housing units; second, promotion of mixed-income communities, by encouragement of private-sector participation and preferences for working families; third, demolition or major renovation of current developments to promote "defensible space" and remove the stigma of the public housing look; fourth, emphasis on New Urbanist design strategies intended to recreate the scale and mixed-use character of older neighborhood fabrics; fifth, encouragement of "family self-sufficiency" programs; and sixth, support for resident involvement in management, often in partnership with private firms. Taken together, these six trends suggest that public housing redevelopment under HOPE VI has become not only a process for redeveloping housing, but a way to redevelop tenants as well. The prevailing media image consists of imploded towers replaced by neo-traditional townhouses,[51] but the real battle is not over housing types, but over the types of tenants these buildings will house. In the 1990s, as before, housing policymakers and frustrated citizens still argued over who deserved to become a public neighbor.

In the 1980s version of public housing redevelopment, the goal was to restructure projects and eliminate troublemakers; in the new round of efforts, the goal is to eliminate troubled projects and restructure occupancy. If the problem is concentrated poverty and unemployment in public housing, however, the HOPE VI initiatives can only begin to redress a systemic flaw. For every large city that has received a grant or two to address the problems of 500 units of distressed public housing, there are thousands of distressed public housing residents living in similarly concentrated poverty in other housing developments. In most large cities, there are certainly significant differences between a city's most distressed public housing development and the average project in that same city, yet there is still a great amount of distress that is shared. The same dire socioeconomic statistics that symbolize the problems facing residents of sites chosen for HOPE VI redevelopment apply equally to the entrenched and concentrated poverty faced by residents in less distressed public housing nationwide.

ONGOING STRUGGLES AT THE BHA

As with the BHA's HOPE VI initiatives, the Authority as a whole faced mixed prospects. In the mid-1990s the agency was again charged with mismanagement, this time centered on its elderly developments. Once the exception to the rule of devastation that characterized the agency at its nadir, these projects now became the focus of scandal and disdain. To blunt criticism while it embarked on internal management reforms, the Authority transferred twelve buildings into the hands of private management companies.[52]

At the same time, the BHA continued to be plagued by persistent claims of racial discrimination. With a waiting list that was by this point more than 80 percent nonwhite, white neighborhoods with predominantly white housing projects struggled to come to terms with the prospect of nonwhite public neighbors (Fig. 5.7). As late as 1988, the three large South Boston family developments housed no black families, and few nonwhites dared enter the public housing in East Boston or Charlestown (see Fig. 4.5).[53] Under the terms of a voluntary compliance agreement entered into with HUD in 1988, and facing another lawsuit from the NAACP, the BHA again pledged to end its discriminatory practices. Eventually, the BHA paid nearly $1.8 million to about 800 families that had been discouraged from living in predominantly white developments.[54] Moreover, to the BHA's credit, the agency did substantially integrate its most notoriously segregated developments during the 1990s. Given the paucity of white applicants and the HUD requirement that tenant assignment to all developments be conducted from a single citywide waiting list, some such integration seemed all but inevitable. It is to the credit of many families who endured difficult circumstances, however, that integration proceeded with far fewer incidents of the violence that met the first pioneers in the 1960s and 1970s. That said, as Bill McGonagle, BHA deputy administrator, noted, "We're pitting poor folks of various races against each other for an ever-dwindling supply of housing."[55]

To reduce further the potential for unrest in white neighborhoods where locally raised low-income whites considered themselves unfairly excluded from a chance to gain entry into nearby public housing, BHA officials still sought ways to preserve a modicum of neighborhood choice. The Authority solicited HUD approval for an "alternate feed" system of selection that would allow prospective public housing tenants to place their names on a waiting list for a specific development rather than the citywide list, with selections to be made alternately from the two lists as openings emerged.[56] As Mayor Menino put it, "Just because you're poor doesn't mean the government should be able to tell you where to live."[57] Faced by counter-charges that the "alternate feed" would contribute to resegregation, however, the plan remained mired in controversy for years. With racially motivated hostility continuing to erupt periodically at some developments, and a federal class-action suit filed against the BHA and the city by tenants who

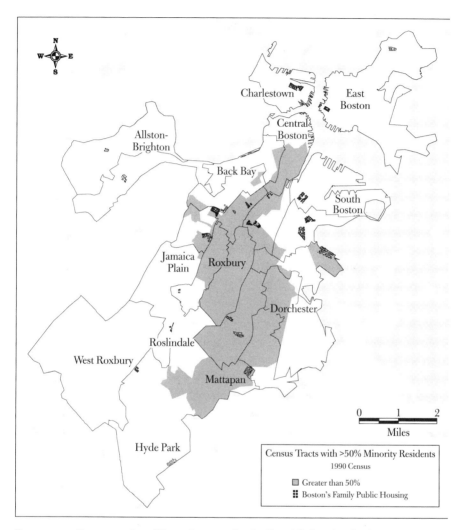

FIGURE 5.7 By 1990, twelve of Boston's twenty-five family public housing developments were located in census tracts that had a nonwhite majority, whereas only three had been located in such neighborhoods at the time they were built (see Fig. 3.19). On the one hand, this reflected the growth and spread of Boston's black, Latino, and Asian populations since 1950. On the other hand, as nearly all Boston public housing moved toward majority occupancy by nonwhites, it meant that many such developments were still located in white-majority neighborhoods, leading to ongoing tensions.

charged that BHA managers responded inadequately to racial harassment at developments in Charlestown and South Boston, any federally sanctioned release from the single citywide waiting list had to be measured against civil rights laws.[58] Making matters worse, a lengthy investigation by HUD in 1995 revealed that the 152 highly desirable townhouse units at the Mary Ellen McCormack development had been systematically reserved for whites only, sparking a public relations nightmare for both the BHA and Menino. The HUD report found evidence of "intentional discrimination as well a discriminatory effect" and concluded that BHA staff had "departed completely" from the official tenant selection process in order to exclude minorities from consideration for the development's best apartments.[59] Whatever the uneasy progress on integration, Boston's racial politics remained the core barrier to reform. Within the BHA, a system within the system continued to operate.

By the mid-1990s, as state and federal officials engaged in new rounds of cutbacks for public housing funding, the BHA's institutional recovery, so dramatically launched under Spence, seemed very much a thing of the past. Even though Boston's public housing projects still contained thousands of whites on public assistance and thousands of nonwhites supported by gainful employment, the tensions of race permeated every discussion of tenant selection and assignment. In a society that remains uncomfortable with racial integration, public housing tenants bore the brunt of public policy initiatives while receiving few of the supposed benefits. The transition from segregated enclaves to integrated ghettoes, like the broader shift from real estate operation to welfare agency, remained contentious, incomplete, and underfunded. Once the BHA belatedly tried to turn itself back toward its original real estate mission, it faced the same problems.

In early 1996, as one more effort to get the BHA's managerial problems under control, Mayor Menino appointed Sandra Henriquez as BHA administrator, the first trained housing professional to hold the post since the departure of Harry Spence. For Henriquez, a black woman who had previously worked for the court-controlled BHA under both Whittlesey and Spence, it marked a return to a much-changed place. During the period of the master and the receiver, she recalled, "We saw ourselves as the reformers and that we were institutionalizing those reforms. Coming back now, I am amazed that there are no vestiges of things I know we worked on in the early 80s." Instead of the new bureaucracy created under Spence, she inherited an agency that had reverted to type, staffed by too many long-tenured employees who "may rail against how awful it is to work for the BHA, but don't leave." It was again an organization that operated according to "political expediency," resisted long-term planning, and remained isolated from the parallel world of private-sector real estate professionals.

Although the administrator faced fewer outside political pressures to house particular tenants in particular developments or to hire or promote specific up-per-level bureaucrats, the Authority remained internally torn by tension between those like Henriquez, who used terms like "portfolio management" and "compet-itive marketing," and those who felt that public housing was already "'good enough for poor people because they're a trapped audience, so we can do what-ever we want.'"[60] Henriquez faced a daunting triple agenda, needing to give re-newed attention to the most basic daily matters, such as hallway maintenance at developments, while also trying again to transform the BHA's internal culture, and struggling to keep the Authority financially able to serve its tenants.

Henriquez returned to the BHA from a successful career in private real estate management because she wished "to prove that we can be good managers of real estate who just happen to be public sector managers." According to her, "Real es-tate is real estate. The principles and the tools and the procedures and the stan-dards should all be the same. It is only who occupies it that should be different."

During the first three years of Henriquez's leadership, the Authority redressed many persistent problems. The BHA and its management partners substantially restored the elderly housing portfolio to the "industry standards" of the private sector. Greater attention to preventive maintenance meant that tenant requests for emergency repairs no longer drove the system, and most work orders could be completed within a one- to three-day turnaround. Tenants at three developments with privatized management actually asked the BHA to come back.

Racial tensions proved more difficult to defuse, but there were signs of prog-ress. Under the terms of a voluntary compliance agreement with HUD, the BHA successfully addressed the fiasco of racial exclusion at the Mary Ellen McCormack townhouses. By 2000 about 40 percent of the townhouses were oc-cupied by nonwhite families. Henriquez also faced the fallout from a three-year HUD investigation into charges that the BHA had downplayed the "system-atic discrimination" against nine minority families living in South Boston and Charlestown developments between 1990 and 1996. HUD secretary Andrew Cuomo termed this bias suit the most serious discrimination case ever brought against a local agency. A subsequent investigation in 1999 to assess the BHA's anti-bias efforts since 1996, while still critical, found evidence of improvement. It credited the city and the housing authority for a reduction in racial and ethnic harassment following adoption of a civil rights protection plan intended to safeguard residents and to discipline managers who failed to follow the plan. In March 1999 the National Black Caucus awarded the BHA a City Cultural Diversity Award for its Diversity and Mediation Project. Even as Henriquez tried to get the BHA back on the right track, however, she faced a contradictory set of complaints: some local white politicians accused her of overzealousness in the enforcement of a "zero tolerance" policy on hate crimes, because she sought eviction of entire white families for the acts committed by one of the children.

In addition to her engagement with the simmering issue of racial bias, Henriquez made another controversial management decision in late 1998 when she temporarily took back the Bromley-Heath development from its Tenant Management Corporation (TMC). She took this extreme step partly as a way to insist upon more rigid enforcement of drug-related evictions. Having made her point about the need for quality management and policing, the BHA returned management control to the TMC in 1999.[61]

By seeking to apply private-sector standards to public housing management, Henriquez wished to "institutionalize changes" that could be sustained after her departure, so that "when we all walk away, the system will operate because it works well and it's the right thing to do." For Henriquez, doing the "right thing" meant improving public housing standards to benefit existing residents. For most other housing policymakers, the more salient challenge had become improving the standard of residents so as to benefit existing public housing.

As the twenty-first century begins, the public sentiment that guides government attitudes toward public housing demands that government get out of the business of providing permanent housing to the long-term unemployed. If this is indeed the motive behind the disposition of the most overtly planned pockets of neighborhood poverty in American cities, it is a policy turn that is not without alternatives or consequences. To reduce systematically the number of subsidized housing units made available to those who need public housing most is to ignore the countervailing lesson of Boston's Commonwealth development. In this one place, at least, a once-devastated project became again a safe and attractive development—run jointly by effective private management and empowered tenants—and re-emerged without resort to income-mixing (even though it is situated in a stable neighborhood that could have happily supported market-rate housing on the site). Most experts agree that such communities are impossible to sustain, yet attempts to destroy them are proceeding slowly, lawsuit by lawsuit, into the new millennium.

IDEOLOGICAL RETRENCHMENT

Efforts to sustain public housing projects as low-income enclaves seem ultimately doomed, especially since even the legal-aid system that supports tenant lawsuits has come under budgetary attack.[62] The prevailing public sentiment wishes to eliminate the projects and, in so doing, seeks ways to recover the means for judging the moral worth of those public neighbors Americans still feel obligated to support. It is as if the entire phylogeny of ambivalent motives for housing marginal people has been recapitulated in the ontogeny of the projects and their tenants. In a society still rooted in expectations of advancement and individual self-reliance, housing authorities—driven by the congressional hold over appropriations—seek every politically possible way to return their projects to the selective collectives of upwardly mobile workers of a half-century earlier. The public rhetoric has reverted to this country's oldest ideological themes, coupling new plans for homeownership by low-income families with insistent calls for self-sufficiency.

In 1984 HUD introduced Project Self-Sufficiency as a demonstration program targeted to 10,000 single mothers in 155 housing authorities. In 1989 the Bush administration followed it with Operation Bootstrap, enrolling an additional 3,000 families. In both programs, housing officials defined self-sufficiency as the ability to achieve enough economic independence through job training to enable families to enter into private-sector housing, while also reducing their dependency on federal entitlement programs. In some instances, such as the Gateway Transitional Families Program in Charlotte, North Carolina, which began in 1987, a housing authority even explicitly phrased the ultimate goal of self-sufficiency in terms of homeownership. Despite a paucity of evidence demonstrating the effectiveness of such programs for all but the most motivated, Congress launched an even more ambitious Family Self-Sufficiency Program (FSS) in 1990, requiring all housing authorities to begin participation by 1993. By 1996, FSS programs across the country had enrolled an estimated 60,000 participants—disproportionately concentrated in the nation's largest housing authorities. In 1998 the BHA's own mission statement called for the Authority to be a "catalyst for the transformation from dependency to economic self-sufficiency."[63]

Although the effectiveness of such self-sufficiency programs is not yet proven, one thing is clear: such programs remain wholly consistent with the language and spirit of deeply rooted American attitudes about housing and personal responsibility.

In the mid-1990s, self-sufficiency programs in public housing got swept up in the current of a broader sea-change in federal welfare policy, reforms that directly affected public housing households receiving AFDC benefits and indirectly affected all the rest. In 1994, with its Work and Responsibility Act (WRA), the Clinton administration proposed a plan to create employment opportunities for welfare recipients, designed to ensure that "anyone who can work, must work—in the private sector if possible, in a temporary subsidized job if necessary." A Republican-led Congress countered with the even more restrictive and contemptuously phrased Personal Responsibility Act (PRA), calling for Congress to "provide States with the resources and authority necessary to help, cajole, lure, or force adults off welfare and into paid employment as quickly as possible, and to require adult welfare recipients, when necessary, to accept jobs that will help end welfare dependency." The PRA not only proposed to cut off welfare benefits to any family after five years but radically increased the discretion of individual states to decide who was deserving of assistance. In this context, Congress sought to scrap the long-standing entitlement program of AFDC, replacing it with the more conditional-sounding Temporary Assistance to Needy Families (TANF). Eventually, in 1996, Congress passed, and Clinton signed, the Personal Responsibility and Work Opportunity Reconciliation Act (PRWORA), modeled closely on the PRA. It included funds for TANF as a block grant to states (as opposed to an entitlement grant to individuals), specified time limits for aid, and required that recipients "engage in work" within two years.[64] Operating in parallel to federal initiatives, Massachusetts replaced its Department of Welfare with the more aptly named Department of Transitional Assistance.

At this writing, most consequences for public housing of such welfare curtailments remain uncertain. In Boston, buoyed by the robust economy of the late 1990s, many BHA residents faced with the curtailment of TANF benefits have found jobs. Unfortunately, Henriquez observes, most of these jobs are "subsistence-level, at break-even with where they were when they were on TANF. We've not seen an increase in rent receipts because people have gone to work. It's not there." As she sees it, welfare reform is "another way of not just hurting poor people but hurting public housing authorities." In theory, "it forces us to take higher-income folks if we want to remain financially viable to offset those decreases in funding." Yet "it's not going to work that way" because, "if housing authorities really do implement this policy, the mayors of those cities where it happens will be screaming about homeless shelter costs and people on the streets and living in cars." Those BHA tenants who cannot find jobs constitute a big problem, according to Henriquez, since the "vast majority" are illiterate. "How do we get people into work if they don't speak English and may not even be literate in their native tongue?" The Massachusetts program is a "work first" program, under which the newly employed are given a variety of additional services to help them hold these jobs or advance from them, yet many public housing tenants cannot meet the minimum threshold to get that initial job.[65] Although the BHA may well choose not to evict its jobless and welfareless tenants who have no place to go (forcing an even greater financial squeeze on the Authority), there are also other potential pressures: caught up in the swirl of rhetoric about temporary assistance, personal responsibility, and family self-sufficiency, Congress may someday set corresponding time limits for residence in public housing.

Despite widespread support in both the House and Senate, however, passage of a landmark overhaul of public housing foundered during House-Senate negotiations in 1996. Congressman Rick Lazio, a Republican from New York who sponsored the House version of the bill, blamed its failure on "a conspiracy between those people who don't give a damn about the poor and those people who are perfectly satisfied maintaining the poor in the federal slums that have been built."[66] Undaunted by the impasse, the Republican-dominated House put this issue at the top of the legislative agenda for 1997, and soon passed it overwhelmingly. Known as the Housing Opportunity and Responsibility Act of 1997 (HORA), the bill clearly and overtly signaled a change in America's public neighbor policy. Declaring that "the Federal Government cannot through its direct action alone provide for the housing of every American citizen," the bill sought new ways to target federal obligation to those "responsible, deserving citizens who cannot provide fully for themselves because of temporary circumstances or factors beyond their control." Just as other local bodies had tried to do in centuries past, Congress asked housing authorities to sift the worthy poor from their undeserving brethren. Assuming a clear division between those self-inflicted causes of poverty that the poor should have been able to control and those forms that resulted from providential misfortune, the national legislature invoked language that sounded more like the close of the seventeenth century than the dawn of the twenty-first.

Congress finally passed its landmark public housing reform bill in October 1998, provocatively entitling it the Quality Housing and Work Responsibility Act.[67] In a country that for centuries had coupled housing benefits to hard work, the new law resonated not only with the Homestead Act but with earlier efforts to link incarceration and forced labor. As in the past, housing reform sought to sort the poor into those the nation should reward and those it should merely endure.

Congress wished to reduce the concentration of poor families in public housing. While stopping short of repealing the thirty-year legacy of the Brooke Amendment legislation that capped rents at 30 percent of income, the legislature nonetheless sought to rein in the amount of public housing targeted to very low-income households.[68] Democrats blocked attempts to restructure rents in ways that would give housing authorities the leeway to price themselves beyond the means of many existing tenants with the lowest incomes, and nearly all legislators wished to set rents in a way that did not seem to penalize existing tenants with jobs, so the new legislation attempted to recalibrate the preferences accorded to the 1 million households still on the nation's public housing waiting lists. Instead of concentrating efforts on getting the old generation of poor out of public housing, Congress found it politically more palatable to focus on keeping the new generation of poor from ever getting in.

At a time when three-quarters of the country's existing public housing population earned less than 30 percent of the median income, the Quality Housing and Work Responsibility Act allowed housing authorities to reserve up to 70 percent of public housing project openings for those earning *more* than this amount, thereby allowing a substantial proportion of apartments to go to those earning between 50 and 80 percent of median. In most cities, this implied that housing authorities should be looking for an entirely new cohort of public housing applicants. In Boston, for example, a family of four earning $55,000 would be eligible, yet the BHA estimates that only about 200 of the 14,000 families on its waiting list earn more than 30 percent of median (about $20,000), clearly indicating that the working poor are not exactly clamoring to gain entrance to its developments. The BHA is able to attract higher-income households to its HOPE VI sites where the housing is brand new, the management is private, and the development has its own separate waiting list. Elsewhere, Henriquez acknowledges, the authority "will not be able to attract" such tenants, mostly because they would re-fuse to place themselves on a citywide waiting list for public housing.[69] Whether or not housing authorities would seek or succeed in recruiting higher-income families, the congressional intent remained clear: public housing should be forc-ibly returned to its earliest incarnation as communities comprised primarily of the temporarily submerged middle class.

Responding to calls by local housing authorities for greater flexibility, the new legislation formally removed the federally mandated preferences for the homeless, those living in substandard housing, and those paying unduly large fractions of their income, and sought increased powers to evict unruly tenants.[70] As a BHA spokeswoman put it, "There are so many families who would kill to live in public housing. I'm sorry, but if you can't make your kids behave, we're giving your apartment to someone who can." In 1996 President Clinton issued an executive order dubbed "One Strike and You're Out," aimed at evicting public housing tenants charged with a felony (even before they had been found guilty by a court), and sought new ways to keep those previously convicted of felonies from ever getting in. The Quality Housing and Work Responsibility Act of 1998 also set limits on the definition of "persons with disabilities," excluding from public housing those who had previously gained preferred eligibility "solely on the basis of drug or alcohol dependence." Moreover, it allowed housing authorities to "prohibit admission" to any households believed to include illegal drug users or alcohol-abusers, and to insist on access to criminal records, sex offender regis-tries, and records from drug abuse treatment facilities during the tenant-screen-ing process. The Act also allowed housing authorities to rent apartments to po-lice officers who would not otherwise be income-eligible as part of efforts to increase security.[71]

Suspicion was still cast upon the least economically advantaged of public housing residents even if they were found to be nonfelonious and nonaddicted. The Act further stipulated that able-bodied unemployed adult residents of public housing perform not less than eight hours of community service work each month or else enter into "economic self-sufficiency" programs.[72] Representative Jesse Jackson Jr. of Illinois vainly tried to eliminate the community service re-quirement from the bill, calling it an unconstitutional form of "involuntary servi-tude." He insisted that tenants be paid at least the minimum wage for any re-quired work. Jackson wondered: "Why are we asking one group—just because they're poor—to work eight hours . . . for nothing?"[73] In the late 1930s, projects like Boston's Old Harbor Village had housed dense networks of voluntary organizations; fifty years later, the federal government crudely sought to impose volunteerism by fiat. Like the nineteenth-century Houses of Industry, the new plan seemed premised on a mildly punitive system of make-work intended to build the character of able-bodied cultural miscreants.[74]

In other ways too, the Quality Housing and Work Responsibility Act of 1998 made it clear which kinds of poor people were welcome to stay in public housing. Although the final version of the bill dropped an earlier requirement that any new tenants who were not working or attending vocational training programs must set actual target dates for leaving public housing, the Act as passed still spoke in terms of a "transition out." For those tenants who were already among the worthy working poor, however, the new law offered a revised rent structure intended to abolish any "disincentive for continued residency." The revised rent structure allowed them the option of paying a maximum ceiling rent (instead of 30 percent of income), encouraging higher-income families to stay on indefinitely. Even as one part of the ideology urged employment as the means to work one's way out of public housing ("graduate" seems the current congressional verb of choice), another part wished those with jobs to stay put and stabilize their communities.[75] As Representative Lazio put it, "The issue boils down to role models. It doesn't help the unemployed to move up the economic ladder if all the people they are surrounded by are also unemployed."[76] Although Congress eventually declined to require a target date for exit from public housing or to specify any sort of eviction procedure should such a date be flouted, the impulse bore more than a passing resemblance to the seventeenth-century custom of warning out. Those who entered the community with the greatest apparent evidence of personal liability received special sanction and no more than conditional endorsement for their ongoing presence. As in Puritan New England, a neo-Puritan Congress sought ways to lessen the long-term obligation to those thought most likely to become an unwelcome public charge.

FROM THE PURITANS TO THE PROJECTS

If the preceding pages have suggested anything, it is that public housing is more than a product of the New Deal. It is also an expression of a lot of old deals, some of them dating back to the earliest days of the Puritans. It is rooted in a belief that communities, aided by government if necessary, have an obligation to care for their marginal members, yet also conditioned by beliefs that jurisdictional transgression or evidence of personal irresponsibility undercut the necessity to care for such public neighbors. The plight of public housing tenants is made more complex by a lingering version of nineteenth-century environmental determinism, now argued in the context of public housing redevelopment rather than tenement reform. Rooted in powerful ideas about the relationship between house form and moral worth, the tragic saga of attempts to house public neighbors—from the Puritan almshouse to the project superblock—reveals a distinctively American brand of cultural unease. Above all, the thorny questions of public housing policy and design point out the underlying iniquities of class, gender, and race relations, just as earlier generations of housing policy conflated slum clearance with efforts to reform or replace the city's least-wanted immigrants.

In contrast to the largely self-sufficient seventeenth-century towns and villages of Puritan New England, however, the global economy of the early twenty-first century inevitably leaves behind a substantial residue of the least-skilled and least-educated, even at times when economists talk of "full employment." In an economic system that deliberately marginalizes some of its potential labor force, and in a metropolitan geography where new jobs are often inaccessible from old ghettoes, the residents of many public housing projects remain socially and spatially separated from economic opportunity. Faced with this situation (or unaware of its existence), many Americans still wish to keep economically marginalized households safely segregated in urban ghettoes—safely, that is, for the rest of a society that resists scattered-site public housing and often rebuffs even the entreaties of individual impoverished families seeking subsidized entry into new urban and suburban neighborhoods via housing vouchers.

In the end, no subsidized housing scheme—save that of the tax breaks for homeowners—seems wholly consistent with American ideological practice. As recently as the presidential campaign of 1996, candidate Bob Dole even revived the oldest of the ideologically driven charges when he lambasted public housing as "one of the last bastions of socialism in the world" during a speech to the National Association of Realtors.[77] To public housing's detractors, the lingering project behemoths and the system of housing authorities that mismanage them symbolize everything wrong with government and everything wrong with the poor. Yet no one stands ready to pay for an alternative solution.

On the face of it, a decentralized system of vouchers seems like the closest possible approximation of the American individualist ethos, since the subsidy travels with the person who is then able—at least in theory—to exercise wide choice among neighborhoods and residential settings. Yet dispersing public neighbors falls short of the ideal solution in one crucially important way: it offers little opportunity for ongoing moral surveillance. Whatever their growing faults, large public housing projects—like the almshouse institutions that preceded them—offer the opportunity for a suspicious electorate to continue to morally classify and spatially distinguish the worthy from the unworthy poor. Seen this way, the idea of "overseers of the poor"—originally imported to New England in the seventeenth century—no longer seems such an outdated notion. To precisely the extent that public housing projects remain cast as unwanted territory—places to fear—they help to clarify and maintain the social order of the city. By contrast, once more prosperous incursions of private development enter into nearby areas, the projects become intensely coveted targets for redevelopment. This seems as true today as it did when the almshouse gave way to the State House in eighteenth-century Boston.

The voucher system, for all its merits, breaks down over the same issue of moral surveillance; all too many private landlords refuse to take on the responsibility for overseeing former public housing families as their tenants. Even with the federal government picking up the tab for the subsidy, most private landlords do not want to take on the obligation to house the public neighbors that public housing could not hold.

It is not only a matter of reluctant landlords; public housing tenants themselves often fear entering into privately managed housing. During the redevelopment of Orchard Park and Mission Main, for instance, dozens of those offered a choice between temporarily exiting the projects with a housing voucher or relocating to other public housing developments for the duration of the construction period chose the latter. This choice continually puzzles Sandra Henriquez: "I'm always surprised. You go to a resident meeting and people hammer and hammer about what you did or didn't do. So you say, 'OK, if you're really unhappy, you can have a certificate and get away from us for awhile.' Then they say no. It's a 'devil you know' thing. There is a comfort in knowing 'here is what your rent will be; here are the expectations for you as a tenant' and that, whatever changes, it's still the housing authority. It's a very strange phenomenon." Henriquez adds that many of these people had spent their adult lives in public housing. They feared alternative housing arrangements where they would be responsible for paying utility costs, and "they really worried about the written guarantee that they would have the right to return to the redeveloped housing only as long as they remained in 'good standing.' They understood what 'good standing' was with the Housing Authority standard, but was that any different than a private landlord's definition?" Yet now, Congress and HUD demand that housing authorities tighten up their standards for tenant behavior. In a world of One Strike evictions, zero tolerance for harassment, greater scrutiny of illegal immigrants, and community service requirements, the overseers of public housing keep a watchful eye on all aspects of tenant "responsibility." As Henriquez comments: "We are much more intrusive on poor people than we are on everybody else, and we are getting more so.[78]

In contrast to Puritan New England, where small communities made it possible to engage in individualized discussion of how to cope with the particular circumstances of each neighborhood pauper and where financial support came out of locally generated funds, public responsibility to assist the needy now operates at a distance. Distance leads people to judge the poor based on category rather than character. For most landlords, whether acting out of racism or out of real or imagined concern for their property, the public neighbor business remains wholly unappealing. Congress, like HUD, has taken a hard look at the prospect of large numbers of public housing families displaced from their projects and unleashed on the private sector: even as they gradually increase funding for vouchers, they fear an expensive political nightmare. As a result, many families who gratefully found their way into public housing will continue to have a difficult time finding their way out. Henriquez has seen the effects of the abolition of rent control in Boston in the late 1990s: "there's no place to move up and out to: There's [no housing] in between. Either you've got a public housing unit or you don't. There's always going to be a need for public housing, and we don't have enough."[79]

Despite the problems of neighborhood resistance to vouchers, the most humane solution for this nation's public neighbors ultimately must be a larger system of public housing with fewer projects. There are certainly individual instances (such as Boston's Commonwealth development) where even large projects can be restored to well-managed communities, yet the institutional mechanisms of most large public housing authorities—after sixty years of straining against the countervailing pressures of private markets—seem wholly incapable of turning around many other diverse communities in highly disadvantaged neighborhoods. At a time when reduced federal and state subsidy for projects seems likely, it makes sense to take inadequate funds in terms of vouchers, and to encourage the least-advantaged among those seeking public housing to use their subsidy in less troubled neighborhoods. Congress seems to recognize this need: the Quality Housing and Work Responsibility Act of 1998 coupled enhanced efforts to deconcentrate the extreme poverty in conventional public housing projects with a requirement that at least 75 percent of tenant-based Section 8 vouchers go to those earning less than 30 percent of the area median income.[80] In other words, place the neediest families in dispersed private housing, rather than gathering them together in large institutional settings. Success will certainly entail both a gradualist approach to deconcentrating poverty and a vigilant and rigorous enforcement of fair housing laws.

Slowly but inexorably, building by building, the country's worst public housing projects will need to be dismantled. Using the HOPE VI program as an example, HUD wants to demolish 145,000 "blighted or obsolete units" by 2003, and to replace fully 60 percent of these with Section 8 vouchers and certificates, rather than "hard units." The Quality Housing and Work Responsibility Act of 1998 allows a housing authority to demolish projects if it can certify that the project is "obsolete as to physical condition, location, or other factors, making it unsuitable for housing purposes," and that "no reasonable program of modifications is cost-effective to return the public housing project . . . to useful life." Similarly, the Act permits sale or transfer of projects if the housing authority can show that "retention of the property is not in best interests of the residents or the public housing agency" either due to adverse conditions or because disposition would allow the "acquisition, development, or rehabilitation of other properties that will be more efficiently or effectively operated as low-income housing."[81]

In this context, the challenge will be to dismantle one system in a way that builds and preserves alternative affordable housing opportunities for those who genuinely need them. Any sincere effort to supersede the projects will be expensive. If one solution is the creation of newly developed mixed-income communities where only one-third of residents have very low incomes, then the equitable thing to do is to build (or lease space in) three times as many such communities to make up for the loss of affordable units. Conversely, if this kind of economic mix is sought more informally through market mechanisms combined with portable subsidized housing vouchers, it makes no sense for Congress to do anything but expand the supply of such vouchers, and for local authorities to make sure that vouchers are targeted to the neediest.

In the end, it is not only the reality of concentrated poverty that must be overcome, but also its image. The worst projects are media targets, and give public housing tenants and those who constantly judge them an unfairly criminalized identity. In addition to all the very real limitations placed on social and economic opportunity, the persistence of the most disastrous projects on the visual and televisual landscape may well act as a symbolic deterrent to other forms of affordable housing progress. Despite a number of remarkable tenant-centered transformations at individual public housing developments and despite the many ways that some projects continue to provide a valuable support network for most families, the stigma attached to a project-based system remains irredeemably acute. As Harry Spence puts it: "Once you've defined public housing the way we've defined it in the last fifteen years, it's almost impossible to turn it around. It's inconceivable to working people today that public housing could be attractive enough to move into, with very rare exceptions. So even if you shift all the rules, the social stigma is so profound now that it's almost impossible to reshape. The assumption about who you are and who you have to be to move in there becomes a screen for self-selection that is endlessly self-perpetuating."[82]

Beginning in 1993, all BHA literature stopped using the term *projects* to refer to its developments because of its "negative connotations," a politically correct gesture that went largely unnoticed by tenants.[83] Clearly, name changes alone will not fix public housing. Nor will it be enough to demolish the worst public housing projects or even to reinvent them as mixed-income communities. Spence noted more than fifteen years ago that this approach eliminates the problem of public housing, but does not solve it. Nationwide, despite the robust economic growth of the 1990s, more than 5 million very low-income renters without housing assistance paid over half their income for housing or lived in "severely substandard" dwellings. Meanwhile, the stock of affordable rental housing was shrinking.[84] As long as the demand for housing by low-income people continues to outstrip the supply of low-rent dwellings, the governmental obligation to serve public neighbors will require attempts to provide new sources of affordable housing.

To succeed in this, however, housing policymakers will need to reframe how such housing subsidy is viewed. Unless "affordable housing" is conceptualized as a continuum of rewards affecting all income groups—encompassing and assisting the two-thirds of American households who receive tax benefits for homeownership just as it helps the 2 percent who receive public housing—public housing will remain firmly detached from the mainstream of society, no more than another coping mechanism for dealing with the poorest of the poor. Yet mainstreaming public housing will not be easy, precisely because hostility toward the jobless remains so deeply rooted. Whatever the broad appeal of a well-housed nation, most American lawmakers still view work responsibility as a prerequisite for quality housing—and regard irresponsibility as the fault of people, not economies.

Many urban public housing systems face a double threat: either projects are too poorly maintained to be desirable or they are too well-located to be retained for use by poor people. Either way, there are renewed pressures to clear away public housing. In some cities, most notably Chicago, housing authorities now seek to demolish the bulk of their existing inventory. Elsewhere, the demise of projects proceeds in a much more gradual and piecemeal manner. In Boston, the BHA can point to a long waiting list for its family developments, and few of these places have substantial numbers of vacancies. Despite widely acknowledged social problems and aging buildings, they still constitute the largest single source of affordable housing in the city. Even so, the BHA continues to compete for more HOPE VI funding, and city leaders would love to see more of the stock transformed in the manner of Orchard Gardens Estates and Mission Main.

Boston may well end up as one of the last hold-outs, but the large public housing project seems headed the way of the old unclassified almshouse—increasingly marginalized and ultimately abandoned. Aside from the many thousands of low-income families that will be dispersed from the low-rent, high-stress environments that they have uneasily but gratefully called home, few others will mourn the downfall of the projects. As a building type and as an institution, they will pass into historical memory like almshouses, bridewells and Houses of Industry. As an index of Puritan-inspired American attitudes toward the poor, and as one stage in the deep-rooted and still ongoing struggle to house public neighbors, however, the projects will long stand as monuments to our collective ambivalence.

NOTES

CREDITS

INDEX

NOTES

INTRODUCTION

1. For a parallel account of this so-called improvement process in debates over twentieth-century American welfare and education policies, see Michael B. Katz, *Improving Poor People: The Welfare State, the "Underclass," and Urban Schools as History* (Princeton: Princeton University Press, 1995).

2. Although this book stresses poverty and race more than the gender dimensions of housing bias, gender issues remain a matter of central importance. Whether one is discussing the demographics of housing projects in which families are overwhelmingly headed by women or reflecting on the long-dominant ideal of the nuclear family in the single-family home, it is clear that housing must be considered as gendered space.

3. Clare Cooper, "The House as Symbol of the Self," in Harold Proshansky, William H. Ittelson, and Leanne G. Rivlin, eds., *Environmental Psychology* (New York: Holt, Rinehart and Winston, 1976), p. 438.

4. Louis Hartz, *The Liberal Tradition in America* (New York: Harcourt Brace Jovanovich, 1955).

5. The term *public neighbor* is meant to be neutral and descriptive. In assessments of poverty, however, terms intended to be merely descriptive all too often become used as pejorative labels. These dangers are discussed in Herbert J. Gans, *The War Against the Poor: The Underclass and Anti-Poverty Policy* (New York: Basic Books, 1995), pp. 18–26, 126.

6. On St. Louis, see Lee Rainwater, *Behind Ghetto Walls* (Chicago: Aldine, 1970); Eugene Meehan, *Public Housing Policy: Myth Versus Reality* (New Brunswick, N.J.: Center for Urban Policy Research, 1975) and *The Quality of Federal Policymaking: Programmed Failure in Public Housing* (Columbia: University of Missouri Press, 1979), as well as works by Roger Montgomery and others. Books on Chicago's public housing include Devereux Bowly, *The Poorhouse: Subsidized Housing in Chicago, 1895–1976* (Carbondale: Southern Illinois University Press, 1978); Arnold Hirsch, *Making the Second Ghetto: Race and Housing in Chicago, 1940– 1960 (Cambridge: Cambridge University Press, 1983);* Martin Meyerson and Edward Banfield, *Politics, Planning, and the Public Interest: The Case of Public Housing in Chicago* (Glencoe,

Ill.: Free Press, 1955); William Moore, *The Vertical Ghetto: Everyday Life in an Urban Project* (New York: Random House, 1969); Gerald Suttles, *The Social Order of the Slum* (Chicago: University of Chicago Press, 1968); Nicholas Lemann, *The Promised Land: The Great Black Migration and How it Changed America* (New York: Knopf, 1991); Alex Kotlowitz, *There are No Children Here* (New York: Doubleday, 1991); and Daniel Coyle, *Hardball: A Season in the Projects* (New York: Putnam's, 1993). On Philadelphia, see John Bauman, *Public Housing, Race, and Renewal: Urban Planning in Philadelphia, 1920-1974* (Philadelphia: Temple University Press, 1987). Peter Marcuse is at work on a history of the New York City Housing Authority, and has already published several incisive articles on the subject. Aspects of New York public housing also have been extensively discussed by Richard Plunz, *A History of Housing in New York City: Dwelling Type and Social Change in the American Metropolis* (New York: Columbia University Press, 1990), among many others. Boston's public housing has been the subject of theses, dissertations, and studies for more than fifty years, and a bibliography may be obtained from the author.

1 Coping with the Poor

1. Herbert J. Gans, *The War Against the Poor: The Underclass and Antipoverty Policy* (New York: Basic Books, 1995), p. 11.

2. The English poor laws with greatest relevance included two *For the Relief of the Poor* 39 Eliz. I c.30 [1598] and, slightly revised, 43 Eliz. I c.2 [1601] and one *For the Punishment of Rogues, Vagabonds and Sturdy Beggars* 39 Eliz. I c. 40 [1598]. The early English poor laws are surveyed in Paul Slack, *The English Poor Law, 1531-1782* (London: Macmillan, 1990). On the American legacy and development of such laws see, for example, Walter I. Trattner, *From Poor Law to Welfare State: A History of Social Welfare in America* (New York: Free Press, 1974), pp. 8-18, and Joe R. Feagin, *Subordinating the Poor: Welfare and American Beliefs* (Englewood Cliffs, N.J.: Prentice-Hall, 1975), pp. 15-26.

3. Slack, *The English Poor Law*, pp. 17-25; David Grayson Allen, *In English Ways: The Movement of Societies and the Transferal of English Local Law and Custom to Massachusetts Bay in the Seventeenth Century* (Chapel Hill: University of North Carolina Press, 1981), pp. 9, 150-151.

4. Andrew Delbanco, *The Puritan Ordeal* (Cambridge, Mass.: Harvard University Press, 1989), pp. 42, 75. See also T. H. Breen and Stephen Foster, "Moving to the New World: The Character of Early Massachusetts Immigration," in Breen, ed., *Puritans and Adventurers: Change and Persistence in Early America* (New York: Oxford University Press, 1980).

5. John Winthrop, "A Model of Christian Charity" (1630), reprinted in Alan Heimert and Andrew Delbanco, eds., *The Puritans in America: A Narrative Anthology* (Cambridge, Mass.: Harvard University Press, 1985), pp. 82-92. Matthew 5:14: "A City that is set on a hill cannot be hid."

6. Elizabeth Wisner makes the important point that "the many orders concerning the poor and the exclusion of strangers were passed by a minority of the inhabitants." As late as 1676, in Massachusetts as a whole, the electorate excluded not only all the women, but also an esti-

mated five-sixths of men, largely because they were not church members; Elizabeth Wisner, "The Puritan Background of the New England Poor Laws," *Social Service Review* 19 (September 1945): 389. See also Edmund S. Morgan, *The Puritan Dilemma: The Story of John Winthrop* (Boston: Little, Brown, 1958).

7. John Winthrop, "Generall Considerations for the Plantation in New England, With an Answer to Several Objections" (Higginson Copy), in *Winthrop Papers, Vol. 2: 1623–1630* (Boston: Massachusetts Historical Society, 1931), p. 120; Chester E. Eisinger, "The Puritans' Justification for Taking the Land," *Essex Institute Historical Collections* 84, 2 (April 1948): 142. It is estimated that between one-third and two-thirds of New England's Indians had died from European-spread diseases even before the arrival of the Puritans; subsequent warfare contributed considerably to the continuation of this near-holocaust. See Delbanco, *The Puritan Ordeal*, pp. 96, 106–107.

8. John Winthrop, *Winthrop's Journal (History of New England)*, vol. 1, ed. James Kendall Hosmer (New York: Charles Scribner's Sons, 1908), p. 294, and "Generall Considerations," p. 120. Though he did not specifically mention a house, Winthrop's contemporary John Cotton agreed: God "admitteth it as a principle in Nature, that in a vacant soyle, hee that taketh possession of it, and bestoweth culture and husbandry upon it, his right it is"; "God's Promise to His Plantations" (London, 1630), cited in Ruth Barnes Moynihan, "The Patent and the Indians: The Problem of Jurisdiction in Seventeenth-Century New England," *American Indian Culture and Research Journal* 2 (1977): 11.

9. Darrett B. Rutman, *Winthrop's Boston: Portrait of a Puritan Town* (New York: W. W. Norton, 1965), p. 4. By the 1640s, there were also some shared duplex houses and even rowhouses (p. 192). Many of the leaders, including Winthrop, who once found themselves among the English gentry, established land holdings through grants of large farming tracts in outlying areas; Delbanco, *The Puritan Ordeal*, p. 77.

10. "Indian Quitclaim," March 19, 1684, reprinted in Caleb H. Snow, *A History of Boston, the Metropolis of Massachusetts, from Its Origin to the Present Period: With Some Account of the Environs*, 2nd ed. (Boston: Abel Bowen, 1828), pp. 389–391; Moynihan, "The Patent and the Indians," p. 10; Jill Lepore, *The Name of War: King Philip's War and the Origins of American Identity* (New York: Knopf, 1997), pp. 79, 83–84. Only much later, when they were displaced onto government-sponsored reservations in New England and elsewhere, were Indians ever fully recognized as public neighbors. As early as 1748, however, "the Massachusetts Council appointed a committee to prepare a bill for the relief and support of Indians who because of age, infirmity, or sickness were in want and incapable of providing for their own subsistence"; Wisner, "Puritan Background of Poor Laws," p. 385. Eventually, government subsidies directed at Indians would become a matter of much paternalism and great controversy. Most tellingly of all, housing benefits for Native Americans of the late twentieth century became taxonomically lumped together with those for the inner-city poor, and placed under the jurisdiction of the Assistant Secretary for Public and Indian Housing.

11. James P. Walsh, "Holy Time and Sacred Space in Puritan New England," *American Quarterly* 32 (Spring 1980): 79–95; Delbanco, *The Puritan Ordeal*, p. 116.

12. Robert W. Kelso, *The History of Public Poor Relief in Massachusetts, 1620–1920* (Boston:

Houghton Mifflin, 1922), pp. 35–37. On the historical origins of settlement restrictions and the actions taken by a variety of New England towns, see Josiah Henry Benton, *Warning Out in New England, 1656–1817* (Boston: W. B. Clarke, 1911). Although the Act of Settlement of 1793 formally repealed the custom of warning out, Massachusetts law continued to make reference to "town consent" as one method for obtaining admission as a town inhabitant, stipulating that a specific warrant item be inserted in the agenda of the town meeting for such a purpose. This provision disappeared only in 1882 (Benton, pp. 52–53).

13. Trattner, *From Poor Law to Welfare State,* pp. 19–20; Rutman, *Winthrop's Boston,* p. 196.

14. John Winthrop, "A Defense of an Order of Court" (1637), reprinted in Heimert and Delbanco, *The Puritans in America,* pp. 164–167; Ellen Smith, "Strangers and Sojourners: The Jews of Colonial Boston," in Jonathan D. Sarna and Ellen Smith, eds., *The Jews of Boston* (Boston: Combined Jewish Philanthropies of Greater Boston, 1995), p. 23.

15. Kelso, *Public Poor Relief,* pp. 37, 41; Rutman, *Winthrop's Boston,* pp. 196, 219.

16. Benton, *Warning Out,* p. 47; Kelso, *Public Poor Relief,* pp. 46–47.

17. Kelso, *Public Poor Relief,* pp. 46–47; Rutman, *Winthrop's Boston,* p. 219; Benton, *Warning Out,* pp. 47, 51, 116; Trattner, *From Poor Law to Welfare State,* pp. 20–21, 29–30; Carl Bridenbaugh, *Cities in the Wilderness: The First Century of Urban Life in America, 1625-1742* (New York: Ronald Press, 1938), p. 81. By the 1650s, in addition to the "Scot's Charitable Society" established by twenty-seven Scots residing in Boston and intended for the "releefe of our selves or any other for which wee may see cause," other philanthropic Bostonians began making bequests to the town for charitable purposes. In 1724 members of the "Irish Nation of Extraction" established the Protestant-run "Charitable Irish Society of Boston," and private individuals continued their benefactions largely through the various churches. See Bridenbaugh, pp. 81–82, 394; Thomas H. O'Connor, *The Boston Irish: A Political History* (Boston: Back Bay Books, 1995), p. 11.

18. Trattner, *From Poor Law to Welfare State,* p. 29; Kelso, *Public Poor Relief,* p. 99; Bridenbaugh, *Cities in the Wilderness,* p. 392; Gerald N. Grob, *Mental Institutions in America: Social Policy to 1875* (New York: Free Press, 1973), pp. 4–9.

19. Bridenbaugh, *Cities in the Wilderness,* p. 82.

20. Cited in Trattner, *From Poor Law to Welfare State,* p. 23; Kelso, *Public Poor Relief.*

21. Kelso, *Public Poor Relief,* p. 108. See also Peter C. Holloran, *Boston's Wayward Children: Social Services for Homeless Children, 1830–1930* (Boston: Northeastern University Press, 1994), p. 18; and see Benjamin Klebaner, "Pauper Auctions: The 'New England Method' of Public Poor Relief," *Essex Institute Historical Collections* 91 (July 1955): 195–210.

22. Kelso, *Public Poor Relief,* pp. 101–107; Holloran, *Boston's Wayward Children,* p. 19; Rutman, *Winthrop's Boston,* p. 219. Massachusetts did, however, pass a statute in 1676 providing for the insane, enjoining town selectmen take care of "distracted persons . . . that are unruly" so that they would not "damnify others" (Trattner, *From Poor Law to Welfare State,* p. 25).

23. Neither New York nor Philadelphia had an almshouse until the early eighteenth century; Bridenbaugh, *Cities in the Wilderness,* pp. 81, 234–236.

24. Minutes of the 1657 Boston Town Meeting, quoted in Lawrence W. Kennedy, *Planning the City upon a Hill: Boston since 1630* (Amherst: University of Massachusetts Press, 1992), p. 19; Bridenbaugh, *Cities in the Wilderness,* p. 82.

25. Bridenbaugh, *Cities in the Wilderness,* p. 82.

26. Grob, *Mental Institutions in America,* pp. 8-9.

27. Heimert and Delbanco, *The Puritans in America,* pp. 261, 275. See Lepore, *The Name of War.*

28. Bridenbaugh, *Cities in the Wilderness,* pp. 234-235. On the early private and church-based charity efforts see Wisner, "The Puritan Background of the New England Poor Laws," pp. 382-385.

29. Bridenbaugh, *Cities in the Wilderness,* pp. 234-235, 385, 393; Kelso, *Public Poor Relief,* pp. 113-114; Trattner, *From Poor Law to Welfare State,* pp. 34-35; Snow, *A History of Boston,* p. 324; David J. Rothman, *The Discovery of the Asylum: Social Order and Disorder in the New Republic* (Boston: Little, Brown, 1971), pp. 4, 39-41; Grob, *Mental Institutions in America,* p. 23. Trattner argues that the combined work of public aid, private giving, and voluntary organizations of eighteenth-century colonial societies following the Great Awakening represented an especially cooperative arrangement, one less prone to the antagonisms that later prevailed among such groups.

30. Bridenbaugh, *Cities in the Wilderness,* pp. 393-394; Rothman, *The Discovery of the Asylum,* pp. 41, 55; Grob, *Mental Institutions in America,* p. 23. See also "Act for Suppressing and Punishing Rogues, Vagabonds, Common Beggars . . . and Also for Setting the Poor to Work" (1699), in *The Acts and Laws of his Majesty's Province of Massachusetts-Bay in New England,* 22, pp. 110-112, cited in Rothman, p. 26.

31. Trattner, *From Poor House to Welfare State,* p. 22; Kelso, *Public Poor Relief,* pp. 117-121.

32. Kelso, *Public Poor Relief,* p. 33.

33. Rothman, *The Discovery of the Asylum,* p. xiii.

34. Ibid., pp. 82-83, 130-133.

35. Boston Prison Discipline Society, *Fourth Annual Report* (Boston, 1829), pp. 54-55, cited in Rothman, *The Discovery of the Asylum,* pp. 83-84. On Boston's orphanages, child placement agencies, juvenile courts, and reformatories see Holloran, *Boston's Wayward Children.*

36. Massachusetts General Court Committee on Pauper Laws, *Report of the Committee on the Pauper Laws of this Commonwealth* "Quincy Report" (Boston, 1821), in David J. Rothman, *The Almshouse Experience: Collected Reports* (New York: Arno Press & The New York Times, 1971). See also Rothman, *The Discovery of the Asylum,* pp. 159-169.

37. Rothman, *The Discovery of the Asylum,* pp. 172-179.

38. Acts of 1834, chapter 151, quoted in Kelso, *Public Poor Relief,* p. 127.

39. Rothman, *The Discovery of the Asylum,* p. 183.

40. Personal communication from Michael B. Katz, January 1997. In 1889, about ten thousand residents of Massachusetts were given relief indoors, whereas fifty thousand benefited from outdoor relief.

41. Snow, *A History of Boston,* p. 325.

42. Walter Muir Whitehill, *Boston: A Topographical History,* 2nd ed. (Cambridge, Mass.: Harvard University Press, 1968), pp. 64–65.

43. Snow, *A History of Boston,* p. 325.

44. Grob, *Mental Institutions in America,* pp. 51–55.

45. Josiah Quincy et al., *Report of the Committee on the Subject of Pauperism and A House of Industry in the Town of Boston,* (Boston: Committee on Pauperism, 1821).

46. To punning Puritans, Jill Lepore comments, praying Indians could easily become preying Indians, and some Bostonians in 1676 petitioned the Council to remove them beyond Deer Island, to "some place farther more from us." Instead, left on the Island, more than half died, mostly from starvation. Lepore, *The Name of War,* pp. 43, 138–145.

47. Quincy et al., *Report of the Committee on Pauperism,* pp. 1–20.

48. Boston officially became a city in 1822.

49. Town records, May 7, 1821, quoted in Snow, *History of Boston,* p. 376.

50. The comparative scarcity of chimneys in the House of Correction building could be a hint that its heating system needed only to serve a few large rooms divided into cells through which air could freely circulate, or even that the amount of heating provided for the House of Correction was less than that provided for the House of Industry. The differences between the two Houses may, however, be due as much to imprecision and inconsistency in the engravings as to any architectural or functional differences.

51. "House of Industry—South Boston," *American Magazine of Useful and Entertaining Knowledge* 1, 2 (October 1834): 52.

52. Ibid., pp. 51–53.

53. Thomas O'Connor, *South Boston: My Home Town* (Boston: Quinlan Press, 1988), p. 30; Kelso, *Public Poor Relief,* pp. 117, 119; "House of Industry—South Boston," p. 51.

54. "House of Industry—South Boston," pp. 51–52.

55. City of Boston, *South Boston Memorial,* city document no. 18, (Boston: Boston Common Council, April 22, 1847).

56. *South Boston Memorial,* pp. 1–29. See also Holloran, *Boston's Wayward Children,* p. 29; O'Connor, *South Boston,* p. 31; Grob, *Mental Institutions in America,* p. 125.

57. *Report on the Removal of the House of Industry and Other Public Institutions at South Boston to Deer Island,* Boston city document no. 30 (Boston: J. H. Eastburn, 1847).

58. David Ward, *Cities and Immigrants* (New York: Oxford University Press, 1970), pp. 51–52, 63, 65.

59. *Report on the Removal of the House of Industry,* p. 12; *Annual Report of the Directors of the Houses of Industry and Reformation,* Boston City Document No. 12, April 1, 1850 (Boston: J. H. Eastburn, 1850).

60. *Report on the Removal of the House of Industry* , p. 14; *Annual Report of the Directors of the Houses of Industry and Reformation,* pp. 17, 20; Holloran, *Boston's Wayward Children,* p. 95; Massachusetts Water Resources Authority, "History of Deer Island" (Boston: MWRA, 1991), pp. 1–3. See also Edward Rowe Snow, *The Islands of Boston Harbor: Their History and Romance, 1626–1935* (Andover, Mass.: Andover Press, 1935), pp. 275, 284–285. In subsequent

decades, Deer Island came to house not only an Almshouse/House of Industry but also, in 1858, the House for the Employment and Reformation of Juvenile Offenders (for boys) and, soon thereafter, a House of Reformation (for girls). These remained on the island until 1877. Between 1882 and 1902, the South Boston House of Correction transferred its inmates to Deer Island, and the House of Industry there was designated as the Suffolk County House of Correction in 1896; this facility continued to house inmates until shortly before it was razed in the 1960s. Another prison, built in 1902, operated until the early 1990s when it was demolished to make way for the world's second largest wastewater treatment plant, part of the massive Boston Harbor clean-up effort. In this way, Deer Island continued to house the public facilities that no one wanted, even after the last public neighbors had been delivered back to the mainland.

61. *Annual Report of the Directors of the Houses of Industry and Reformation,* Boston city document no. 12, April 1, 1850 (Boston: J. H. Eastburn, 1850), pp. 17–19.

62. O'Connor, *The Boston Irish,* pp. 71–80, 94.

63. *Annual Report of the Directors of the Houses of Industry and Reformation,* Boston city document no. 12, April 1, 1850 (Boston: J. H. Eastburn, 1850), p. 5; Rothman, *The Discovery of the Asylum,* pp. 237–240, 288, 290.

64. City of Boston, Board of Aldermen, *Report of Committee on the Overseers of the Poor,* Boston city document no. 27 (Boston, 1859), pp. 3, 5, 11, 16–22, 25.

65. Rothman, p. 288.

66. Lawrence Veiller, *A Model Housing Law* (New York: Russell Sage Foundation, 1920), p. 27. On Veiller and Riis, see Roy Lubove, *The Progressives and the Slums* (Pittsburgh: University of Pittsburgh Press, 1962), especially chapters 3, 5, and 6.

67. Veiller, quoted in David M. Culver, "Tenement Reform in Boston, 1846–1898" (Ph.D. diss., Boston University, 1972), p. 233n15. Veiller's observations about Boston's tenement problems were confirmed in 1910 by the findings of the Housing Committee of the "Boston-1915" movement. Based on population statistics collected in 1905, the Committee's "Special Agent" H. K. Estabrook concluded that parts of Boston's North and West Ends were "more densely populated than any other American city or district—except in New York." Indeed the "chief difference is that New York's densely populated district is several times as extensive as Boston's" (H. K. Estabrook, "Congestion in the North and West Ends," in Boston-1915, Inc., *Report of the Housing Committee of Boston-1915,* April 11, 1910, pp. 6, 8.

68. Sam Bass Warner, Jr., *Streetcar Suburbs: The Process of Growth in Boston, 1870–1900* (Cambridge, Mass.: Harvard University Press, 1962), p. 162.

69. Culver, "Tenement Reform," p. 55.

70. Whitehill, *Boston: A Topographical History,* chap. 4; Henry Binford, *The First Suburbs: Residential Communities on the Boston Periphery, 1815–1860* (Chicago: University of Chicago Press, 1985).

71. On average, 34 percent of residents in American cities with populations over 25,000 were foreign-born in 1870; Ward, *Cities and Immigrants,* Fig. 2-5, pp. 75–77.

72. Oscar Handlin, *Boston's Immigrants: A Study in Acculturation* (Cambridge, Mass.: Harvard University Press, 1979, original 1941), p. 91 and table 7 ("Nativity of Bostonians, 1855");

Stephan Thernstrom, *The Other Bostonians: Poverty and Progress in the American Metropolis, 1880–1970* (Cambridge, Mass.: Harvard University Press, 1973), pp. 113–114; Culver, "Tenement Reform," pp. 6–9; Ward, *Cities and Immigrants,* pp. 105–107.

73. Ward, *Cities and Immigrants,* pp. 106–108.

74. *Report of the Committee on the Expediency of Providing Better Tenements for the Poor* (Boston: Eastburn's Press, 1846), pp. 6, 16, 29–32.

75. Handlin, *Boston's Immigrants,* pp. 101–102.

76. *Quarterly Report of the City Physician* (1853), in Culver, "Tenement Reform," p. 18; Handlin, *Boston's Immigrants,* p. 109.

77. Handlin, *Boston's Immigrants,* pp. 104–108.

78. *Report of the Committee of Internal Health on the Asiatic Cholera, Boston City Documents,* 1849, no. 23, p. 13, quoted in Culver, "Tenement Reform," p. 22.

79. *Second Annual Report of the Massachusetts Bureau of Statistics of Labor,* 1871, p. 520, quoted in Culver, "Tenement Reform," p. 125.

80. Charles Eliot Norton, "Dwellings and Schools for the Poor," *North American Review* 82 (April 1852): 465.

81. Culver, "Tenement Reform," pp. 47–54, 58–59.

82. Several subsequent acts and amendments aimed at maximizing light and ventilation. Increasingly stringent fire safety codes followed in 1892, 1895, and 1897, and sanitation standards gradually rose, although toilets in individual apartments were not required until 1920; Christine Cousineau, "Tenement Reform in Boston, 1870–1920: Philanthropy, Regulation, and Government Assisted Housing," working paper, Society for American City and Regional Planning History, 1990, pp. 14–19.

83. Culver, "Tenement Reform," pp. 67–68, 70, 93, 119.

84. Charles E. Buckingham, et al., *The Sanitary Condition of Boston* (Boston, 1875), p. 77, quoted in Culver, "Tenement Reform," p. 115n96.

85. Lubove, *The Progressives and the Slums;* Robert Fogelson, "The Parsimony of 'the large-hearted rich': The City and Suburban Homes Company and the Model Tenement Movement," unpublished ms.; and "Limited Dividend Roll Call," *Architectural Forum* 62 (January 1935): 98–103.

86. A 6 percent return, however, compared poorly to the returns possible from investment in the worst class of tenements; annual returns of more than 15 percent continued into the twentieth century; Cousineau, "Tenement Reform," p. 12.

87. Culver, "Tenement Reform," pp. 45–46, 130–134.

88. *Annual Reports of the Boston Co-operative Building Company,* quoted in Culver, "Tenement Reform," pp. 147–148, 174.

89. In all this, Bowditch and the Company's other directors seemed oblivious to the extent that the depression of 1873—rather than character flaws and environmental shortcomings—contributed to the inability of many tenants to pay their rent. The directors knew that many tenants had lost their jobs and were increasingly unable to afford their payments, yet demanded that rent be paid in advance; Bowditch seemed genuinely surprised when it proved "impossible to get it." He could have predicted the ultimate fate of the "Lincoln Building": less than a

decade after it was abandoned by the Boston Co-operative Building Company, it was condemned and ordered vacated by the Board of Health. For the full saga of the Crystal Palace fiasco, see Culver, "Tenement Reform," pp. 129-164, and David P. Handlin, *The American Home: Architecture and Society, 1815-1915* (Boston: Little, Brown, 1979), pp. 254-257.

90. David Handlin, *American Home*, pp. 259-263; Culver, "Tenement Reform," pp. 205-212.

91. Dwight Porter, *Report Upon a Sanitary Inspection of Certain Tenement-House Districts of Boston* (Boston, 1889), p. 5.

92. Benjamin Orange Flower, *Civilization's Inferno, Or Studies in the Social Cellar* (Boston, 1893).

93. Flower, *Civilization's Inferno*, pp. 13-14, 24, 36, 52, 60, 63, 84-86, 89, 99-102, 133, 195, 236. See also Culver, "Tenement Reform," pp. 241, 247, 256-259.

94. Alexander Keyssar, *Out of Work: The First Century of Unemployment in Massachusetts* (Cambridge: Cambridge University Press, 1986), pp. 4, 12-19, 36-37, 152-156.

95. The taxonomy of poverty in Table 2 notably omits mention of tenement conditions as a proximate cause; private charitable organizations concerned themselves primarily with relief of distress rather than with reform of social institutions.

96. Other famous studies reached diverse conclusions: Amos G. Warner's multicity analysis of persons relieved by charities concluded that lack of work constituted the chief cause of poverty, in marked contrast to the findings of Charles S. Hoyt's survey of 12,614 paupers in New York State's almshouses, which tied poverty to personal vices and behaviors; Warner, *American Charities: A Study in Philanthropy and Economics* (New York and Boston: Thomas Y. Crowell, 1894); Hoyt, "The Causes of Pauperism," in *Tenth Annual Report of the State Board of Charities* (New York, 1877), quoted in Michael B. Katz, *Poverty and Policy in American History* (New York: Academic Press, 1983), pp. 90-113.

97. Culver, "Tenement Reform," pp. 251-271.

98. H. K. Estabrook, *Some Slums in Boston* (Boston: Twentieth Century Club, 1898); Chandler, in Woods, ed., *Americans in Process: A Settlement Study* (Cambridge: Riverside Press, 1903), pp. 87-89; City of Boston, *Report of Committee Appointed By Mayor Peters on Housing*, Boston city document no. 121 (1918), p. 8.

99. Allen F. Davis, *Spearheads for Reform: The Social Settlements and the Progressive Movement* (New York: Oxford University Press, 1967), pp. 18-19. The rise of charitable organizations in nineteenth-century Boston is chronicled in Nathan Irvin Huggins, *Protestants Against Poverty: Boston's Charities, 1870-1900* (Westport, Conn.: Greenwood, 1971). A broader range of Protestant, Catholic, and Jewish reform movements during the last two decades of the nineteenth century are discussed in Arthur Mann, *Yankee Reformers in the Urban Age* (Cambridge, Mass.: Harvard University Press, 1954).

100. Robert A. Woods and Albert J. Kennedy, eds., *The Settlement Horizon* (New Brunswick, N.J.: Transaction, 1990; 1922 original), p. 388; Judith Ann Trolander, *Professionalism and Social Change: From the Settlement House Movement to Neighborhood Centers, 1886 to the Present* (New York: Columbia University Press, 1987), p. 246.

101. Jane Addams, *Newer Ideals of Peace* (New York: Macmillan, 1907), p. 182.

102. The centrality of the Bostonian intellectual contribution to the movement is made clear in Da-

vis, *Spearheads for Reform*; Clarke A. Chambers, *Seedtime of Reform: American Social Service and Social Action, 1918–1933* (Minneapolis: University of Minnesota Press, 1963); Judith Ann Trolander, "Introduction," in Woods and Kennedy, eds., *The Settlement Horizon;* Sam Bass Warner, Jr., "Preface," in Kennedy and Woods, *The Zone of Emergence* (Cambridge, Mass.: MIT Press, 1962).

103. Woods and Kennedy, *The Settlement Horizon,* pp. 64–65.

104. Woods, "The Total Drift," in Woods, ed., *The City Wilderness: A Settlement Study* (Cambridge: Riverside Press, 1898), p. 310.

105. Woods and Kennedy, *The Settlement Horizon,* p. 65; Woods, "The Total Drift," in Woods, ed., *The City Wilderness,* p. 305.

106. Woods, "The Total Drift," in Woods, ed., *The City Wilderness,* p. 296; Woods and Kennedy, *The Settlement Horizon,* p. 71. On parallels in public education, see Stanley K. Schultz, *The Culture Factory: Boston Public Schools, 1789–1860* (New York: Oxford University Press, 1973); Michael B. Katz, *The Irony of Early School Reform: Educational Innovation in Mid-Nineteenth-Century Massachusetts* (Cambridge, Mass.: Harvard University Press, 1968); and Marvin Lazerson, *Origins of the Urban Public School: Public Education in Massachusetts, 1870–1915* (Cambridge, Mass.: Harvard University Press, 1971).

107. Warner, preface to Kennedy and Woods, *Zone of Emergence,* p. 9. The high number of settlements at this time can be attributed in part to the rather lax criteria for counting them. Approximately half of these had an explicit religious mission, whereas more restrictively granted membership in the National Federation of Settlements (NFS) required no extensive proselytizing; Trolander, *Professionalism and Social Change,* pp. 3–4.

108. Tucker, "Andover House Circular No. 1, October 1891," cited in Woods and Kennedy, eds., *Handbook of Settlements* (New York: Russell Sage Foundation, 1911), p. 125.

109. Tucker, "The Work of the Andover House in Boston," in Woods, et al., *The Poor in Great Cities: Their Problems and What is Doing to Solve Them* (New York: Scribner's, 1895), pp. 182, 184–186.

110. Woods, "Social Recovery," in Woods, ed., *The City Wilderness,* p. 275.

111. Woods, "The University Settlement Idea" (1892), p. 29; and Woods, "University Settlements as Laboratories in Social Science," in Woods, *The Neighborhood in Nation-Building: The Running Comment of Thirty Years at the South End House* (Cambridge: Riverside Press, 1923), p. 36. Though a few settlement residents devoted their entire working lives to this cause—such as Woods, Addams, Graham Taylor in Chicago, and Lillian Wald in New York—such longevity was exceptional. Davis reports that the median number of years spent in settlement work was three. Davis concludes that most residents were "only artificially a part of the neighborhood" since they had their own life within the settlement and since most spoke no language except English (Davis, *Spearheads for Reform,* pp. 33, 87).

112. Woods and Kennedy, *Handbook of Settlements,* p. 127.

113. Ibid., pp. 125–128.

114. Robert A. Woods and Albert J. Kennedy, *The Settlement Horizon,* pp. 207, 169–170.

115. Charles D. Underhill, M.D., "Public Health," in Robert A. Woods, ed., *The City Wilderness,* p. 69.

116. Catherine S. Atherton and Elizabeth Y. Rutan, "The Child of the Stranger," in Woods, ed., *Americans in Process,* p. 292.

117. Robert Woods, "Assimilation: A Double-Edged Sword," in Woods, ed., *Americans in Process,* p. 358.

118. William I. Cole, "Introductory," in Woods, ed., *The City Wilderness,* p. 2.

119. Underhill, "Public Health," in Woods, ed., *The City Wilderness,* p. 69.

120. Woods and Kennedy, *The Settlement Horizon,* p. 326n2.

121. Ibid., pp. 419–420.

122. Thorstein Veblen, *The Theory of the Leisure Class: An Economic Study of Institutions* (New York: Modern Library, 1934; original 1899, rev. 1912), pp. 345, 342.

123. Barbara Miller Solomon, *Ancestors and Immigrants: A Changing New England Tradition* (Cambridge, Mass.: Harvard University Press, 1956), p. 153.

124. O'Connor, *Boston Irish,* pp. 129, 148–153; Solomon, *Ancestors and Immigrants,* pp. 5–6, 44, 60.

125. Francis A. Walker, "Occupations and Mortality of Our Foreign Population, 1870," in Davis R. Dewey, ed., *Discussions in Economics and Statistics* (New York, 1899).

126. Walker, "Immigration and Degradation" *Forum* XI (1891): 640.

127. Woods, "Progress at the South End House Measured By Decades," in Woods, *The Neighborhood in Nation-Building,* p. 299. There were often polar disagreements among settlement leaders about the advisability of immigration restrictions. While some, such as New York's Lillian Wald, favored few restrictions, many others agreed with Woods. For most, the principal reason for favoring restrictions was a serious economic one: an unrestricted flood of immigrants would create an excess of low-wage workers and contribute to their greater exploitation, while also threatening the gains being made by organized labor (Davis, pp. 90–92).

128. Solomon, p. 151. The story of the Immigration Restriction League is addressed in considerable detail in Solomon, chaps. 5–9.

129. Woods and Kennedy, *The Settlement Horizon,* p. 336.

130. See Frederick A. Bushée, "Population," and William I. Cole, "Criminal Tendencies," in Woods, ed., *The City Wilderness,* pp. 44–45, 168, 173–174; Bushée, "The Invading Host," and Jesse Fremont Beale and Anne Withington, "Life's Amenities," in Woods, ed., *Americans in Process,* pp. 55, 60, 66, 248–249.

131. "Report of the Committee to Study Conditions of Negroes in the Pleasant Street District," South End House, cited in Davis, *Spearheads for Reform,* pp. 95–96.

132. John Daniels, *In Freedom's Birthplace: A Study of the Boston Negroes* (New York: Houghton Mifflin, 1914, reprinted 1968), pp. 174ff, 198, 215, 223, 404, 419, 421, 423, 426, 437.

133. Thernstrom, *The Other Bostonians,* pp. 210–213. Thernstrom's conclusions draw heavily on the work of Elizabeth Pleck, Herbert Gutman, and Tamara Haraven. See also Elizabeth Pleck, *Black Migration and Poverty, Boston 1865–1900* (New York: Academic Press, 1979), pp. 162–196.

134. Robert Woods, *The Neighborhood in Nation-Building,* p. 3; Sam Bass Warner, Jr., "Introduction," Kennedy and Woods, *Zone of Emergence,* p. 17.

135. Settlement residents, at least in some cities, took unusual initiative in racial matters, and "were

exceptions in an era that usually thought of the progressive movement as progress for whites only." All founders of the National Association for the Advancement of Colored People (NAACP), for instance, had settlement connections. Certainly, Robert Woods himself was far less preoccupied with "race traits" than many of his South End House colleagues, though his own views were far less farsighted than those of Jane Addams and others who were early advocates of civil rights. Davis, *Spearheads for Reform*, pp. 85–86, 94–96, 102; Trolander, *Professionalism and Social Change*, p. 93.

136. Statistics on the black population of Boston, from the U.S. Census and the Massachusetts State Census, are tabulated in Pleck, *Black Migration and Poverty*, table A-1, p. 209, and Thernstrom, *The Other Bostonians*, p. 179.

137. Daniels, *In Freedom's Birthplace*, pp. 213–214, 219–220; Pleck, *Black Migration and Poverty*.

138. Ibid., pp. 27–30, 85.

139. Although a black population of 2 percent seems small by today's standards, it should be noted that Boston housed a higher percentage of blacks in 1900 than did many other major northern cities such as New York, Chicago, Detroit, and Cleveland; by 1920, however, Boston's percentage of black population lagged behind all of these places.

140. Woods, in Daniels, *In Freedom's Birthplace*, pp. x–xi.

141. Shaw, who had led the first Negro troops into battle during the Civil War, and had died with many of them in an ill-conceived charge on South Carolina's Fort Wagner, was widely revered as a nineteenth-century martyr for the abolitionist cause. The heroism of the Massachusetts Fifty-Fourth regiment, made up of free blacks from across the nation, was seen as an important confirmation of black abilities and commitment to their country. Shaw's role, which inspired poetry by Emerson and Lowell as well as countless eulogies, also was viewed as proof that the Brahmin aristocracy could still produce Christian heroes. This dual interpretation of Shaw surely underpinned the apt selection of his name for such a settlement. See George M. Fredrickson, *The Inner Civil War: Northern Intellectuals and the Crisis of the Union* (New York, Harper & Row, 1965), pp. 151–155.

142. Woods and Kennedy, *Handbook of Settlements*, pp. 121–122.

143. Daniels, *In Freedom's Birthplace*, p. 194.

144. Trolander, *Professionalism and Social Change*, pp. 93–94.

145. Derived from Thernstrom, *The Other Bostonians*, p. 180.

146. Woods, "The Total Drift," in Woods, ed., *The City Wilderness*, p. 293; Woods and Kennedy, *The Settlement Horizon*, p. 189.

147. Woods and Kennedy, *The Settlement Horizon*, p. 190.

148. Woods, "The Total Drift," in Woods, ed., *The City Wilderness*, pp. 291–292. Regarding his wish for disincentives to vagrants, Woods noted two decades later that "For some years tramps have found it increasingly difficult to approach large cities in Massachusetts, which are by a happy chance at a distance from other state lines, without facing the disagreeable necessity of working" (Woods and Kennedy, *The Settlement Horizon*, p. 194).

149. Woods, "The Total Drift," in Woods, ed., *The City Wilderness*, p. 293; Woods, "Assimilation: A Double-Edged Sword," in Woods, ed., *Americans in Process*, pp. 371–372.

150. Woods and Kennedy, *The Settlement Horizon,* p. 174; Woods, "Work and Wages," in Woods, ed., *The City Wilderness,* p. 92.

151. As staff members professionalized, the mission of settlements gradually shifted toward more recreation-oriented "neighborhood centers" and, by the 1930s, even the concept of neighborhood residence was under challenge. In 1949, the National Federation of Settlements added "and Neighborhood Centers" to its official title. Subsequently, this organization—under black leadership since the early 1970s—eliminated the term "settlement" completely. The national group was officially renamed "United Neighborhood Centers of America" in 1979. In Boston, however, the umbrella organization long known as the United South End Settlements still persists to this day. Chambers, *Seedtime of Reform,* p. 123; Trolander, *Professionalism and Social Change,* pp. 39, 48, 217–218, 232; Trolander, *Settlement Houses and the Great Depression* (Detroit: Wayne State University Press, 1975), p. 45; Davis, *Spearheads for Reform,* pp. 231–232.

152. City of Boston, *The North End: A Survey and a Comprehensive Plan,* Report of the City Planning Board, city document no. 121 (Boston: City of Boston Printing Department, 1919), p. 46.

153. Lawrence Veiller, "Slum Clearance," in *Housing Problems in America,* Proceedings of the Tenth National Conference on Housing (Philadelphia, 1929), pp. 74–75; Mabel L. Walker, *Urban Blight and Slums: Economic and Legal Factors in Their Origin, Reclamation, and Prevention* (Cambridge, Mass.: Harvard University Press, 1938), pp. 357–418. The language of slum clearance permeated discussions at the National Conference of City Planning and at the National Conference on Housing by the late 1910s. See, for example, Veiller, "Slumless America," in *Proceedings of the Twelfth National Conference on City Planning* (Cincinnati, 1920), pp. 154–161.

154. Cousineau, "Tenement Reform," pp. 19–23.

155. Ralph Adams Cram, "Scrapping the Slum," in *Housing Problems in America,* pp. 242–250.

156. City of Boston, *The North End: A Survey and a Comprehensive Plan,* pp. iii, 9–10, 19, 36, 42–43; George Gibbs, Jr., "A Boston Slum to be Eradicated," *The City Plan* (Boston, January 1917), p. 5; Cram, "Scrapping the Slum," pp. 245, 249. See also Max Page, "The Creative Destruction of New York City: Landscape, Memory, and the Politics of Place, 1900–1930" (Ph.D. diss., University of Pennsylvania, 1995), chap. 3.

2 REWARDING UPWARD MOBILITY

1. Walt Whitman, *Democratic Vistas,* in Whitman, *Leaves of Grass and Selected Prose* (New York: Modern Library, 1981; 1871 original), pp. 486–487.

2. Thomas Jefferson, in letter to James Madison (October 28, 1785), quoted in Henry Nash Smith, *Virgin Land* (Cambridge, Mass.: Harvard University Press, 1950), p. 128.

3. Thomas Jefferson, *Notes on the State of Virginia,* Query XIX, quoted in Leo Marx, *The Machine in the Garden* (New York: Oxford University Press, 1964), pp. 124–125.

4. "An Ordinance for Ascertaining the Mode of Disposing of Lands in the Western Territory," May 20, 1785, *Journals of American Congress, from 1774 to 1788,* vol. IV (Washington, D.C.:

1823), in Payson Jackson Treat, *The National Land System, 1785-1820* (New York: E.B. Treat, 1910), pp. 395-400.

5. Treat, *National Land System*, pp. 22-27, 30; William Haller, Jr., *The Puritan Frontier: Town-Planting in New England Colonial Development, 1630-1660* (New York: Columbia University Press, 1951), pp. 31-42.

6. Address to the Massachusetts Constitutional Convention, 1820; and U.S. Congress, *Register of Debates in Congress*, vol. 3, 19th Cong., 1st sess., 1826, p. 727, quoted in Peter Marcuse, "The Ideologies of Ownership and Property Rights," in Richard Plunz, ed., *Housing Form and Public Policy in the United States* (New York: Praeger, 1980), p. 45.

7. "Letter from Thomas Jefferson to C. F. C. de Volney, February 8, 1805," quoted in John W. Reps, *The Making of Urban America: A History of City Planning in the United States* (Princeton: Princeton University Press, 1965), p. 317.

8. There is a vast literature on the development of American public lands policy during the nineteenth century, and it would be inappropriate to review it here. Historians in the early twentieth century, following Frederick Jackson Turner, interpreted the development of nineteenth-century American democracy in terms of development of frontier lands. The next generation of historians, most notably Paul W. Gates, stressed the ways that speculative practices distorted the aims of federal policy and led to land monopolies and excessive rates of tenancy, while more recent accounts have found evidence that many tenants eventually became owners, and cast doubt on the importance of monopolies. Since the 1950s, building on the work of Allan Bogue, many scholars have employed social science methods to emphasize the behavior of private markets on the western frontier. See, for example, Thomas Donaldson, *The Public Domain: Its History with Statistics* (Washington, D.C.: GPO, 1884); George M. Stephenson, *Political History of the Western Lands, from 1840 to 1862* (Boston: Richard G. Badger, 1917); Benjamin F. Hibbard, *History of the Public Land Policies* (New York: Macmillan, 1924); Roy M. Robbins, *Our Landed Heritage: The Public Domain, 1776-1970* (Lincoln: University of Nebraska Press, 2nd ed., rev., 1976); Allan G. Bogue, *From Prairie to Corn Belt* (Chicago: University of Chicago Press, 1963); Vernon Carstensen, ed., *The Public Lands* (Madison: University of Wisconsin Press, 1963); Paul W. Gates, *History of Public Land Law Development* (Washington, D.C.: U.S. GPO, 1968), which contains an enormous bibliography; James W. Oberly, *Sixty Million Acres: American Veterans and the Public Lands before the Civil War* (Kent, Ohio: Kent State University Press, 1990).

9. Treat, *National Land System*, pp. 81, 87.

10. Jerry A. O'Callaghan, "The War Veteran and the Public Lands," and Rudolf Freund, "Military Bounty Lands and the Origins of the Public Domain," in Carstensen, ed., *The Public Lands*, pp. 109-119 and 15-34.

11. George Washington, "Public Lands for Veterans," in William Parker Cutler and Julia Perkins Cutler, *Life, Journals, and Correspondence of Rev. Manasseh Cutler* (Cincinnati, 1888), vol. I, pp. 172-174.

12. "The Disposition of Lands in the Western Territory," in *Journals of the American Congress: From 1774 to 1788* (Washington, D.C., 1823), vol. 4: Friday, May 20, 1785; quoted in Treat, *National Land System*, pp. 237-238, 245.

13. Treat, *National Land System,* pp. 247, 255–256; Oberly, *Sixty Million Acres,* pp. 3, 9–12, 14–21, 28–53.

14. Though military service after 1855 was not rewarded with bounty lands (despite attempts in 1872 and 1873 to implement them for Civil War veterans), by the early twentieth century the amount of land granted for military service totaled about seventy million acres. Treat, *National Land System,* pp. 259–260; O'Callaghan, "The War Veteran and the Public Lands," pp. 116–117; Robbins, *Our Landed Heritage,* pp. 214–216.

15. Oberly, *Sixty Million Acres,* p. 159. Oberly estimates that receipt and sale of a quarter-section land warrant would net the veteran the equivalent of almost half a year's average earnings, so it formed quite a significant one-time pension (pp. 161–163).

16. Cited in Walter I. Trattner, *From Poor Law to Welfare State: A History of Social Welfare in America* (New York: Free Press, 1974), pp. 60–62; see also Gates, *History of Public Land Law Development,* pp. 18–19.

17. Paul W. Gates, "The Homestead Act: Free Land Policy in Operation, 1862–1935," in Howard Ottoson, ed., *Land Use Policy and Problems in the U.S.* (Lincoln: University of Nebraska Press, 1963), pp. 28–29.

18. U.S. Congress, *Congressional Globe,* appendix, June 20, 31st Congress, 1st sess., 1850, part 3: p. 951, quoted in Marcuse, "The Ideologies of Ownership and Property Rights," p. 46.

19. Thomas Le Duc, "U.S. Land Policy to 1862," in Ottoson, ed., p. 5.

20. Treat, "National Land System," p. 386. See also Marion Clawson, *Man and Land in the United States* (Lincoln: University of Nebraska Press, 1964), pp. 68–69; and Robbins, *Our Landed Heritage,* pp. 72–91.

21. Jan Cohn, *The Palace or the Poorhouse: The American House as a Cultural Symbol* (East Lansing: Michigan State University Press, 1979), pp. 175–189.

22. Cohn, pp. 139–145, 170, 215. To a large extent, these "models" were transmitted through architectural pattern books, notably the work of Andrew Jackson Downing: *Cottage Residences* (1842), *Landscape Architecture* (1844), *The Architecture of Country Houses* (1850); as well as Alexander Jackson Davis's *Rural Residences* (1842), Edward Shaw's *Rural Architecture* (1843), Calvert Vaux's *Villas and Cottages* (1854), and Charles P. Dwyer's *Economic Cottage Builder* (1856) and *The Immigrant Builder* (1859). See David Schuyler, *Apostle of Taste: Andrew Jackson Downing, 1815–1852* (Baltimore: Johns Hopkins University Press, 1996), pp. 1–8, 74, 96, and Gwendolyn Wright, *Building the Dream: A Social History of Housing in America* (New York: Pantheon, 1981), pp. 80–85.

23. Quoted in James T. Dubois and Gertrude S. Mathews, *Galusha Grow: Father of the Homestead Law* (Cambridge: Riverside Press, 1917), p. 110.

24. Eric Foner, *Free Soil, Free Labor, Free Men: The Ideology of the Republican Party before the Civil War* (New York: Oxford University Press, 1970), p. 27.

25. Quoted in Foner, *Free Soil, Free Labor, Free Men,* p. 29.

26. Quoted in Dubois and Mathews, *Galusha Grow,* p. 259.

27. Fred A. Shannon, *The Farmer's Last Frontier, 1860–1897* (New York: Farrar and Rinehart, 1945), p. 51.

28. Foner, *Free Soil, Free Labor, Free Men,* p. 27. Many others, both contemporaneously and sub-

sequently, questioned the "safety-valve" contention. See, for example, Clarence H. Danhof, "Farm-Making Costs and the 'Safety Valve': 1850–1860," and Fred A. Shannon, "The Homestead Act and the Labor Surplus," in Carstensen, ed., *The Public Lands,* pp. 253–314.

29. *Annual Report of the Directors of the Houses of Industry and Reformation,* Boston city document no. 12, April 1, 1850 (Boston: J.H. Eastburn, 1850), pp. 4–5.

30. *Report of Committee on the Overseers of the Poor.* Boston city document no. 27, April 11, 1859, pp. 4–8, 26.

31. By contrast, some northern industrialists feared that homestead legislation might drain off too much of the cheap labor force they required or could threaten their profits from western markets. Robbins, *Our Landed Heritage,* pp. 176–181; Gates, *History of Public Land Law Development,* p. 393.

32. Thomas H. O'Connor, *The Boston Irish: A Political History* (Boston: Back Bay Books, 1995), pp. 53–54.

33. Gates, "The Homestead Act," pp. 29–30, 42, and Shannon, "The Homestead Act," in Carstensen, ed., *The Public Lands,* p. 298; Shannon, *Farmer's Last Frontier,* p. 51.

34. Daniel Feller, *The Public Lands in Jacksonian Politics* (Madison: University of Wisconsin Press, 1984), pp. 196–197.

35. Robbins, *Our Landed Heritage,* p. 423.

36. Theda Skocpol, *Protecting Soldiers and Mothers* (Cambridge, Mass.: Harvard University Press, 1992), p. 7.

37. Lawrence W. Kennedy, *Planning the City on a Hill,* p. 65.

38. Warner, *Streetcar Suburbs,* pp. 136–137, 144, 149–153.

39. Ibid., pp. 46–47, 55–58.

40. Woods and Kennedy, "Introduction," in Kennedy and Woods, *The Zone of Emergence,* pp. 35–39.

41. *Report of the Committee on the Expediency of Providing Better Tenements for the Poor* (Boston: Eastburn's Press, 1846), pp. 14–16; Edward H. Chandler, "City and Slum," in Robert A. Woods, ed. *Americans in Process* (Boston: Houghton Mifflin, 1903), pp. 80–81; Handlin, *The American Home,* p. 257.

42. Horace B. Sargent, *Homesteads for the Poor* (Boston, 1854), cited in David Culver, "Tenement Reform in Boston, 1846–1898" (Ph.D. diss., Boston University, 1972), p. 169.

43. Rodwin, *Housing and Economic Progress,* pp. 28–32.

44. Edward Everett Hale, "Workingmen's Homes," "Co-operative Homes," and "Homes for Boston Laborers," in *Workingmen's Homes: Essays and Stories* (Boston: Osgood and Company, 1874), pp. 2–3, 8–9, 25, 65–66.

45. Robert Treat Paine, "Homes for the People," *Journal of Social Science* 15 (February 1882): 105, 110–116.

46. David Handlin, *The American Home,* pp. 242–243; Warner, *Streetcar Suburbs,* pp. 102–105. In all, Paine and the Workingmen's Building Association produced more than 250 houses, yet this was dwarfed by the thousands of new tenements constructed during the same years. See

Christine Cousineau, "Tenement Reform in Boston, 1870–1920: Philanthropy, Regulation, and Government Assisted Housing," working paper, Society for American City and Regional Planning History, 1990, p. 10.

47. Robert Treat Paine, "The Housing Conditions in Boston," *Annals of the American Academy of Political and Social Science* 20, 1 (July 1902): 129.

48. Culver, "Tenement Reform," p. 253.

49. Boston Dwelling House Company, "Woodbourne: A Description of Single and Semi-De-tached Houses Offered at This Attractive Site By the Boston Dwelling House Company" (Boston: Boston Dwelling House Company, n.d. [c. 1916]), pp. 3–5.

50. "Boston Dwelling House Company About to Start on Unique Project to Show Possibilities of Scientific Housing," *Boston Herald,* December 20, 1911; *Boston Traveler,* December 19, 1911, quoted in Robert Campbell, "Forgotten Utopias," *Boston Globe Sunday Magazine,* May 21, 1995, p. 18; "Two Groups of Houses Built for the Boston Dwelling House Company," *The Brickbuilder* 22, 4 (1913): 93.

51. A. D. F. Hamlin, "The Workingman and His House," *Architectural Record* 44 (October, 1919): 302, 305.

52. A. D. F. Hamlin, "The Charm of the Small House," *Architectural Record* 44 (October 1918): 277.

53. Roy Lubove, *Community Planning in the 1920's: The Contribution of the Regional Planning Association of America* (Pittsburgh: University of Pittsburgh Press, 1963), pp. 6, 9–11.

54. MHC reports are quoted in Lubove, *Community Planning in the 1920's,* pp. 6–15; and the MHC's Fourth Annual Report is reprinted in Roy Lubove, ed., *The Urban Community: Housing and Planning in the Progressive Era* (Englewood Cliffs, N.J.: Prentice-Hall, 1964), pp. 99–102.

55. Commonwealth of Massachusetts, *Fourth Annual Report of the Homestead Commission, 1916,* public document no. 103 (Boston, 1917), reprinted in Lubove, ed., *The Urban Community,* pp. 99–102; "For a State Housing Experiment," *The Survey* 35, 10 (April 22, 1916).

56. Sam Bass Warner, Jr., *The Way We Really Live: Social Change in Metropolitan Boston Since 1920* (Boston: Boston Public Library, 1977), p. 70, and *The Urban Wilderness: A History of the American City* (New York: Harper and Row, 1972), pp. 28–32. See also Seymour I. Toll, *Zoned American* (New York: Grossman, 1969), pp. 27–29; Higham, *Strangers in the Land,* p. 25.

57. Marc A. Weiss, *The Rise of the Community Builders: The American Real Estate Industry and Urban Land Planning* (New York: Columbia University Press, 1987), p. 11.

58. Province Law of 1692, chap. 32; now chap. 3, sec. 3 of the General Laws, quoted in Kennedy, *Planning the City on a Hill,* p. 17.

59. *Village of Euclid v. Ambler Realty Co.,* "Brief and Argument for Appellee," and Court opinion, cited in Toll, pp. 232–253; Charles M. Haar, *Land-Use Planning: A Casebook on the Use, Mis-use and Re-Use of Urban Land* (Boston: Little, Brown, 1959), p. 163; Constance Perin, *Every-thing in Its Place: Social Order and Land Use in America* (Princeton: Princeton University Press, 1977), pp. 45–47; William M. Randle, "Professors, Reformers, Bureaucrats, and

Cronies: The Players in *Euclid v. Ambler*," in Charles M. Haar and Jerold S. Kayden, eds., *Zoning and the American Dream* (Chicago: American Planning Association, 1989), pp. 42, 50.

60. Weiss, *The Rise of the Community Builders*, pp. 11–12.

61. Allan David Heskin, *Tenants and the American Dream: Ideology and the Tenant Movement* (New York: Praeger, 1983), p. xi.

62. Perin, *Everything In Its Place:* p. 62.

63. Manuel Castells, *The Urban Question* (Cambridge, Mass.: MIT Press, 1977), p. 166.

64. Matthew Edel, Elliott D. Sclar, and Daniel Luria, *Shaky Palaces: Homeownership and Social Mobility in Boston's Suburbanization* (New York: Columbia University Press, 1984), p. 295. These data involve further analysis of data originally collected by Stephan Thernstrom, as well as new attempts to follow a sample of Thernstrom's families into the suburbs. Edel, Sclar, and Luria acknowledge that this sample underestimated the homeownership rate of family heads in 1880, since it included sons who were not yet living apart from their parents (pp. 51, 138–139).

65. The most thorough study of twentieth-century homeownership in metropolitan Boston casts considerable doubt over the social and financial advisability of home purchases. Examining data between 1890 and 1970, its authors debunk prevailing assumptions about the expectation of increased property values and augmented social and economic mobility so often associated with the ownership of a home. Edel, Sclar, and Luria, *Shaky Palaces,* pp. 7, 169; see also Rodwin, *Housing and Economic Progress*, pp. 26–52.

66. For these purposes, the "home magazines" are defined to include such nationally circulated standards as *House Beautiful, Good Housekeeping, Ladies' Home Journal, American Home,* and *Journal of Home Economics,* as well as opinion magazines such as *Literary Digest, The New Republic, Outlook, The Atlantic Monthly, Survey Graphic,* and *Scribner's.*

67. Quoted in Campbell, "Forgotten Utopias," p. 18; Boston Dwelling House Company, "Woodbourne: A Description," p. 3.

68. Marc A. Weiss, "Own Your Own Home: Housing Policy and the Real Estate Industry." Paper presented to the Conference on Robert Moses and the Planned Environment, Hofstra University, June 11, 1988, pp. 3–5.

69. M. W. Folsom, *A Home of Your Own* (Chicago: National Association of Real Estate Boards, 1922), n.p.

70. John F. Bauman, *Public Housing, Race, and Renewal: Urban Planning in Philadelphia, 1920–1974* (Philadelphia: Temple University Press, 1987), pp. 15–16.

71. *Report of the Committee on Home Ownership, Income, and Types of Dwellings,* President's Conference on Home Building and Home Ownership, vol. IV (Washington, D.C.: GPO, October 1932), pp. 2, 30.

72. "Housing versus Ownership," *The New Republic,* December 16, 1931, p. 123. In 1940, the Census of Housing showed that more than 20 percent of urban owner-occupied homes were "substandard" in terms of basic amenities, construction quality, and maintenance (quoted in Weiss, "Own Your Own Home," p. 3).

73. Edith Elmer Wood, *Recent Trends in American Housing* (New York: Macmillan, 1931).

74. *Report of the Committee on Large-Scale Operations*, President's Conference on Home Building and Home Ownership (Washington, D.C.: GPO, October 1932), pp. 68, 85.

75. Quoted in Bauman, *Public Housing, Race, and Renewal*, p. 20.

76. *Report of the Committee on Blighted Areas and Slums*, President's Conference on Home Building and Home Ownership (Washington, D.C.: GPO, October 1932), pp. xiv, 31–32.

77. See, for example, Leonardo Benevolo, *History of Modern Architecture: Vol. 2, the Modern Movement* (Cambridge, Mass.: MIT Press, 1977), chaps. 13–17; Peter G. Rowe, *Housing and Modernity* (Cambridge, Mass.: MIT Press, 1993), especially chap. 2. On European housing schemes thought especially relevant by one major U.S. public housing pioneer, see Catherine Bauer's classic *Modern Housing* (Boston: Houghton Mifflin, 1934).

78. Edward Relph, *The Modern Urban Landscape* (Baltimore: Johns Hopkins University Press, 1987), p. 71.

79. Davis, *Spearheads for Reform*, pp. 23, 61.

80. Woods and Kennedy, *The Settlement Horizon*, p. 329.

81. Robert A. Woods, "The University Settlement Idea," in Woods, *The Neighborhood in Nation-Building* (Boston: Houghton Mifflin, 1923), p. 25.

82. Woods and Kennedy, *The Settlement Horizon*, p. 31.

83. Ebenezer Howard, *Garden Cities of To-Morrow*, edited by Frederick J. Osborn (Cambridge, Mass.: MIT Press, 1965 [original 1902]).

84. "Two Groups of Houses Built for the Boston Dwelling House Company," *The Brickbuilder* 22, 4 (1913): 93–96.

85. Roy Lubove, "Homes and 'A Few Well Placed Fruit Trees': An Object Lesson in Federal Housing," *Social Research* 27 (1960): 469.

86. Wood, *Recent Trends in American Housing*, pp. 66–68.

87. Lubove, "Homes and 'A Few Well Placed Fruit Trees,'" pp. 474–477. See also William J. O'Toole, "A Prototype of Public Housing Policy: the USHC," *Journal of the American Institute of Planners* 34, 3 (May 1968): 140–152; and Miles L. Colean, "The Factual Findings," in The Twentieth Century Fund, *Housing for Defense: A Review of the Role of Homes in Relation to America's Defense and a Program for Action"* (New York: Twentieth Century Fund, 1940).

88. John Taylor Boyd, Jr., "Industrial Housing Reports," *Architectural Record* 47 (January 1920): 89.

89. Christian Topolov, "Scientific Urban Planning and the Ordering of Daily Life: The First 'War Housing' Experiment in the United States, 1917-1919," *Journal of Urban History* 17, 1 (November 1990): 15–17, 40. In the end, the USHC and EFC managed to serve the housing needs of an estimated 360,000 workers and their families, though most of this entailed transportation improvements rather than newly constructed homes. Lubove, "Homes and 'A Few Well Placed Fruit Trees,'" pp. 476–477; Wood, *Recent Trends*, pp. 69–74. In addition to these efforts, the Ordnance Department also housed upwards of 45,000 people in sixteen temporary towns designed for the manufacture of explosives, located in isolated areas. The largest of these, at Old Hickory, Tennessee, housed 10,000 workers; Wood, *Recent Trends*, p. 71; Richard S. Childs, "The Government's Model Villages," *The Survey* 41 (February 1, 1919): 585–587.

90. Raymond Unwin, *Nothing Gained By Overcrowding! How the Garden City Type of Development May Benefit Both Owner and Occupier* (London: P.S. King, 1912).

91. Litchfield, quoted in Topolov, "Scientific Urban Planning," p. 19, and in Lubove, "Homes and 'A Few Well Placed Fruit Trees,'" p. 482.

92. Sylvester Baxter, "The Government's War Housing Program at Bridgeport, Conn.," *Architectural Record* 45, 2 (1919): 137.

93. Lawrence Veiller, "Industrial Housing Developments in America: Part II, The Government's Standards for War Housing of Permanent Construction," *Architectural Record* 43, 4 (April 1918): 344–359.

94. Rogers Flannery, speaking before the House Committee on the Merchant Marine and Fisheries, *Housing for Employees of Shipyards*, 65th Cong., 2nd sess., January 25, 28, 1918, p. 32, quoted in Topolov, "Scientific Urban Planning," p. 38.

95. Topolov, "Scientific Urban Planning," pp. 37–38; O'Toole, "Prototype of Public Housing Policy," p. 149.

96. Sylvester Baxter, "The Government's Housing Project at Quincy, Mass.," *Architectural Record* 45, 3 (March 1919): 247.

97. Topolov, "Scientific Urban Planning," pp. 21, 28.

98. Ibid., pp. 28–29, 36; Baxter, "The Government's Housing Project at Quincy, Mass.," p. 253.

99. Topolov, "Scientific Urban Planning," pp. 22, 24; Robert Anderson Pope, "Governmental Housing," *The New Republic* 13 (November 24, 1917): 93–94.

100. Veiller, "Industrial Housing Developments in America," p. 351.

101. Topolov, "Scientific Urban Planning," pp. 34–37.

102. Lubove, "Homes and 'A Few Well Placed Fruit Trees,'" pp. 485–486; Wood, *Recent Trends*, pp. 77–78; John Ihlder, "Uncle Sam as Auctioneer," *The Survey* 41 (February 8, 1919): 659–660.

103. United States Department of Labor, Bureau of Industrial Housing and Transportation, *Report of the United States Housing Corporation*, vol. II: *Houses, Site-Planning, Utilities* (Washington, D.C.: GPO, 1919), excerpted in Lubove, ed., *The Urban Community*, pp. 113–114.

104. Lubove, "Homes and 'A Few Well Placed Fruit Trees,'" pp. 472–486.

105. Ibid., p. 485.

106. Lawrence Veiller, *A Model Housing Law* (New York: Russell Sage Foundation, 1920), pp. 7, 344–345, and Veiller, "Industrial Housing Developments in America," pp. 344–345.

107. It is also worth noting the prominent role of the state government in New York, whose sponsorship of limited-dividend housing activities following creation of the New York State Board of Housing in 1926 predated state-based efforts elsewhere (aside from the precocious MHC experiment in Lowell, Massachusetts).

108. Woods, "The Neighborhood in Social Reconstruction" (1914), in Woods, *The Neighborhood in Nation-Building*, pp. 148, 151; Woods, "The Settlement Reconsidered in Relation to Other Neighborhood Agencies (1921), in Woods, *The Neighborhood in Nation-Building*, pp. 282–283; Woods, "The City and its Local Community Life" (1917), in Woods, *The Neighborhood in Nation-Building*, p. 196.

109. Clarence Arthur Perry, *The Neighborhood Unit: A Scheme of Arrangement for the Family-Life*

Community. In *Neighborhood and Community Planning.* (New York: Committee on Regional Plan of New York and Its Environs, 1929) vol. 7, monograph 1, pp. 22–141; *The Rebuilding of Blighted Areas: A Study of the Neighborhood Unit in Replanning and Plot Assemblage* (New York: Regional Plan Association, 1933); *Housing for the Machine Age* (New York: Russell Sage Foundation, 1939).

110. Tridib Banerjee and William C. Baer, *Beyond the Neighborhood Unit: Residential Environments and Public Policy* (New York: Plenum, 1984), p. 2.

111. Perry, *The Neighborhood Unit,* p. 25.

112. Harrison, "Introduction," in Perry, *The Neighborhood Unit,* p. 23.

113. Perry, *The Neighborhood Unit,* pp. 35–44, 58, 108.

114. Harrison, "Introduction," in Perry, *The Neighborhood Unit,* p. 23.

115. Perry's principles also included ideas derived from housing sponsored by the Metropolitan Life Insurance Company in New York City, as well from several other early community designs, such as those for Mariemont, Ohio; Baltimore's Roland Park, and Kansas City's Country Club District and, on a smaller scale, Boston's Woodbourne. Perry's neighborhood unit idea attempted to update and Americanize the celebrated English precedents designed by Parker and Unwin.

116. Perry, *The Neighborhood Unit,* pp. 90–100, and 132–140, which contains a lengthy appendix, "Forest Hills Restrictions"; Perry, *Housing for the Machine Age,* pp. 211–214.

117. Mumford, introduction to Clarence Stein, *Toward New Towns for America* (Cambridge: MIT Press, 1989 [1950 original]), pp. 16–17.

118. Perry, *Housing for the Machine Age,* p. 197.

119. Ibid., pp. 20–21, 108.

120. These successors include Chatham Village in Pittsburgh and Baldwin Hills Village in Los Angeles, as well as the Greenbelt new towns of the 1930s, and the postwar new towns in Britain and elsewhere. In a diluted way, the Radburn idea affected a great deal of postwar American suburban subdivision practice.

121. Stein, *Toward New Towns for America,* p. 48.

122. Wayne D. Heydecker, with Ernest P. Goodrich, *Sunlight and Daylight for Urban Areas: A Study of Suggested Standards for Site Planning and Building Construction* (New York: Committee on Regional Plan of New York and Its Environs, 1929), vol. 7, monograph 2, pp. 141–209. There is also an extensive and influential European literature on such matters.

123. Perry, *The Rebuilding of Blighted Areas,* p. 51.

124. Perry, *The Neighborhood Unit,* pp. 53, 59, 104.

125. Quoted in Perry, *The Rebuilding of Blighted Areas,* p. 4.

126. Ibid., p. 9.

127. Ibid., p. 10.

128. Ibid., p. 12.

129. Ibid., p. 58.

130. Ibid., pp. 47, 58.

131. Timothy McDonnell, *The Wagner Housing Act* (Chicago: Loyola University Press, 1957), chap. 3; Gail Radford, *Modern Housing for America: Policy Struggles in the New Deal Era*

(Chicago: University of Chicago Press, 1996), pp. 75–76, 181–186; Wood, *Recent Trends in American Housing*, p. 1; Bauer, *Modern Housing*.

3 BUILDING SELECTIVE COLLECTIVES

1. Alvin Schorr, *Slums and Social Insecurity* (Washington, D.C.: GPO, 1963), p. 110. For more elaborate versions of this argument, see Peter Marcuse, "Interpreting 'Public Housing' History," *Journal of Architectural and Planning Research* 12, 3 (Autumn 1995): 240–258 and "Mainstreaming Public Housing: A Proposal for a Comprehensive Approach to Housing Policy," in David Varady, Wolfgang Preiser, and Francis Russell, eds., *New Directions in Urban Public Housing* (New Brunswick, N.J.: Center for Urban Policy Research, 1998), pp. 23–44.

2. Quoted in Nathan Straus, *The Seven Myths of Housing* (New York: Alfred A. Knopf, 1944), p. 20.

3. In a 1937 report, Harold Ickes, PWA administrator, listed unemployment relief as the first objective of the Housing Division. See Robert Moore Fisher, *Twenty Years of Public Housing* (New York: Harper, 1959), p. 83; Charles Abrams, *Revolution in Land* (New York: Harper & Bros., 1939), p. 250.

4. Eugenie Ladner Birch, "Edith Elmer Wood and the Genesis of Liberal Housing Thought, 1910–1942" (Ph.D. diss., Graduate School of Arts and Sciences, Columbia University, 1975), pp. 183–185.

5. Harold Wolman, *Politics of Federal Housing* (New York: Dodd Mead, 1971), pp. 26–27; Harry C. Bredemeier, *The Federal Public Housing Movement* (New York: Arno Press, 1980), pp. 108, 115.

6. Charles Abrams, *Forbidden Neighbors: A Study of Prejudice in Housing* (New York: Harper & Bros., 1955), pp. 229–243.

7. William E. Leuchtenburg, *Franklin D. Roosevelt and the New Deal, 1932–1940* (New York: Harper Colophon, 1963), p. 136.

8. *Congressional Record* 81 (August 21, 1937): 9639, quoted in Lawrence M. Friedman, *Government and Slum Housing: A Century of Frustration* (Chicago: Rand McNally, 1968), p. 114; *Proceedings of the Boston City Council*, January 22, 1934, p. 20.

9. Leuchtenburg, *Roosevelt and the New Deal*, pp. 136–140; Friedman, *Government and Slum Housing*, pp. 114–116.

10. Charles H. Trout, "Curley of Boston: The Search for Irish Legitimacy," in Ronald P. Formisano and Constance K. Burns, eds. *Boston 1700–1980: The Evolution of Urban Politics* (Westport, Conn.: Greenwood Press, 1984), pp. 186–187; Milton Lewis Kerstein, "Old Harbor Housing Project: A Study of the Development of Public Housing Policy, 1930–1938" (master's thesis, University of Massachusetts at Boston, 1981).

11. Aside from Ihlder, whose principal influence in Washington occurred much later, after he moved there, the national leadership on public housing matters in the 1930s did not come

from Boston. In the effort to initiate federal action on behalf of public housing, Boston had no nationally active counterpart to Langdon Post of the New York City Housing Authority who, together with Charles Abrams and Mary Simkhovitch, led a New York contingent seeking to ensure that Senator Robert Wagner would introduce legislation. Simultaneously, working from Philadelphia, Catherine Bauer joined with labor leader John Edelman and architect Oscar Stonorov to draft a housing bill for Representative Henry Ellenbogen of Pittsburgh to introduce. In addition to the New York and Philadelphia centers of influence, Ernest Bohn in Cleveland, Alfred Stern in Chicago, and Coleman Woodbury and Warren Vinton in Washington all pressed the Roosevelt administration and Congress for legislative action on a decentralized public housing program; see Bredemeier, *Federal Public Housing Movement*, pp. 82–83.

12. John Ihlder, "A Housing Program" (Boston: Boston Housing Association, March 1934), pp. 2, 8.

13. Kerstein, "Old Harbor Housing Project," pp. 55–56; "$4,000,000 Home Project for E. Boston," *Boston Herald*, August 18, 1933, p. 1. The site of the proposed Neptune Gardens project now lies under the tarmac of Boston's Logan Airport; a vestigial spur is called Neptune Road.

14. "South Boston Site Selected: Government Will Take 19 Acres, Build Homes and Rent Them at Low Rates," *Boston Daily Globe*, January 31, 1935, pp. 1, 15; "U.S. to Condemn 11 City Blocks in Low-Rent Plan," *Boston Herald*, January 31, 1935, pp. 1, 15; State Board of Housing, *Annual Report of the State Board of Housing, from September 27, 1933 to November 30, 1934* (Boston: Department of Public Welfare, 1935), p. 3.

15. "South Boston Residents Dejected at Losing Homes," *Boston Herald*, January 31, 1935, pp. 1, 15; "Householders of South Boston Cheer Call to Defend Homes from Confiscation," *Boston Herald*, February 16, 1935, pp. 1, 6; "Crowd Boos High Rent in Housing Plan," *Boston Evening Transcript*, March 13, 1935, pp. 1, 6.

16. "Crowd Boos High Rent in Housing Plan," pp. 1, 5; "Big Firm Fights Housing Plan," *Boston Herald*, March 13, 1935, pp. 1, 5.

17. A federal district court ruled in *United States v. Certain Lands in City of Louisville* that the use of eminent domain powers to acquire slum property in order to clear it for use as public housing did not constitute a proper public use, since it was not a proper "governmental function to construct buildings in a state for the purpose of selling or leasing them to private citizens for occupancy as homes." Part of the basis of the ruling centered on the alleged illegality of federal initiatives in the various states and did not preclude locally initiated projects [9 F. Supp. 137, 141 (D.C.W.D. Ky. 1935), affirmed by a divided court in 78 Fed. 2d 684 (C.C.A. 6, 1935); dismissed on motion of the solicitor general, 294 U.S. 735 (1935), 297 U.S. 726 (1936). The case is discussed in Friedman, *Government and Slum Housing*, p. 102.

18. "Mayor Joins in So. Boston Protest Over $5,000,000 Housing Site Shift," *Boston Herald*, July 31, 1935, pp. 1, 7; Kerstein, "Old Harbor Housing Project," pp. 65–69.

19. Kerstein, "Old Harbor Housing Project," pp. 69–71. Land-use maps of the day show that the site contained only two small structures, and much of it had been used as a dump. Finance

Commission of the City of Boston, *Reports and Communications* (Boston: City of Boston Printing Department, 1940), p. 35, cited in John A. Carter, "Distributional Patterns in Boston Public Housing" (master's thesis [Geography], Boston University Graduate School, 1958), p. 27; "Mayor Joins in So. Boston Protest," p. 7.

20. "PWA Abandons South Boston Plan," *Boston Herald*, September 27, 1935, p. 23; "Wave of Protest in South Boston," *Boston Post*, September 27, 1935, pp. 1, 13; *Proceedings of the Boston City Council*, September 30, 1935, pp. 394-395.

21. Kerstein, "Old Harbor Housing Project," pp. 71-75.

22. Blame for delays should be widely shared: the state legislature failed to establish a municipal corporation in time to receive federal funds for slum removal; the Boston City Planning Board resisted receipt of federal loan money unless ultimate "responsibility and control" could remain in local hands; the lawyers for large real estate interests blocked the government's eminent domain proceedings; the state refused to pass legislation that would have let the City of Boston acquire land; the Massachusetts Emergency Finance Board unsuccessfully argued that the federal government should pay all project expenses; and the City Council (as well as Mayor Mansfield) argued that the Old Harbor project should be required to pay municipal taxes. Charles H. Trout, *Boston, the Great Depression, and the New Deal* (New York: Oxford University Press, 1977), pp. 152-153; Kerstein, "Old Harbor Housing Project," pp. 81-88; "Puts Mixup on Housing Up to City: Joseph Lee, Jr., Blames Mayor and Council for Situation," *Boston Post*, September 29, 1935, p. 8; *Proceedings of the Boston City Council*, September 30, 1935, p. 398.

23. Trout, *Boston, the Great Depression, and the New Deal*, p. 153.

24. *Boston Traveler*, October 14, 1935, pp. 1, 14. Here, as everywhere else in Boston, many complained that too many jobs went to "outsiders," whose connections to contractors and politicians were more pronounced than their attachments to the local neighborhoods where the work would take place.

25. "Country Fortunate in Stopping Housing Projects Says Paul," *South Boston Tribune*, August 11, 1939, pp. 1, 3.

26. John Breen, quoted in *Proceedings of the Boston City Council*, January 24, 1938, p. 27; May 22 and December 4, 1939, pp. 274, 480. Breen's statement was originally made in December 1938.

27. Boston City Directory, 1940; Boston "Police List," 1940; 1940 U.S. Census; *Proceedings of the Boston City Council*, December 5, 1938, p. 397.

28. Greater Boston Community Council, *What Do You Know About South Boston and Its Neighborhoods: Andrew Square, City Point, Old Harbor Village, Telegraph Hill, West Broadway?* (Boston: Community Studies Research Bureau, November 1944), pp. 11, 14, 23, 25, 27, 29, 33.

29. The mayor and city councilors squabbled for years over what it meant to have four board members "appointed by the mayor and the city council," but Mansfield's choices prevailed. They included, initially, an architect, two attorneys, and a union leader; and the governor, acting through the State Board of Housing, chose a minister. See *Proceedings of the Boston City Council*, August-December 1935, pp. 345, 397-399, 402, 416-417, 431-432; 435-436, 443-444,

470–471, 487, 506–507, 521, 532; February 3, 1936, p. 38; May-June 1937, pp. 193, 209–210, 235–236.

30. Boston City Planning Board, *Land Use Maps of Boston* (Boston: City Planning Board, 1935); Carter, "Distributional Patterns," p. 32.

31. Boston Housing Authority (hereafter BHA), *Rehousing the Low Income Families of Boston: Review of the Activities of the Boston Housing Authority, 1936–1940* (Boston, 1941), n.p. Other well-documented WPA and early USHA projects seem to have been similarly criss-crossed by an intricate web of social, recreational, and civic networks.

32. BHA, *Rehousing the Low Income Families of Boston;* Straus, *The Seven Myths of Housing,* p. 161. The Boston Municipal Research Bureau decried the paltry annual "service payment" as "an arbitrary sum which bears no relationship to any established policy," since it was not calculated on the basis of "rental income, operating surplus, or municipal services actually rendered to the project," Boston Municipal Research Bureau, *Payments in Lieu of Taxes on Public Housing in Boston* (Boston, January 1944), p. 7.

33. Calvin H. Yuill, "A Review of Housing Activity in Boston" (Housing Association of Metropolitan Boston, 1940), vertical files, Rotch Library, MIT, p. 14. This organization was a successor to the Boston Housing Association.

34. Friedman, *Government and Slum Housing,* pp. 106, 100n107. Wagner is quoted on p. 109.

35. Beatrice G. Rosahn and Abraham Goldfeld, *Housing Management: Principles and Practices* (New York: Covici Friede, 1937), p. 35.

36. United States Housing Authority, *What the Housing Act Can Do For Your City* (Washington, D.C., 1938).

37. G. M. Stout, "What Price Low-Cost Housing?" *National Apartment Journal,* May 1935, p. 10, quoted in M. B. Schnapper, ed., *Public Housing in America* (New York: H. W. Wilson Company, 1939), p. 343.

38. Cited in John P. Dean, *Home Ownership: Is It Sound?* (New York: Harper & Bros., 1945), p. 36.

39. Housing Act of 1937, quoted in Friedman, *Government and Slum Housing,* pp. 112–113.

40. Straus, *Seven Myths,* p. 104. The infamous decision to omit closet doors—almost always now remembered as an economy measure—in fact has a more complex origin. In his discussion of World War I guidelines for government housing, Lawrence Veiller pointed out that "in some parts of the country" closet doors were omitted out of a belief that "the clothes of workers need special fumigation and airing"; "Industrial Housing Developments in America: Part II, The Government's Standards for War Housing," *Architectural Record* 43 (April 1918): 347.

41. Edith Elmer Wood, *Slums and Blighted Areas in the United States* (Washington, D.C.: GPO, 1935), p. 19; Mabel L. Walker, *Urban Blight and Slums: Economic and Legal Factors in Their Origin, Reclamation, and Prevention* (Cambridge, Mass.: Harvard University Press, 1938), pp. 3–7.

42. State Board of Housing, *Annual Report of the State Board of Housing from September 27, 1933 to November 30, 1934* (Boston: Department of Public Welfare, 1935).

43. State Board of Housing (Massachusetts), *Annual Report of the State Board of Housing, for the year ending November 30, 1936* (Boston: Department of Public Welfare, 1937), p. 12.

44. State Board of Housing, *Annual Report for 1933-34*. Setting aside the methodological difficulties of attributing the pro-rated costs of city services, the study also conveniently ignored the fact that all but the wealthiest residential districts constitute a net drain on city resources; it is chiefly the central business district that generates a surplus.

45. Boston Municipal Research Bureau, *Payments in Lieu of Taxes on Public Housing in Boston* (Boston, 1944), pp. 2, 11.

46. BHA and City of Boston, "Cooperation Agreement Between the City of Boston, Massachusetts, and the Boston Housing Authority," October 25, 1938; BHA, *Rehousing the Low Income Families of Boston*. Based on BHA-supplied figures for its first four projects, the 4.75 percent payments in lieu of taxes were expected to generate yearly revenues of about $23,000—substantial, yet well short of $134,603 annual tax liability if the projects had been privately held properties. In addition, however, the BHA reported having paid the city approximately $210,000 in unpaid taxes on the slum properties it obtained and also having purchased approximately $85,000 of city-owned property.

47. *Report on The Income and Cost Survey of the City of Boston,* analyzed in Walker, *Urban Blight and Slums,* pp. 64-66.

48. City Planning Board study, quoted in BHA, *Rehousing the Low Income Families of Boston*.

49. BHA, *Rehousing the Low Income Families of Boston*.

50. Ibid.

51. Ibid.

52. Board of Zoning Adjustment, *Zoning Petitions,* nos. 272, 273, 274, and 275.

53. Rheable M. Edwards, Laura B. Morris, and Robert M. Coard, "The Negro in Boston" (Boston: Action for Boston Community Development, November 1961), p. 24; U.S. Census, 1940.

54. Walter Firey, *Land Use in Central Boston* (Cambridge, Mass.: Harvard University Press, 1947), p. 133.

55. BHA, *Rehousing the Low Income Families of Boston*.

56. The Boston city directories, updated annually, provide information about those living at every known address, including the name and occupation of the household head. The police lists are an even more comprehensive census of all Boston adult residents conducted annually by the Boston Police Department from 1917 through 1959. The latter, intended to be used primarily for voter registration procedures, are organized by ward and precinct, and provide the full name and sex of each adult, as well as his or her age, type of employment, citizenship status, and place of residence the preceding year. Using the city directories as a cross-check makes it possible to follow the residential movements (or lack thereof) of most adult residents of public housing over time with a high degree of reliability.

57. *Allydonn Realty Corp. v. Holyoke Housing Authority* (Mass. Adv. Sh. [1939] 1719), 24 *North Eastern Reporter,* 2nd ser., 665. Holyoke is a small city in western Massachusetts.

58. *Stockus et al. v. Boston Housing Authority,* 24 *North Eastern Reporter,* 2nd ser., 333; Report and Rescript in re *Stockus, et als., vs. Breen, et als.,* Massachusetts Supreme Judicial Court, equity no. 3954, and bill of complaint, related motions, and demurrers, Massachusetts Supe-

rior Court, equity no. 50577, archives, Massachusetts Supreme Judicial Court; BHA, *Rehousing the Low Income Families of Boston.*

59. *Stockus et al. v. Boston Housing Authority,* pp. 336–338.

60. "The Housing Decision," editorial, *South Boston Tribune,* December 22, 1939, p. 2.

61. "Notice to Vacate," letter from John A. Breen, Chairman, Boston Housing Authority, to Baltramieus and Annie M. Stockus, May 20, 1939.

62. BHA, *Rehousing the Low Income Families of Boston.*

63. Ibid.

64. Anna L. Kenney, "The Boston Housing Authority" (master's thesis, Boston University, 1941).

65. Boston city directories and police lists, 1938–1943.

66. Kenney, "The Boston Housing Authority," p. 49A.

67. Quoted in *Proceedings of the Boston City Council,* May 22, 1939, p. 274.

68. Kenney, "The Boston Housing Authority," pp. 38–54; *Charlestown News,* June 23, 1939, December 22, 1939, and October 18, 1940, p. 1; John A. Malloy, "A Discussion of the Method of Tenant Selection Used by the Boston Housing Authority under the Provisions of the United States Housing Act of 1937" (master's thesis, School of Social Work, Boston College, 1941), pp. 23–46. Boston police lists and Boston city directories, 1939, 1942. The figure of 8 percent was derived by following a 10 percent sample (n = 120) of households who were residents of the site in 1939. Only nine (7.5 percent of the sample) were listed as residents of the Charlestown project by the time it was first fully occupied in early 1942. The claim by J. Anthony Lukas that 36 percent of the families evicted from the Charlestown site gained new apartments in the project is wildly out of line with the data from the police lists and city directories for this project and others of its era. J. Anthony Lukas, *Common Ground: A Turbulent Decade in the Lives of Three American Families* (New York: Vintage, 1986), pp. 146, 151.

69. Quoted in *Proceedings of the Boston City Council,* May 22, 1939, p. 275.

70. Fortunately for the BHA, attorneys for the Stockus family never saw these figures.

71. Kenney, "The Boston Housing Authority"; *Proceedings of the Boston City Council,* February 3, 1941, p. 41 and August 4, 1941, p. 268; Boston police lists and Boston city directories, 1939, 1942. The project rehousing statistic was computed by tracing the residential mobility of a 10 percent sample of the households who had lived on the site in 1939 before it was razed. These were followed to 1942, and only one couple out of sixty-two (1.6 percent) was found to have gained an apartment at Old Colony.

72. "Mission Hill Housing Area Is Seized by Boston Authority: Removal of 2500 Required as Mr. Average Citizen Belatedly Realizes 'There is No Santa Claus,'" *Roxbury Gazette and South End Advertiser,* June 2, 1939, p. 1.

73. Quoted in *Proceedings of the Boston City Council,* April 7, 1941, and June 5, 1939, pp. 148–149, 296; "Carey Insists Housing Authority Be More Liberal with Local Applicants," *Jamaica Plain Citizen,* April 10, 1941, pp. 1, 6. According to the Overseers of Public Welfare, only four evicted households were added to the welfare rolls between May 20 and July 20, 1939 (quoted in *Proceedings of the Boston City Council,* August 7, 1939, p. 372).

74. The Looker On, "Housing Project Residents Unable to Get Tenements," *Roxbury Gazette and South End Advertiser,* June 23, 1939, p. 1.

75. Housing Association of Metropolitan Boston, "Comparative Survey of Present and Former Dwellings of Families Displaced by the Development of a Public Housing Project in Boston" (mimeograph, October 1939), vertical files, Rotch Library, MIT.

76. Ibid.

77. Ibid.; BHA, *Rehousing the Low Income Families of Boston.*

78. Housing Association of Metropolitan Boston, "Comparative Survey"; *Proceedings of the Boston City Council,* February 10, 1941, p. 54; Boston police list, 1939. The handful of noncitizens found among the tenant lists of early Boston public housing projects seem to have been either spouses or elderly parents of citizens.

79. Housing Association of Metropolitan Boston, "Comparative Survey"; Kenney, "The Boston Housing Authority," pp. 47A, 49, 49A; police lists and Boston city directories, 1939, 1942. The figures are based on a 10 percent sample of all listed adults on the site, drawn by taking every tenth last name. The assumption of marriage is based on the co-presence of two consecutively listed persons having the same last name, one of whom is male and one of whom is female, whose ages are within fifteen years of each other.

   The accounts of employment given for the purpose of the police lists were unverified. Given the high reported incidence of relief payments to those living on the site in 1939 and the fact that no person was recorded as "unemployed," these are probably accounts of the jobs they would have if they were employed. Despite this uncertainty, these figures seem worth reporting for the purpose of comparison of occupational categories.

80. "Constitutionality of Housing Projects Challenged Here," *Roxbury Gazette and South End Advertiser,* November 17, 1939, p. 1. The Boston City Council and the mayor formally requested that the BHA "name the streets, courts, and ways" of the Lenox Street project "in honor of colored citizens of Boston who attained prominence in the affairs of the city"; *Proceedings of the Boston City Council,* September 9, 1940, p. 339.

81. *Proceedings of the Boston City Council,* January 24, February 14, February 28, October 24, November 21, and December 19, 1938, pp. 27–29, 71–73, 77, 335–336, 375, 417, 419–420; December 4, 1939, pp. 479–483; January 29, February 19, April 15, October 28, 1940, pp. 43, 56, 152, 395.

82. *Proceedings of the Boston City Council,* August 28, 1939, p. 391; "Pleased Tenants Move Into Roxbury's First Housing Project," *Roxbury Gazette and South End Advertiser,* December 20, 1940, p. 1; "Council Asks That Local Labor Be Used on Housing Project," *Roxbury Gazette and South End Advertiser,* September 1, 1939, p. 1.

83. "No More Housing," editorial, *The South Boston Tribune,* June 16, 1939, p. 2.

84. "Stop Housing Projects," editorial, *The South Boston Tribune,* June 23, 1939, p. 2.

85. "Forget It, Mr. Mayor," editorial, *South Boston Tribune,* February 7, 1941.

86. "John A. Breen Wins Praise for Work on Housing Projects," *Parkway Transcript,* March 9, 1939, p. 13; "Praises Government for Boston Slum Clearance," *Parkway Transcript,* March 30, 1939, p. 4; "Work for 5000 Men in Gigantic Housing Projects in Boston," *Parkway Transcript,* May 4, 1939.

87. "New Housing Project Slated for the Roxbury District," *Roxbury Gazette and South End Advertiser,* March 15, 1940, p. 1.

88. Brief from *Stockus v. Boston Housing Authority,* quoted in BHA, *Rehousing the Low Income Families of Boston.*

89. BHA, *Rehousing the Low Income Families of Boston.*

90. Straus, *Seven Myths,* p. 154; Straus, *Housing and Recreation* (Washington, D.C., United States Housing Authority, November 1939), pp. 2, 8, 14–16. Straus stressed the importance of gardening to nonwhite groups: "A housing project which is wholly or predominantly of colored or Latin-American occupancy is often the most attractive spot in the town" since "the love of flowers characteristic of these groups finds expression in beautifying project grounds"; Straus, *Seven Myths,* p. 162.

91. The issue of where to site public housing was influenced by two key court decisions. *United States v. Certain Lands in City of Louisville* (1935) required the PWA to build on vacant land, and the government did not appeal the decision. In 1936, however, the New York Court of Appeals in *New York City Housing Authority v. Muller* held that it could be considered a "public use" for the *state* to use its eminent domain for public housing. In combination, these two cases contributed to the decision to let individual cities administer public housing, under the terms of the 1937 Housing Act. See Friedman, *Government and Slum Housing,* pp. 102–103.

92. Straus, *Seven Myths,* pp. 53, 56.

93. Edith Elmer Wood, *Introduction to Housing: Facts and Principles* (Washington, D.C.: United States Housing Authority, 1939), p. 34.

94. Joseph Hudnut, "Housing and the Democratic Process," *Architectural Record,* June 1943: 44.

95. Straus, *Housing and Recreation,* p. 3; *Seven Myths,* p. 163.

96. Hudnut, "Housing and the Democratic Process," p. 44.

97. G. Lynde Gately, M.D., "Letter to Boston Housing Authority," January 15, 1941, and Joseph F. Timilty, "Letter to Boston Housing Authority," January 15, 1941, reprinted in BHA, *Rehousing the Low Income Families of Boston.* The comments about the relationship between project design and police patrols were echoed in many other places over the next several years, including an April 1949 telegram from Mayor James M. Curley to Senator Hubert Humphrey, urging passage of the Housing Act of 1949 partly on the basis that the "layout of buildings makes for ease of patrol and better housing conditions help juvenile delinquent problem" (quoted in *Boston City Record,* April 16, 1949, p. 393).

98. BHA, *Rehousing the Low Income Families of Boston.*

99. BHA, *Annual Report, 1944–1945* (Boston, 1945), n.p.

100. Ibid.

101. Ibid.

102. Ibid.

103. Groups such as the Boston Municipal Research Bureau argued that because local municipalities absorbed the bulk of the government subsidy themselves (through lost revenues due to tax exemption), it was only fair that the cities also garner the bulk of the surplus. In 1944, at a time when the city struggled with a declining tax base made more serious by increased amounts of

tax-exempt real estate, the Bureau warned that public housing currently forced the city into an annual "tax loss" of about $1 million, and that an "additional loss of $164,000 would be incurred for each thousand families rehoused under an expanded program." Boston Municipal Research Bureau, *Payments in Lieu of Taxes on Public Housing in Boston,* pp. 9–10.

104. "Housing Projects Discussion Subject during Past Week," *South Boston Gazette,* February 7, 1941; *Proceedings of the Boston City Council,* February 3 and February 17, 1941, pp. 46–47, 70–71.

105. *Proceedings of the Boston City Council,* August 4, 1941, pp. 268–269 and November 22, 1942, p. 310. Data on occupation and prior residence come from the 1942 police lists, cross-referenced with the city directories. For 1956, BHA payments to Boston in lieu of taxes totaled $132,516 for the ten state-aided projects and $266,600 for federally aided projects; Carter, "Distributional Patterns," p. 46.

106. BHA, *Annual Report, 1944–1945.*

107. Ibid.

108. "Woodland Hill Fights Proposed FHA Housing Project," *Parkway Transcript,* September 17, 1942, pp. 1, 3; "Lull in Woodland Hill Row," *Parkway Transcript,* September 24, 1942, pp. 1, 4; "WPB Gets Woodland Hill Protest," *Parkway Transcript,* October 22, 1942, pp. 1, 12; "Woodland Hill Wins Protest as WPB Acts," *Parkway Transcript,* December 10, 1942, pp. 1, 4.

109. Richard O. Davies, *Housing Reform during the Truman Administration* (Columbia: University of Missouri Press, 1966), p. 11; Massachusetts State Housing Board, *Annual Report, July 1, 1953–June 30, 1954* (Boston, 1954), p. 7.

110. Raymond Foley, testimony of April 20, 1949, cited in U.S. Congress, Housing of Representatives, *Housing Act of 1949 Hearings,* pp. 355–356.

111. *Housing Act of 1949,* Section 201 (8)(c).

112. In *Housing Reform during the Truman Administration,* Davies charts the battles over housing policies in the immediate postwar period, including a blow-by-blow description of the fisticuffs on the House floor between eighty-three-year-old Adolph Sabath (Democrat, Illinois), chairman of the House Rules Committee, and sixty-nine-year-old E. E. Cox (Democrat, Georgia) (p. 110).

113. "Nationwide Survey," *Fortune,* December 1943, cited in Dean, *Homeownership: Is It Sound?* p. 168; *Behind the Blueprints: Better Homes and Gardens Special Report,* 1946, pp. 1, 6; "Declaration of National Housing Policy," in U.S. Congress, House of Representatives, *Housing Act of 1949: Hearings before the Committee on Banking and Currency on H.R. 4009,* 81st Cong., 1st sess., April 7, 1949, p. 1.

114. Fitch and Maenner, quoted in Davies, *Housing Reform during the Truman Administration,* pp. 18, 109–110.

115. In 1947 Nathan Straus stated flatly that the real estate lobby "has shaped our 'policy' in Congress." Nathan Straus, "Why You Can't Get That New Home," *American Magazine,* December 1947, pp. 21, 30. See also Harry C. Bredemeier, *The Federal Public Housing Movement* (New York: Arno Press, 1950), p. 130; U.S. Congress, House Select Committee on Lobbying

Activities, 81st Cong., 2nd sess., 1950, *Hearings,* Part 2, pp. 351–352; and "Press Release of Harry S. Truman to Sam Rayburn," June 17, 1949, quoted in Davies, p. 110.

116. Bredemeier, *Federal Public Housing Movement,* pp. 141, 147; Davies, *Housing Reform,* pp. 16–17.

117. "Public Housing Promotes Home Ownership," *American City,* May 1951, p. 163.

118. Nathan Straus, "Public Housing and American Tradition," address of July 20, 1938, p. 3, in the vertical files of the Loeb Library, Harvard Graduate School of Design; Straus, *The Seven Myths of Housing,* pp. 167–169. Catherine Bauer made similar arguments in *A Citizen's Guide to Public Housing* (Poughkeepsie, N.Y.: Vassar College, 1940), pp. 70–71.

119. *Housing Act of 1949,* quoted in Friedman, *Government and Slum Housing,* pp. 110–111; NAHB, "The Ten Basic Steps of Public Housing" (1949), quoted in Leonard Freedman, *Public Housing: The Politics of Poverty* (New York: Holt, Rinehart, and Winston, 1969), p. 43.

120. Massachusetts Housing Bureau, "Supporting Data for 20 Percent Gap Determination—Boston, Massachusetts," August 7, 1950, pp. 2–3; "Establish Housing Center for Vets," *Jamaica Plain Citizen,* August 29, 1946, pp. 1–2; "An Act to Relate the Housing Authority Law to Federal Legislation, to Give Preference to Families of Servicemen and Veterans in Housing Authority Projects . . ." Chapter 574, *Acts and Resolves of Massachusetts,* 1946, pp. 619–641, especially sect. 26FF. Though these homes remained part of the BHA's portfolio for only a few years, and all were sold by 1956, they remained financially controversial. A Boston Finance Commission report to the City Council in 1953 charged that the Chapter 372 "social experiment" had cost the city millions of dollars beyond any likely receipts, concluding that this city-financed effort, like all other public housing, failed to produce "enough income in rentals to pay operating and financing costs"; "Finance Commission Warns that the Sales of Veterans' Housing as Proposed May Cost City and Taxpayers a Considerable Sum Over and Above All Other Receipts—Costs to Mount with Each Succeeding Year," *Boston City Record,* February 28, 1953, pp. 229, 232. See also Chapter 372, *Massachusetts Acts and Resolves, 1946,* pp. 380–386, and its amendment, Chapter 481, *Massachusetts Acts and Resolves, 1952;* Massachusetts State Housing Board, *Annual Report, July 1, 1953–June 30, 1954* (Boston, 1954), pp. 9–11.

121. Chapter 200, *Acts and Resolves of Massachusetts,* 1948, pp. 195–200; State Housing Board, *Primer for Use of Local Housing Authorities* (Boston, June 1948), p. 3; Commonwealth of Massachusetts, *The Commonwealth of Massachusetts Report of the Special Commission to Make a Survey and Study of Problems Relating to Veterans Including Housing and Hospital Facilities,* Part I—Veterans Housing, December 1947, p. 6. The definition of "veteran" changed several times during the decade after World War II. Chapter 200 defined a veteran as "a man or woman who served for at least ninety consecutive days in the armed forces of the United States of America and has been separated therefrom under conditions other than dishonorable. The term shall also include the widow, mother, or other dependent of a person who so served and who died while in such service and the wife, mother or other dependent of a person who is so serving." In subsequent years, the definition was expanded to encompass service in the Korean conflict (Chapter 403, *Massachusetts Acts and Resolves,* 1955).

122. Governor Robert F. Bradford, letter to Albert S. Bigelow, chairman, State Housing Board,

September 8, 1948, reprinted in State Housing Board, *Massachusetts Housing for Veterans, 1948* (Boston, 1948).

123. "Collins Urges Private Capital Aid Housing," *Jamaica Plain Citizen*, January 15, 1948, pp. 1, 10.

124. Boston Municipal Research Bureau, *Payments in Lieu of Taxes on Public Housing in Boston*, p. 15; Chapter 200, *Acts and Resolves of Massachusetts*, 1948, pp. 195-200.

125. Massachusetts State Board of Housing, "Veterans' Housing Act, Chapter 200 of the Acts of 1948," memorandum from A. S. Bigelow, chairman, State Board of Housing to Massachusetts mayors, selectmen, chairmen of housing authorities and committees, April 13, 1946, p. 2.

126. Controversy surrounding these delays contributed to the resignation of BHA chairman Breen in 1944; *Proceedings of the Boston City Council*, February 7, 1944, pp. 70-71.

127. BHA, "Housing Authority Announces Radical Change in Policy," press release, January 21, 1946.

128. *Proceedings of the Boston City Council*, February 28 and March 6, 1944, pp. 89, 104-105; July 30, October 22, November 26, December 3, 1945, pp. 278, 375, 404, 420-422; January 7, 1946, pp. 13-15; April 28, 1947, pp. 277-280.

129. BHA, *Rehousing the Low-Income Families of Boston, 1949* (Boston, 1949), n.p.; "Boston Housing Authority Can Accept No More Applications for Tenancy for Some Time Due to the Lack of Construction Available for Needs and Demands," *Boston City Record*, October 16, 1948, p. 1035. When the lists reopened, 11,000 more families applied by mid-1952, with new applications coming in at a rate of a hundred a week; "Boston Housing Authority Has Record of Supplying Needed Housing Facilities Comparing Favorably with Any City in the Country," *Boston City Record*, July 26, 1952, p. 737.

130. "Rep. Collins Rebukes State Housing Board," *Jamaica Plain Citizen*, September 2, 1948, p. 1.

131. State Housing Board, *Primer for Use of Local Housing Authorities* (Boston, June 1948), pp. 13-15. Chapter 260 of the Acts of 1948 substituted the name State Housing Board for the previously existing State Board of Housing, and transferred all powers, duties, and obligations to the chairman of the new entity, now lodged in the Executive Department rather than in the Department of Public Welfare.

132. State Housing Board, *Primer*, pp. 13-15. In 1954, the year the last of the Boston Veterans Housing Projects opened, fully 98 percent of the families living in Chapter 200 housing statewide had one or more children. See Massachusetts State Housing Board, *Annual Report, July 1, 1953–June 30, 1954* (Boston: State Housing Board, 1954), p. 3.

133. "Boston Housing Authority Plans Huge Building Program," *Boston City Record*, July 26, 1952, p. 739.

134. "Information for Commission against Discrimination," memorandum from W. J. Hutchinson, supervising housing manager to Paul Liston, BHA general counsel, March 13, 1956.

135. "Mayor Curley in Broadcast Recounts Successful Efforts in Securing Approval of Housing Plans for Veterans, with Work Starting at Cathedral Site and in Brighton," *Boston City Record*, October 29, 1949, pp. 1211-1212.

136. "Rep. Hailer Proposes Two New Vet Housing Projects," *Jamaica Plain Citizen*, March 3,

1949, pp. 1-2; "Break Ground for New Veteran Housing Project in Forest Hills," *Jamaica Plain Citizen*, February 17, 1949, p. 1; "Final Plans Are Drawn for New Housing Project," *Jamaica Plain Citizen*, August 16, 1951, p. 1.

137. Board of Zoning Adjustment, zoning petitions nos. 287 and 313; Carter, "Distributional Patterns," pp. 94-95.

138. Board of Zoning Adjustment, zoning petition no. 321.

139. Ibid.; Carter, "Distributional Patterns," p. 95.

140. Carter, "Distributional Patterns," pp. 69-79; Emilie Tavel, "'We're All Taxi Poor:' Are Public Housing Projects Meeting the Needs of the Tenants as Fully as They Should?" *Christian Science Monitor*, January 22, 1955, p. 1, sect. 2.

141. Carter, "Distributional Patterns," pp. 69-79.

142. Irwin Deutscher, "The Gatekeeper in Public Housing," in *Among the People: Encounters With the Poor*, ed. Irwin Deutscher and Elizabeth J. Thompson (New York: Basic Books, 1968), pp. 44-50.

143. Quoted in May B. Hipshman, *Public Housing at the Crossroads: The Boston Housing Authority* (Boston: Massachusetts Committee on Discrimination in Housing, Commission on Housing [Metropolitan Boston Association, United Church of Christ], and Citizens' Housing and Planning Association of Metropolitan Boston, August 1967), p. 27.

144. BHA, *Report of the Activities . . . and Accomplishments of the Boston Housing Authority, January 1, 1950–December 31, 1952* (Boston, 1953), n.p.

145. "Evictions and Collections," memorandum from John C. Conley, assistant counsel to Paul F. Liston, BHA general counsel, January 15, 1946; "Nuisance Cases," memorandum from John C. Conley to all managers, August 22, 1946.

146. Jeremiah F. Sullivan, BHA acting executive director, letter to the area rent director, Office of Price Administration (OPA), February 21, 1947; William F. Riley, area rent director, OPA, letter to Jeremiah F. Sullivan, acting executive director, BHA, March 7, 1947; and Harry W. Sturges, assistant director for management, Federal Public Housing Authority, letter to BHA, March 27, 1947.

147. In 1951 the "lowest monthly gross rents being achieved by private enterprise" in the Boston area were $97 for one bedroom, $99 for two bedrooms, and $121.75 for three bedrooms; the corresponding ceiling rents for BHA apartments were $46, $52, and $58. Moreover, the BHA offered four- and five-bedroom apartments at a time when the private sector could provide "no substantial supply"; BHA, "Proposal for Revised Maximum Income Limits," March 30, 1951, pp. 2-3; Massachusetts Housing Bureau, "Supporting Data for 20 Percent Gap Determination—Boston, Massachusetts," pp. 2-3. Data on occupations and prevailing wages are calculated from tables supplied by the Massachusetts Department of Labor and Industries, "Average Weekly Earnings—Production Workers in Manufacturing Plants"; from the U.S. Department of Labor, Bureau of Labor Statistics, "Union Scale of Wages—Boston, Massachusetts"; from the National Metal Trades Association, "Wage Survey—Boston Area (Lowest Paid Male Employees)"; and from the City of Boston, "Weekly Salary of Laborers," all listed in the BHA "Proposal for Revised Maximum Income Limits," pp. 4a-9.

148. The BHA also included an alternative "minimum adequate budget" prepared by the Visiting

Nurse Association of Boston in January 1951. Using a similar family of four but employing slightly more generous assumptions—including an itemized provision for a weekly forty-cent church donation—this version projected a necessary annual family income of $2,619.48, a figure above the maximum for that family's admission to Boston public housing. Both budgets are included in BHA, "Proposal for Revised Maximum Income Limits," March 30, 1951, pp. 10-11. All these figures are for the BHA's federally funded developments. The state developments, with somewhat different admissions criteria and a different subsidy structure, had a somewhat higher set of income ceilings. Though administered jointly by the BHA, the federally aided Public Housing Administration developments and the state-assisted Veterans Housing projects initially did differ both in their clientele and rent structure. Because the state subsidy was smaller, the BHA faced an increased need to maintain a larger rent roll at those developments, and consequently set higher income limits for continued occupancy. In 1956 the city-wide average income of families in state-aided developments was nearly $3,500, about $730 more than that of families in federal public housing; Charles E. Slusser, chairman, Public Housing Administration, letter to Thomas J. Lane, U.S. Representative, May 21, 1956; Frederick Cronin, chairman, BHA, "Request for Revision of Income Limits on All State-Aided Developments," letter to Massachusetts State Housing Board, July 17, 1956.

149. "Some 300 Housing Unit Tenants Benefit By Raised Income Limits," *Boston City Record*, June 30, 1956, p. 760.

150. O'Connor, *The Boston Irish*, pp. 206, 222.

151. "Housing Head to Ask Probe of 'Shakedown,'" *Boston Globe*, May 1, 1951; *Proceedings of the Boston City Council*, April 28, 1947, p. 280, and April 30, 1951, p. 126; Jonathon Morris Pynoos, "Breaking the Rules: The Failure to Select and Assign Public Housing Tenants Equitably" (Ph.D. diss., Harvard University, 1974), pp. 12-13.

152. "Status of Police and Firemen Clarified by Housing Authority," *Boston City Record*, May 9, 1959, p. 411.

153. BHA, *Report of Activities . . . and Accomplishments, January 1, 1950–December 31, 1952;* BHA, "Public Housing in Boston," January 31, 1957, p. 6.

154. Paul F. Liston, letter to Mary Driscoll, chairman, Boston Licensing Board, February 19, 1946.

155. Carter, "Distributional Patterns," table VII.

156. BHA, *Report of Activities . . . and Accomplishments, January 1, 1950–December 31, 1952.*

157. BHA, "Conditions of Occupancy," 1949, nos. 5, 10, 12, 13, 22, 23, and 29.

158. BHA, *Report of Activities . . . and Accomplishments, January 1, 1950–December 31, 1952.*

159. Emilie Tavel, various articles, *Christian Science Monitor*, January 17-21, 1955.

160. Abrams, *Forbidden Neighbors*, p. 282.

4 MANAGING POVERTY AND RACE

1. 1960 U.S. Census. Oliver Wendell Holmes coined the phrase as "hub of the Solar System."

2. See Arnold Hirsch, *Making the Second Ghetto: Race and Housing in Chicago, 1940–1960* (New York: Cambridge University Press, 1982), pp. 215, 232–266; Devereux Bowly, Jr., *The Poorhouse: Subsidized Housing in Chicago, 1895–1976* (Carbondale, Ill.: Southern Illinois Uni-

versity Press, 1978), pp. 111–135; Martin Meyerson and Edward Banfield, *Politics, Planning and the Public Interest* (Glencoe, Ill.: Free Press, 1955); John F. Bauman, *Public Housing, Race, and Renewal: Urban Planning in Philadelphia, 1920–1974* (Philadelphia: Temple University Press, 1987), pp. 167–173; Eugene J. Meehan, *The Quality of Federal Policymaking: Programmed Failure in Public Housing* (Columbia, Mo.: University of Missouri Press, 1979), p. 219, and *Public Housing Policy: Convention Versus Reality* (New Brunswick, N.J.: Center for Urban Policy Research, 1975).

3. BHA archives.

4. James M. Curley, "Mayor Curley Making Plans for Rebuilding of Blighted Areas in Boston . . . ," *Boston City Record,* February 12, 1949, p. 164.

5. Lawrence W. Kennedy, *Planning the City upon a Hill: Boston since 1930* (Amherst: University of Massachusetts Press, 1992), p. 159.

6. BHA, *Report of The Activities . . . and Accomplishments of the Boston Housing Authority, January 1, 1950–December 31, 1952* (Boston, 1953); John B. Hynes, in *Boston Globe,* May 12, 1955, quoted in Thomas H. O'Connor, *Building a New Boston: Politics and Urban Renewal 1950 to 1970* (Boston: Northeastern University Press, 1993), p. 77.

7. Housing and Home Finance Agency, *The Workable Program: What It Is* (Washington, D.C.: GPO, September 1955), pp. 1, 3, 6.

8. O'Connor, *Building a New Boston,* pp. xii–xiii, 75–76, 127; Housing Association of Metropolitan Boston, "New Boston Committee's Housing Rehabilitation Plan for Boston" (Boston, December 1952).

9. Herbert Gans, *The Urban Villagers: Group and Class in the Life of Italian-Americans* (New York: Free Press, 1962); Marc Fried, "Grieving for a Lost Home," in *The Urban Condition,* ed. Leonard J. Duhl (New York: Basic Books, 1963); Fried, *The World of the Urban Working Class* (Cambridge, Mass.: Harvard University Press, 1973); and Chester Hartman, "The Housing of Relocated Families," *Journal of the American Institute of Planners* 30 (November 1964): 266–286.

10. Boston Municipal Research Bureau, "Charting the Future of Urban Renewal," (Boston, July 1959), p. iv; John B. Hynes, letter accompanying "Order for Loan of $4,500,000 for West End Redevelopment Project Area," August 5, 1957, *Proceedings of the Boston City Council,* August 5, 1957, p. 213; BHA, *West End Redevelopment Plan: Declaration of Findings,* May 1957; O'Connor, *Building a New Boston,* pp. 134–135; William J. Foley, "Finance Commission Report," *Proceedings of the Boston City Council,* July 30, 1959, p. 355.

11. "$20 Million Home Project for West End Revealed: City Would Demolish 682 Houses to Make Way for Over 2000 Families," *Boston Globe,* April 12, 1953, pp. 1, 58.

12. Urban Redevelopment Division, BHA, "Urban Redevelopment and the West End" n.d. (1953?), p. 7; Urban Redevelopment Division, BHA, *West End Project Report: A Preliminary Redevelopment Study of the West End of Boston,* March 1953, pp. 1, 36; Urban Redevelopment Division, BHA, "Urban Redevelopment and the West End," p. 4. When the Boston City Council debated the West End redevelopment plan in 1957, the initial resolution called the neighborhood "a substandard and decadent area" that was "detrimental to the safety, health, morals, and welfare of the inhabitants and users thereof and of the City of Boston at large . . ."

One councilor asked that the word *morals* be stricken. The motion carried and, with this amendment, the resolution was unanimously adopted [*Proceedings of the Boston City Council,* July 22, 1957, p. 207].

13. Urban Redevelopment Division, BHA, "Urban Redevelopment and the West End," pp. 2–3, 5, and "West End Progress Report," January 1956, p. 5.

14. Urban Redevelopment Division, BHA, "Urban Redevelopment and the West End." See also *West End Project Report: Preliminary Study*; "Urban Redevelopment and the West End," March 1954; "Relocation Plan: West End Land Assembly and Redevelopment Project," March 16, 1955; and "West End Progress Report," January 1956.

15. Urban Redevelopment Division, BHA, "Urban Redevelopment and the West End," March 1954. Those who owned land in the West End were promised "a fair price," and business proprietors were told that they could "bid on land in the proposed retail area" within the redeveloped complex, but were warned that "it must be recognized that with only one-third as many people in the redeveloped areas, there just will not be enough business to support most of the retail stores in the West End now" (p. 7).

16. Urban Renewal Division, BHA, "West End Progress Report," January 1956; Chester Hartman, "The Limitations of Public Housing: Relocation Choices in a Working-Class Community," *Journal of the American Institute of Planners* 29 (November 1963): 283–296, iand "The Housing of Relocated Families," pp. 266–286; O'Connor, *Building a New Boston*, pp. 135–139.

17. Hartman, "The Limitations of Public Housing," pp. 284–285.

18. Ibid., pp. 284–286.

19. Ibid., pp. 288–290. Italics in original.

20. Ibid., p. 293.

21. Ibid., pp. 285, 293–295.

22. John Stainton, *Urban Renewal and Planning in Boston: A Review of the Past and a Look at the Future* (Boston: Citizens' Housing and Planning Association and Boston Redevelopment Authority, November 1972), pp. 10–11.

23. Management Services, Inc., "A Comprehensive Program," pp. 4, 39, 54–57.

24. United South End Settlements and BHA, "First Evaluation Report of the Community Services Center Operating in the South End Housing Project, September 1960 to October 1961," November 1961, pp. 3–11, Mayor John F. Collins Papers (hereafter JFC Papers), box 68.

25. Management Services, Inc., "A Comprehensive Program," pp. 57, 61.

26. Ibid., pp. 61–63.

27. State Housing Board, *Housing for the Elderly: Standards of Design* (Boston: State Housing Board, March 1954), p. 13; "Architects' Fees—Housing for the Elderly Program," Memorandum from Harland A. McPhetres, director, Massachusetts State Housing Board, to Daniel Tyler, Jr., chairman, March 1954; "Housing for the Elderly," memorandum from Daniel Tyler, Jr., chairman, Massachusetts State Housing Board to all Massachusetts architects registered with the Massachusetts Board of Registration of Architects, July 1954.

28. State Housing Board, *Housing for the Elderly,* p. 13.

29. "Housing Project for Elderly People," *Proceedings of the Boston City Council,* October 1, 1956,

p. 283; "Additional Federally Aided Low-rent Housing," January 28, 1957, p. 18; "Report of Finance Commission for 3,000 Federally Aided Housing Units," August 19, 1957, p. 227–229.

30. "Report of Committee to Evaluate Request of Boston Housing Authority to Build Additional Public Housing," *Proceedings of the Boston City Council,* May 19, 1958, pp. 184–186; Overseers of the Public Welfare, "Housing Survey RE Elderly Persons," *Proceedings of the Boston City Council,* June 30, 1958, p. 236.

31. "Statement by Councilor Foley RE Housing for the Elderly," *Proceedings of the Boston City Council,* July 28, 1958, p. 271; "Study of Public Housing for Elderly People," ibid., August 4, 1958, p. 276.

32. Ibid.

33. Research Division, Boston City Planning Department, "Statistical Analysis of the Report to Mayor Hynes from the Overseers of the Public Welfare on the Housing Needs of the Elderly," *Proceedings of the Boston City Council,* August 18, 1958, pp. 280–282; "Executive Committee Report," ibid., September 15, 1958, p. 325.

34. "Approval for Reservation for Low-Rent Housing," *Proceedings of the Boston City Council,* May 23, 1960, pp. 111–112; "Report of Committee on Public Housing," ibid., May 22, 1961, pp. 116–117; "Information on Housing Program for the Elderly," ibid., October 31, 1966, pp. 212–214.

35. Meehan, *The Quality of Federal Policymaking,* pp. 36–37.

36. James H. Henderson (President, Rental Housing Association, Division of Greater Boston Real Estate Board), "Our Housing Competitor," *The Realtor,* 1960.

37. Ibid.

38. Management Services, Inc., "A Comprehensive Program," pp. 58, 60; BHA, "U.S. Bureau of the Census Report on Housing Conditions of Elderly Families in Boston," press release, May 12, 1961; "Name of Old Harbor Village Changed to Mary Ellen McCormack Project," *Proceedings of the Boston City Council,* May 22, 1961, p. 119.

39. "Franklin Field Elderly Project Wins Attention," *Boston City Record,* March 14, 1964, p. 212; JFC Papers, boxes 209, 257, 303.

40. BHA, *Annual Report, January 1, 1962–December 31, 1963* (Boston, 1964), p. 22.

41. Thomas H. O'Connor, *The Boston Irish* (Boston: Northeastern University Press, 1995), pp. 123–125.

42. *Proceedings of the Boston City Council,* January 11 and January 18, 1960, pp. 9, 14.

43. JFC Papers, boxes 60, 62. These lists initially did no more than generate "reports," and in many cases no housing could be immediately forthcoming.

44. Letter, Edward Hassan, BHA to Edward J. Logue, BRA, July 31, 1963, JFC Papers, box 61.

45. JFC Papers, box 315.

46. JFC Papers, boxes 60, 234, 235, 288.

47. James H. Crowley, Chief of Tenant Relations, BHA, letter to John H. O'Neill, Administrative Assistant to Mayor Collins, August 10, 1964, JFC Papers, box 62.

48. Public Housing Committee of the United Community Services, "A Proposal for the Establishment of a Department of Social Services and Community Relations Within the Boston Housing Authority," December 1963.

49. Alan Gartner, letter to Edward Hassan, April 9, 1963. BHA Administrative Files, Massachusetts State Archives.

50. Edward Hassan, letter to John F. Collins (in response to Robert Drinan's Advisory Committee on Minority Housing Report), March 12, 1964. JFC Papers, box 244.

51. Edward Hassan, "Memo to John F. Collins Re: Adoption by Boston Housing Authority of Statements titled 'Public Housing and Urban Renewal Interagency Policies and Procedures,'" June 8, 1964, JFC Papers, box 244; Hassan to Gartner, April 16, 1963.

52. Interview with Edward Logue, April 1996. See also Logue, quoted in Jane Roessner, *A Decent Place to Live: From Columbia Point to Harbor Point* (Boston: Northeastern University Press, 2000), p. 88.

53. Boston Redevelopment Authority, "Final Report on Family Relocation, Government Center Project Area," December 31, 1963, p. 2.

54. Boston Redevelopment Authority, "Final Relocation Report, New York Streets Project—UR Mass, 2-1," March 1958, p. 2, Exhibit A and Exhibit C; Boston Redevelopment Authority, "Final Report on Family Relocation, Government Center Project Area," December 31, 1963, pp. 3–4, 10, 22.

55. United South End Settlements, "Castle Square Residential Relocation Program: Final Report," February 1, 1964, p. 23.

56. Ibid., pp. 28–29.

57. Ibid.

58. Ibid., p. 53.

59. Boston Redevelopment Authority, Family Relocation Department, "Diagnostic Report: Residents of the South End Urban Renewal Project," June 1967; Edward Logue, memorandum to John F. Collins, "Relocation in Washington Park," March 15, 1963, JFC Papers, box 172; Langley Carleton Keyes, Jr., *The Rehabilitation Planning Game: A Study in the Diversity of Neighborhood* (Cambridge: MIT Press, 1969), pp. 186–187, 207; USES, Castle Square, p. 30.

60. Massachusetts General Laws, Chapter 479, Laws of 1950, approved May 23, 1950; State Housing Board, "Resolution No. 1, Establishing Tenant Selection Policies, Rental Schedules, Income Limits, and Policies and Standards for the Management of Veterans' Housing Developments," draft for discussion and final version, dated August 19, 1949; Francis X. Lane, BHA administrator, memorandum to the members of the Authority on "Management Resolution Suggested by State Housing Board for Chapter 200 Developments," June 7, 1949, BHA Administrative Files, Massachusetts State Archives; John Ihlder, executive director, National Capital Housing Authority, letter to Francis X. Lane, BHA administrator, January 4, 1952.

61. Edward D. Hassan, BHA Board chairman, to New York Regional Office, Public Housing Administration, responding to request for annual breakdown of federal projects by race, April 4, 1960.

62. Boston Branch NAACP vs. Boston Housing Authority, Complaint filed before Commonwealth of Massachusetts, Massachusetts Commission Against Discrimination, PH XIII-2-C, May 31, 1962.

63. James A. Travers, Mayor's Youth Activities Bureau, memorandum to mayoral aide John H.

O'Neill Jr. Re: "Mission Hill Racial Incident," June 26, 1962; Henry Leen, Roche and Leen, Attorneys at Law, memorandum to James A. Travers, July 6, 1962, JFC Papers, box 120.

64. Elmer (Emmy) Foster, Director of Citizens Relations, memorandum to John F. Collins, RE: "Columbia Point," July 17, 1962, JFC Papers, box 120. See also Roessner, *A Decent Place to Live,* pp. 56-64.

65. BHA, Central Administrative Files, Massachusetts State Archives.

66. *Boston Globe,* May 30, 1962; BHA Board, "Statement of the Boston Housing Authority to the Commonwealth of Massachusetts Commission Against Discrimination," April 1 and April 18, 1963.

67. May Boulter Hipshman, "Public Housing in Boston: Changing Needs and Role" (master's thesis, MIT, 1967), pp. 37-40, 44-45, and *Public Housing at the Crossroads: The Boston Housing Authority* (Boston: Massachusetts Committee on Discrimination in Housing; Commission on Housing, Metropolitan Boston Association, United Church of Christ; and Citizens' Housing and Planning Association of Metropolitan Boston, 1967), pp. xv, 60-61; JFC papers, boxes 60, 62.

68. Hipshman, "Public Housing in Boston," pp. 37-40, 44-45, and *Public Housing at the Crossroads,* pp. xv, 60-61; Anthony J. Yudis, "Public Housing Role—III: Social Work Experts Contend That Politics Hurts Hub Program, Want Full-Time Director," *Boston Globe,* January 29, 1963, p. 24.

69. "Choice of Housing Chief Postponed after Protest," *Boston Globe,* March 28, 1963; Jon Pynoos, "Breaking the Rules: Bureaucracy and Reform in Public Housing" (Ph.D. diss., Harvard University, 1974), p. 17.

70. Hipshman, "Public Housing in Boston" pp. 40, 48; Pynoos, "Breaking the Rules," p. 18; Massachusetts Committee on Discrimination in Housing, "Citizen Housing Group Lauds Ash Appointment as B.H.A. Director," press release, May 16, 1963.

71. Ellis Ash, BHA acting administrator to Ben Shapiro, MCAD commissioner, May 16, 1963.

72. Quoted in Philip MacDonnel, "The Process of Change at the Boston Housing Authority," (A.B. thesis, Harvard College, 1971), p. 46.

73. Interview with Ellis Ash, May 1997.

74. "Text of Housing Authority Statement" (June 19, 1963), *Boston Globe,* June 20, 1963; Anthony J. Yudis, "Hub Adopts Fair Housing," *Boston Globe,* June 20, 1963.

75. "Text of Housing Authority Statement," *Boston Globe,* June 20, 1963.

76. Edward D. Hassan, BHA chairman; Kenneth I. Guscott, president of the Boston branch of the NAACP, Alan Gartner, chairman, Greater Boston Chapter of the Congress on Racial Equality, "Joint Statement of Policy on Tenancy in Public Housing," November 15, 1963.

77. BHA, "Mission Statement: Department of Tenant and Community Relations," 1964, JFC Papers, box 244; Jim Travers, memorandum ("Important-Confidential") to John Collins Re: "Boston Housing Integration," March 1964; Ellis Ash, memorandum to John F. Collins, "Staffing of Department of Tenant and Community Relations," July 22, 1964, JFC Papers, box 244. More than thirty years later, when asked about the charge of anti-Catholic bias, Ash responded, "I am fascinated . . . My reaction is primarily one of interest and amusement. I cer-

tainly don't think that anything I did was related in a focal manner to Catholics"; interview, May 1997.

78. Tom Francis, executive secretary, Committee for Civic Unity, to John H. O'Neill, "[Confidential] Memo on 'Richard Scobie,'" March 24, 1964. JFC Papers, box 245.

79. BHA, "Evaluations of Intergroup Relations Orientation Institutes," July 1963, BHA Central Administrative Files, Massachusetts State Archives.

80. Hipshman, "Public Housing in Boston," pp. 41–42; interview with Ash, May 1997; Advisory Committee to the BHA, "Summary of Minutes," November 15, 1963–November 12, 1964, p. 3, BHA Central Administrative Files.

81. Robert Drinan and the Advisory Committee on Minority Housing, "[Confidential] Memo to Mayor," March 5, 1964, JFC Papers, box 244.

82. Interview with Ellis Ash, May 1997; Ellis Ash, "Statement to Special Commission on Low-Income Housing, Commonwealth of Massachusetts," November 23, 1964.

83. Robert C. Weaver to Ellis Ash, December 22, 1964, JFC papers, box 257; interview with Ellis Ash, May 1997.

84. Ellis Ash, "Memo to John F. Collins Re: Utilization of the Services of Mr. Richard Scobie on a Loan Basis from the United Community Services," March 1964, JFC Papers, box 244; Victor C. Bynoe, "[Confidential] Letter to John F. Collins," March 13, 1964, JFC Papers, box 244.

85. Ellis Ash to John F. Collins, February 4, 1965, JFC Papers, box 257; interview with Ellis Ash, May 1997.

86. Richard S. Scobie, director, Tenant and Community Relations Department, memorandum to Cornelius J. Connors, director, Research and Administrative Methods, "Boston Housing Authority Policies for Admittance and Continued Occupancy," January 26, 1965; BHA, "Resolution Establishing Policies and Standards Governing Occupancy of Federally Aided Developments," as approved November 3, 1965, pp. 16–17.

87. BHA, Department of Tenant and Community Relations, "Follow-up Study of a Selected Group of Tenants, Identified during Application Process as Potential Problem Families," July 1967, BHA Central Administrative Files; Pynoos, "Breaking the Rules," p. 21.

88. George Schermer Associates, *More than Shelter: Social Needs in Low- and Moderate-Income Housing,* prepared for the National Commission on Urban Problems, research report no. 8 (Washington, D.C.: U.S. GPO, 1968), pp. 75–76.

89. Albert J. Palmer, acting assistant administrator and director of management, memorandum to all housing managers, "Re: New Minimum Welfare Rent," October 26, 1964, BHA Central Administrative Files; BHA, "Resolution Establishing Policies and Standards Governing Occupancy of Federally Aided Developments," as approved November 3, 1965, pp. 15, 17, 19.

90. Ellis Ash, acting administrator, memorandum to James H. Crowley, chief of Tenant Selection and Tenant Status Review, "Re: Relationships Between Tenant Selection and the Department of Tenant and Community Relations," December 15, 1964; Hipshman, *Public Housing at the Crossroads,* p. 33; BHA, "Responses to Recommendations Made by Advisory Committee," February 3, 1964. This last document details the procedures used to prepare "pioneer" black families for placement in white projects.

91. Advisory Committee on Minority Housing, "Analysis of the Principal Impediments to Effec-

tive Implementation of the Agreement to Integrate," December 15, 1964, BHA Central Administrative Files.

92. Chester Hartman, "The Impact of Federal Housing and Community Development Programs on the Poverty Problem," report prepared for the Office of Economic Opportunity (OEO), 1966, quoted in Hipshman, *Public Housing at the Crossroads*, p. 33.

93. BHA, "Resolution Establishing Policies and Standards Governing Occupancy of Federally Aided Developments," as approved November 3, 1965, p. 19.

94. Interview with Ellis Ash, October 1972, cited in Citizens Housing and Planning Association et al., *A Struggle for Survival: The Boston Housing Authority, 1969-1973* (Boston, 1973), pp. iv-10; Advisory Committee to the BHA, "Third Annual Report and Recommendations of the Advisory Committee to the Boston Housing Authority," November 10, 1966, pp. 1-2; Boston Municipal Research Bureau, "Survey of Boston Departments and Agencies Concerned with Housing, Development and Environmental Control," March 1969, p. 16; Lewis Michael Popper, "The Boston Housing Authority: A Study of Conflict in Bureaucracy" (honors thesis, Harvard College, 1968), pp. 40, 42, 75, 85, 94.

95. BHA Advisory Committee, "Minutes," February 10, 1966; Pynoos, "Breaking the Rules," p. 25.

96. Ellis Ash to Joseph J. Kohler, assistant director for management, Public Housing Administration, New York Regional Office, March 23, 1966; Ash to Edward Siegfried, CC Housing Committee, December 21, 1966; BHA, "Responses to Recommendations Made by Advisory Committee," February 3, 1965; Pynoos, "Breaking the Rules," p. 29.

97. BHA Advisory Committee, "Fourth Annual Report of the Advisory Committee to the Boston Housing Authority," November 1967, BHA Central Administrative Files; Subcommittee on Minority Housing, "Minutes of Meeting with Mayor," July 15, 1964, JFC Papers, box 62. BHA efforts to hire more nonwhites were hampered both by the tenure system that encouraged older employees to hold onto their jobs, and by the relative absence of blacks in the eleven unions that held considerable power over appointments (BHA Advisory Committee, "Minutes of the Meeting," October 20, 1966, BHA Central Administrative Files).

98. Pynoos, "Breaking the Rules," p. 28.

99. Orchard Park Tenants, "Petition to the Boston Housing Authority," June 12, 1964, BHA Central Administrative Files; Edward Hassan, memorandum to John H. O'Neill, "Re: Transfers," January 7, 1964, JFC Papers, box 120. During the first nine months of 1964, more than one-third of all transfers systemwide had been granted, without Ash's knowledge, to white tenants wishing to move out of Orchard Park; Ellis Ash, "Transfer Policies and Practices," January 19, 1965, BHA Central Administrative Files.

100. BHA, "Responses to Recommendations Made by Advisory Committee," February 3, 1965; BHA Advisory Committee, "Report of Subcommittee to Analyze Responses to Recommendations of the Advisory Committee," July 22, 1965, p. 3.

101. National Committee against Discrimination in Housing, *How the Federal Government Builds Ghettos* (New York, 1967), pp. 17, 25.

102. Ibid., pp. 17, 25.

103. *Boston Globe,* April 19, 1969, quoted in Pynoos, "Breaking the Rules," p. 36.

104. Pynoos, "Breaking the Rules," p. 40.

105. Quoted in Pynoos, "Breaking the Rules," p. 72.

106. Pynoos studied the relationship between race and housing conditions among BHA applicants, and found that blacks were much more likely than whites to be living in housing classified as "bad" or "terrible," and that those who lived in the worst housing conditions were much more likely to accept public housing under the 1-2-3 plan; ibid., pp. 73–75, 80.

107. Hipshman, "Public Housing in Boston," p. 76. By this time, the BHA began acknowledging that its nonwhite tenants were not all "Negro." In 1967, 43 percent of the applicants were listed as black, and an additional 16 percent were classified as Puerto Rican (many of whom may have preferred to self-identify, in racial terms, as white).

108. Pynoos, "Breaking the Rules," pp. 68–69.

109. Ibid., p. 153.

110. Ibid., pp. 82–83.

111. Ibid., pp. 96–97. Pynoos also identified two other groups: "survivalists," who changed their views according to what was thought necessary to preserve their jobs, and "avoiders," who simply tried to minimize their contact with applicants and tended to be the lowest ranked employees in their division, with little decisionmaking control.

112. Hipshman, "Public Housing in Boston," pp. 62–66. Compared to the national public housing authority average, Boston managers were disproportionately white males and considerably less well-educated; Chester Hartman and Margaret Levi, "Public Housing Managers: An Appraisal," *Journal of the American Institute of Planners* (March 1973), pp. 127, 131–132. Other studies showed that Housing Authority Boards (94 percent white and 91 percent male) and executive directors (97 percent white and 79 percent male) were even less likely to resemble the race, ethnicity, and gender of the households they served; Chester Hartman and G. Carr, "Housing Authorities Reconsidered," *Journal of the American Institute of Planners* 35 (January 1969), pp. 10–21, and "Local Public Housing Administration: An Appraisal," working paper no. 137 (Berkeley: Center for Planning and Development Research, University of California, 1970).

113. Pynoos, "Breaking the Rules," pp. 195–199, 245. For case studies revealing the wildly different practices at Mary Ellen McCormack and Columbia Point, see Jeffrey Manditch Prottas, "Techniques of the Weak in Bureaucratic Conflict: The Case of Public Housing" (Department of City and Regional Planning, Harvard University, April 1978).

114. Interview with Elaine Werby, December 1995.

115. Interview with Doris Bunte, November 1995; *Proceedings of the Boston City Council,* February 19, 1968, January 12, 1970; Julius Bernstein, Doris Bunte, and John Connolly, "A Statement of Objectives," included in CHPA et al., *A Struggle for Survival: The Boston Housing Authority, 1969–1973,* app. B, p. 3.

116. Interview with Ellis Ash, May 1997.

117. Interview with Doris Bunte, November 1995; Herbert P. Gleason, corporation counsel, City of Boston Law Department, letter to Mayor Kevin H. White, February 2, 1971, BHA Administrative Files; Herbert P. Gleason, letter to the Boston City Council, February 2, 1971, BHA Administrative Files; "Appointment and Confirmation of Doris Bunte as a Member of the Boston

Housing Authority," and "Certified Copy of Final Judgment, Bunte vs. Kevin White et al.," *Proceedings of the Boston City Council,* February 14 and 28, 1972, pp. 76-77, 92; Stephen Curwood, "Court orders Bunte reinstated to BHA Board," *Bay State Banner,* February 10, 1972, pp. 1, 8; "Mrs. Bunte's reinstatement delayed," *Bay State Banner,* February 17, 1972, pp. 1, 24; "Bunte rejoins BHA, model lease adopted," *Bay State Banner,* March 9, 1972, p. 1.

118. J. Anthony Lukas, *Common Ground: A Turbulent Decade in the Lives of Three American Families* (New York: Vintage, 1986), p. 220.

119. Pynoos, "Breaking the Rules," pp. 84-85, 93-94; interview with Doris Bunte, November 1995. A HUD audit of the BHA in 1972 found evidence that one doctor had written more than thirty nearly identical letters for various patients requesting exceptional placements; Pynoos, p. 225.

120. Pynoos, "Breaking the Rules," p. 110; interview with Doris Bunte, November 1995; Daniel Finn, BHA administrator to Herman D. Hillman, assistant regional administrator, Housing Assistance, HUD, March 16, 1970.

121. Pynoos, "Breaking the Rules," pp. 89, 232.

122. Welfare Department letters to the mayor's office are in JFC Papers, box 244.

123. BHA, Central Administrative Files. See Henry J. Aaron, *Shelter and Subsidies: Who Benefits from Federal Housing Policies?* (Washington, D.C.: The Brookings Institution, 1972), pp. 116-117.

124. Pynoos, "Breaking the Rules," pp. 44, 129-130, 149, 161.

125. Ibid., pp. 60-61, 225; U.S. Department of Housing and Urban Development, Boston Area Office, *Comprehensive Consolidated Management Review Report on the Housing Authority of the City of Boston* (Boston, 1972), p. 144.

126. Pynoos, "Breaking the Rules," pp. 64-65, 67.

127. Richard S. Scobie, *Problem Tenants in Public Housing: Who, Where, and Why Are They?* (New York: Praeger, 1975), pp. 65, 73, 75.

128. Ibid.; Gerald Taube, "Social Structural Sources of Residential Satisfaction-Dissatisfaction in Public Housing" (Ph.D. diss., Brandeis University, 1972), p. 226.

129. "Redesignation of Housing Projects," *Proceedings of the Boston City Council,* August 20, 1973, pp. 627-628.

130. Wright Patman (D-Texas), quoted in R. Allen Hays, *The Federal Government and Urban Housing* (New York: State University of New York Press, 1985), p. 87; HUD handbook quoted in U.S. Department of Housing and Urban Development, "Interest Rate Subsidies: National Housing Policy Review," in *Federal Housing Policy & Programs: Past and Present,* ed. J. Paul Mitchell (New Brunswick, N.J.: Center for Urban Policy Research, 1985), p. 337; John F. Bauman, "Public Housing: The Dreadful Saga of a Durable Policy," *Journal of Planning Literature* 8 (May 1994): 356.

131. Robert Whittlesey, "Planning for BHA Developments," in "Report of the Master in the Case of *Perez v. Boston Housing Authority*," CA 03096, July 1976, p. VII-3; CHPA et al., *A Struggle for Survival,* pp. III-1-3.

132. Rachel G. Bratt, "Public Housing: The Controversy and the Contribution," in *Critical Per-*

spectives on Housing, ed. Rachel Bratt, Chester Hartman, and Ann Meyerson (Philadelphia: Temple University Press, 1986), pp. 341–342; Bauman, "Public Housing," p. 358.

133. Hays, *The Federal Government and Urban Housing*, pp. 144–145; CHPA et al., *A Struggle for Survival*, pp. III-2, 6–10; Bauman, "Public Housing," p. 356; Charles Tilly, Joe R. Feagin, and Constance Williams, "Rent Supplements in Boston: An Evaluation of the Boston Housing Authority Program of Rent Supplements for Large Low-Income Families, 1964–1967" (Joint Center for Urban Studies, Massachusetts Institute of Technology and Harvard University, 1968), p. 216.

134. U.S. Department of Housing and Urban Development, "1997 Picture of Subsidized Households Quick Facts" (Office of Policy Development and Research, 1998); "Approving Application to HUD for 2,120 Units under Leased Housing Program," *Proceedings of the Boston City Council*, July 22, 1974, p. 454.

135. Robert Moore Fisher, *Twenty Years of Public Housing: Economic Aspects of the Federal Program* (Westport Conn.: Greenwood Press, 1959).

136. Aaron, *Shelter and Subsidies*, p. 116.

137. BHA, "A Fiscal Crisis in State-Aided Public Housing," March 1970, pp. 1–11; CHPA et al., *A Struggle for Survival*, pp. II-1–3; Robert Taggart, *Low Income Housing: A Critique of Federal Aid* (Baltimore: Johns Hopkins Press, 1970), p. 32. See also Frank deLeeuw, assisted by Eleanor Littman Jarutis, *Operating Costs in Public Housing: A Financial Crisis* (Washington, D.C., The Urban Institute, 1969).

138. Lisa Peattie, "Conventional Public Housing," working paper no. 3 (Cambridge, Mass.: Joint Center Working Papers, Massachusetts Institute of Technology, February 1972), p. 4; Robert B. Whittlesey, "Financial Condition of BHA," in "Report of the Master in the Case of *Perez v. Boston Housing Authority*," CA 03096, July 1976, pp. II-1–14. The state legislation occurs as Chapter 854 of the Laws of 1970, Chapter 694 of the Laws of 1970, and Chapter 1114 of the Laws of 1971; *Proceedings of the Boston City Council*, February 9, November 22, and December 21, 1976, pp. 132–133, 951, 1049.

139. Whittlesey, "Report of the Master," pp. I-1–3.

140. Ibid.

141. Interview with Robert Whittlesey, April 1996; Robert Whittlesey, "Report of the Master," pp. I-8, 22. Whittlesey credits Dan Sullivan with having written much of the 1,500-page report.

142. Interview with Robert Whittlesey, April 1996.

143. Interview with John Murphy, chief of Tenant Selection, November 1995; Samuel Thompson, BHA administrator, letter to Robert Whittlesey, December 13, 1976. Master's Files, Massachusetts State Archives; interview with Robert Whittlesey, April 1996.

144. Interview with Robert Whittlesey, April 1996. The master's report echoed and updated the sorts of disparaging conclusions already reached in 1972; HUD, *Comprehensive Consolidated Management Review Report of the Housing Authority of the City of Boston*, pp. 48, 50–51, 57–60, 74.

145. Interview with Robert Whittlesey, April 1996.

146. Whittlesey, "Report of the Master," pp. I-52–53; IX-30–39. When the BHA sent out letters to a

thousand households on its waiting list to inform them of the preferences given to those willing to move into developments where they would be in the racial minority, only five applicants indicated an interest in such an option; Jon Pynoos, *Breaking the Rules: Bureaucracy and Reform in Public Housing* (New York: Plenum, 1987), p. 162.

147. Whittlesey, "Report of the Master," pp. IX-14–15, 22–24, 31, 39; Robert Schafer, "Racial Discrimination in the Boston Housing Market," *Journal of Urban Economics* 6 (1979): 176–196.

148. Interview with John Murphy, chief of Tenant Selection, November 1995.

149. Interview with Murphy, November 1995; Whittlesey, "Report of the Master," pp. IX-66–76.

150. Whittlesey, "Report of the Master," pp. VI-1, 26–27.

151. Bradley Biggs, BHA administrator, "Memorandum to All Employees Re: 'Employee Attitudes,'" August 18, 1978, BHA Central Administrative Files.

152. BHA, "Occupancy Analysis by Development Classification," January 31, 1979, receiver's files, Massachusetts State Archives.

153. Paul Garrity, "Findings of the Massachusetts Superior Court, with Memorandum of Recorded Observations at the Commonwealth Development During the View on April 11, 1979" and "Memorandum of Recorded Observations at the Orient Heights, D Street, and Mission Hill Main Developments During the View on April 19, 1979," *Perez* case, July 25, pp. 102–103.

154. Alan Sheehan, "State Court Backs BHA Receivership," *Boston Globe*, February 4, 1980, p. 1.

5 THE BOSTON HOUSING AUTHORITY SINCE 1980

1. BHA Planning Department, *State of the Development Report,* October 1979; Esther Scott, *Managing the Boston Housing Authority: The Receivership Begins,* John F. Kennedy School of Government Case Program (Cambridge, Mass.: Harvard University, 1985), pp. 1–3; Bernard Cohen, "Is Harry Spence God? Or Is He Just Damn Good?" *Boston Magazine,* December 1981, p. 170.

2. Cohen, "Is Harry Spence God?" p. 170.

3. Quoted in Eric T. Schneiderman, *Perez v. Boston Housing Authority: A Case Study in Institutional Reform Legislation,* Harvard Law School case (Cambridge, Mass.: Harvard Law School, 1982), p. 40.

4. *Perez et al. v. Boston Housing Authority, Order of Appointment of Receiver,* Superior Court Civil Action No. 17222, February 4, 1980, pp. 1–9.

5. Lewis H. Spence, "The Plight of Public Housing," speech delivered at the annual meeting of United Community Planning Corporation, April 23, 1980, p. 4.

6. Ibid., pp. 5–6.

7. Cohen, "Is Harry Spence God?" p. 44; Robert Lovinger, "Can This Man Save Public Housing? The Boston Housing Authority's Harry Spence," *Boston Globe Magazine,* August 23, 1981, p. 26.

8. Spence, "Plight of Public Housing," p. 8.

9. Ibid.

10. Interview with Harry Spence, September 1995.

11. Harry Spence, "Speech to the United Community Planning Corporation" (April 1981), quoted in Lovinger, "Can This Man Save Public Housing?," p. 41.

12. Interview with John Murphy, November 1995.

13. Interview with Basil Tommy, February 1994.

14. *Perez v. Boston Housing Authority*, "Findings, Rulings and Orders," Superior Court No. 17222, November 13, 1984. On efforts to reform management practices, see Rochelle Bates Lee, "A Report on the Boston Housing Authority's Management Program During Court Receivership, 1980-1984" (master's thesis, MIT, 1984).

15. Quoted in Elizabeth Laurance March, "Money Makes It Easier: Turning Around Large Troubled Housing Projects" (master's thesis, MIT, 1983), p. 42.

16. Interview with Spence, September 1995. See also Jane Roessner, *A Decent Place to Live: From Columbia Point to Harbor Point* (Boston: Northeastern University Press, 2000), pp. 184-203.

17. For details of the Commonwealth redevelopment effort, see Lawrence J. Vale, "The Revitalization of Boston's Commonwealth Development," in Willem van Vliet, ed., *Affordable Housing and Urban Development in the United States,* Urban Affairs Annual Reviews 46 (Thousand Oaks, Calif.: Sage, 1996), pp. 100-134.

18. In 1992, Commonwealth was featured as one of only four public housing "turnaround" efforts nationwide deemed worthy of inclusion in a book of case studies sponsored by the National Commission on Severely Distressed Public Housing; *National Commission on Severely Distressed Public Housing, Case Studies and Site Examination Reports,* chap. 4, "Commonwealth Development" (Washington, D.C.: U.S. GPO, 1992). The redevelopment effort has also received an Urban Design Award from the Boston Society of Architects in 1985, a Governor's Design Award in 1986, a Merit Award for landscaping for multifamily housing from the Boston Society of Landscape Architects in 1987, and the Urban Land Institute's 1989 Award for Excellence in the category of Rehabilitation Development.

19. Lawrence J. Vale, "Public Housing Redevelopment: Seven Kinds of Success," *Housing Policy Debate* 7 (1996): 491-534, and "Empathological Places: Residents' Ambivalence Toward Remaining in Public Housing," *Journal of Planning Education and Research* 16 (1997): 159-175.

20. See Lawrence J. Vale, "Transforming Public Housing: The Social and Physical Redevelopment of Boston's West Broadway Development," *Journal of Architectural and Planning Research* 12 (Autumn, 1995): 278-305; interview with Sandra Henriquez, Janurary 2000. Commonwealth received $31.6 million (in 1983 dollars) for 392 units, Franklin Field received approximately $26 million for 346 units, and West Broadway received about $26.5 million, which was expected to cover only the first phases of the redevelopment, with the full costs for 675 apartments estimated to be upwards of $60 million; Executive Office of Communities and Development (Massachusetts), *Redevelopment Handbook: Procedures and Guidelines for Redeveloping Public Housing* (Boston, 1990), p. 74. Per-unit total redevelopment costs were therefore in the range of $75,000-$80,000 (in 1983 dollars).

21. This account of Columbia Point's transformation draws upon Lawrence J. Vale, "Columbia Point," *Encyclopedia of Housing* (Thousand Oaks, Calif.: Sage, 1998). See also Roessner, *A Decent Place to Live,* pp. 191-192.

22. Spence, "The Plight of Public Housing," pp. 3-4.

23. Lewis Harry Spence, "Reagan's Big Lie," *Boston Observer,* May 1982, p. 6.

24. Michael H. Schill, "Distressed Public Housing: Where Do We Go From Here?" *University of Chicago Law Review* 60 (1993): 517; Lewis H. Spence, "Rethinking the Social Role of Public Housing." *Housing Policy Debate* 4,3 (1993): 359.

25. Interview with Harry Spence, September 1995.

26. Jon Pynoos, *Breaking the Rules: Bureaucracy and Reform in Public Housing* (New York: Plenum, 1986), pp. 177–181; "Housing Boston's Poor" [Editorial], *Boston Globe,* April 26, 1984; Interview with Harry Spence, September 1995.

27. Pynoos, *Breaking the Rules,* pp. 179–180; Monica Hileman, "Wrong Way to Select Tenants," *Boston Globe,* April 28, 1984; Coalition for Basic Human Needs, "Letter to the Editor of the *Boston Globe,*" May 21, 1983; Michael K. Frisby, "BHA Shelves Plan Giving Housing Preference to Working Poor," *Boston Globe,* July 17, 1984.

28. Interview with Harry Spence, September 1995.

29. *Armando Perez et al. v. Boston Housing Authority,* "Findings, Rulings and Orders," November 13, 1984, pp. 1–2, 5, 20–26.

30. Ibid., p. 24.

31. Interview with Don Gillis, former BHA community organizer and subsequent executive director of Boston's Economic Development and Industrial Corporation (EDIC), March 1994; interview with Harry Spence, September 1995.

32. National Commission on Severely Distressed Public Housing, *The Final Report of the National Commission on Severely Distressed Public Housing* (Washington, D.C.: U.S. GPO, 1992); U.S. Department of Housing and Urban Development, "The Transformation of America's Public Housing: A 1996 Status Report," http://www.hud.gov/pih/pihcont.html.

33. David J. Cortiella, "Diversity in Housing: Working Poor Families Never Even Had a Chance," editorial, *Boston Globe,* April 24, 1994, p. 71; Michael Rezendes, "Opening Doors? Police Sweeps Have Gotten the Headlines, But New Eligibility Guidelines are What May Change the Face of Public Housing," *Boston Globe,* April 24, 1994, p. 65.

34. Cortiella, "Diversity in Housing," p. 71; Peter S. Canellos, "BHA Seeks OK to Limit Priority for Homeless," *Boston Globe,* September 11, 1992, pp. 25, 31.

35. Quoted in Canellos, "BHA Seeks OK to Limit Priority for Homeless," p. 25.

36. Hitov and Marsh are quoted in ibid., p. 31.

37. Lawrence J. Vale, "Beyond the Problem Projects Paradigm: Defining and Revitalizing 'Severely Distressed' Public Housing," *Housing Policy Debate* 4, 2 (1993); HUD, "The Transformation of America's Public Housing: A 1996 Status Report," p. 2; Wayne Sherwood, *Demographic Characteristics of Public and Indian Housing Residents,* CLPHA Report 95-1 (Washington, D.C., 1995). Many critics of such figures—including some public housing residents—point out that a lot of earned income goes unreported.

38. Interview with John Murphy, November 1995.

39. Jack Kemp, "Passage Out of Poverty," editorial, *Washington Post,* August 12, 1992, in response to Lawrence J. Vale, "Jack Kemp's Pet Delusion," editorial, *Washington Post,* August 3, 1992.

40. U.S. Department of Housing and Urban Development, "Notice of Funding Availability (NOFA) for Public Housing Demolition, Site Revitalization, and Replacement Housing

Grants (HOPE VI)," *Federal Register,* July 22, 1996; HUD, "The Transformation of America's Public Housing: A 1996 Status Report", and *A New HUD: Opportunity For All, 1997 Consolidated Report* (Washington, D.C.: HUD, 1998), pp. 53-55.

41. Charles Adams, Elsa Gutierrez, Langley Keyes, Mary Quesada, and David Thacher, "HOPE VI Baseline Study: Mission Main, Boston, Massachusetts." In U.S. Department of Housing and Urban Development, *An Historical and Baseline Assessment of HOPE VI, Volume II: Case Studies* (Washington, D.C.: U.S. Department of Housing and Urban Development, Office of Policy Development and Research, August 1996), pp. 16-19.

42. Adams et al., "HOPE VI Baseline Study," p. 8; BHA, *"Mission Main Redevelopment: HOPE VI Program, Phase 2, Request for Development Proposals* (Boston: BHA, January 31, 1996), pp. 9, 12.

43. Adams et al., "HOPE VI Baseline Study," p. 30.

44. Winn/Peabody/Cruz Management Company, "Mission Main: A World of New Beginnings," n.d. (c. 1999); BHA, "Media Advisory: A Mission Main Grand Opening and Ribbon Cutting Ceremony," November 8, 1999; BHA, "HOPE 6 Mission Main Project Summary," n.d.; interview with Sandra Henriquez, January 2000.

45. BHA, *Orchard Park Neighborhood Revitalization: Final Submission, Implementation Grant Application, HOPE VI Plus* (Boston: BHA and Orchard Park Tenants Association [OPTA], September 1, 1995), pp. ES-1, 2.

46. BHA, *Orchard Park Revitalization Initiative: HOPE VI program, Phase 2, Request for Development Proposals* (Boston: BHA, February 2, 1996), p. 8; Richard Chacón, "Orchard Park Set for $50m Makeover," *Boston Globe,* April 7, 1996, pp. 29, 31.

47. BHA, *Orchard Park Neighborhood Revitalization,* p. ES-2.

48. Ibid., p. ES-7; BHA, "Hope 6 Orchard Park," October 1998.

49. U.S. Department of Housing and Urban Development, *An Historical and Baseline Assessment of HOPE VI* (3 vols.) (Washington, D.C.: U.S. Department of Housing and Urban Development, Office of Policy Development and Research, August 1996).

50. Ibid., vol. 1, p. 5-4.

51. See, for example, Sharon Cohen, "The Great Bulldozing," *Associated Press Newsfeatures,* February 25, 1996; Rob Gurwitt, "Breaking Up the Ghetto: The Projects Come Down," *Governing* 8 (November 1995): 16-22.

52. BHA Elderly Housing Task Force, "Mayor Thomas M. Menino's BHA Elderly Housing Task Force Final Report," February 21, 1995, 29 pp.; Don Aucoin, "Mayor Eyes Privatizing Elderly Housing: Report Cites Poor Conditions, Mismanagement," *Boston Globe,* February 2, 1995, pp. 17, 19; Adrian Walker, "Panel: Privatization Won't Cure All of BHA's Elderly Housing Woes," *Boston Globe,* February 23, 1995; interview with Sandra Henriquez, August 1998.

53. Michael K. Frisby, "Integration Goes Slowly at Boston Housing Projects," *Boston Globe,* October 21, 1987, pp. 1, 17.

54. Michael Rezendes, "BHA Seeks OK on Choice Plan: Backers of 'Alternate Feed' Proposal Hope It Will Ease Racial Tension," *Boston Globe,* August 28, 1992, p. 25.

55. Michael Grunwald, "A Fresh Path to Public Housing," *Boston Globe,* pp. E1-E2; Charles A. Radin, "Public Housing Turns Back on Past: Despite Trouble Spots, Many See Racial Ten-

sions Easing at BHA Developments," *Boston Globe,* February 4, 1998, pp. A1, B4; Charles A. Radin, "BHA's Eviction Statistics Rebut Critics: Figures Show Blacks, Not Whites, Are More Likely to Be Removed," *Boston Globe,* January 27, 1998; Tatsha Robertson, "Racial Tension Mars Development," *Boston Globe,* August 13, 1998, pp. B1, B5; McGonagle quoted in Derrick Z. Jackson, "Squeeze Is On for Housing," *Boston Globe,* February 6, 1998, p. A25.

56. Michael Rezendes, "Housing Choice Plan OK Seen Near," *Boston Globe,* August 5, 1992, pp. 23, 26.

57. Cited in Michael Grunwald, "Issues of Rights, Bias Raised by BHA Attempt to Give Tenants Choice," *Boston Globe,* September 22, 1994.

58. Donald Martelli, "2 S. Boston Youths Held in Racially Tied Street Fight," *Boston Globe,* March 4, 1996; Karen Avenoso, "Looking Out For Trouble: Racial Discord Weighs Heavily on Residents of Old Colony," *Boston Globe,* April 29, 1996, pp. 1, 8; Mike Barnicle, "About Racism at Old Colony," *Boston Globe,* May 3, 1994; Stephanie McLaughlin, "S. Boston Woman's Windows Vandalized: BB Attack Seen as Racially Motivated," *Boston Globe,* February 17, 1995; Zachary R. Dowdy and Ric Kahn, "Youth Pleads Not Guilty in Stabbings," *Boston Globe* January 3, 1996; Kevin Cullen, "S. Boston Says Its Problems Ignored: Change Has Brought Stress With It," *Boston Globe,* May 5, 1993, pp. 29, 36; Ric Kahn, "Suspect Charged in Racial Attack at South Boston Project," *Boston Globe,* February 21, 1997, p. B2; "Housekeeping at the BHA," editorial, *Boston Globe,* January 18, 1997; interview with Sandra Henriquez, August 1998.

59. Michael Grunwald, "U.S. Says BHA Held Units For Whites: Probe Focuses on S. Boston Project," *Boston Globe,* December 13, 1995; Michael Grunwald, "Menino on BHA: Mixed Feelings," *Boston Globe,* December 14, 1995.

60. Interview with Henriquez, August 1998.

61. Interview with Sandra Henriquez, January 2000; Stephanie Ebbert, "BHA Director Facing a History of Problems; After 3 years, she wins some accolades," *Boston Globe,* February 21, 1999, pp. B1, B4; Judy Rakowsky and Louise Palmer, "U.S. Officials fault BHA for 'Systematic' Bias," *Boston Globe,* February 18, 1999, pp. A1, A22; Tatsha Robertson, "HUD Chief Sees BHA Gains," *Boston Globe,* May 16, 1999, pp. B1, B5; Marie Bernard, "BHA Honored for Diversity Program," *Boston Globe,* March 7, 1999; Brian MacQuarrie, "Evictions Pit BHA Against 3 Families," *Boston Globe,* January 15, 1998, pp. B1, B6; Anne Kornblut, "Bromley-Heath Officers Cite Lack of Support," *Boston Globe,* pp. B1, B6; Judy Rakowsky, "Bromley Ex-managers Fault BHA Approach," *Boston Globe,* December 31, 1998; Judy Rakowsky, "Bromley, BHA Reach Agreement," *Boston Globe,* January 30, 1999, p. B1.

62. Indira A. R. Lakshmanan, "Curbs Near in Legal Aid for the Poor," *Boston Globe,* March 26, 1996, pp. 1, 9.

63. William M. Rohe and Rachel Garshick Kleit, "From Dependency to Self-Sufficiency: An Appraisal of the Gateway Transitional Families Program," *Housing Policy Debate* 8 (1997): 75–108, and "Returning Public Housing to its Roots: An Assessment of the Family Self-Sufficiency Program," paper presented at the Housing in the 21st Century Conference, sponsored by the Housing and Built Environment Committee of the International Sociological Association, Alexandria, Virginia, June 1997, p. 7; BHA, "Mission Statement," 1998.

64. Michael Wiseman, "Welfare Reform in the United States: A Background Paper," *Housing Policy Debate* 7, 4 (1996): 595–648.

65. Interview with Henriquez, August 1998; Doris Sue Wong and Francie Latour, "For 5,800 Families, Reckoning Near," *Boston Globe,* November 27, 1998, pp. A1, A12–A13, A15; Zachary R. Dowdy, "Homelessness Rising Despite Brisk Economy," *Boston Globe,* October 12, 1998, pp. B1, B4.

66. "Congress Drops Last-Ditch Effort at Overhauling Public Housing," *Washington Post,* September 28, 1996; Lazio, cited in Flynn McRoberts, "Public Housing Reform Bill Dies Political Death: Congress Itching to Work Instead on Re-election," *Chicago Tribune,* September 28, 1996.

67. Quality Housing and Work Responsibility Act (QHWRA) of 1998 (H.R. 4194).

68. Edward W. Brooke, "Save the Brooke Amendment," editorial, *Boston Globe,* May 8, 1996; "Tenant Advocates Oppose Bill Lifting Cap on Rents," *Richmond Times-Dispatch,* April 26, 1996; "[Un]affordable Housing," editorial, *Christian Science Monitor,* May 6, 1996; Laura Barrett and Timothy Saasta, "Hitting the Poor While They're Down," editorial, *St. Louis Post-Dispatch,* May 2, 1996; Michael Grunwald, "GOP Seeks to Repeal Public Housing Bill: Shift from Income-Based to Market Rents Sought," *Boston Globe,* April 30, 1996; James Dao, "Bill to Open Up Public Housing Is Near Accord: More Working Families Instead of Very Poor," *New York Times,* August 19, 1998, pp. A1, A33; QHWRA of 1998, sec. 523.

69. QHWRA of 1998, sec. 513; interviews with Henriquez, August 1998, January 2000; Stephanie Ebbert, "Housing Bill Offers New Options for Middle Class," *Boston Globe,* October 12, 1998, pp. B1, B4.

70. The abolition of federal preferences for public housing initially appeared, in January 1996, as a rule passed as part of a "continuing resolution" during protracted federal budget negotiations, and was subsequently included as sec. 514 of the QHWRA of 1998, and sec. 575 dealt with eviction procedures; Michael Grunwald, "Housing Deal Hits Needy Hard," *Boston Globe,* March 2, 1996, pp. 1, 6.

71. Hillary Jones, quoted in Grunwald, "A Fresh Path to Public Housing," p. E2; "'One Strike and You're Out': U.S. Seeks to Banish Felons from Public Housing," *CNN Interactive,* March 28, 1996; QHWRA of 1998 (H.R. 4194), secs. 506, 524, 575–578.

72. QHWRA of 1998, secs. 502, 512. The community service requirement exempts those tenants who are elderly or disabled, as well as those who are working, attending school or vocational training or complying with public assistance work requirements.

73. Quoted in Mike Dorning, "House Passes Overhaul of Public Housing: Goal is to Boost Access for Families of Working Poor," *Chicago Tribune,* May 15, 1997, p. 22.

74. On the other hand, it is a policy that finds favor in many quarters. In Boston, Henriquez acknowledges concerns about equity and stigma, but nonetheless hopes that a mandatory community service program could be defined broadly enough to provide useful activities based in housing developments; interview with Henriquez, January 2000.

75. In Boston, in advance of a concerted effort to recruit more working families, the question of ceiling rents seemed a moot point. As of 1996, BHA officials determined that only 65 out of 15,000 public housing tenant families were paying more than fair market rent for their apart-

ments, and promised these few a reduction (Grunwald, "Housing Deal Hits Needy Hard," p. 6); QHWRA of 1998, secs. 519, 523.

76. Quoted in Mike Dorning, "Congress Ready to OK Public Housing Overhaul," *Chicago Tribune,* March 27, 1997.

77. Quoted in Clarence Page, "Will Dole's Olive Branch to Poor Hurt His Presidential Bid?" *Chicago Tribune,* May 1, 1996.

78. Interview with Henriquez, January, 2000. For another account of the reasons why so many public housing residents prefer to stay put, see Lawrence J. Vale, "Empathological Places: Residents' Ambivalence Toward Remaining in Public Housing," *Journal of Planning Education and Research* 16 (1997), pp. 159–175.

79. Interview with Henriquez, August 1998.

80. QHWRA of 1998, sec. 513.

81. Ibid., sec. 531; U.S. Department of Housing and Urban Development, *A New HUD: Opportunity for All,* p. 53; U.S. Department of Housing and Urban Development, *HUD Budget: F.Y. 2001* (Washington, D.C.: HUD, February 2000), p. 31.

82. Interview with Spence, September 1995.

83. Kevin Cullen, "'Project' Label Dropped by BHA," *Boston Globe,* June 11, 1993.

84. U.S. Department of Housing and Urban Development, Office of Policy Development and Research, *Rental Housing Assistance: The Crisis Continues* (Washington, D.C., April 1998), p. 1.

CREDITS

Fig. 1.1 John Winthrop, *Winthrop's Journal (History of New England)*, vol. 1, ed. James Kendall Hosmer (New York: Charles Scribner's Sons, 1908).

Figs. 1.2, 1.4, 1.9 Courtesy of the Norman B. Leventhal Map Collection.

Figs. 1.3, 1.5, 1.6, 1.7 Caleb H. Snow, *A History of Boston* (Boston: Abel Bowen, 1828), pp. 322a, 52a, i, 376a.

Fig. 1.8 *The American Magazine of Useful and Entertaining Knowledge*, 1, 2 (October 1834): 51.

Figs. 1.11, 1.14, 3.9 Michael P. Conzen and George K. Lewis, *Boston: A Geographical Portrait* (Cambridge: Ballinger, 1976), p. 37.

Fig. 1.12 *Report of the Committee on Internal Health on the Asiatic Cholera* (Boston, 1849), p. 171.

Fig. 1.13 Benjamin O. Flower, *Civilization's Inferno* (Boston, 1893).

Fig. 2.1 Adapted from maps by Anne Beamish.

Fig. 2.2 Sam Bass Warner, Jr., *Streetcar Suburbs* (Cambridge, Mass.: Harvard University Press, 1962). Reprinted with permission of Harvard University Press.

Fig. 2.3 The Boston Dwelling House Company, *Woodbourne: A Description of Single and Semi-Detached Houses Offered at This Attractive Site By the Boston Dwelling House Company* (Boston, 1916).

Figs. 2.4, 2.10 Author's photos, 1996.

Fig. 2.5 A. D. F. Hamlin, "The Workingman and His House," *Architectural Record* 44 (October 1918).

Figs. 2.6, 2.7, 2.8 M. W. Folsom, *A Home of Your Own* (Chicago: National Association of Real Estate Boards, 1922).

Fig. 2.9 Kilham and Hopkins, architects, *The Brickbuilder* 22 (1913): 93.

Fig. 2.11 U.S. Housing Corporation, reprinted in Christian Topolov, "Scientific Urban Planning and the Ordering of Daily Life: The First 'War Housing' Experiment in the United States, 1917–1919," *Journal of Urban History* 17, 1 (November 1990).

Fig. 2.12 *Architectural Record* 45 (March 1919), p. 10.

Figs. 2.13, 2.14, 2.15 Clarence Arthur Perry, *Housing for the Machine Age* (New York: Russell Sage Foundation, 1939), pp. 75, 58, 122b. Reprinted with permission.

Figs. 2.16, 2.17 Clarence Stein, *Toward New Towns for America* (Cambridge, Mass.: MIT Press, 1966). Reprinted with permission.

Fig. 3.1 Boston Housing Authority; U.S. Bureau of the Census, *Historical Statistics of the United States, Colonial Times to 1970, Bicentennial Edition, Part 1* (Washington, D.C., 1975), pp. 639–642, and *Statistical Abstract of the United States: 1989* (Washington, D.C., 1989), p. 699.

Figs. 3.2, 3.3, 3.4, 3.10, 3.11, 3.12, 3.13, 3.15 Boston Housing Authority, *Rehousing the Low Income Families of Boston: Review of the Activities of the Boston Housing Authority, 1936–1940* (Boston, 1941).

Fig. 3.5 State Board of Housing, *Annual Report of the State Board of Housing from September 27, 1933 to November 30, 1934* (Boston: Department of Public Welfare, 1935). Reprinted with permission.

Fig. 3.6 Mabel L. Walker, *Urban Blight and Slums* (Cambridge, Mass.: Harvard University Press, 1938), p. 65. Reprinted with permission.

Fig. 3.7 Boston Housing Authority; 1940 U.S. Census.

Figs. 3.8, 3.22, 3.24 Adapted from Boston Redevelopment Authority maps by Geneviève Vachon.

Figs. 3.14, 3.16, 3.17, 3.18, 3.19, 3.20 Boston Housing Authority, *Annual Report, 1944–1945* (Boston, 1945).

Figs. 3.21, 4.2 Boston Housing Authority; 1950 U.S. Census.

Fig. 3.23 State Housing Board, *Primer for Use of Local Housing Authorities* (Boston, June 1948). Reprinted with permission.

Figs. 4.1, 4.5, 4.6 Compiled from Boston Housing Authority data.

Fig. 4.3 Boston City Planning Board, *General Plan for Boston* (Boston, 1950), pp. 42–43. Reprinted with permission.

Fig. 4.4 John Stainton, *Urban Renewal and Planning in Boston: A Review of the Past and a Look at the Future* (Boston: Citizens' Housing and Planning Association and Boston Redevelopment Authority, November 1972). Reprinted with permission.

Fig. 4.7 Boston Housing Authority archives.

Fig. 5.1 *Boston Globe Magazine*, August 23, 1981. Reprinted with permission. Photograph copyright © John Goodman.

Fig. 5.2 Stephen E. Tise, AIA. Reprinted with permission.

Fig. 5.3 Stephen E. Tise, AIA; Lane, Frenchman and Associates, Inc. Reprinted with permission.

Fig. 5.4 Boston Housing Authority, *Your Home* (August 1951); Corcoran, Jennison, Inc./Joan Goody, AIA.

Figs. 5.5, 5.7 Boston Housing Authority; 1990 U.S. Census.

Fig. 5.6 Author's photo, 2000.

INDEX

Massachusetts Housing Authority law, 196, 197, 241

Massachusetts Housing Finance Agency (MHFA), 335, 359

Massachusetts Housing for Veterans, 249, 252

Massachusetts Real Estate Owners Association, 172–173

Massachusetts Sanitary Code, 338–339, 344, 348

Massachusetts Special Commission on Low-Income Housing, 313

Massachusetts State Archives, 358

Massachusetts State Board of Housing, 162, 171–173, 185–187, 189, 243, 246–249, 285–286, 302, 418n29, 426n131

Massachusetts State House, 37, 39, 44, 185, 232, 234, 388

Massachusetts State Housing Board. *See* Massachusetts State Board of Housing

Massachusetts Supreme Judicial Court, 198–199, 216, 328, 339, 346

Massachusetts Veterans' Housing program (Chapter 200), 236, 242–250, 290, 305, 307, 313, 325, 329, 337, 425n121, 426n132, 428n148

Mather, Cotton, 27

Mattapan (Boston), 246

Maverick development (East Boston). *See* East Boston development

May, Ernst, 129

McCormack, John, 175, 233, 290, 297

McGonagle, Bill, 376

McLean Insane Asylum, 12, 38–39

Meehan, Eugene, 288

Mellan, Barbara, 365

Menino, Thomas, 371, 376, 378

Metropolitan Life Insurance Company housing, 415n115

Mission Hill (Main) development, 191, 193, 205–207, 223, 226, 230, 295, 301, 303–304, 308, 312, 323, 338, 370–373, 388, 392

Mission Hill Extension development, 251, 252, 295, 302, 303–304, 312, 320, 323, 324, 329, 338, 366

Mixed-income housing, 354–355, 357–364, 371–375, 380, 390–391

Model Housing Law, 141

Model Lodging House Association (Boston), 12, 63

"Model of Christian Charity," 2, 22

Model tenements, 10, 13, 63–66, 348

Modern Housing, 156

Moral classification, 8–9, 15, 19–21, 26–27, 40–52, 59, 66–68, 77–78, 85–87, 89, 99, 116, 120–126, 135, 139–140, 143, 152, 157–158, 182, 196, 216, 223, 227–229, 256–260, 262–265, 276, 277, 283, 291, 294–297, 299–300, 309–310, 314–315, 325–326, 327, 331–332, 334, 335, 342–343, 351, 363, 369, 380–381, 383–384, 387–388, 429–430n12

Morris, William, 130

Mumford, Lewis, 147, 218

Murphy, John, 342–343, 351–352

National Affordable Housing Act of 1990, 164

National Association for the Advancement of Colored People (NAACP), 163, 170, 303–307, 309–310, 313, 365, 376, 406n135

National Association of Home Builders (NAHB), 238–241

National Association of Housing Officials, 156, 240

National Association of Mental Hygiene, 82

National Association of Real Estate Boards (NAREB), 120–125, 127, 135, 238–241

National Commission on Severely Distressed Public Housing, 164, 370, 440n18

National Commission on Urban Problems, 315

National Committee against Discrimination in Housing, 322–323

National Federation of Settlements, 74, 404n107

National Housing Act (1934), 162, 169

National Industrial Recovery Act of 1933, 162, 168, 170

National Origins Act of 1924, 82

National Public Housing Conference, 156, 237

National Retail Lumber Dealers' Association, 183

Native Americans, 22–24, 29, 40–41, 95, 397nn7,10, 400n46

Nativism, 52–53, 50–61

Neighborhood centers, 88, 407n151. *See also* Settlement houses

Neighborhoods, 73–76, 80, 86–89, 91, 142–155, 169–171, 210–211, 248, 249, 255–256, 258, 280, 286, 372–373, 376

Neighborhood Unit, 14, 129, 276, 415n115